The Political Economy of Human Behaviour and Economic Development

Sangaralingam Ramesh

The Political Economy of Human Behaviour and Economic Development

Psychology and Economic Development

palgrave
macmillan

Sangaralingam Ramesh
University of Oxford
Oxford, UK

ISBN 978-3-031-12665-9 ISBN 978-3-031-12666-6 (eBook)
https://doi.org/10.1007/978-3-031-12666-6

This Palgrave Macmillan imprint is published by the registered company Springer Nature Switzerland AG.
The registered company address is: Gewerbestrasse 11, 6330 Cham, Switzerland

For my father and my mother,
Nallathamby Sangaralingam and Pathmarani Sangaralingam,
Inuvil and Karinagar, Ceylon,
For their duty and for their courage.

Preface

The big emphasis in scholarly activity associated with contemporary Economics is the acquisition and the analysis of data using Machine Learning and Artificial Intelligence techniques to determine how people make decisions. However, this does not necessarily involve an analysis of the underlying sequential processes such as different parenting strategies, and cultural and economic environment that may impact on childhood and adult cognitive, social, and cultural development. It will be the study of the feedback mechanism between these factors and childhood and adolescent development which will allow for a better understanding of how decisions are made by adults and how these decisions may either positively or negatively impact on society. Moreover, the results of such an analysis will give policymakers robust information which can be used for the formulation of policies associated with government spending on helping families with childcare costs and the provision of education services for children from an exceedingly early age. Furthermore, policymakers can encourage the development and the implementation of specific and personalised curriculums and school activities which will better help children develop into mature and rational adults. Increased government expenditure in these areas will help improve equality in society and help reduce the social costs associated with crime and drug dependency. In addition, a qualitative analysis of the factors associated with human development and economic activity will help to better understand how and why such activity takes place. This may lead to overcoming the problems associated with the abstract results which are obtained from using mathematical models, constructed based on simplifying assumptions, to analyse a complex real world. Moreover, while contemporary economic theory assumes that consumers maximise utility, it may be the case that consumers want to escape poverty and embrace prosperity. This may be the fundamental mechanism behind human behaviour which drives economic activity and not the maximisation of utility or rational choices. It may also be the case that this mechanism of human behaviour develops independently of the economic system in which individuals develop from birth, as infants, in childhood, into adolescence and into adulthood. For example, individuals born and brought up in former command economies (USSR, Central Europe, China, Vietnam) seek a better life in the developed economies of the West either through formal or informal migration. The same is true of people born and bred in developing economies. The former command economies (except China) and the developing economies lack the infrastructure, institutions, state of development, responsible governance, resources, systems of education, health, and freedoms to facilitate the flowering of economic prosperity. This would facilitate not only economic development but also the promotion of well-being. Lacking such economic development and well-being, individuals seek a better life by migrating from countries mired in poverty to countries relatively better off. In this case, the fundamental driving force behind human behaviour in the context of economic activity may not be the maximisation of utility or rational choice but the biological need to reproduce and to perpetuate the transmission of one's genes to subsequent generations. Following reproductive activities, the development of a human being begins from conception, in the womb, as an infant, as a child, as an adolescent and then into adulthood. The factors which affect each stage of this development will have an impact on the physical, physiological as well as the cognitive functioning of the adult who through their behaviour will take part in economic activity. Therefore, a better understanding of each stage of human development may lead to a better understanding of the nature of not only economic activity but also economic development. This is because economic activity may facilitate rising incomes and innovation (through greater competition). These changes will facilitate economic growth and then over time economic development. To optimise economic activity and economic development, the determination of the factors which optimise the development of human behaviour through its various stages will allow policymakers to develop and implement more effective social and economic programmes. This in turn will benefit the development of human society and help to sustain our civilisation.

This book is the author's fifth book and as such expands on the search for the roots of economic growth and economic development. This search emphasises the role of cognition and its development through the adult life cycle as being at the heart of human development. It is the development and growth of the latter which facilitates economic development and economic growth over time. The authors previous books include *China's Lesson's for India: Volume 1—The Political Economy of Development*, *China's Lessons for India : Volume 2—The Political Economy of Change*, *The Rise of Empires—The Political Economy of Innovation* and *China's Economic Rise—Lessons from Japan's Political Economy.*

London, UK

Sangaralingam Ramesh

Acknowledgements

I would like to thank the library service at the University of Oxford, where the idea for this book was formulated, and where writing of the book began in July 2019. However, due to the Covid pandemic and the lock-downs I had to find an alternative location to continue my work. In this case, I was lucky to meet Mr Alexander Tardios, through his wife, Dr Janja Tardios, the Headmaster of St John's Senior School, Cockfosters, London. Mr Tardios kindly allowed me to use a classroom at the school where I continued to write this book. For his kind help and generosity, I am truly indebted. Furthermore, I would also like to thank Wyndham Hacket Pain, the Editor for Economics publications at Palgrave Macmillan, as well as Karthika Devi, Production Editor (Books), Springer Nature, for their continuous support throughout the book publication process. I would also like to thank my research assistant, Ms Ludovica Ardente, for proofreading the final manuscript and for writing the abstracts of the book chapters. These would allow for concise information about the book and its contents to be located via the Internet.

Contents

CHAPTER 1

Introduction

China's economic rise has primarily been due to the incremental economic reforms instigated by the Chinese government since 1978 when the country began the transition from a centrally planned command economy to a mixed-market economy in which state intervention and free market forces co-exist. However, from a human perspective the key drivers of China's economic growth have been entrepreneurship and improvements in the possibilities for quality childcare due to the adoption of the one child policy in 1980. In the case of entrepreneurship, the government's economic and market reforms have allowed opportunity-based and necessity-based entrepreneurs to engage in economic activity by setting up businesses and fuelling China's economic phenomenal economic growth, which became more pronounced after China joined the World Trade Organization (WTO) in 2001. Moreover, improvements in the possibilities for childcare have been brought about by China's one child policy, which became a state-sanctioned policy in 1980 due to China's ever-growing population and fears that the country's economy would not be able to support it. The policy remained until 2015 and was quickly dismantled due to China's ever-shrinking population and fears that the slow growth in the population would reduce the workforce available to the economy and a reliance upon a smaller younger population to support a larger and growing elderly population. However, China's one child policy has facilitated the opportunity for the wider family to save and invest in the well-being and

S. Ramesh, *The Political Economy of Human Behaviour and Economic Development*,
https://doi.org/10.1007/978-3-031-12666-6_1

development of one child, the prince or the princess. The level of investment in the one child of the family would have led to higher levels of educational attainment and facilitated China's transition to some knowledge economy—perhaps matching if not surpassing the innovativeness enshrined in the US economy. Furthermore, in the case of China, entrepreneurship and the knowledge economy may be correlated because needs-based entrepreneurs make the money required to educate their children, whether in China or abroad. However, a negative impact of China's one child policy has perhaps been the growing selfishness of children brought up with the undivided attention of parents, the maternal and paternal set of grandparents as well as aunts and uncles. This selfishness may lead to a less caring and cohesive society in which the young no longer look after the well-being of elders and where divorce rates and levels of abuse soar.

The purpose of economic activity should be to facilitate human development. While the occurrence of this causation is in no doubt, what is in doubt is the mechanisms efficacy in ensuring that human development is spread evenly throughout the population. However, the problem with economic growth is that it usually facilitates human development amongst a small proportion of the population while inequality between the rich and the poor increases over time. This phenomenon is true within countries as well as between countries. The reasons as to why this phenomenon persists may be due to two factors. The first is the lack of quality of human development within and between countries. And the second is the efficacy of government policy in allowing for the factors requisite for quality human development to permeate and diffuse throughout society. The lack of quality human development and government policy may be entwined. For example, it has been found that if children and adolescents are given educational opportunities, they will be able to develop the characteristic of resilience, which will allow them to overcome adverse environments. As a result, they will be able to enter adulthood with better emotional stability and cognitive capabilities. These characteristics will in turn allow them to make better decisions. However, if a country spends a small proportion of its GDP on the public provision of education and/or if the quality of the educational services or in the school's infrastructure, then the impact on childhood development would be negative. Educational services may be represented by the quality of teaching, the developmental and learning opportunities a child receives and the quality of the relationship with the instructor/teacher. On the other hand, the schooling infrastructure may be represented by the quality of the buildings, the availability of Wi-Fi, the availability of computing equipment as well as library resources. Nevertheless, the question also arises as to whether inequality would persist amongst peoples between and in countries even if government policies towards eradicating inequality and promoting quality human development were in place in the context of economic activity and economic growth. If inequality does persist, then the implication is that inequality may arise from human existence and economic activity due to differences in upbringing, cultural differences and economic circumstances. In this case, the aim of this volume is to evaluate whether differences in upbringing represent a source of persistent inequality in society. This may be evident from the fact that people who were born and grew up in a prosperous country struggle to achieve while those individuals who were born and grew up in a less prosperous developing country do well when they migrate to a prosperous country which has better physical (roads, railway networks etc.) and soft infrastructure (public educational system, public healthcare system, law and order). In this case, the objective of this volume is to determine how the policies of government should be focused to eradicate the emergence of such inequalities at source. If government policies are not so attuned to the reality of human development, then the implication would be that there will be increases in inequality because of economic growth. In other words, prosperity will become concentrated in the hands of the few and out of the grasp of the many. Furthermore, merely changing the focus of government policy from economic growth to quality of life may not have that much effect on eradicating inequality in society if inequality is so pervasive due to differences in upbringing. The best ways to bring up infants and enable their development through childhood into adolescence and beyond into adulthood in the best way possible to achieve optimal development is something that is neither taught nor learned. The implication is that some parents will achieve the right balance of strategies and use of resources in bringing up their children while other parents may not. The result of varying degrees of upbringing is that the development of individuals through infancy, childhood, adolescence and into adulthood will vary. This will be characterised by the development of differing levels of cognitive and non-cognitive skills.

The dynamism of technological innovation through the accumulation of wealth and human cognition co-exists with the constancy of the variation of human behaviour. Innovation can be driven by circumstance, necessity or opportunity though still dependent on human cognition. On the other hand, variations in human behaviour may be dependent on the combined effects of genes, the environment and upbringing. In any case, new technological innovations are made, based on the foundations of previous innovations. However, the variability of human behaviour has stayed constant through the ages. For example, innovation took place when the round wheel replaced the square wheel in the times of ancient Sumeria. And in late eighteenth-century England, James Watt invented the steam engine. The round wheel and the steam engine were then integrated into the design of the railway engine, the movement of which was powered by the release of compressed steam. This enabled the transport of people and goods over long distances. However, the ability of an individual to kill another individual in anger has remained unchanged from the time of ancient Sumeria, to the seventeenth century AD, to the eighteenth century AD, remaining true in today's world. Therefore, while the capacity to innovate increases over time, the variability of human behaviour remains constant over the lifetimes of different individuals—although, as a result of ongoing evolution, there may be minor changes in the genes which are inherited from one generation to the next: typically, the genes which are passed from parent to child and not the same as those passed from grandparents to the parents. Individual lifetime experiences and environments will change an individual's transmissible genes in a different way. However, over the lifetime of an individual, the nature of behaviour will depend on the different life cycle stages, infant, child, adolescent and adult, and the environment associated with each.[1] Therefore, in the case of human behaviour, it is also important to consider the link between the person and the environment rather than that of the person in the environment.[2] This is because the nature of human behaviour depends on the environment. For example, the behaviour of someone constantly facing deadlines will be different from the behaviour of someone who has no deadlines to meet but instead has a carefree life. This is because someone who is constantly having to meet deadlines will always be under stress.[3] The person and the environment are a multi-dimensional phenomenon with specific dimensions contributing to the wider impact on human behaviour. In other

[1] Hutchison, E. (2019), Dimensions of Human Behaviour: Person and Environment, Sage Publications, Singapore.

[2] Ibid.

[3] Herbert, D., Coveney, J., Clarke, P., Graves, N., and Barnett, A. (2013), The impact of funding deadlines on personal workloads, stress and family relationships: a qualitative study of Australian Researchers, BMJ Open, Vol. 4, Issue 3.

words, analysing just one dimension will not be enough in understanding the wider impact.[4] A better understanding of human behaviour can be reached if it can be modelled as a multi-dimensional entity which integrates the systems associated with the biology, physiology and social aspects of every individual.[5] And, in the context of this integrated super-system, the most vital component, the co-ordinator in chief, is the brain.[6]

The Brain

The structure of the human brain is shown in Fig. 1.1. The shape of the brain is as such that the cerebrum, the easily recognisable wrinkled structure, represents three-quarters of the brain's volume.[7]

In turn the cerebrum itself is divided into two hemispheres which 'sit' on a thick stalk called the brain stem.[8] The two hemispheres are connected by the corpus callosum, a bridge of nerve fibres.[9] At the back of this structure, the main brain or cerebrum, is the protruding, cauliflower-shaped cerebellum or 'little brain'.[10] The cerebrospinal fluid (CSF) circulates the outer space of the brain as well as the spinal column.[11] The entire brain is constituted of billions of cells, supported by seven times more glial cells, each of which has thousands of connections to other brain cells.[12] The brain is the organ which co-ordinates our interaction with each other as well as with the world.[13] It also allows us to distinguish between 'self' and 'non-self'.[14] Each brain cell is like any other cell in the human body except its main purpose is communicating with other cells. In this case, each brain cell will receive an input signal through its soma end via dendrites.[15] The shape and the size of the dendritic trees will be different in different parts

[4] Hutchison, E. (2019), Dimensions of Human Behaviour: Person and Environment, Sage Publications, Singapore.

[5] Sapolsky, R. (2018), Behave: The Biology of Humans at Our Best and Worst, Penguin Books, New York.

[6] Ibid.

[7] Carter, R. (2019), The Brain Book, DK, London.

[8] Greenfield, S. (2014), The Human Brain: A Guided Tour, Weidenfeld & Nicolson.

[9] Carter, R. (2019), The Brain Book, DK, London.

[10] Greenfield, S. (2014), The Human Brain: A Guided Tour, Weidenfeld & Nicolson.

[11] Ibid.

[12] Dubin, M. (2002), How the Brain Works, Blackwell Sciences Inc, Oxford.

[13] Carter, R. (2019), The Brain Book, DK, London.

[14] Ibid.

[15] Ibid.

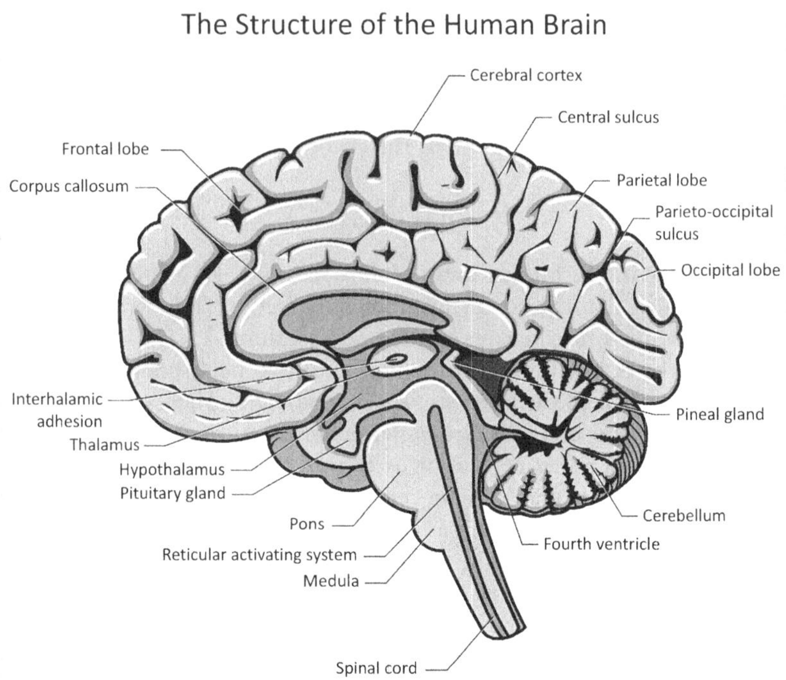

Fig. 1.1 The structure of the human brain

of the brain, as will the point of origin of the axon from each neuron.[16] The axons themselves end in a very large number of button-sized objects called boutons, which make contact with the dendrites of thousands of other neurons by forming synaptic points.[17] The signal then passes along the cell through the axon before exiting through terminals at the cell end, which form synapses with other brain cells.[18]

The higher-level mental functions occur in the cerebral cortex, and the lower-level brain functions such as those associated with the regulation of

[16] Ibid.
[17] Ibid.
[18] Ibid.

the heartbeat and breathing occur in the brainstem. Therefore, it is easy to see that the brain has a vertical zoning, with the level of cognition falling as one moves down the zone.[19] The inner brain also has a system of four interconnected ventricles. The two hemispheres of the cerebellum each have a ventricle; these are connected to a third ventricle in the mid-brain, which is linked to a fourth ventricle in the medulla and the pons.[20] The ventricles are filled with the CSF, which drains from the brain into the blood stream through the subarachnoid space.[21] The brain also houses 30 concentrations of neurons, called nuclei, which are paired left and right as the hemispheres are, which serve specific purposes.[22] However, the main nuclei in the human brain include the basal, the caudate, the subthalamic, the thalamus, the amygdala and the facial nucleus.[23] For cognition the most important of these nuclei are the caudate, the thalamus and the amygdala. It is these areas of the brain which are impacted upon by the external environment in which the embryo develops in its mother's womb or the child or the adolescent grows up in.

The caudate is responsible for processing feedback, the thalamus is a processing area for inputs and the amygdala is responsible for learning, memory and emotions. However, in the process of evolutionary development, other parts of the brain may have played a role. For example, the parieto-frontal 'mirror neuron' systems may have been important for language development in humans.[24] Moreover, the parietal and frontal connections of the brain may be where the action system is located.[25] In Macaque monkeys it has been observed that this area of the brain is modified when the monkeys are learning by trial and error to use sticks to reach fruit.[26] The innovative learning of the monkeys may suggest how human

[19] Ibid.

[20] Ibid.

[21] Ibid.

[22] Ibid.

[23] Ibid.

[24] Rizzolatti, G., and Buccino, G. (2005), The Mirror Neuron System and its Role in Imitation and Language, IN From Monkey Brain to Human Brain, A Fyssen Foundation Symposium (Ed), MIT Press, Cambridge, Massachusetts.

[25] Luppino, G. (2005), Organisation of the Posterior Parietal Lobe and of Parieto frontal Connections, IN From Monkey Brain to Human Brain, A Fyssen Foundation Symposium (Ed), MIT Press, Cambridge, Massachusetts.

[26] Iriki, A. (2005), A Prototype of Homo Faber: A Silent Precursor of Human Intelligence in the Tool Making Monkey Brain, IN From Monkey Brain to Human Brain, A Fyssen Foundation Symposium (Ed), MIT Press, Cambridge, Massachusetts.

evolution may also have followed the same pattern, with the results of such learning embedded in the human genetic code through gene expression.[27] The frontal lobes of the human brain have also been identified as the areas responsible for maintaining concentration. The stronger the ability to concentrate, the stronger will be the level of cognition.[28] This is because thoughts can be coherently organised, such that a consistent thought pattern will emerge. The frontal cortex is not only the slowest part of the brain to develop but also the part which reflects the ageing process first.[29]

The frontostriatal system of the brain encompasses both the neocortex and the basal ganglia.[30] The basal ganglia is further divided into the dorsal striatum and the ventral striatum, with the latter being smaller than the former.[31] The ventral striatum receives inputs from the orbital prefrontal cortex and is responsible for generating craving impulses.[32] While the orbital frontal cortex is associated with behaviours associated with compulsion, it is also an area of the brain which is important in terms of the transition from compulsive behaviours to goal-directed behaviours.[33] On the other hand, the posterior region of the frontal lobe provides inputs to the dorsal striatum.[34] This is divided into the caudate and the putamen.[35] The selection from a number of possible alternative strategies to determine a behaviour to achieve a specific objective is made possible by the caudate.[36] However, the putamen is responsible for behaviours associated with responses to stimuli and to learning by performing actions repeatedly.[37]

[27] Iriki, A. (2005), A Prototype of Homo Faber: A Silent Precursor of Human Intelligence in the Tool Making Monkey Brain, IN From Monkey Brain to Human Brain, A Fyssen Foundation Symposium (Ed), MIT Press, Cambridge, Massachusetts.

[28] Dempster, F. (1992), The Rise and Fall of the Inhibitory Mechanism: Toward a Unified Theory of Cognitive Development and Ageing, Developmental Review, 12, pp. 45-75.

[29] Ibid.

[30] Striedter, G. (2016), Neurobiology: A Functional Approach, Oxford University Press, Oxford.

[31] Ibid.

[32] Ibid.

[33] Brann, A. (2017), Neuroscience for Coaches: How to Use the Latest Insights for the Benefits of Your Clients, 2nd Edition, Kogan Page Limited, London.

[34] Striedter, G. (2016), Neurobiology: A Functional Approach, Oxford University Press, Oxford.

[35] Ibid.

[36] Grahn, J., Parkinson, J., and Owen, A. (2008), The Cognitive Functions of the Caudate Nucleus, Progress in Neurobiology, 86, pp. 141-155.

[37] Ibid.

The dorsal striatum and the ventral striatum 'feed' into the dorsal pallidum and into the ventral pallidum, respectively.[38] The respective parts of the pallidum then 'feed' into different regions of the thalamic nuclei.[39] In this case, the ventral pallidum-thalamus route leads to the anterior prefrontal cortex, but the dorsal pallidum-thalamus route leads to the frontal lobe posterior region.[40] The organisation of the brain with regard to the frontostriatal system leads to contextual behavioural selections and responses, especially with regard to the environment faced by children and adolescents.[41] While the psychological structures and the organisation of the brain are important for the development of cognitive and non-cognitive skills, theories of the mind allow for a better understanding of the emotional aspects of human behaviour.

Theories of the Mind

Theories of the Mind (ToM) relate to the concept that children can understand human behaviour by identifying their mental states as well as those of others.[42] Theories of the Mind (ToM) fall into two categories, 'theory theory'[43] and 'simulation theory'[44]. The 'theory theory' ToM is based on the notion that states of belief and the transition from one belief to another can be inferred or deduced from a set of rules and laws.[45] On the other hand, 'simulation theory' asserts that we infer or deduce the mental states of others based on a 'projection' of our own mental states.[46] From a wider perspective, a Theory of the Mind (ToM) considers whether mental states

[38] Striedter, G. (2016), Neurobiology: A Functional Approach, Oxford University Press, Oxford.

[39] Ibid.

[40] Ibid.

[41] Ibid.

[42] Premack, D., and Woodruff, G. (1978), Does the chimpanzee have a theory of mind? The Behavioral and Brain Sciences, 4, 515-526.

[43] Gopnik, A. (1993), How we know our minds: The illusion of first-person knowledge of intentionality, Behavioral and Brain Sciences, 16, pp. 1-14.

[44] Goldman, A. I. (2002), Simulation theory and mental concepts: IN Simulation and knowledge of Action, Dokic, J., and Proust, J. (Eds), John Benjamins, Amsterdam.

[45] Gordon, R. (1996), Radical Simulationism, IN Theories of theories of Mind, Carruthers, P., and Smith, P. (Ed), Cambridge University Press, Cambridge.

[46] Ibid.

are physical or non-physical.[47] From a narrower perspective, the ToM can be defined as an explanation of how mental reasoning processes develop and are used by individuals to think about and to predict other people's behaviour.[48] ToM therefore represents one's awareness of others as well as an awareness of one's self. Indeed, to predict others' behaviour there is a need for self-awareness. This necessitates a set of inherent beliefs and desires[49]—as well as emotions.[50] An analysis of human behaviour using a ToM approach is therefore more realistic but in sharp contrast with the approach taken by neoclassical economics. The analytical approach taken by the latter is very much dependent on the assumption of rationality. In other words, human decisions are based on pure logic and as such beliefs, desires or emotions have no impact on the choices which are made. In this case, in the context of the assumption of perfect knowledge, individuals are expected to continuously update probabilities associated with specific choices.[51]

There are two main reasons as to why ToM may be of general interest to scholars, with the findings of research being of specific interest to policymakers in government.[52] Firstly, ToM is an important aspect of cognitive development. And secondly, this cognitive development will lead to other developments. One important aspect of the study of and research into ToM is with regard to how children acquire their ToM skills.[53] At a generic level this could happen because of an interplay between genes and the environment.[54] However, with regard to policy formulation, it would be beneficial if this causal relationship could be broken down into its specific processes. For example, how is the cognitive development of children affected by experiences.[55] It is with regard to the conceptualisation of experience that ToMs differ.[56] However, it would be beneficial for

[47] Campbell, N. (2005), A Brief Introduction to the Philosophy of Mind, Broadview Press Ltd, Ontario, Canada.

[48] Doherty, M. (2009), Theory of Mind: How Children Understand Others Thoughts and Feelings, Psychology Press, Hove and New York.

[49] Ibid.

[50] Miller, S. (2016), Parenting and Theory of Mind, Oxford University Press, Oxford.

[51] Kuzmics, C. (2004), Stochastic Evolutionary Stability in Extensive Form Games of Perfect Information, Games and Economic Behavior, Vol. 48, Issue 2, pp. 321-336.

[52] Miller, S. (2016), Parenting and Theory of Mind, Oxford University Press, Oxford.

[53] Ibid.

[54] Ibid.

[55] Ibid.

[56] Miller, S. (2016), Parenting and Theory of Mind, Oxford University Press, Oxford.

policymakers to be able to understand and know what formative experiences beneficially develops cognitive abilities so that suitable policies can be developed for schools and for society in general.

There are four specific types of ToM.[57] These include modularity theories, Piagetian theories, matching theories and intersubjectivity theories. Modularity theories suggests that ToM is acquired as brain structures develop over time and individuals become conscious of themselves as well as of others.[58] On the other hand, the Piagetian theories associated with ToM suggest that one's view of oneself and of others develops over time on a subjective basis as opposed to an objective one.[59] But matching theories assert that causal reasoning and a recognition of ToM occurs not via the use of language but by observation.[60] Intersubjectivity theory relates to understanding ToM in the case of individuals with autism. In this case, the emphasis needs to be on understanding intersubjective engagement of the autistic child with other children as well as the extent of the empathy in them in the context of ToM.[61] Nevertheless, regardless of the number of ToMs, any ToM has several characteristic features.[62] Firstly, any theory of the mind recognises a psychological relationship between human agents and objects which may not be face to face but at a distance. Secondly, in any theory of the mind, there is the recognition of the equivalence of 'self' and 'other' with regard to the conceptualisation of psychological relationships. Thus, any theory which seeks to explain the development of ToM should be able to put forward an explanation which helps in achieving an understanding of these two features. And whereas ToM is normally thought about in the context of psychological states such as desire, belief and emotions, this could also be thought of in the context of psychological

[57] Moore, C. (2006), Theories of Mind in Infancy, British Journal of Developmental Psychology, 14, pp. 19-40.

[58] Scholl, B., and Leslie, A. (2002), Modularity, Development and 'Theory of Mind', Mind & Language, Vol. 14, Issue 1, pp. 131-153.

[59] Perner, J., Stummer, S., Sprung, M., and Doherty, M. (2002), Theory of Mind find its Piagetian perspective: why alternative naming comes with understanding belief, Cognitive Development, Vol. 17, Issues 3-4, pp. 1451-1472.

[60] Varley, R., and Siegal, M. (2000), Evidence for Cognition without grammar from causal reasoning and 'theory of mind' in an agrammatic aphasic patient, Current Biology, Vol. 10, Issue 12, pp. 723-726.

[61] Dant, T. (2014), In Two Minds: Theory of Mind, Intersubjectivity, and autism, Theory and Psychology, https://doi.org/10.1177/0959354314556526

[62] Moore, C. (2006), Theories of Mind in Infancy, British Journal of Developmental Psychology, 14, pp. 19-40.

states between 'agents' and 'objects'.[63] This relational construct exists simply because an agent may be in a specific psychological state which is held against an object. Furthermore, psychological relations consist not just of states such as desires, beliefs and emotions held against objects but also actions directed against objects.[64] The nature of psychological states is not directly observable and so presents observers with a challenge in understanding, explaining and justifying such states. Moreover, just because agents and objects may be observable, there is no guarantee that the psychological states of agents can be deciphered. It may also be the case that psychological relations may be associated with agents and objects in locations which are far apart. For example, Jim hates the university canteen because it is overcrowded at lunch time. In this case, Jim does not have to be in the canteen to hate it. He can hate it from a distance with the knowledge that at a specific time of the day, when he most needs to use it, it is crowded.

Modularity theories of ToM focus on stipulating the biological structures which are necessary for processing information in order to facilitate the development of human cognition.[65] Modularity theories assert that ToM development occurs due to embedded neural network mechanisms solely devoted to the emergence of reasoning.[66] In other words, the entire neural network may not be homogenous but specific parts or modules could be dedicated to different information processing requirements, which acting as a whole would facilitate cognitive development.[67] As the brain develops, specific modules could become activated over time. Furthermore, there may be a part of the brain dedicated to ToM such that it becomes active by the second year of the life of an individual.[68] And although experiences may trigger its development, the core structure of the brain responsible for its development will not have been changed.[69]

[63] Barresi, J., and Moore, C. (1996), Intentional Relations and Social Understanding, Behavioral and Brain Sciences, Vol. 19, Issue 1, pp. 107-122.

[64] Moore, C. (2006), Theories of Mind in Infancy, British Journal of Developmental Psychology, 14, pp. 19-40.

[65] Moore, C. (2006), Theories of Mind in Infancy, British Journal of Developmental Psychology, 14, pp. 19-40.

[66] Mahy, C., Moses, L., and Pfeifer, J. (2014), How and Where: Theory of Mind in the Brain, Developmental Cognitive Neuroscience, 9, pp. 68-81

[67] Moore, C. (2006), Theories of Mind in Infancy, British Journal of Developmental Psychology, 14, pp. 19-40.

[68] Ibid.

[69] Ibid.

On the other hand, unlike modularity theories, mental file theory explains how children of approximately four years of age are able to pass the false belief test as well as are able to process identity statements.[70] It is at the age of 4/5 that children may be able to construe that a person's views about the world may be mistaken, in other words the recognition that a person may hold false beliefs.[71] Moreover, at the same time as the development of the ability to identify false beliefs, children are also able to play the alternative naming game.[72] For example, if someone identifies the picture of a rabbit as a rabbit, the child in response will call out bunny.[73] Another approach to a better understanding of ToM can be associated with Piagetian theories. These theories suggest that cognitive development, social awareness and an awareness of the minds of others emerges and develops due to the interaction between the infant and its social environment.[74] Over time, the interactions between the infant and its environment may allow for a growing awareness of the equivalence of 'self' and 'other'. As the awareness of the equivalence of 'self' and 'other' develops over time, so does the level of human cognition. Theories which seek to explain the development of ToM and cognition as the growing awareness of the equivalence of 'self' and 'other' over time are known as matching theories.[75] A rising awareness of the equivalence of 'self' and 'other' could occur over time through the infant's observation and recognition of events which result from their interactions with the immediate environment. As a result, the infant will develop an understanding of the 'self' and the 'other' and, as a result, over time will be able to exhibit different

[70] Perner, J., Mauer, M. C., & Hildenbrand, M. (2011). Identity: Key to children's understanding of belief. Science, 333(6041), 474–477. https://doi.org/10.1126/science.1201216

[71] Wilde-Astington, J., Pelletier, J., and Homer, B. (2002), Theory of Mind and epistemological development; the relation between children's second order false-belief understanding and their ability to reason evidence, New Ideas in Psychology, Vol. 20, Issues 2-5.

[72] Perner, J., & Leahy, B. (2016). Mental files in development: Dual naming, false belief, identity and intentionality. Review of Philosophy and Psychology, 7, 491–508. https://doi.org/10.1007/s13164-015-0235-6

[73] Perner, J., Stummer, S., Sprung, M., and Doherty, M. (2002), Theory of mind finds its Piagetian perspective; why alternative naming comes with understanding belief, Cognitive Development, Vol. 17, Issues 3-4, pages 1451-1472.

[74] Moore, C. (2006), Theories of Mind in Infancy, British Journal of Developmental Psychology, 14, pp. 19-40.

[75] Moore, C. (2006), Theories of Mind in Infancy, British Journal of Developmental Psychology, 14, pp. 19-40.

psychological states with other objects.[76] However, the events in which 'self' and 'other' are matched must occur frequently as well as in a non-random fashion such that the infant will be able to intuitively understand the connection between the two.[77] Thus, on the whole, ToM asserts that there is a separation between 'self' and 'others', and in order to bridge this gap individuals need to simulate the minds of others.[78] It is this 'bridge' which contextualises the need for different theories to explain how the minds of others may be simulated by individuals. An alternative to a ToM explanation and understanding of the development of cognition can be based in the context of an intersubjectivity approach. This is specifically with regard to a process of social cognition and then individual cognition.[79] In other words, child and individual consciousness interacts with its socio-economic environment and at the same time remains malleable to change.[80] The intersubjectivity approach can be decomposed into primary, secondary and tertiary intersubjectivity. Primary intersubjectivity revolves around the evolving ability of infants to be able to discern the intention of others through the observation of their expressions and actions.[81] Thus, infants begin to develop an awareness of 'self' through the emotional communication and expression with parents and immediate family members.[82] Once a sense of 'self' has been developed by the infant at around the age of 1, abilities emerge such that infants realise that minds can be 'interfaced' by direct communication. It is this intentionality and directness of communication of the infant which denotes secondary

[76] Ibid.

[77] Ibid.

[78] Zlatev, J., Racine, T., Sinha, C., Itkonen, E. (2008), Intersubjectivity – What makes us human? IN The Shared Mind – Perspectives on Intersubjectivity, Zlatev, J., Racine, T., Sinha, C., Itkonen, E. (Eds), John Benjamins Publishing Company, Amsterdam.

[79] Ibid.

[80] Allen, M., and Williams, G. (2011), Consciousness, plasticity, and connectomics: the role of intersubjectivity in human cognition, Front. Psychol. https://doi.org/10.3389/fpsyg.2011.00020

[81] Gallagher, S., and Hutto, D. (2008), Understanding Others Through Primary Interaction and Narrative Practice, IN The Shared Mind – Perspectives on Intersubjectivity, Zlatev, J., Racine, T., Sinha, C., Itkonen, E. (Eds), John Benjamins Publishing Company, Amsterdam.

[82] Bard, K. (1998), Social-experiential Contributions to Imitation and Emotion in Chimpanzees, IN Intersubjective Communication and Emotion in Early Ontogeny, Braten, S. (Ed), Cambridge University Press, Cambridge.

intersubjectivity.[83] Language development occurs around the age of 2 and this facilitates communication in more advanced social contexts.[84] Tertiary intersubjectivity involves a growing awareness of third parties in the environment during the process of communication with other actions, which could be sideward glances at individuals standing nearby.[85]

A key question faced by researchers for decades is the role of language in the context of the development of ToM.[86] Indeed, some studies have found that the level of language ability of children is positively related to the level of mental reasoning ability.[87] More, specifically children's understanding of epistemic states is developed in response to being exposed to verbs and syntax which are representative of epistemic states.[88] The verbs which are linguistically expressive of epistemic states would be expressive of either 'belief' or 'knowledge' in some form.[89] In this case, epistemic states result from experiences, which give rise to knowledge, which may lead to belief formation. In this case, decisions may be made on the basis of beliefs, which may not be true and therefore not rational.[90] Furthermore, due to the fact that epistemic states are based on belief, they are unlikely to change when new facts emerge.[91] Nevertheless, it has been shown that

[83] Bretherton, I. (1992), Social Referencing, Intentional Communication and the Interfacing of Minds in Infancy, IN Social Referencing and the Social Construction of Reality in Infancy, Feinman, S. (Ed), Springer Science + Business Media, New York.

[84] Gallagher, S., and Hutto, D. (2008), Understanding Others Through Primary Interaction and Narrative Practice, IN The Shared Mind – Perspectives on Intersubjectivity, Zlatev, J., Racine, T., Sinha, C., Itkonen, E. (Eds), John Benjamins Publishing Company, Amsterdam.

[85] Linell, P. (2017), Intersubjectivity in Dialogue, IN The Routledge Handbook of Language and Dialogue, Weigand, E. (Ed), Routledge, New York.

[86] Juan, V., and Astington, J. (2017), Does Language Matter for Implicit Theory of Mind? The Effects of Epistemic Verb Training on Implicit and Explicit False-Belief Understanding, Cognitive Development, 41, 19-32.

[87] Milligan, K., Astington, J. W., & Dack, L. A. (2007). Language and theory of mind: Meta-analysis of the relation between language ability and false-belief understanding, Child Development, 78(2), 622–646.

[88] Hale, C. M., & Tager-Flusberg, H. (2003). The influence of language on theory of mind: A training study. Developmental Science, 6(3), 346–359.

[89] Martinez-Navarro, B. (2017), Epistemic States of Convincement: A Conceptualisation from the Practice of Mathematicians and neurobiology, IN Understanding Emotions in Mathematical Thinking and Learning, Eligio, U. (Ed), Academic Press.

[90] Bochman, A. (2007), The Many Valued and Nonmonotonic Turn in Logic, Handbook of the History of Logic, Vol. 8, pp. 13-689.

[91] Ibid.

epistemic verb training produced significant effects on epistemic reasoning with regard to implicit measures of both true and false belief reasoning.[92] This is specifically in the case of children who received epistemic verb training, leading them to achieve a greater improvement in the proportion of correct fixations in the context of measures of false belief.[93] In the case of true belief reasoning, there were significant declines in the proportion of correct fixations between the pre- and the post-assessment periods.[94] These findings associated with the impact of epistemic (conditions required for the acquisition of knowledge) training on true/false belief reasoning throws into contradiction the forecasts related to working memory capacity. This is because training did not impose any additional burdens on the processing capacity of cognition.[95] Therefore, the concurrent development of cognitive ability and experience may directly affect the implicit processing of epistemic states.[96] The latter can be associated with propositions believed. For example, the proposition could be that the 'sun rises each morning'. Associated with this proposition would be the epistemic state of 'know' or 'believe'.

Socio-Economic Status, Family Processes and Human Development

Evolutionary psychologists seek to better understand how human beings function in the context of psychological mechanisms which have evolved over time.[97] It is the interaction of the individual's environment with these psychological mechanisms which facilitates survival through infancy, childhood and to adulthood. This process may suggest that natural selection has been active in early life to allow for its extension to later life.[98] However, at a deeper level in the context of evolutionary developmental psychology,

[92] Juan, V., and Astington, J. (2017), Does Language Matter for Implicit Theory of Mind? The Effects of Epistemic Verb training on Implicit and Explicit False-Belief Understanding, Cognitive Development, 41, 19-32.

[93] Ibid.

[94] Ibid.

[95] Ibid.

[96] Ibid.

[97] Bjorklund, D., and Pellegrini, A. (2000), Child Development and Evolutionary Psychology, Child Development, November/December 2000, Volume 71, Number 6, pp. 1687-1708.

[98] Ibid.

the process of human development involves the interaction of genetically wired reactions and adaptations to various levels of external stimuli. But these genetically wired reactions and adaptations will differ from individual to individual due to genetic variations. In this way some individuals are better able to adapt to their environment and survive, reproduce and pass genetic variations onto future generations—although a better understanding will be required of how long-evolved psychological mechanisms impact on the development of human behaviour.[99] If psychological mechanisms are equivalent to cognitive processes, then it is the interplay between these processes and the individual's physical and social environment which not only characterises the development but also typifies the extent of human behaviour. This would suggest that Darwin's Natural Selection is caused by the interplay between cognition and the environment.[100] Therefore, it must follow that the development of human cognition over time took place to facilitate the resolution of real-world problems.[101] Nevertheless, although cognition may be considered as a whole, different cognitive processes may have evolved in order to allow for adaptation to different environmental conditions.[102] These different cognitive processes may be compared to having a unique computer programming language but different algorithms performing different functions. In an analogous way the human brain facilitates the emergence of different cognitive processes to deal with different physical and social environmental situations. The specificity of the application of cognitive processes suggests that cognition may not be a tool which allows for general problem solving[103]—in which case there may be a constraint to the extent of learning,[104] although the level of the performance of cognition allows for the expected gain to be higher

[99] Ibid.

[100] Cosmides, L., & Tooby, J. (1987), From evolution to behavior: Evolutionary psychology as the missing link, IN The latest on the Best Essays on Evolution and Optimality, Dupre, J. (Ed), MIT Press, Cambridge, MA.

[101] Ibid.

[102] Ibid.

[103] Bjorklund, D., and Pellegrini, A. (2000), Child Development and Evolutionary Psychology, Child Development, November/December 2000, Volume 71, Number 6, pp. 1687-1708.

[104] Gelman, R., and Williams, E.M. (1998), Enabling Constraints for Cognitive Development and Learning: Domain-Specificity and Epigenesis, IN Handbook of Child Psychology: Vol. 2, Cognition, Perception and Language, Kuhn, D., and Siegler, R.S. (eds.), Wiley, New York.

than the level of mental effort expended.[105] But while the disconnect between cognition and general problem solving may be thought of as having a negative impact on human development, it may actually be beneficial by allowing learning to occur in smaller 'bytes', leading to the accumulation of knowledge gained through experience. Moreover, the ability to learn will be different according to the state of individual development. For example, a child may not be able to learn as much or to deal with situations as effectively as an adult would be able to. However, whether an adult or a child, it may be the case that different environmental experiences activate different genes, which leads to different behaviours.[106] But just as behaviours are shaped by the environment, behaviours will also shape the environment.[107] Furthermore, childhood experiences may impact on adult behaviour.[108] But the childhood environment may be different to the adult environment.[109] In this case, in contrast to adults and older children, younger children may be more biologically tuned to receiving specific stimuli during their phase of development.[110] Therefore, it would be worthwhile for governments to analyse the costs and the benefits associated with early childhood interventionist policies with regard to policy formulation.[111] On the whole, governments would have a better understanding in the formulation of public policy with the knowledge that the cognitive processes used by modern humans to adapt to their environments have changed little since the dawn of civilisation 10,000 years ago.[112] However, the problems faced by modern humans are very different from those faced by our ancestors centuries ago.

[105] Anderson, J. (1991), Is human cognition adaptive, Behavioural and Brain Sciences, 14, pp. 471-517.

[106] Bjorklund, D., and Pellegrini, A. (2000), Child Development and Evolutionary Psychology, Child Development, November/December 2000, Volume 71, Number 6, pp. 1687-1708.

[107] Ibid.

[108] Ibid.

[109] Ibid.

[110] Bjorklund, D. F. (1997), The Role of Maturity in Human Development, Psychological Bulletin, 122, pp. 153-169.

[111] Hyson, M.C., Hirsh-Pasek, K., and Rescorla, L. (1990), Academic Environments in Preschool: Challenges or Pressures? Early Education and Development, 1, pp. 401-423.

[112] Bjorklund, D., and Pellegrini, A. (2000), Child Development and Evolutionary Psychology, Child Development, November/December 2000, Volume 71, Number 6, pp. 1687-1708.

An understanding of the psychological transformation of a newborn baby through infancy, childhood and then to adolescence and adulthood, the first 20 years of life, has always been a challenge for psychologists.[113] This psychological transformation also embodies a cognitive transformation which is facilitated by the formation of a hierarchical set of skills.[114] The hierarchy is composed of ten levels grouped into three categories associated with specific skills, abstract, sensory-motor and representational skills.[115] Each skill can be characterised as an exchange between the individual and the environment.[116] Moreover, skills develop continuously through levels not stages, although individuals' skills categories may not be at the same level at a point in time.[117] The development of specific skills is entirely dependent on the environment, with the best-developed skills being those which have been induced most often by the environment.[118] However, the extent to which individual skills can be induced by the environment will depend on the state of development of the individual, which will in turn dictate the highest skill level which can be attained.[119] But as the individual passes from infancy to childhood to adolescence and thence to adulthood, the highest skill level attainable will also increase.[120] Environmental stimulation rather than the genetic makeup of the individual facilitates the myelination of nerves in the cortex of the brain.[121] At birth, the infant has limited motor functions but a functioning sensory system which enables it to feel pain, hunger and discomfort, allowing it to alert its parents through its cries. The myelination of nerves in the cortex of the brain of the infant occurs mostly in the first eight months of the infant's life, although the process of myelination could also extend into adulthood. The myelination of the nerves allows for the development of insulation, which will facilitate the efficient transmission of electrical

[113] Fischer, K. (1980), A Theory of Cognitive Development: The Control and Construction of Hierarchies of Skills, Psychological Review, Vol. 87, No. 6.

[114] Ibid.

[115] Ibid.

[116] Sameroff, A. (1975), Transactional models in early social relations. Human Development, 18, 65-79.

[117] Fischer, K. (1980), A Theory of Cognitive Development: The Control and Construction of Hierarchies of Skills, Psychological Review, Vol. 87, No. 6.

[118] Ibid.

[119] Ibid.

[120] Ibid.

[121] Fischer, K.W., and Lazerson, A. (1984), Human Development: From conception through adolescence, W.H. Freeman, New York.

impulses from neuron to neuron via axons. Therefore, the greater is the extent of the myelination of nerves in the cortex of the brain, the greater will be the motor development of the individual. This in turn will facilitate cognitive development.

An understanding of the factors responsible for the successive cognitive development of the child into adolescence and adulthood will also provide policymakers with insights into how public policy may be better formulated to prevent the occurrence of behavioural, psychological and health disorders later in life. The development of cognition through childhood, adolescence and adulthood is dependent not only on individual factors such as genes but also on the nature of the individual's environment. This is because the structural development of the nerve fibres in the cortex of the brain is not dependent on genes. However, their structural development is dependent on the stimulations the nerve fibres receive through the environment in which an individual inhabits.[122] In this case, the extent and the number of neuron connections will determine the individual's level of cognition and even reason. Cognition can be defined as the extent of individual control in each environmental context.[123] Effective cognitive development will allow individuals to make better decisions regarding their daily lives as well as with regard to the long term too. Addiction to drugs, tobacco and/or alcohol will denigrate optimal individual decision-making capacity. In such instances individuals may engage in risky and wasteful decision making, which may result in poor lifestyle choices. An example would include a poor diet, which would incur healthcare costs borne by society. Another example would be domestic violence, which would require the involvement of the social services departments of local governments. The social costs associated with drug addiction and domestic violence can be avoided if the effective cognitive development of children can be facilitated through government policy. Moreover, once an adult individual can make better decisions, then an environment will exist in which individuals can decide whether to have children, how many children to have and when to have them. Government policy focused on childhood development is important because historic studies have emphasised the positive link between bad homes/schools and the emergence of

[122] Fischer, K., and Lazerson, A. (1984), Human Development, From Conception through adolescence, W.H. Freeman & Co Ltd, New York.

[123] Catania, A. C. (1978), The psychology of learning: Some lessons from the Darwinian revolution, Annals of the New York Academy of Sciences, 309, 18-28.

behavioural problems.[124] But the impact of growing up in a bad home/school will vary from individual to individual and will be transactional in nature rather than unidirectional. In other words, the effects of growing up in a bad home or going to a bad school may lead to behavioural problems, but these problems may be resolved as the personality develops.[125] Moreover, the result of not being able to grow and develop in a harmonious home will be that children may develop psychiatric disorders.[126] However, the positive link between the development of behavioural problems and having grown up in an inharmonious home can also be examined from other perspectives.[127] Firstly, the development of behavioural problems may be more dependent on genetic factors than they are on environmental factors. Secondly, the child may have an impact on parenting, rather than parenting having an impact on the child. For example, if the child is compliant to its parents' requests, the latter will be under less stress and may even treat the child better. In the case of the impact on adolescent mental health, it has been found that poor parenting styles do have a big impact.[128]

Lastly, behavioural problems may arise due to social disadvantages and/or because of circumstances in the child's physical environment. Although there are many factors which may lead to the emergence of behavioural problems in children, the evidence suggests that one factor may not be solely responsible.[129] Furthermore, long-term personality development is not just dependent on childhood experiences but on a fusion of these experiences with ongoing life experiences.[130] The characteristics of this

[124] Rutter, M., and Giller, H. (1983), Juvenile Delinquency: Trends and Perspectives, Penguin, Harmondsworth, Middlesex.

[125] Rutter, M. (1981), Maternal deprivation reassessed, 2nd Edition, Penguin, Harmondsworth, Middlesex.

[126] Rutter, M. (1985), Family and School Influences on Behavioural Development, J. Child Psychol. Psychiat, Vol. 26, No. 3, pp. 349-368.

[127] Rutter, M. (1985), Family and School Influences on Behavioural Development, J. Child Psychol. Psychiat, Vol. 26, No. 3, pp. 349-368.

[128] Joseph, M., and John, J. (2008), Impact of Parenting Styles on Child Development, Global Academic Society Journal, Social Science Insight, Vol. 1, No. 5, pp. 16-35.

[129] Sackett, G.P. (1982), Can single processes explain effects of postnatal influences on primate development, IN The development of attachment and affiliative systems, Emde, R.N., and Harmon, R. J. (Eds), Plenum Press, New York.

[130] Rutter, M., Quinton, D., and Liddle, C. (1983), Parenting in two generations: looking backwards and looking forwards, IN Families at Risk, Madge, N. (Ed), Heinemann Educational, London.

chain of experiences are that they are 'incomplete', vary from individual to individual and are subject to modification.[131] Therefore, the implication is that it will be possible to change an individual's behaviour pattern throughout his/her life.[132] However, a good upbringing with positive emotional and educational experiences can give a head start to a child—for example, by preventing the development of anxiety and nervousness in the child,[133] because this might foster earlier maturity and therefore bestow the advantage on the individual of being able to make informed decisions. Thus, scarce family resources can be more effectively invested in the optimal upbringing of children. One of the benefits of China's one child policy is that greater investment has been made in each child, with an entire family's resources contributing to this endeavour. Better decisions can also be made about what to eat, how much to eat and when and how much to exercise. Such decisions will not only allow for a better quality of life and longevity but also serve to reduce society's healthcare costs. When optimal decisions can be made in these circumstances, parental and family resources can be more efficiently and effectively used in bringing up children. As a result, as adolescents and adults, individuals will be better educated, cultured and emotionally and psychologically well adjusted. This will lead to a reduction in substance abuse, delinquency, better performance at school as well as overall good citizenship. One of the factors which is directly relevant to effective parenting in the context of the outcomes discussed above relates to parental socio-economic status.

In general, three approaches, social causation, social selection and the interactionist perspective, provide an understanding to the relationship between socio-economic status and human development.[134] Socio-economic status can be associated with economic security as well as with social recognition.[135] It can be measured in the context of occupational

[131] Rutter, M. (1985), Family and School Influences on Behavioural Development, J. Child Psychol. Psychiat, Vol. 26, No. 3, pp. 349-368.

[132] Ibid.

[133] Denham, S., and Liverette, K. (2019), The Emotional Basis of Learning and Development in Early Childhood Education IN Handbook of Research on the Education of Young Children, Saracho, O. (Ed), 4th Edition, Routledge, New York.

[134] Conger, R., and Donnellan, M. (2007), An Interactionist Perspective on the Socioeconomic Context of Human Development, Annu. Rev. Psychol, 58, pp. 175-99.

[135] Liu, W.M., Ali, S.R., Soleck, G., Hopps, J., Dunston, K., and Pickett, T.J. (2004), Using social class in counselling psychology research. J. Counsel. Psychol. 51:3–18.

status, educational attainment as well as income level.[136] These measures have a different impact on human development and so must be treated as separate and independent data measures in any type of empirical analysis.[137] Due to the unique relationship between each measure and human development, suitable analytical techniques which can separate these complex interactions must also be used in any empirical analysis.[138]

The idea that family stress processes as well as the effects of family investments in children has a direct impact on childhood development reflects the social causation view of the relationship between socio-economic status and human development. It is a view which is supported by empirical evidence.[139] The Family Stress Model (FSM) suggests that poverty has a negative impact on parents, which in turn leads to poor parenting.[140] On the other hand, the Family Investment Model (FIM) suggests that parents lacking an education, time and financial resources will be able to invest little in the emotional and cognitive development of their children compared to parents who are better endowed with an education, time and finances.[141] Nevertheless, the social selection perspective that socio-economic development itself results from differences between individuals is also supported by empirical evidence.[142] Although empirical evidence supports both social causation and social selection, recent research is supportive of the dynamic relationship between socio-economic status and developmental change, the interactionist approach.[143] This approach stresses the links between socio-economic status and the different approaches to parenting and childhood development.[144] In this case, parental social status and parental access to economic and financial resources may have a direct impact on the development of their

[136] Ensminger, M.E., and Fothergill, K. (2003), A decade of measuring SES: what it tells us and where to go from here, IN Socioeconomic Status, Parenting, and Child Development, Bornstein, M.H., and Bradley, R.H., (Eds), Mahwah, NJ: Erlbaum.

[137] Conger, R., and Donnellan, M. (2007), An Interactionist Perspective on the Socioeconomic Context of Human Development, Annu. Rev. Psychol, 58, pp. 175-99.

[138] Ibid.

[139] Ibid.

[140] Ibid.

[141] Ibid.

[142] Ibid.

[143] Conger, R., and Donnellan, M. (2007), An Interactionist Perspective on the Socioeconomic Context of Human Development, Annu. Rev. Psychol, 58, pp. 175-99.

[144] Ibid.

children.[145] Economically and psychologically disadvantaged children may grow into adulthood with behavioural problems.[146] But the effects of the impacts may vary between boys and girls.[147] Both endure a transition in development in the context of reaching a compromise in gaining their adulthood voice and developing relationships. The transition may leave a psychological impact, which may facilitate psychological illnesses, which boys experience in childhood and girls in adolescence.[148] In this case, girls experience optimal psychological risk during adolescence.[149] However, at the same time, these children may develop a desire to succeed despite the negative circumstances of their birth through the strength of character bestowed upon them through the parenting they received. Nevertheless, unless the children have an ardent desire to succeed, the negative parenting aspects of childhood may impact on the day-to-day choices they make, which has an impact not only on their own economic well-being but also on the well-being of society.

Poverty may cause deficits not only in terms of economic, cultural and educational opportunities but also in the context of emotional and parental support. Poverty may mean that parents will have to work away from home for longer periods of time, resulting in the children receiving less emotional parental support—although this could be substituted for by emotional and economic support from grandparents and extended family. However, a negative link between poverty and mental well-being has been empirically established.[150] In other words as poverty goes up, mental well-being goes down. In fact because of this causal relationship between poverty and mental well-being, it would seem that persistent poverty not only denigrates childhood development[151], but that it also denigrates the

[145] Conger, R and Conger, K.J. (2002), Resilience in Midwestern families: selected findings from the first decade of a prospective, longitudinal study, J. Marriage Fam. 64:361–73.

[146] Oakes, J.M., and Rossi, P.H, (2003), The measurement of SES in health research: current practice and steps toward a new approach, Soc. Sci. Med. 56:769–84.

[147] Brown, L., and Gilligan, C. (1993), meeting at the Crossroads: Women's Psychology and Girls Development, Feminism & Psychology, Vol. 3 (1):11-35.

[148] Ibid.

[149] Ibid.

[150] Ackerman, B.P., Brown, E.D., and Izard, C.E., (2004), The relations between persistent poverty and contextual risk and children's behavior in elementary school. Dev. Psychol. 40:367–77.

[151] Duncan, G.J., and Magnuson, K.A. (2003), Off with Hollingshead: socioeconomic resources, parenting, and child development. IN Socioeconomic Status, Parenting, and Child Development, Bornstein, M.H., and Bradley, R.H., (Eds), Mahwah, NJ: Erlbaum.

efficient functioning of the family unit.[152] There is scholarly empirical work to support this idea, with the measures of poverty being associated with a low income level, high debt levels relative to level of assets as well as occupational instability.[153] Poverty leads to an inability to meet material demands, especially for necessities, let alone luxuries, as well as an inability to pay bills.[154] It is the psychological stress which results from this which leads to parental behaviours which may not optimise the bringing up of children and therefore the children's childhood development. Psychological stress will trigger biochemical pathways which will lead to emotional distress such as depression or behavioural problems such as substance addiction.[155] Addiction may occur due to the genetic dispositions of the individual.[156] But the emotional distress and the behavioural problems of parents will lead to negative parental behaviours, including neglect of the child. Moreover, emotional distress and behavioural problems arising from psychological stress on the part of either or both parents will lead to conflict within the marriage and this will lead to a negative nurturing environment for the children.[157] On the other hand, the lower the level of parental psychological stress, the less will be parental emotional distress and behavioural problems, leading to parental emotional stability and a positive nurturing environment from which children will be able to positively benefit in the context of physical, emotional, behavioural and cognitive development.[158] In this case, children's cognitive ability, social and emotional competence, behaviour and social compliance will be much better if parental income was higher, as this would relieve parents of the effects of stress, leading to better parenting.[159] Links have also been established between socio-economic status and the development of thinking

[152] Elder, G.H.J., and Caspi, A. (1988), Economic stress in lives: developmental perspectives, J. Soc. Issues 44:25–45.

[153] Conger, R and Conger, K.J. (2002), Resilience in Midwestern families: selected findings from the first decade of a prospective, longitudinal study, J. Marriage Fam. 64:361–73.

[154] Ibid.

[155] Ibid.

[156] Agrawal, A., and Lynskey, M. (2008), Are there genetic influences on addiction: evidence from family, adoption and twin studies, Addiction, Vol. 103, Issue 2, pp. 1069-1081.

[157] Conger, R and Conger, K.J. (2002), Resilience in Midwestern families: selected findings from the first decade of a prospective, longitudinal study, J. Marriage Fam. 64:361–73.

[158] Ibid.

[159] Gennetian, L.A., and Miller, C. (2002), Children and welfare reform: a view from an experimental welfare program in Minnesota, Child Dev. 73:601–20.

ability[160] as well as between the relative position in the social hierarchy and health.[161] This may be because parents from a lower social hierarchy background are more likely to be less educated than their counterparts at high levels of the social hierarchy; and thus more likely to use physical punishment in their children's upbringing rather than reasoning with them.[162] Harsher, stricter, unreasoned parenting can be associated with poor emotional and social development during the first two decades of life[163]—although such an earlier upbringing may also serve to instil in children a deep desire to succeed if the negative emotional and behavioural effects can be conquered through the strength of the child's willpower. But middle-class parents are more likely to be educated and to have a stable financial and economic background. In this case, it is this type of parent who will be able to reason with their children, using a richer vocabulary than would parents from a low socio-economic background. Moreover, middle-class parents would also be better able to engage in activities which would cognitively stimulate their children's minds.[164] Reasoning with a richer vocabulary would also allow children to develop emotional stability and better cognition in adulthood. Thus, the Financial Investment Model asserts that when parents have greater financial resources and social and human capital, then children would stand a higher probability of being able to develop cognitively, emotionally, physically and behaviourally.[165] This is because such parents will be able to access resources for their children such as private tutoring and babysitting facilities in addition to meeting immediate family needs. However, parents with lower financial resources and social and human capital will be struggling just to meet the

[160] Mezzacappa, E. (2004), Alerting, orienting, and executive attention: developmental properties and sociodemographic correlates in an epidemiological sample of young, urban children. Child Dev. 75:1373–86.

[161] Evans, G.W., and English, K. (2002), The environment of poverty: multiple stressor exposure, psychophysiological stress, and socioemotional adjustment, Child Dev. 73:1238–48.

[162] Hoffman, L.W. (2003), Methodological issues in the studies of SES, parenting, and child development, IN Socioeconomic Status, Parenting, and Child Development, Bornstein, M.H., and Bradley, R.H., (Eds), Mahwah, NJ: Erlbaum.

[163] Steinberg, L. (2001), We know some things: parent-adolescent relationships in retrospect and prospect, J. Res. Adolesc. 11:1–19.

[164] Conger, R., and Donnellan, M. (2007), An Interactionist Perspective on the Socioeconomic Context of Human Development, Annu. Rev. Psychol, 58, pp. 175-99.

[165] Conger, R and Conger, K.J. (2002), Resilience in Midwestern families: selected findings from the first decade of a prospective, longitudinal study, J. Marriage Fam. 64:361–73.

day-to-day needs of the family.[166] It is through the findings of empirical studies that it has become established that the child-rearing strategies adopted by parents serve as a link to determine the causal relationship between the family economic circumstances and childhood and adolescent development.[167] Dire family economic circumstances may have a bigger negative impact on parents in the context of more stress than the simple desire to do better for the family.[168] The negative impact on parents will have a negative impact on their optimal parenting strategy, perhaps exhibited by neglect of the children or unreasoned behaviour towards them. This may cause distress to the child, leading to a lowering of self-esteem, causing damage to childhood development.[169] The child may feel neglected, unwanted, unloved and unable to understand his/her parents' negative behaviour towards him/her. The child may then become paranoid and think negatively of itself, whereas the real culprit is/are the parent/parents. As the child develops into adulthood, the implication is that the earlier life experiences will have a direct impact on decisions and choices which are taken in adulthood.[170]

Empirical studies have found that increases in the levels of family income help to reduce the anti-social behaviour of children as well as their susceptibility to suffer depression.[171] While there has been significant empirical investigation of the Family Stress Model, not much research has been conducted in order to evaluate the Family Investment Model.[172] Nevertheless, those studies which have been conducted do show that family income level matters when it comes to a question of parental investment

[166] Bradley, R.H., and Corwyn, R.F. (2002), Socioeconomic status and child development. Annu. Rev. Psychol. 53:371–99.

[167] Conger, R and Conger, K.J. (2002), Resilience in Midwestern families: selected findings from the first decade of a prospective, longitudinal study, J. Marriage Fam. 64:361–73.

[168] Mistry, R.S., Biesanz, J.C., Taylor, L.C., Burchinal, M., and Cox, M.J. (2004), Family income and its relation to preschool children's adjustment for families in the NICHD Study of Early Child Care. Dev. Psychol. 40:727–45.

[169] Sobolewski, J.M., and Amato, P.R. (2005), Economic hardship in the family of origin and children's psychological well-being in adulthood. J. Marriage Fam. 67:141–56.

[170] Lähdepuro, A., Savolainen, K., Lahti-Pulkkinen, M. et al. (2019), The Impact of Early Life Stress on Anxiety Symptoms in Late Adulthood. Sci Rep **9,** 4395. https://doi.org/10.1038/s41598-019-40698-0

[171] Strohschein, L. (2005), Household income histories and child mental health trajectories, J. Health Soc. Behav. 46:359–75.

[172] Conger, R., and Donnellan, M. (2007), An Interactionist Perspective on the Socioeconomic Context of Human Development, Annu. Rev. Psychol, 58, pp. 175-99.

in the development of their children.[173] The ability of parents to be able to hire tutors for their children to support school-based academic learning as well as to allow them to take up a hobby to develop a particular skill will enable the children to achieve occupational fulfilment when they become adults.[174] Furthermore, a link has also been found between the cognitive development of children between the ages of three and five and parental income levels.[175] In reality if such a link does exist, then the implication is that there should be greater state involvement in monitoring and supporting the parenting of children from a very early age. Such state intervention would allow for better citizenship in adulthood and reduce the social costs associated with delinquency, and with wrong decision making. The case for strong state intervention in the parenting of children from an early age may also ensure that children's cognitive development begins earlier, leading to academic success in adolescence. Educated children and adolescents will ensure that as they themselves become parents, their children will benefit from a parenting strategy based on reasoned thinking and a richer vocabulary. Empirical evidence supports the idea that there is a positive correlation between the level of education of parents and the cognitive development of children as well as a negative relationship between the level of parental education and negative childhood and adolescent behaviours.[176] However, this is not to say that the children of uneducated parents will themselves be uneducated. This is because uneducated, poor parents may tend to push their children harder to study so that they can have a more prosperous future by entering a profession, for example. In contrast to the social causation models such as FSM and FIM, the social selection perspective with regard to parental socio-economic status and childhood and adult development suggests that generational advantages

[173] Bradley, R.H., and Corwyn, R.F. (2002), Socioeconomic status and child development, Annu. Rev. Psychol. 53:371–99.

[174] Teachman, J.D., Paasch, K.M., Day, R.D., and Carver, K.P. (1997), Poverty during adolescence and subsequent educational attainment. IN Consequences of Growing Up Poor, Duncan, G.J., and Brooks-Gunn, J. (Eds), Russell Sage Found, New York.

[175] Linver, M.R., Brooks-Gunn, J., and Kohen, D. (2002), Family processes as pathways from income to young children's development. Dev. Psychol. 38:719–34.

[176] Bradley, R.H., and Corwyn, R.F. (2003), Age and ethnic variations in family process mediators of SES, IN Socioeconomic Status, Parenting, and Child Development, Bornstein, M.H., and Bradley, R.H. (Eds), Mahwah, New Jersey, Erlbaum.

are passed from one generation to the next.[177] For example, income accumulated by grandparents may benefit their grandchildren. On the other hand, a counter-argument to the social selection perspective, the obvious being better genetics[178], is that poorer parents will simply drive their children to work harder at school with the knowledge that a better education will increase employability in adulthood. Alternatively, poor parents may allow their children to develop social skills and the confidence to take advantage of educational opportunities.[179] From the author's experiences, this is something that happens a lot in Chinese society, in which the immediate and the extended family will contribute towards the financing of the education of a family member (child). So, although the social selection perspective offers an alternative explanation for the link between parental socio-economic status and childhood and adolescent development, it remains one strand of thinking amongst the many. Nevertheless, the debate is whether social causation, social selection or a dynamic interplay of both has the most impact on parental socio-economic status and childhood development.[180]

Theories of Human Development

The Capability Approach can be thought of as the philosophical basis for thinking about human development.[181] In this case, the Capability Approach does not give a specific qualitative or quantitative indicator of human development. So, while the Capability Approach does not recognise GNP per capita or healthcare as indicators of human development, it would recognise the growth in human potential or capability as being an indicator of development.[182] The Capability Approach encapsulates the

[177] Lerner, R.M. (2003), What are SES effects effects of? A developmental systems perspective, IN Socioeconomic Status, Parenting, and Child Development, Bornstein, M.H., and Bradley, R.H. (Eds), Mahwah, New Jersey, Erlbaum.

[178] Conger, R., and Donnellan, M. (2007), An Interactionist Perspective on the Socioeconomic Context of Human Development, Annu. Rev. Psychol, 58, pp. 175-99.

[179] Comer, J. (1988), Educating Poor Minority Children, Scientific American, Vol. 259, No. 5.

[180] Ibid.

[181] Alkire, S. (2002), Dimensions of Human Development, World Development, Vol. 30, No. 2, pp. 181-205.

[182] Sen, A. K. (1990). Development as capability expansion, IN Human development and the international development strategy for the 1990s, K. Griffin, & J. Knight (Eds.), London: Macmillan.

different combinations of abilities which an individual may be capable of doing.[183] These abilities may be associated with either a survival event or a non-survival event.[184] In the Capability Approach there is neither a pre-determined list of capabilities nor an indication of which capability has priority over another.[185] The indiscernibility of which capability may have priority over another is a frequent criticism of the Capability Approach.[186] However, what the Capability Approach does show is that only if government policies facilitate the emergence of opportunities, then and only then can individuals become capable by taking up those opportunities.[187] Initiative, for example, is a skill which cannot be taught at school, college or university for it to emerge.[188] Moreover, initiative is best learnt or acquired through the undertaking of structured activities such as volunteering or on-the-job training. However, the process of how initiative is acquired and used remains a mystery.[189] But the development of initiative may involve the construction of an algorithm in the brain which stimulates individual motivation.[190] In the context of motivation, it has been found that time plays a critical role.[191] In this case, when time is short, then the regulation of emotional states becomes a motivational priority in order to achieve the most urgent objective.[192] Although, chronological age may be used to explain changes in cognitive, motivational and emotional developments, time left seems to be a better one.[193] But the older people become, chronological age is no longer an ideal way in which to identify states of human psychology. This is because individuals are exposed to different

[183] Sen, A. K. (1992). Inequality re-examined. Cambridge: Harvard University Press.

[184] Alkire, S. (2002), Dimensions of Human Development, World Development, Vol. 30, No. 2, pp. 181-205.

[185] Sen, A. K. (1999). Development as Freedom, New York, Knopf Press.

[186] Alkire, S. (2002), Dimensions of Human Development, World Development, Vol. 30, No. 2, pp. 181-205.

[187] Vizard, P., Fukuda-Parr, S., and Elson, D. (2011), Introduction: The Capability Approach and Human Rights, Journal of Human Development and Capabilities, Vol. 12, Issue 1.

[188] Larson, R. (2000), Toward a Psychology of Positive Youth Development, Vol. 55, No. 1, pp. 170-183.

[189] Ibid.

[190] Ibid.

[191] Carstensen, L. (2006), The Influence of a Sense of Time on Human Development, Science, Vol. 312.

[192] Ibid.

[193] Ibid.

experiences and opportunities and so may be at various levels of development.[194] Moreover, as people become older, there is a greater appreciation of the time they have left, which becomes more important than the time since birth.[195] This appreciation may motivate older people to achieve more in the time that they have left. However, regardless of age, when time is short people tend to get things done faster.[196]

The Capability Approach recognises that individuals can only achieve their potential if the opportunities to do so exist. This approach has been strengthened by a shift of thinking within the field of psychology itself. Traditionally, psychologists may have thought that children's development and personality could be sculptured. But in recent times it has become more and more evident that young people can be the agents of their own development.[197] The reason for this change in perspective is the realisation that human behaviour cannot be reduced to a set of laws because human beings are intentional creatures and agents of their own and environmental change.[198] In other words, human beings have an inherent psychological mechanism which leads to a desire for change and development.[199] The traditional perspective of psychology of viewing human behaviour in the context of laws is very similar to the way in which contemporary economic thought allows for the mathematical modelling of human behaviour in an economic context. This is achieved by assuming that human beings make rational choices, consumers maximise utility and firms maximise profits. Nevertheless, in the context of the new psychological approach, there may also be a biological mechanism which calls for successful adaptation to the environment inspired through children's learning.[200] Learning becomes efficient when intrinsic human motivation becomes ignited.[201] However, while this is dependent on the individuals environment, once it occurs the extent of control by the individual of

[194] Ibid.

[195] Ibid.

[196] Ibid.

[197] Larson, R. (2006), Positive Youth Development, Wilful Adolescents, And Mentoring, Journal of Community Psychology, Vol. 34, No. 6, pp. 677-689.

[198] Ibid.

[199] Ibid.

[200] Piaget, J. (1967), Biology and knowledge, University of Chicago Press, Chicago.

[201] Ryan, R.M., & Deci, E.L. (2003), On assimilating identities to the self: A self-determination theory perspective on internalization and integrity within cultures. In Handbook of self and identity, Leary, M.R., and Tangney, J.P. (Eds.), Guilford Press, New York.

agency also improves.[202] The stage of individual development at which this occurs is adolescence, during which levels of cognitive competence improve, facilitating better control over degrees of individual agency.[203]

Conclusion

The growth of the Chinese economy since 1978 has been facilitated by a by a number of four-year plans, carefully crafted by the government, which have allowed for infrastructure, markets and institutions to develop over time. As a result, a mixed-market economy has developed in which the state sector and private interests co-exist. However, the specific mechanisms which have driven China's economic growth since 1978 have been widespread entrepreneurship amongst China's population and globalisation. Nevertheless, another less-thought-of feature of China's economic reforms is the one-child policy instigated in 1978 in order to reduce the size of a rapidly increasing population but removed in 2015 due to a rising ageing population amongst a dwindling number of younger people. One less-recognised feature to emerge from China's one child policy was that the time, care and financial resources afforded to that one child were seen as an investment by the entire family. Furthermore, many families in China are entrepreneurial in nature and are wealthy enough to send the one child to study abroad. However, even though the entire family would have invested in the future of the one child, the one child would have grown up in an environment in which the parents would have been very demanding in terms of his/her achievement. In the years up to adolescence, the one child would have been emotionally blackmailed by the parents to achieve in academia and extracurricular activities. This kind of parental behaviour would leave a scar on the one child's psyche, but the resulting drive for achievement and success would become part of him/her over time. But the one child would have escaped the emotional ravages and competition for the family's scarce resources due to sibling rivalry. Instead of having a brother or a sister, the one child would have a cousin brother or a cousin sister. Nevertheless, some families who were wealthy enough to pay the

[202] Ibid.

[203] Moshman, D. (1998), Cognitive development beyond childhood. IN Handbook of child psychology: Vol 2. Cognition, perception, and language. (pp. 947–978), Kuhn, D., and Siegler, R.S.(Eds.), John Wiley & Sons, New York.

fines incurred by having more than one child were able to do so—although these kinds of families remained a minority.

China's economic reforms of 1978 increased the pace of economic activity, this being the backdrop to China's one child policy. The connection between the two perhaps can be seen as the facilitation of human development, which should form the foundation of economic development. However, while in the case of China, economic activity via entrepreneurship has facilitated human development due to the one child policy, this perhaps as not been the case in other countries. While the one child policy may have arisen out of a need to reduce the numbers of a rising population, it was simultaneously timed with the start of China's economic reforms, which had a huge positive impact on economic activity in the country. The correlation between the two, the increase in economic activity and the investment in the one child, was perhaps unseen at the time but now resonates around the world, as China's economy at least in the long term is on a never-ending path of ascendancy. In the light of China's experience, it can be safely stated that the purpose of economic activity should be to facilitate human and therefore economic development. However, at a generic level, the problem with economic growth is that it usually facilitates human development amongst a small proportion of the population while the degree of inequality between the rich and the poor increases over time. There are two reasons as why this may happen. Firstly, there may be a lack in the equality of opportunity for human development. Secondly, there may a lack of government initiatives in promoting the equalities of opportunities for human development. However, government programmes and schemes for promoting such opportunities may exist but may not be efficient in facilitating the emergence and development in the equality of opportunities for all in a society. Programmes which would promote equality of opportunities would, for example, be those associated with education. This is due to the fact that access to education for children and adolescents will allow them to develop the characteristic of resilience. This will allow them to cope with and to overcome adverse environments. The development of a resilient character before and during adolescence will allow the adolescent to enter adulthood with better emotional stability and cognitive abilities. This will allow them to make better decisions, which would result in better life outcomes. Nevertheless, despite the existence of government programmes facilitating the emergence and the development of the equality of opportunities for the population of a country, inequalities may still persist in societies. Despite the existence of such programmes, the focus and the emphasis of government economic policy may be solely on maximising economic growth. In such a case, inequality between the rich and the poor persists, with the smaller proportion of a country becoming richer while the larger proportion becoming poorer. The persistence of inequality in society would suggest that inequality may arise from human existence and economic activity due to differences in upbringing, cultural differences and economic circumstances. Therefore, the aim of this volume is to evaluate whether differences in upbringing represent a source of persistent inequality in society. The objective of this volume is to determine how the social and the economic policies of governments should be focused to eradicate the emergence of such inequalities at source. If a government's social and economic policies are not so attuned and correlated with the realities and the needs of human development, then the implication would be that there will be increases in inequality because of economic growth. Therefore, changing the emphasis of government policy from facilitating economic growth to promoting improvements in the quality of life may not have much effect if the causes of inequality are due differences in upbringing. This will give rise to differences in the trajectory of human development. However, differences in upbringing result in different developmental paths, some resulting in the emergence and enhancement of positive characteristics while others lead to the emergence and the enhancement of negative characteristics. The former will result in an adult who is emotionally stable and who exhibits strong cognitive and non-cognitive skills, while, on the other hand, an upbringing which leads to the emergence and the enhancement of negative characteristics may result in an adult who is emotionally unstable and who exhibits poor cognitive and non-cognitive skills. In order to better understand how upbringing and developmental outcomes can be better aligned, human behaviour should be modelled as a multidimensional entity which incorporates the integration of the biological, physiological and social aspects associated with every individual. The entity responsible for 'managing' and 'co-ordinating' this integrated system is the human brain. While in the latter there are many different nuclei, the most important for these for the emergence of effective cognition are the caudate, the thalamus and the amygdala. It is these areas of the brain which are impacted upon by the external environment, whether it be the foetus developing in the mother's womb or the infant, the child, the adolescent or the adult. The thalamus is the part of the brain in which the processing of inputs from the senses occurs. The amygdala is responsible for memory, learning and emotions. On the other hand, the caudate is responsible for processing the feedback from different behavioural responses, which may help in selecting the best strategy from a series of alternative strategies. While certain parts of the brain are associated with cognitive development, there are also theories associated with this development. For example, the Theory of Mind relates to one's awareness of others as well as an awareness of oneself. The Theory of Mind is an important feature of cognitive development, and this may lead to other developments. Such developments arise due to the interplay between psychological processes and the individual's physical and social environment, which characterises not only development but also the extent of the development of human behaviour. Therefore, in the context of a young person and their environment, the young person can only become agents of their own development if they are given opportunities. This correlates with the Capability Approach, which recognises that individuals can only achieve their potential if the opportunities to do so exist.

References

Ackerman, B. P., Brown, E. D., & Izard, C. E. (2004). The Relations Between Persistent Poverty and Contextual Risk and Children's Behavior in Elementary School. *Developmental Psychology, 40*, 367–377.

Agrawal, A., & Lynskey, M. (2008). Are There Genetic Influences on Addiction: Evidence from Family, Adoption and Twin Studies. *Addiction, 103*(2), 1069–1081.

Alkire, S. (2002). Dimensions of Human Development. *World Development, 30*(2), 181–205.

Allen, M., & Williams, G. (2011). Consciousness, Plasticity, and Connectomics: The Role of Intersubjectivity in Human Cognition. *Frontiers in Psychology*. https://doi.org/10.3389/fpsyg.2011.00020

Anderson, J. (1991). Is Human Cognition Adaptive. *Behavioural and Brain Sciences, 14*, 471–517.

Bard, K. (1998). Social-Experiential Contributions to Imitation and Emotion in Chimpanzees. In S. Braten (Ed.), *Intersubjective Communication and Emotion in Early Ontogeny*. Cambridge University Press.

Barresi, J., & Moore, C. (1996). Intentional Relations and Social Understanding. *Behavioral and Brain Sciences, 19*(1), 107–122.

Bjorklund, D. F. (1997). The Role of Maturity in Human Development. *Psychological Bulletin, 122*, 153–169.

Bjorklund, D., & Pellegrini, A. (2000). Child Development and Evolutionary Psychology. *Child Development, 71*(6), 1687–1708.
Bochman, A. (2007). The Many Valued and Nonmonotonic Turn in Logic. *Handbook of the history of logic, 8*, 13–689.
Bradley, R. H., & Corwyn, R. F. (2002). Socioeconomic Status and Child Development. *Annual Review of Psychology, 53*, 371–399.
Bradley, R. H., & Corwyn, R. F. (2003). Age and Ethnic Variations in Family Process Mediators of SES. In M. H. Bornstein & R. H. Bradley (Eds.), *Socioeconomic Status, Parenting, and Child Development*. Erlbaum.
Brann, A. (2017). *Neuroscience for Coaches: How to Use the Latest Insights for the Benefits of Your Clients* (2nd ed.). Kogan Page Limited.
Bretherton, I. (1992). Social Referencing, Intentional Communication and the Interfacing of Minds in Infancy. In S. Feinman (Ed.), *Social Referencing and the Social Construction of Reality in Infancy*. Springer.
Brown, L., & Gilligan, C. (1993). Meeting at the Crossroads: Women's Psychology and Girls Development. *Feminism & Psychology, 3*(1), 11–35.
Campbell, N. (2005). *A Brief Introduction to the Philosophy of Mind*. Broadview Press Ltd.
Carstensen, L. (2006). The Influence of a Sense of Time on Human Development. *Science, 312*.
Carter, R. (2019). *The Brain Book*. DK.
Catania, A. C. (1978). The Psychology of Learning: Some Lessons from the Darwinian Revolution. *Annals of the New York Academy of Sciences, 309*, 18–28.
Comer, J. (1988). Educating Poor Minority Children. *Scientific American, 259*(5).
Conger, R., & Conger, K. J. (2002). Resilience in Midwestern Families: Selected Findings from the First Decade of a Prospective, Longitudinal Study. *Journal of Marriage and the Family, 64*, 361–373.
Conger, R., & Donnellan, M. (2007). An Interactionist Perspective on the Socioeconomic Context of Human Development. *Annual Review of Psychology, 58*, 175–199.
Cosmides, L., & Tooby, J. (1987). From Evolution to Behavior: Evolutionary Psychology as the Missing Link. In J. Dupre (Ed.), *The Latest on the Best Essays on Evolution and Optimality*. MIT Press.
Dant, T. (2014). In Two Minds: Theory of Mind, Intersubjectivity, and Autism. *Theory and Psychology*. https://doi.org/10.1177/0959354314556526
Dempster, F. (1992). The Rise and Fall of the Inhibitory Mechanism: Toward a Unified Theory of Cognitive Development and Ageing. *Developmental Review, 12*, 45–75.
Denham, S., & Liverette, K. (2019). The Emotional Basis of Learning and Development in Early Childhood Education. In O. Saracho (Ed.), *Handbook of Research on the Education of Young Children* (4th ed.). Routledge.

Doherty, M. (2009). *Theory of Mind: How Children Understand Others Thoughts and Feelings*. Psychology Press.

Dubin, M. (2002). *How the Brain Works*. Blackwell Sciences.

Duncan, G. J., & Magnuson, K. A. (2003). Off with Hollingshead: Socioeconomic Resources, Parenting, and Child Development. In M. H. Bornstein & R. H. Bradley (Eds.), *Socioeconomic Status, Parenting, and Child Development*. Erlbaum.

Elder, G. H. J., & Caspi, A. (1988). Economic Stress in Lives: Developmental Perspectives. *Journal of Social Issues, 44*, 25–45.

Ensminger, M. E., & Fothergill, K. (2003). A Decade of Measuring SES: What It Tells Us and Where to Go from Here. In M. H. Bornstein & R. H. Bradley (Eds.), *Socioeconomic Status, Parenting, and Child Development*. Erlbaum.

Fischer, K. (1980). A Theory of Cognitive Development: The Control and Construction of Hierarchies of Skills. *Psychological Review, 87*(6).

Fischer, K., & Lazerson, A. (1984). *Human Development, from Conception Through Adolescence*. W.H. Freeman.

Gallagher, S., & Hutto, D. (2008). Understanding Others Through Primary Interaction and Narrative Practice. In J. Zlatev, T. Racine, C. Sinha, & E. Itkonen (Eds.), *The Shared Mind – Perspectives on Intersubjectivity*. John Benjamins Publishing Company.

Gelman, R., & Williams, E. M. (1998). Enabling Constraints for Cognitive Development and Learning: Domain-Specificity and Epigenesis. In D. Kuhn & R. S. Siegler (Eds.), *Handbook of Child Psychology: Vol. 2, Cognition, Perception and Language*. Wiley.

Gennetian, L. A., & Miller, C. (2002). Children and Welfare Reform: A View from an Experimental Welfare Program in Minnesota. *Child Development, 73*, 601–620.

Goldman, A. I. (2002). Simulation Theory and Mental Concepts. In J. Dokic & J. Proust (Eds.), *Simulation and Knowledge of Action*. John Benjamins.

Gopnik, A. (1993). How We Know Our Minds: The Illusion of First-Person Knowledge of Intentionality. *Behavioral and Brain Sciences, 16*, 1–14.

Gordon, R. (1996). Radical Simulationism. In P. Carruthers & P. Smith (Eds.), *Theories of Theories of Mind*. Cambridge University Press.

Grahn, J., Parkinson, J., & Owen, A. (2008). The Cognitive Functions of the Caudate Nucleus. *Progress in Neurobiology, 86*, 141–155.

Greenfield, S. (2014). *The Human Brain: A Guided Tour*. Weidenfeld & Nicolson.

Hale, C. M., & Tager-Flusberg, H. (2003). The Influence of Language on Theory of Mind: A Training Study. *Developmental Science, 6*(3), 346–359.

Herbert, D., Coveney, J., Clarke, P., Graves, N., & Barnett, A. (2013). The Impact of Funding Deadlines on Personal Workloads, Stress and Family Relationships: A Qualitative Study of Australian Researchers. *BMJ Open, 4*, 3.

Hoffman, L. W. (2003). Methodological Issues in the Studies of SES, Parenting, and Child Development. In M. H. Bornstein & R. H. Bradley (Eds.), *Socioeconomic Status, Parenting, and Child Development*. Erlbaum.
Hutchison, E. (2019). *Dimensions of Human Behaviour: Person and Environment*. Sage.
Hyson, M. C., Hirsh-Pasek, K., & Rescorla, L. (1990). Academic Environments in Preschool: Challenges or Pressures? *Early Education and Development, 1*, 401–423.
Iriki, A. (2005). A Prototype of Homo Faber: A Silent Precursor of Human Intelligence in the Tool Making Monkey Brain. In *From Monkey Brain to Human Brain, A Fyssen Foundation Symposium*. MIT Press.
Joseph, M., & John, J. (2008). Impact of Parenting Styles on Child Development. *Global Academic Society Journal, Social Science Insight, 1*(5), 16–35.
Juan, V., & Astington, J. (2017). Does Language Matter for Implicit Theory of Mind? The Effects of Epistemic Verb Training on Implicit and Explicit False-Belief Understanding. *Cognitive Development, 41*, 19–32.
Kuzmics, C. (2004). Stochastic Evolutionary Stability in Extensive Form Games of Perfect Information. *Games and Economic Behavior, 48*(2), 321–336.
Lähdepuro, A., Savolainen, K., Lahti-Pulkkinen, M., et al. (2019). The Impact of Early Life Stress on Anxiety Symptoms in Late Adulthood. *Scientific Reports, 9*, 4395. https://doi.org/10.1038/s41598-019-40698-0
Larson, R. (2000). Toward a Psychology of Positive Youth Development. *American Psychologist, 55*(1), 170–183.
Larson, R. (2006). Positive Youth Development, Willful Adolescents, and Mentoring. *Journal of Community Psychology, 34*(6), 677–689.
Lerner, R. M. (2003). What Are SES effects of? A Developmental Systems Perspective. In M. H. Bornstein & R. H. Bradley (Eds.), *Socioeconomic Status, Parenting, and Child Development*. Erlbaum.
Linell, P. (2017). Intersubjectivity in Dialogue. In E. Weigand (Ed.), *The Routledge Handbook of Language and Dialogue*. Routledge.
Linver, M. R., Brooks-Gunn, J., & Kohen, D. (2002). Family Processes as Pathways from Income to Young Children's Development. *Developmental Psychology, 38*, 719–734.
Liu, W. M., Ali, S. R., Soleck, G., Hopps, J., Dunston, K., & Pickett, T. J. (2004). Using Social Class in Counselling Psychology Research. *Journal of Counseling Psychology, 51*, 3–18.
Luppino, G. (2005). Organisation of the Posterior Parietal Lobe and of Parieto-frontal Connections. In A. F. Brain (Ed.), *From Monkey Brain to Human*. MIT Press.
Mahy, C., Moses, L., & Pfeifer, J. (2014). How and Where: Theory of Mind in the Brain. *Developmental Cognitive Neuroscience, 9*, 68–81.

Martinez-Navarro, B. (2017). Epistemic States of Convincement: A Conceptualisation from the Practice of Mathematicians and Neurobiology. In U. Eligio (Ed.), *Understanding Emotions in Mathematical Thinking and Learning*. Academic Press.

Mezzacappa, E. (2004). Alerting, Orienting, and Executive Attention: Developmental Properties and Sociodemographic Correlates in an Epidemiological Sample of Young, Urban Children. *Child Development, 75*, 1373–1386.

Miller, S. (2016). *Parenting and Theory of Mind*. Oxford University Press.

Milligan, K., Astington, J. W., & Dack, L. A. (2007). Language and Theory of Mind: Meta-Analysis of the Relation Between Language Ability and False-Belief Understanding. *Child Development, 78*(2), 622–646.

Mistry, R. S., Biesanz, J. C., Taylor, L. C., Burchinal, M., & Cox, M. J. (2004). Family Income and Its Relation to Preschool Children's Adjustment for Families in the NICHD Study of Early Child Care. *Developmental Psychology, 40*, 727–745.

Moore, C. (2006). Theories of Mind in Infancy. *British Journal of Developmental Psychology, 14*, 19–40.

Moshman, D. (1998). Cognitive Development Beyond Childhood. In D. Kuhn & R. S. Siegler (Eds.), *Handbook of Child Psychology: Vol 2. Cognition, Perception, and Language* (pp. 947–978). Wiley.

Oakes, J. M., & Rossi, P. H. (2003). The Measurement of SES in Health Research: Current Practice and Steps Toward a New Approach. *Social Science & Medicine, 56*, 769–784.

Perner, J., & Leahy, B. (2016). Mental Files in Development: Dual Naming, False Belief, Identity and Intensionality. *Review of Philosophy and Psychology, 7*, 491–508. https://doi.org/10.1007/s13164-015-0235-6

Perner, J., Stummer, S., Sprung, M., & Doherty, M. (2002). Theory of Mind Find Its Piagetian Perspective: Why Alternative Naming Comes with Understanding Belief. *Cognitive Development, 17*(3–4), 1451–1472.

Perner, J., Mauer, M. C., & Hildenbrand, M. (2011). Identity: Key to Children's Understanding of Belief. *Science, 333*(6041), 474–477. https://doi.org/10.1126/science.1201216

Piaget, J. (1967). *Biology and Knowledge*. University of Chicago Press.

Premack, D., & Woodruff, G. (1978). Does the Chimpanzee Have a Theory of Mind? *The Behavioral and Brain Sciences, 4*, 515–526.

Rizzolatti, G., & Buccino, G. (2005). The Mirror Neuron System and Its Role in Imitation and Language. In A Fyssen Foundation Symposium (Ed.), *From Monkey Brain to Human Brain*. MIT Press.

Rutter, M. (1981). *Maternal Deprivation Reassessed* (2nd ed.). Penguin.

Rutter, M. (1985). Family and School Influences on Behavioural Development. *Journal of Child Psychology and Psychiatry, 26*(3), 349–368.

Rutter, M., & Giller, H. (1983). *Juvenile Delinquency: Trends and Perspectives*. Penguin.
Rutter, M., Quinton, D., & Liddle, C. (1983). Parenting in Two Generations: Looking Backwards and Looking Forwards. In N. Madge (Ed.), *Families at Risk*. Heinemann Educational.
Ryan, R. M., & Deci, E. L. (2003). On Assimilating Identities to the Self: A self-Determination Theory Perspective on Internalization and Integrity Within Cultures. In M. R. Leary & J. P. Tangney (Eds.), *Handbook of Self and Identity*. Guilford Press.
Sackett, G. P. (1982). Can Single Processes Explain Effects of Postnatal Influences on Primate Development. In R. N. Emde & R. J. Harmon (Eds.), *The Development of Attachment and Affiliative Systems*. Plenum Press.
Sameroff, A. (1975). Transactional Models in Early Social Relations. *Human Development, 18*, 65–79.
Sapolsky, R. (2018). *Behave: The Biology of Humans at Our Best and Worst*. Penguin Books.
Scholl, B., & Leslie, A. (2002). Modularity, Development and 'Theory of Mind'. *Mind & Language, 14*(1), 131–153.
Sen, A. K. (1990). Development as Capability Expansion. In K. Griffin & J. Knight (Eds.), *Human Development and the International Development Strategy for the 1990s*. Macmillan.
Sen, A. K. (1992). *Inequality Re-examined*. Harvard University Press.
Sen, A. K. (1999). *Development as Freedom*. Knopf Press.
Sobolewski, J. M., & Amato, P. R. (2005). Economic Hardship in the Family of Origin and Children's Psychological Well-Being in Adulthood. *Journal of Marriage and the Family, 67*, 141–156.
Steinberg, L. (2001). We Know Some Things: Parent-Adolescent Relationships in Retrospect and Prospect. *Journal of Research on Adolescence, 11*, 1–19.
Striedter, G. (2016). *Neurobiology: A Functional Approach*. Oxford University Press.
Strohschein, L. (2005). Household Income Histories and Child Mental Health Trajectories. *Journal of Health and Social Behavior, 46*, 359–375.
Teachman, J. D., Paasch, K. M., Day, R. D., & Carver, K. P. (1997). Poverty During Adolescence and Subsequent Educational Attainment. In G. J. Duncan & J. Brooks-Gunn (Eds.), *Consequences of Growing Up Poor*. Russell Sage Foundation.
Varley, R., & Siegal, M. (2000). Evidence for Cognition Without Grammar from Causal Reasoning and 'Theory of Mind' in an Agrammatic Aphasic Patient. *Current Biology, 10*(12), 723–726.
Vizard, P., Fukuda-Parr, S., & Elson, D. (2011). Introduction: The Capability Approach and Human Rights. *Journal of Human Development and Capabilities, 12*, 1.

Wilde-Astington, J., Pelletier, J., & Homer, B. (2002). Theory of Mind and Epistemological Development; The Relation Between Children's Second Order False-Belief Understanding and Their Ability to Reason Evidence. *New Ideas in Psychology, 20*, 2–5.

Zlatev, J., Racine, T., Sinha, C., & Itkonen, E. (2008). Intersubjectivity – What Makes Us Human? In J. Zlatev, T. Racine, C. Sinha, & E. Itkonen (Eds.), *The Shared Mind – Perspectives on Intersubjectivity*. John Benjamins Publishing Company.

CHAPTER 2

The Dimensions of Human Development

Introduction

Whenever the issues of human and economic development are analysed, there is always a need to consider a set of criteria which must be fulfilled to judge whether such development has been successful or not.[1] These criteria are the same as 'dimensions' of the same problem. A key feature of 'dimensions' are that they co-exist with other factors of the same problem.[2] For example, in the context of human development, it is essential for an individual to have access to a balanced diet, access to healthcare, access to sanitation and drinking water, education and equal opportunities. The latter, in the context of human development, requires that there be a reasonable recognition of the human rights of an individual—reasonable in the context that the behaviour of any individual should not have any negative impact either on society or on other individuals. Unfortunately, in Western society 'reasonable freedom' is not recognised because society and injured parties have recourse to the law. And access to this tends to be expensive and the results of the legal process do not always lead to justice for those whose human rights have been violated by others. Nevertheless,

[1] Alkire, S. (2002), Dimensions of Human Development, World Development, Vol. 30, No. 2, pp. 181-205.

[2] Ibid.

S. Ramesh, *The Political Economy of Human Behaviour and Economic Development*,
https://doi.org/10.1007/978-3-031-12666-6_2

the consideration of these 'dimensions' allows for the development and implementation of policies which enable the accomplishment and fulfilment of all the dimensions required for as complete human development as possible. In effect these dimensions serve as a benchmark for the elucidation of policies which would serve the purpose of achieving the multidimensional objective of human development.[3] This would embrace full access to public, private, economic, social, political and spiritual resources.[4] In this case, the evaluation of human development can be seen as a re-evaluation of economic activity as a process which merely satisfies the basic human needs to a process which provides opportunities for people to achieve valuable functionings.[5] These functionings could range from those required for survival to those more simple such as visiting a relative.[6] This would signify a shift from a unidimensional approach to understanding human development as a multidimensional problem requiring a multidimensional approach.[7] This multidimensional approach to assessing development reflects the Capability Approach to assessing development, in which case the extent of development is measured on the basis of an expansion of capability.[8] This could be an expansion of capability associated with survival, the ability to drink water or something as trivial as being able to visit a relative.[9] A similar approach to the Capability Approach which also does not determine either basic needs or basic capabilities can be associated with a 'no need to reason' approach to the way in which people behave.[10] In this case, by behaving in the way that they do, people are reflecting on a multidimensional view of their lives—access to resources, relationships, life experiences, beliefs and preferences, and thus can

[3] Ibid.

[4] Ibid.

[5] Ibid.

[6] Ibid.

[7] Seth, S., and Santos, ME. (2020), *Multidimensional Inequality and Human Development.* In: Cambridge Handbook of the Capability Approach. Cambridge University Press, pp. 392-416. ISBN 978-1107115286.

[8] Sen, A. K. (1990). Development as capability expansion. In Human development and the international development strategy for the 1990s, Griffin, K., & Knight, J. (Eds.), London: Macmillan.

[9] Alkire, S. (2002), Dimensions of Human Development, World Development, Vol. 30, No. 2, pp. 181-205.

[10] Grisez, G., Boyle, J., & Finnis, J. (1987), Practical principles, moral truth and ultimate ends, American Journal of Jurisprudence, 32, 99–151.

determine the best way in which they should behave.[11] However, although these approaches take a multidimensional approach to human development, there is a better need to understand the ways in which behaviour and functioning can be improved. This improvement can be achieved by reducing the inequality in society and improving the mechanisms for opportunities to arise and be grasped. Economic growth could be one way in which inequality in society can be reduced. However, the maximisation of economic growth and GDP has been the centre piece of the economic policy of governments around the world since 1945. In conjunction with the rapid rise of globalisation after the late 1970s, the impact on human society regardless of country has been to polarise prosperity in the hands of the few and poverty in the hands of the many. Therefore, in the last few years there has been a shift away from the mainstream view that government economic policies aimed at maximising economic growth will lead to increasing prosperity for all to a non-consensus view that the focus of government socio-economic policy should be on enhancing and maximising human well-being and the quality of life. Two countries which have embraced this economic ideology are Bhutan and New Zealand. It is about time that other countries also followed suit so that human well-being is enhanced, and the uneven distribution of wealth reduced.

Economic Growth and Human Development

The transition in policy thought from per capita income growth as being the focus of development to the human development approach reached a climax in 1990.[12] This was essentially due to the publication of a report in the same year on human development by the UNDP.[13] In this case, economic activity was seen as a means of human development, measured by the extent of the choices and opportunities which were becoming available to individuals.[14] The most important of the increasingly accessible choices and opportunities were those associated with achieving a healthy life, a long lifespan, becoming educated and being able to earn enough income to be able to enjoy an acceptable standard of living. Whilst these

[11] Alkire, S. (2002), Dimensions of Human Development, World Development, Vol. 30, No. 2, pp. 181-205.

[12] Stewart, F., Ranis, G., and Samman, E. (2018), Advancing Human Development: Theory and Practice, Oxford University Press, Oxford.

[13] UNDP (1990), Human Development Report 1990, Oxford University Press, Oxford.

[14] Ibid.

features were seen as the basic features of the advancement of human development, the other higher-level features of the advancement of human development were associated with enforceable human rights, freedom of thought, the freedom of political preferences and the ability to respect oneself.[15] However, in most countries in today's world, the focus of government policy has been on economic growth regardless of whether there is any human development at all—with economic growth being seen as a substitute for the level of general welfare in society as well as a mechanism for facilitating human development.[16] It may also be the case that human development will have an impact on economic growth when the expression of individual freedom is unhindered such that developing capabilities has a positive impact on economic performance.[17] Moreover, incomes will increase as a result of increased economic performance and this will allow for increased choices and perhaps better opportunities to develop individual capabilities.[18]

After the end of World War II in 1945, the pursuit of economic growth was seen as the way amongst policymakers and governments to alleviate poverty in their countries, with increases in GDP per capita being seen as a quantification of improvements in human development.[19] But it had been recognised in the mid-1950s that the quality of life is and should be the end product of economic activity.[20] Around this time it was also recognised that the economic performance of an economy allowed for greater choice.[21] The capabilities and functionings of the Capability Theory are very similar to the human capability formation and the use to which acquired capabilities are put to use in the context of the Human Capability Report.[22] The distinction between economic growth and human development had already been recognised, as well as the supposed causation between the two variables. However, the problem with the causation was

[15] Ibid.

[16] Ranis, G. (2004), Human Development and Economic Growth, Center Discussion Paper No. 887, Yale University.

[17] Ibid.

[18] Ibid.

[19] Srinivasan, N.T (1994), Human Development: A New Paradigm or Reinvention of the Wheel, The American Economic Review, Vol. 84, No. 2.

[20] Buchanan, N. S. and Ellis, H. S. (1955), Approaches to economic development. Twentieth Century Fund, New York.

[21] Lewis, A. (1955), The theory of economic growth. Irwin, Homewood, IL.

[22] Sen, A. (1992), Inequality re-examined. Russell Sage Foundation, New York.

that it only impacted a few, leaving in its wake the rising income disparity between the rich and the poor. This disparity in income between the rich and the poor in countries throughout the world has accelerated in the era of globalisation. Moreover, since 1990 increasing globalisation has meant that the few in countries around the world have become affluent whilst the many have remained poor. The impact of this has been that in contemporary times, in countries such as Bhutan and New Zealand, the focus of government policy has shifted away from an emphasis on economic growth to an emphasis on human development. This has become quantified in the context of the Human Development Index (HDI). The HDI was introduced by the UNDP in 1990 in order to quantify the extent of human development in the context of the level of income required to maintain a basic standard of living, the opportunity to acquire knowledge as well as longevity.[23] While the latter two are required for the development of human capabilities, income levels determine the extent to which capabilities can be utilised.[24] Each of the three factors associated with human development is quantified in terms of the level of deprivation at country level by real income per head, and literacy and life expectancy as an equally weighted sum in the HDI.[25] However, while all three factors can be quantified, there is a question as to the legitimacy of this quantification. Any valuation of capabilities and functionings will be subjective and so will vary from individual to individual and from circumstance to circumstance.[26] Similarly, educational attainment and life expectancy in the context of the HDI, being like the functionings of the Capability Theory, do not need to have the same relative values between countries, individuals and groups. Moreover, longevity is not effectively quantified in the HDI, as a decrease in life expectancy from an initial base of 40 years is not comparable to a decrease in life expectancy from an initial base of 60 years.[27] Thus, in comparing the HDI with the Capability Theory, it is not possible to find the conceptual approach of the latter with regard to poverty and the standard of living in the former.[28] Nevertheless, the complementation of real income growth with other measures will help to assess development performance

[23] Srinivasan, N.T (1994), Human Development: A New Paradigm or Reinvention of the Wheel, The American Economic Review, Vol. 84, No. 2.

[24] Ibid.

[25] Ibid.

[26] Ibid.

[27] Ibid.

[28] Ibid.

and this approach is justifiable in order to achieve a better understanding of the development process itself.[29] However, the multidimensional nature of the development process has been recognised by economists prior to the publication of the HDR in 1990. This is evidenced by the implementation of the International Suffering Index, which incorporates ten quantifiable variables associated with well-being.[30] But the question arises as to whether variables other than income give any further information which can be used to evaluate the process of development. In this case, if the additional variables complement the explanatory depth of how differing income levels may result in different development processes in different countries, then the inclusion of such variables will be justified. However, because there is no standard measure which can be applied country by country on an equal basis, complementing the explanatory power of income is not commonly used to evaluate the development process.[31] On the other hand, different indicators could be used to measure distinct aspects of the development process. In this case, if the indicators are mutually orthogonal then these indicators quantify different unrelated facets of the development process, whereas if indicators are perfectly correlated then these indicators measure the same aspect of the development process.[32] But in the context of the UNDP's HDI it is not clear what the combination of income levels, longevity and knowledge is evaluated in the context of the development process itself.[33] Indeed, the weakness of the quantification of the data associated with each component of the index in not allowing for the universal conformity of the index across countries at differing levels of the development process is clear. For example, the GNP data of countries is not easily comparable due to biases and errors in estimation as well as gaps in the time for which the data is available.[34] Similarly, there may also be inaccuracies in the estimation of life expectancies within and between countries. And such data may be quantified and estimated using sophisticated mathematical models rather than based on a system of

[29] Ibid.

[30] Camp, S., and Speidel, J. J, (1987), The international human suffering index, Population Crisis Committee, Washington, DC.

[31] Srinivasan, N.T (1994), Human Development: A New Paradigm or Reinvention of the Wheel, The American Economic Review, Vol. 84, No. 2.

[32] Ibid.

[33] Ibid.

[34] Ibid.

national measurement.[35] Furthermore, with regard to literacy levels—the quantification of the knowledge indicator in the HDI—different countries may define literacy in diverse ways and school enrolment rates do not have a global standard. Moreover, the length of the school year, dropout rates and the quality of schools will vary from country to country.[36] This makes it difficult to use the HDI as the basis of comparison as well as across countries. Therefore, for the reasons discussed so far, it becomes evident that not only does the HDI lack a robust conceptual framework but also it lacks solid theoretical foundations.[37] Therefore, evaluating the human development process between countries becomes problematic and any policy recommendations become ill founded. This may lead to inappropriate policies being devised for countries such that human development and well-being goals cannot be achieved. Furthermore, even before the Human Development Report of 1990, countries such as Sri Lanka and the Indian state of Kerala were making headway with regard to human development. And in the case of Kerala, earlier achievements in human development, especially in the context of education and health, may have helped to facilitate economic growth.[38] This is because with a good education and health, workers will be more productive in the context of being skilled as well as physically fit. This empirical finding was found in the context of 15 Indian states: cross-sectional growth regressions have shown that there has been a convergence with respect to human development amongst the states but a divergence in the growth of real per capita income.[39] Thus, while the poorer states failed to catch up with the richer states, they were able to catch up in terms of human development.[40] This indicates that well-formulated human development policies are effective in stimulating the features of human development. This finding, in conjunction with the earlier finding, would suggest that economic growth induced by human development processes should be strengthened to promote a virtuous cycle rather than a vicious cycle.[41] A virtuous cycle results when superior

[35] Ibid.

[36] Ibid.

[37] Ibid.

[38] Chakraborty, A. (2005), Kerala's Changing Development Narratives, Economic and Political Weekly, Vol. 40, No. 6, pp. 541-547.

[39] Ghosh, M. (2006), Economic Growth and Human Development in Indian States, Economic and Political Weekly, Vol. 41, No. 30, pp. 3321-3329.

[40] Ibid.

[41] Ibid.

performance in human development causes a positive long-term impact on economic growth[42]—while a vicious cycle has the opposite effect, leading to unstable economic growth. However, in the case of Nigeria it has been found that while there is a long-run relationship between economic growth and human development, only economic growth has a positive impact on human development and not vice versa.[43] Furthermore, it has been found that increasing the level of public expenditure, especially on female health and education, has a positive impact on the link between economic growth and human development.[44] Moreover, the distribution of income and the rate of investment have a positive impact on the transition chain from human development to economic growth.[45] Remittances from relatives working overseas has also helped to further human development back in their home countries, where families may be dependent on the remittances of relatives working overseas.[46] However, the nature of the impact of economic growth on human development depends on the extent to which government policy is able to allocate public spending effectively to promote the uptake of education in a country.[47] Nevertheless, in Latin America it has been found that good health is important for income generation.[48] But in the case of African countries it has been found that there was a negative impact on economic growth due to public expenditure on health and education, whereas levels of human capital stock have some positive impact on economic growth.[49] The negative impact of public expenditure on health and education on economic growth may be

[42] Ranis, G., Stewart, F., and Ramirez, A. (2000), Economic Growth and Human Development, World Development, Vol. 28, No. 2, pp. 197-219.

[43] Chikalipah, S., and Okafor, G. (2018), Dynamic Linkage Between Economic Growth and Human Development: Time Series Evidence from Nigeria, Journal of International Development, 31, 22-28.

[44] Ibid.

[45] Ranis, G., Stewart, F., and Ramirez, A. (2000), Economic Growth and Human Development, World Development, Vol. 28, No. 2, pp. 197-219.

[46] Ratha, D. (2013), The Impact of Remittances on Economic Growth and Poverty Reduction, Migration Policy Institute, Policy Brief No. 8.

[47] Shome, S., and Tondon, S. (2010), Balancing Human Development with Economic Growth: A Study of ASEAN 5, Annals of University of Petrosani, Economics, 10(1), pp. 335-348.

[48] Mayer, D. (2001), The Long-Term Impact of Health on Economic Growth in Latin America, World Development, Vol. 29, No. 6, pp. 1025-1033.

[49] Eggoh, J., Houeninvo, H., Sossou, Gilles-Armand (2015), Education, Health and Economic Growth in African Countries, Journal of Economic Development, Volume 40, No.

because the African population is sparsely spread in rural areas, making access to health centres difficult, and the population may also be agriculturally based and poor. In this case, education may be the furthest thing in their minds that they would want. Although, the greater skill level may facilitate greater productivity and greater levels of economic growth. Another general finding based on an analysis of 79 developing countries, but not including Eastern European countries, using World Bank Development Indicators 2003 suggests that an early policy emphasis on promoting human development is important, as this not only facilitates short-run economic growth but sustains it in the long run.[50] Moreover, besides the investment in human capital, institutional quality may also be important in the context of human capital accumulation, specifically with regard to building a sustainable development path.[51] This may be because superior institutions may allow for a more effective and efficient allocation of resources. This may lead to a more effective educational system.

Some argue that economic growth by itself will be enough to reduce the disparities in income and human development in India.[52] Yet other studies find that the greater is the level of financial inclusion in terms of the demand and supply of financial services, the greater will be the impact on India's economic growth.[53] However, it has also been found that while financial inclusion promotes economic growth, economic growth does not promote financial inclusion.[54] However, this finding may differ when countries are natural resource dependent.[55] For example, in the case of Saudi Arabia, it has been found that there is a strong and positive relationship between financial inclusion and the Human Development Index, while there is a negative and insignificant correlation between financial inclusion and economic growth. Moreover, financial inclusion is also highly negatively correlated with both the share of the rural population

[50] Suri, T., Boozer, N., Ranis, G., and Stewart, F. (2010), Paths to Success: The Relationship Between Human Development and Economic Growth, World Development, Vol. 39, No. 4, pp. 506-522.

[51] Costantini, V., and Monni, S. (2008), Ecological Economics, 64, pp. 867-880.

[52] Dholakia, R. (2003), Regional Disparity in Economic and Human Development in India, Economic and Political Weekly, Vol. 38, No. 39, pp. 4166-4172.

[53] Sethi, D., and Sethy, S. (2017), Financial Inclusion Matters for Economic Growth in India, International Journal of Social Economics, Vol. 46, No. 1, pp. 132-151.

[54] Ibid.

[55] Hathroubi, S. (2019), Inclusive Finance, Growth and Socio-Economic Development in Saudi Arabia: A Threshold Cointegration Approach, Journal of Economic Development, Volume 44, No. 2.

and the share of women in the population.[56] This could be because neither the rural population nor women in the economy are engaged in any significant economic activity and thus will not be contributing to the country's economic growth. On the other hand, in general there was found to be a non-linear causal relationship between economic growth, financial inclusion and human development in the long run[57]—while in the short run there was no causation between financial inclusion and economic growth and vice versa.[58] This could be because investment and savings only have long-term impacts on economic growth. This is perhaps because the factors associated with human development such as longevity, knowledge and increases in real GDP per capita can only be thought of as being long-term phenomena because they can only be accessed over an extended period. Furthermore, long-run living standards also depend upon the availability of the factors of production. These factors of production include labour and capital. With regard to labour, this can be viewed as human capital which absorbs and uses knowledge but at the same time also generates knowledge through innovation and invention. Thus, human capital innovation allows for technological innovation, which allows for the creation of jobs as the population grows and facilitates economic growth through increases in productivity.[59] And strong institutions in a country facilitate potentially high levels of economic growth, both linked but causality flowing from strong institutions to economic growth.[60] This could be because strong institutions allow for a more efficient management, organisation and allocation of resources, resulting in increased productivity, profitable use of resources and higher standards of living as income levels increase in society. Nevertheless, it has also been found using standard covariance accounting that it is the variation in inputs which explains 46% of the variability in long-run living standards.[61] In addition, using capital intensity covariance accounting, it has been found that 25%

[56] Ibid.

[57] Ibid.

[58] Ibid.

[59] Mincer, J. (1984), Human Capital and Economic Growth, Economics of Education Review, Vol. 3, No. 3, pp. 195-205.

[60] Siddiqui, D., and Ahmed, Q. (2019), The Causal Relationship Between Institutions and Economic Growth: An Empirical Investigation for Pakistan Economy, International Economics and Business, Vol. 5, No. 1.

[61] Tamura, R., Dwyer, J., Devereux, J., and Baier, S. (2019), Economic Growth in the Long Run, Journal of Development Economics, 137, pp. 1-35.

of the variation in long-run living standards is explained by variations in the levels of the factors of production.[62] And using intergenerational human capital accumulation, it has been found that up to 50% of the variation in long-run living standards can be explained by the variability in inputs.[63]

Despite the progress of Sri Lanka and Kerala with regard to human development, there has been no noticeable change in the policies of countries or regions within countries which are lagging behind.[64] This may be indicative of the fact that impediments to progressing human development within and across countries may lie in the political processes of national and multinational institutions. Recommendations for improvements in the political processes so that decisions about how human development can be efficiently progressed seem to be lacking in the Human Development Report and this needs to be addressed.[65]

Quality of Life Versus Human Development

Explicitly, quality of life is associated with better living conditions as well as with perceptions of what quality of life should be.[66] However, implicitly, quality of life can be emphasised in terms of longevity, improved health and nutrition, opportunities to improve living standards and the diffusion and uptake of democracy in the wider society[67]—although the latter would be more effective if it was representative of society and functioned as a technocracy as well as a meritocracy. Some may argue that China's model of 'democracy' may be more effective at stimulating economic growth and development rather than the Western model of democracy. This may be because even though its economic reforms began in 1978, China's

[62] Tamura, R., Dwyer, J., Devereux, J., and Baier, S. (2019), Economic Growth in the Long Run, Journal of Development Economics, 137, pp. 1-35.

[63] Ibid.

[64] Srinivasan, N.T (1994), Human Development: A New Paradigm or Reinvention of the Wheel, The American Economic Review, Vol. 84, No. 2.

[65] Ibid.

[66] Glatzer, W. (2015), Monitoring and Analysing Quality of Life – An Introduction, IN Global Handbook of Quality of Life: Exploration of Well-Being of Nations and Continents, Glatzer, W., Camfield, L., Moller, V., and Rojas, M. (Eds), Springer, London.

[67] Glatzer, W. (2015), Monitoring and Analysing Quality of Life – An Introduction, IN Global Handbook of Quality of Life: Exploration of Well-Being of Nations and Continents, Glatzer, W., Camfield, L., Moller, V., and Rojas, M. (Eds), Springer, London.

economic growth as well as economic development took off rapidly and now may even be surpassing that of Western, developed countries.

In the context of evaluating poverty, quality of life seems to have superseded traditional measures of poverty such as income levels.[68] This is probably because the limitations of using income as a measure of poverty have become well known over time.[69] In this case, disposable income as a measure of poverty fails to take into account inflation, accumulated debt, state benefits, the nature of the working circumstances of the self-employed and the individual's long-term command over resources.[70] Moreover, wealth and income may not be suitable substitutes for happiness[71]—the former two being objectively quantifiable, while the latter is subjectively qualitative. Furthermore, relative measures of income are static measures which do not consider the state of the economy which may impact on poverty levels. It is the recognition that income and wealth are not sufficient measures to evaluate poverty which has given rise to other approaches to analyse well-being such as the Quality-of-Life approach (QoL).[72] QoL is concerned with not just the control of resources and living conditions across a lifespan but also the ways in which individuals think and feel about their lives and how they respond to this.[73] QoL is evaluated on the basis of the Capability Theory, which focuses on the activities that individuals are enabled to conduct instead of focusing purely on the material resources which may be available to them.[74] In this case, there had been a growing disillusionment with GDP growth as the focus of government economy

[68] Whelan, C., Watson, D., and Maitre, B. (2019), From Income Poverty to Multidimensional Quality of Life, The Economic and Social Review, Vol. 50, No. 4, pp. 683-705.

[69] Watson, D., C. T. Whelan and B. Maitre, 2017. "Non-Monetary Indicators and Multiple Dimensions: The ESRI approach to Poverty Measurement", *The Economic and Social Review*, Vol. 48, No. 4, pp. 369-392.

[70] Nolan, B. and C. T. Whelan, 2007. "On the Multidimensionality of Poverty and Social Exclusion" in Micklewright, J. and S. Jenkins, (eds.), *Poverty and Inequality: New Directions*. Oxford: Oxford University Press.

[71] Yaya, S., Ghosh, S., Ghose, B. (2019), Subjective Happiness, Health and Quality of Life and Their Sociocultural Correlates among Younger Population in Malawi, Soc. Sci, 8, 55.

[72] Whelan, C., Watson, D., and Maitre, B. (2019), From Income Poverty to Multidimensional Quality of Life, The Economic and Social Review, Vol. 50, No. 4, pp. 683-705.

[73] Ibid.

[74] Sen, A. (1992), Inequality: Re-examined, Oxford: Clarendon Press, Sen, A. (1993), Capability and Well-Being IN Nussbaum, M. and Sen, A. (Eds.), The Quality of Life, Oxford: Clarendon Press.

policy because increasing prosperity was concentrated rather than widely dispersed throughout the population. The result was the increasing disparities in income between the rich and the poor. Therefore, policymakers shifted away from using GDP to promote and assess economic development and towards promoting development based on environmental, social and economic indicators. The end game of policy shifting away from GDP to these indicators was to ensure that the well-being of households and individuals improved.[75] This objective was furthered in 2011 with the launch of the OECD's Better Life Initiative, which was made up of two components. The first of these was the Your Better Life Index, which facilitated OECD countries to compare well-being.[76] And the second component of the Better Life Initiative is a framework for assessing how well-being develops across OECD countries.[77] Another study on the quality of life in Latvia analysed factors associated with the state of finances, the level of economic activity, levels of education, access to housing, law and order, the state of the environment and the quality of health.[78] However, an alternate framework for establishing, promoting and measuring well-being had already been established by the United Nations (UN) in 2000. As globalisation rapidly expanded throughout the world, disparities in income increased amongst populations in countries as well as amongst populations between countries. Nevertheless, one study has shown that globalisation improved the quality of life in Pakistan[79]—although, the improvement in the quality of life seems to vary between Pakistani provinces, with districts in Punjab being at the higher end of improvements in the quality of life.[80] This could be because Punjab is a rich agricultural province which has benefitted from the export of agricultural products as a direct result of globalisation. However, because of growing disparities in income the United Nations developed and implemented the Millennium

[75] OECD (2013), OECD Guidelines on Measuring Subjective Well-being, OECD publishing, Paris. https://doi.org/10.1787/9789264191655-en

[76] OECD, 2011a. Compendium of OECD Well-being Indicators, OECD Publishing, Paris.

[77] OECD, 2011b. "How's Life? Measuring Well-being". Paris: OECD publishing. https://doi.org/10.1787/9789264121164-en

[78] Judrupa, I., and Pipare, A. (2019), Measurement of the Quality of Life in the Regions of Latvia, Proceedings of the 2019 International Conference 'Economic Science for Rural Development', No. 51, pp. 152-159.

[79] Majeed, M. T. (2019). Quality of life and globalization: Econometric evidence from Asian economies, Journal of Quantitative Methods, 3(1), 84-113.

[80] Ihsan, N., and Aziz, B. (2019), A Multidimensional Analysis of Quality of Life: Pakistan's Context, Soc Indic Res 142, pp. 201-227.

Development Goals (MDGs) in 2000. The MDGs are a set of objectives relating to reducing poverty, reducing sickness and hunger, improving opportunities for people, reducing gender inequality and improving the environment.[81] Although the MDGs were put in place in 2000, they represented a set of universal objectives which all countries around the world were expected to achieve by the year 2015. The annual publication of the information relating to the extent to which each country had achieved with regard to attaining the MDGs allowed for greater scrutiny of each government's achievements in the public sphere as well as provided an incentive for countries to compete with each other in improving MDG achievements.[82] However, the main uncertainties with the latter rested with the extent to which rich, developed economies would be willing to financially help the poorer developing nations, and the commitment of politicians within countries to champion the fulfilment of the MDG objectives.[83] In 2015, the MDGs were replaced by the Sustainable Development Goals (SDGs). There were 17 SDGs identified by the United Nations, with the aim of achieving each by the year 2030.[84] The word 'sustainable' is associated with nature, life support and the community, while 'development' is best associated with people, economy and society.[85] The SDGs followed on from the MDGs but with a greater emphasis on sustainable development. Sustainable development is measured in the context of the Sustainable Development Index (SDI), which in essence reflects the level of development achieved in the context of ecological efficiency.[86] The SDGs focus on bringing poverty within and between countries to an end and ensuring prosperity and inclusiveness in a society which is both just

[81] Glatzer, W. (2015), Monitoring and Analysing Quality of Life – An Introduction, IN Global Handbook of Quality of Life: Exploration of Well-Being of Nations and Continents, Glatzer, W., Camfield, L., Moller, V., and Rojas, M. (Eds), Springer, London.

[82] Sachs, J. (2012), From Millennium Development Goals to Sustainable Development Goals, Lancet, 379, pp. 2206-11.

[83] Sachs, J. (2012), From Millennium Development Goals to Sustainable Development Goals, Lancet, 379, pp. 2206-11.

[84] United Nations, 2015. Transforming our world: the 2030 agenda for sustainable development. https://www.un.org/ga/search/view_doc.asp?symbol¼A/RES/70/1&Lang¼E

[85] US National Research Council, Policy Division, Board on Sustainable Development, (1999), Our Common Journey: A Transition Toward Sustainability, National Academy Press, Washington, DC.

[86] Hickel, J. (2020), The Sustainable Development Index: Measuring the ecological efficiency of human development in the Anthropocene, Ecological Economics, 167.

and peaceful.[87] The financial means required for countries to successfully achieve the SDGs need to be provided by both the public sector and the private sector. However, while the public sector should play a larger role in financing the achievement of the SDGs in developed economies, private sector financing in the form of foreign direct investment will be important for developing economies, especially because the public sector of such countries is not big enough to play such a role.[88] Within the category of developing economies, there are least developed economies, which includes 34 African economies. In such countries, not only there is a lack of public sector financial resources, but such countries also face unstable and volatile governments, endemic corruption as well as the impact of varying seasonal factors, including droughts.[89] Nevertheless, the main difficulties faced by African countries in achieving the SDGs were a lack of political co-ordination and the organisation of resources required to do so.[90] Another problem with countries achieving the SDGs is a precise universal definition of 'sustainable'.[91] However, the flexibility with which 'sustainable' can be defined, quantified and measured could perhaps be one of its advantages in allowing for diverse contributions to an evolving idea.[92] This approach allows for 'sustainable' to be adapted and applied to an ever-changing global socio-economic and cultural environment. Moreover, in contrast to the MDGs, the SDGs have allowed for the concepts of economic development and environmental protection to be given greater width and depth such that it has now become possible for governments to focus on the human and social aspects of development while at the same time emphasising protection of the environment at the expense

[87] United Nations, 2015. Transforming our world: the 2030 agenda for sustainable development. https://www.un.org/ga/search/view_doc.asp?symbol¼A/RES/70/1&Lang¼E

[88] UNCTAD, 2014. World Investment Report 2014 - Investing in the SDGs: an Action Plan. https://unctad.org/en/PublicationsLibrary/wir2014_en.pdf

[89] Aust, V., Morais, A., and Pinto, I. (2020), How does foreign direct investment contribute to Sustainable Development Goals? Evidence from African countries, Journal of Cleaner Production, 245.

[90] Ibid.

[91] Robert, K., Parris, T., Leiserowitz, A. (2005), What is Sustainable Development? Goals, Indicators, Values and Practice, Environment: Science and Policy for Sustainable Development, 47:3, pp. 8-21.

[92] Ibid.

of its exploitation just to further human existence.[93] Therefore, what is 'sustainable' lies between established concepts and concepts which are dynamic and changing according to socio-economic, political, cultural and ecological circumstances.[94] And whatever perspective of sustainable development is followed, it may be true to say that all perspectives adhere to the three-dimensional approach to human well-being associated with social inclusion, environmental sustainability and economic development.[95] Thus, sustainable development needs the interaction and dialogue of a diverse group of stakeholders in order to facilitate collective action such that a number of values can be achieved at the same time.[96] However, it may not be possible to quantify all the SDGs because of their complex interactions.[97]

Even though well-being has been singled out as the best way in which to assess the development and progression of the individual, the household and society shifting away from the post-World War II emphasis on GDP growth as the universal signal of well-being for all, the development framework is lacking in one respect. This is with regard to childhood development, as this is where the seeds of inequality and an inferior quality of life are sowed. Moreover, whereas childhood development has been linked to the level of household wealth, it has also been found that other factors such as the extent of maternal education and the quality of the home environment are also important.[98] Furthermore, it is evident that human development is not just an outcome of a preconfigured genetic programme that an individual is born with.[99] But instead, human development is unique to each individual, dependent on the culture, relationships

[93] Robert, K., Parris, T., Leiserowitz, A. (2005), What is Sustainable Development? Goals, Indicators, Values and Practice, Environment: Science and Policy for Sustainable Development, 47:3, pp. 8-21.

[94] Ibid.

[95] Sachs, J. (2012), From Millennium Development Goals to Sustainable Development Goals, Lancet, 379, pp. 2206-11.

[96] Ibid.

[97] Bhayana, S., and Kakkar, A. (2019), Sustainable development goals, going beyond GDP: India's Case, Indian Journal of Economics and Development, Vol. 7(2).

[98] Miller, L., Neupane, S., Neupane, S., Lohani, M., Joshi, N., Shrestha, M., Thorne-Lyman, A. (2019), Diet quality over time is associated with better development in rural Nepali Children, Matern Child Nutr. 2020;e12964, https://doi.org/10.1111/mcn.12964

[99] Osher, D., Cantor, P., Berg, J., Steyer, L., and Rose, T. (2020), Drivers of Human Development: How relationships and context shape Learning and Development, Applied Developmental Science, Vol. 24, No. 1, pp. 6-36.

and environment to which each individual is exposed, with adaptations taking place over an entire lifetime.[100] This ideological stance stems from an integration of knowledge from the fields of biology, neuroscience, psychology and the social sciences.[101] The integrated approach to childhood development leads to the idea that genes act only when stimulated by the environment, and as such are followers rather than prime movers.[102] Therefore, the social and physical environments and the interaction of the child with these contexts become very important to the way in which genes are expressed.[103] In this case, human development can thus be considered to be both constructive and progressive and, importantly, dependent on context and relationships and adversity and resilience in shaping individual personality.[104] If an individual is in a context and relationships from which adversity results, then the individual may become stressed and this could lead to alcoholism, drug addiction, bullying or other harmful behaviours. However, owing to childhood intervention with appropriate educational, cultural, health and behavioural policies, the individual may have instead become resilient enough to overcome the stress in a positive way without resorting to alcohol. Furthermore, an environment in which a child is brought up amongst quarrelling parents may lead to the child in adulthood being unable to form close relationships. And if primary education is of poor quality, then the positive externalities associated with increased mobile phone penetration in a country may be reduced.[105] Therefore, with regard to human development, context plays a powerful

[100] Ibid.

[101] Fedyk, M. (2015). How (not) to bring psychology and biology together. Philosophical Studies, 172(4), 949–967.

[102] Cantor, P., Osher, D., Berg, J., Steyer, L., and Rose, T. (2019), Malleability, plasticity, and individuality: How children learn and develop in context, Applied Developmental Science, 23:4, 307-337, DOI: https://doi.org/10.1080/10888691.2017.1398649

[103] Keating, D. P. (2016). Transformative role of epigenetics in child development research: Commentary on the special section. Child Development, 87(1), 135–142. doi: https://doi.org/10.1111/cdev.12488

[104] Osher, D., Cantor, P., Berg, J., Steyer, L., and Rose, T. (2020), Drivers of Human Development: How relationships and context shape Learning and Development, Applied Developmental Science, Vol. 24, No. 1, pp. 6-36.

[105] Asongu, S., and Odhiambo, N. (2019), Basic Formal Education Quality, Information Technology, and Inclusive Human Development in Sub-Saharan Africa, Sustainable Development, 27, pp. 419-428.

role and thus needs to be 'managed' so that a positive outcome results.[106] For example, in infancy and early childhood, physical contact between the parent and the infant/child can, in the absence of a spoken language, act as a substitute for communication, allowing for reinforced learning.[107] It is, therefore, evident that the upbringing and educational pathways of children should be designed in such a way that individual responses in context and relationships over lifetimes will reflect resilience and positive adaptation in an environment which promotes well-being, learning and health.[108] The development of resilience in childhood and adolescence will be more fully evaluated in Chap. 7.

Social Institutions and Social Capabilities

A social institution can be thought of as a network of relationships bound by norms and customs which are codified in a standard way so as to be understood by individuals and thus by society at large.[109] A social institution is comparable to an institutional domain.[110] Examples of major institutional domains or social institutions include the family, the macroeconomy, education, law, politics and religion.[111] The best way in which to study social institutions is through the use of the Rational Choice Theory.[112] The use and development of the Rational Choice Theory has become more interdisciplinary over time, involving anthropologists, sociologists and political scientists, whereas during the time of its conception,

[106] Cremin, L. (1980). American education: The national experience. New York, NY: Harper and Row.

[107] Cascio, C., Moore, D., and McGlone, F. (2019), Social Touch and Human Development, Developmental Cognitive Neuroscience, 35, 5-11.

[108] Osher, D., Cantor, P., Berg, J., Steyer, L., and Rose, T. (2020), Drivers of Human Development: How relationships and context shape Learning and Development, Applied Developmental Science, Vol. 24, No. 1, pp. 6-36.

[109] Turner, J. (2010), Theoretical Principles of Sociology, Volume 1: Macrodynamics, Springer, New York.

[110] Ibid.

[111] Turner, J. (1997), The Institutional Order: Economy, Kinship, Religion, Polity, Law and Education in Evolutionary and Comparative Perspective, Longman, New York.

[112] Hechter, M., Opp, Karl-Dieter., and Wippler, R. (2017), Introduction, IN Social Institutions: Their Emergence, Maintenance and Effects, Hechter, M., Opp, Karl-Dieter and Wippler, R. (Eds), Routledge, New York.

the main proponents were economists and psychologists.[113] At the heart of the Rational Choice Theory there are three assumptions.[114] These include the Preference Hypothesis, the Constraint Hypothesis and the Utility Maximisation Hypothesis. The Preference Hypothesis suggests that individuals can rank choices and act in such a way that they are able to attain the highest-ranking choice. However, the Constraint Hypothesis suggests that individuals may be constrained in attaining their highest-ranking choice because of social institutions or because they may not control the resources necessary. Lastly, the Utility Maximisation Hypothesis suggests that given the constraints, individuals will attain the highest-ranking choice possible. Based on these three assertions, one of the key outcomes of the Rational Choice Theory is that social institutions result only when they are favourable to the private interests of individuals.[115] However, the social optimal outcomes of the allocation of resources may not match the private optimal outcomes. Therefore, social institutions which result from private interests may not fulfil the needs of society. The implication is that governments should play a key role in ensuring the effective development and maintenance of social institutions. Examples of the latter would include the family, the monarchy, religious groups and groups of individuals with the same values and beliefs.[116] The latter would include social entrepreneurship.

An effective social institution such as family would, by creating a positive environment, ensure that children's behaviours are guided and that the choices they face are clear.[117] Moreover, a childhood upbringing in a positive environment which helps to build the qualities of resilience and flexibility in individuals can lead to a reduction in inequality, because in such an environment, opportunities are available to activate an individual's mental and physical functioning. However, some changes in individual behaviour are intergenerational. In this case, social change can be considered in the context of developmental change. This is specifically with

[113] Hechter, M., Opp, Karl-Dieter., and Wippler, R. (2017), Introduction, IN Social Institutions: Their Emergence, Maintenance and Effects, Hechter, M., Opp, Karl-Dieter and Wippler, R. (Eds), Routledge, New York.

[114] Ibid.

[115] Ibid.

[116] Fraser, J. (2020), Social Institutions and International Human Rights Law Implementation, Cambridge University Press, Cambridge.

[117] Kaplan, S. (2018), Huma Rights in Thick and Thin Societies: The Universal Declaration and Bridging the Gap, Cambridge University Press.

regard to change which occurs across generations in contrast to change which occurs across a lifetime.[118] An objective associated with the theory of human development and social change is to explain how values and cultural norms and practices change across generations, as there is social, economic as well as cultural change.[119] However, a better understanding of human development in the context of social change may not lead to a better understanding of how income inequality in society may arise. In this regard, a better understanding of how inequality in human capability arises may lead to a better understanding of how income inequality may arise in society.[120] The inequality in human capability may begin to become apparent by the late teens in adolescents because preferences and skills are determined early in the life of a child.[121] Indeed, empirical evidence suggests that in the United States, individuals will be aware of the factors which give rise to half of the lifetime inequality in the present value of future earnings by the age of 18.[122] The origins of these factors may lie in the early years of childhood, during which the child's context, environment and genes may play a crucial role in the development of character and cognition. Cognition may play a key role in the development of skills as well as the development of sound judgement and the ability to make sound judgements. But to 'put yourself in someone else's shoes' perhaps requires the development of a higher level of cognition.[123] The role of the father in childhood development in the context of how much time the father spends with the children has been an area of extensive research.[124] The findings of such research are supported by the findings of other scholarly works which suggest that a positive relationship between the child and its primary caregiver as well the child's accessibility to educational

[118] Greenfield, P. (2009), Linking Social Change and Developmental Change: Shifting Pathways of Human Development, Developmental Psychology, Vol. 45, No. 2, pp. 401-418.

[119] Ibid.

[120] Cunha, F., and Heckman, J. (2009), The Economics and Psychology of Inequality and Human Development, Journal of the European Economic Association, 7(2-3) pp. 320-364.

[121] Ibid.

[122] Cunha, F., and Heckman, J. (2007), The Evolution of Uncertainty in Labor Earnings in the US Economy, Working Paper, University of Chicago.

[123] Bradford, E., Jentzsch, I., and Gomez, J. (2015), From Self to Social Cognition: Theory of Mind Mechanisms and their relation to Executive Functioning, Cognition, 138, pp. 21-34.

[124] Lamb, M., and Tamis-Lemonda, C. (2004), The Role of the Father: An Introduction IN The Role of the Father in Childhood Development, Lamb, M. (Ed), John Wiley & Sons, Inc.

opportunities will impact on its development, particularly in the context of building a resilient character. The development of this is particularly important when the child enters puberty and adolescence, successive periods of human development in which genetic and psychological mechanisms unleash a torrent of hormones into the human body, facilitating transition into adulthood. Furthermore, from one perspective, the social learning theory is very much dependent on the interactions between the child and the parents and society in the context of the physical maturation of the child, to explain cognitive development. This perspective is based on the ideas that learning occurs in stages on the basis of stimulus-response, with the child initially acquiring actions and responses, the physical maturation of the child which brings about different learning experiences as the child interacts with wider society over time.[125] On the other hand, another perspective on the social learning theory suggests that the 'manipulation' of a child's emotions with regard to reinforcement and motivation is important for the development of cognitive processes in conjunction with memory, imagery and problem solving.[126]

Social entrepreneurship can be thought of as a social institution which facilitates social capabilities—although the nature of social entrepreneurship and its social value remains to be clarified through further empirical research.[127] The same can also be said for a multi-level analysis of social entrepreneurship because empirical analysis so far has only analysed social entrepreneurship one level at each stage of the analysis.[128] Social entrepreneurship and sustainable development may be interconnected.[129] In this case, social entrepreneurs are able to bring change in the context of social and environmental problems.[130] Social entrepreneurs usually engage with

[125] Sears, R. (1957), Identification as a form of behavioural development, IN The Concept of Development, Harris, D. (Ed), University of Minnesota Press, Minneapolis.

[126] Bandura, A. (1977), Self-efficacy: Toward a unifying theory of behavioural change, Psychological Review, 84, pp. 191-215.

[127] Saebi, T., Foss, N., Linder, S. (2018), Social Entrepreneurship Research: Past Achievements and Future Promises, Journal of Management, Vol. 45, No. 1, pp. 70-95.

[128] Ibid.

[129] Picciotti, A. (2017), Towards Sustainability: The Innovation Paths of Social Enterprise. Ann. Public Coop. Econ. 88, 233–256.

[130] Partzsch, L. and Ziegler, R. (2011), Social entrepreneurs as change agents: A case study on power and authority in the water sector. Int. Environ. Agreem. Polit. Law Econ, 11, 63–83.

society through small- and medium-sized enterprises (SMEs)[131] in developing economies, where financial development may not be as advanced as in developed economies. Therefore, social entrepreneurs will have to rely on government sources to finance the activities of the SMEs. Nevertheless, in order to bring the opportunities for sustainable development to fruition, the knowledge and innovation of entrepreneurs is paramount.[132] However, it is the life experiences of entrepreneurs since childhood in the context of not only their education but also other personal experiences which give them knowledge about social issues and problems.[133] But in order to learn through education and personal experiences in childhood, upbringing and the quality of the environment are important for the beneficial development of cognition.

The emergence and growth of social entrepreneurship is dependent on three types of capital, financial capital, human capital and a combination of both.[134] Financial systems which are subject to a philanthropic approach will have a positive impact on financial capital investment.[135] And human capital investment is positively impacted by the quality of educational systems.[136] But investment in financial and human capital is positively impacted by the quality and effectiveness of political systems.[137] However, social capital is improved especially in rural areas of Ukraine when the whole community works on multidimensional projects, the results of which generate spillovers in the context of economic and socio-ecological effects.[138] Social enterprises fulfil social purposes and their roles can be

[131] Simón, F.J.G.; González-Cruz, T.; Contreras-Pacheco, O. (2017), Policies to enhance social development through the promotion of SME and social entrepreneurship: A study in the Colombian construction industry. Entrep. Reg. Dev, 29, 51–70.

[132] Hall, J.K.; Daneke, G.A.; Lenox, M.J. (2010), Sustainable development and entrepreneurship: Past contributions and future directions. J. Bus. Ventur, 25, 439–448.

[133] Singh, A. (2018), The Process of Social Value Creation: A Multiple-Case Study on Social Entrepreneurship in India, Springer, India.

[134] Sahasranamam, S., and Nandakumar, M. (2010), individual capital and social entrepreneurship: Role of formal institutions, Journal of Business Research, 107, pp. 104-117.

[135] Ibid.

[136] Ibid.

[137] Ibid.

[138] Sandal, Jan-Urban, Yakobchok, V., Lytvynchuk, I., and Plotnikova, M. (2019), Institutions for Forming Social Capital in Territorial Communities, Management Theory and Studies for Rural Business and Infrastructure Development, Vol. 41, No. 1, pp. 67-76.

wide ranging and variable from one country to another country.[139] To reduce homelessness, social entrepreneurship may be geared towards the provision of social housing.[140] On the other hand, social entrepreneurship may be geared towards providing opportunities for those existing on the fringes of society[141] or on providing social services.[142] Marginalised people in developing countries are those most likely to be living in forested, rural areas.[143] In this case, peoples living in rural, forested areas will be concerned with the lack of infrastructure associated with transport and the digital economy, demographic decline and the provisioning of adequate housing.[144] However, the peoples of rural, forested areas will also be concerned with the problems associated with climate change, as well as the problems of food and energy availability.[145] In order to address and resolve these issues, the best strategy is one of social innovation.[146] Innovation and social innovation are the mechanisms associated with facilitating sustainable development, helping to revitalise the economy as well as increasing the quality of people's lives.[147] The theoretical framework behind innovation led to the importance of human capital and trust as being two vital components required for its success.[148] However, the importance of social capital in the context of the success of innovation also came to be

[139] Henderson, F., and Hall, K. (2019), Social enterprise, social innovation and self-directed case: Lessons from Scotland, Social Enterprise Journal, Vol. 15, No. 4, pp. 438-456.

[140] Fitzpatrick, S. and Watts, B. (2017), "Competing visions: security of tenure and the welfarisation of English social housing", Housing Studies, Vol. 32 No. 8, pp. 1021-1038.

[141] Gidron, B. and Monnickendam-Givon, Y. (2017), "A social welfare perspective of market-oriented social enterprises", International Journal of Social Welfare, Vol. 26 No. 2, pp. 127-140.

[142] Henderson, F., Reilly, C., Moyes, D. and Whittam, G. (2018), "From charity to social enterprise: the marketization of social care", International Journal of Entrepreneurial Behavior and Research, Vol. 24 No. 3, pp. 651-666.

[143] Nijnik, M., Secco, L., Miller, D., Melnykovych. (2019), Can Social Innovation Make a Difference to Forest Dependent Communities? Forest Policy and Economics, 100, pp. 207-213.

[144] Ibid.

[145] Ibid.

[146] BEPA (2011), Empowering People, Driving Change: Social Innovation in the European Union. 34 p. http://ec.europa.eu/bepa/pdf/publications_pdf/social_innovation.pdf

[147] Nijnik, M., Secco, L., Miller, D., Melnykovych. (2019), Can Social Innovation Make a Difference to Forest Dependent Communities? Forest Policy and Economics, 100, pp. 207-213.

[148] Fukuyama, F. (1995), Trust: Social Virtues and the Creation of Prosperity, Free Press, NY.

recognised.[149] Following this, there was a shift towards the role of institutions and interactions between the different stakeholders in the innovation process. This led to the next stage of development theory, where hybrid institutions such as coalitions and partnerships became the key to innovation.[150] Institutions were seen to be the foundations of the strength and robustness of the systems and networks of specific industries.[151] Managers will also benefit from having knowledge of the evolution of technology across different products and sectors over time.[152] This will give them an opportunity to assess whether the technology will be beneficial or not and thus allow them to be incentivised or dis-incentivised in promoting the technology with stakeholders if the technology will allow the firm to achieve its strategic goals.[153]

The role of intermediaries in the process of innovation has attracted the attention of researchers.[154] One particular type of intermediary can be associated with social innovation and one category of this is represented by social procurement.[155] Over time, policymakers have recognised that not only does social procurement create value but it is also conducive to facilitating social enterprise.[156] Furthermore, social procurement is also a process by which economic development is facilitated via the generation of spillover effects. Nevertheless, some empirical studies have suggested that positive spillover effects, such as the creation of jobs due to large firms transacting with smaller supplying firms, are dependent on the level of

[149] Coleman, J. (1988), Social capital in the creation of human capital. Am. J. Sociol. 94, 95–120.

[150] Defourny, J., Nyssens, M., 2008. Social enterprise in Europe: recent trends and developments. Soc. Enterp. J. 4 (3).

[151] Gim, C., Miler, C., and Hirt, P. (2019), The resilience work of institutions, Environmental Science and Policy, 97, pp. 36-43.

[152] Suddaby, R., Coraiola, D., Harvey, C., and Foster, W. (2020), History and the microfoundations of dynamic capabilities, Strat Mgmt J, pp. 530-556.

[153] Ibid.

[154] Agogue, M., Berthet, E., Fredberg, T., Le Masson, P., Segrestin, B., Stoetzel, M., Wiener, M., and Ystrom, A. (2017), "Explicating the Role of Innovation Intermediaries in the 'Unknown': A Contingency Approach." Journal of Strategy and Management 10(1): 19–39. doi: https://doi.org/10.1108/JSMA-01-2015-0005

[155] Barraket, J. (2019), The Role of Intermediaries in Social Innovation: The Case of Social Procurement in Australia, Journal of Social Entrepreneurship, DOI: https://doi.org/10.1080/19420676.2019.1624272

[156] Ibid.

investment undertaken by firms in an uncertain economic environment.[157] However, strong leadership in large firms facilitated investment in their link with smaller firms to overcome the uncertain economic environment in which smaller firms were unwilling to invest.[158] Social procurement acts as an intermediary and a facilitator of social innovation by bringing together different stakeholders.[159] This allows for the diffusion of knowledge and generation of new ideas, particularly in the context of procedures and practices.[160] It has also been found that the innovation capability of service firms is improved by greater customer involvement, such that this involvement becomes a complementary capability.[161] Moreover, in the context of Chinese firms, network centrality has a much bigger impact on the innovation performance of the firm when the levels of marketisation (formal institutions) are stronger than are the levels of social cohesion (informal institutions).[162] The mechanism through which social procurement acts to facilitate innovation arises mainly because of its capacity to bring together different stakeholders and thereby to diffuse ideas rather than through transactions.[163] In this case, the effects of social procurement intermediation on social innovation have also been supported by the findings of other scholarly work.[164] However, the findings differ in that social

[157] Weber, R., and S. Schnell, S. (2003), Contracting in: How a Business Intermediary Sought to Create Supplier Networks and Jobs in the Inner City, Economic Development Quarterly, 17(2): 148–164. doi: https://doi.org/10.1177/0891242403017002003

[158] Ibid.

[159] Barraket, J. (2019), The Role of Intermediaries in Social Innovation: The Case of Social Procurement in Australia, Journal of Social Entrepreneurship, DOI: https://doi.org/10.1080/19420676.2019.1624272

[160] Theodorakopoulos, N., Ram, M., and Beckinsale, M. (2013), Human Resource Development for Inclusive Procurement by Intermediation: A Situated Learning Theory Application, The International Journal of Human Resource Management 24(12): 2321–2338. doi: https://doi.org/10.1080/09585192.2013.781433

[161] Anning-Dorson, T. (2019), Complementary Capabilities Across Cultures, Cross Cultural & Strategic Management, Vol. 26, No. 4, pp. 567-586.

[162] Wang, H., Zhao, Y., Dang, B., Han, P., and Shi, X. (2019), Network centrality and innovation performance: the role of formal and informal institutions in emerging economies, Journal of Business and Industrial Marketing, 34/6, pp. 1388-1400.

[163] Barraket, J. (2019), The Role of Intermediaries in Social Innovation: The Case of Social Procurement in Australia, Journal of Social Entrepreneurship, DOI: https://doi.org/10.1080/19420676.2019.1624272

[164] Jenner, P. (2016), The Role of the Intermediary in Social Enterprise Sustainability: An International Comparative Study, Journal of New Business Ideas and Trends, 14(1), pp. 23–40.

procurement generates spillover effects not just for social enterprises but amongst other types of enterprises.[165]

In an economy all firms are interdependent and networked. As a result, in an uncertain environment the impact on one firm will impact on how capabilities develop in other firms. Moreover, Sen's Capabilities Approach can be extended to evaluate the uneven global distribution of the capacity for scientific innovation.[166] In this case, once expanded to a social level, Sen's Capabilities Approach identifies scientific knowledge as a social good, becoming a social capability in the context of a country being capable to produce it.[167] And in order to develop and improve the innovation capability of a country, it becomes necessary to integrate and make stronger the economic, political and social structures which form a country's innovation system.[168] Moreover, in the era of globalisation, in a country such as Malaysia, institutions need to be better enhanced in order to provide better social protection to citizens.[169] Furthermore, at a generic level, the principles of corporate governance should be dictated by the basic institutions of society which assign rights to capabilities and primary goods in society, so that capabilities can be transformed into functionings through the interaction of stakeholders in firms.[170]

Social networks are based on positive past experiences of working with others directly or indirectly or on acquaintances through kinship, forming an important part of social capital.[171] In this case, social networks and organisation of economic activities through such networks represent an efficient alternative informal institution to formal institutions associated

[165] Barraket, J. (2019), The Role of Intermediaries in Social Innovation: The Case of Social Procurement in Australia, Journal of Social Entrepreneurship, DOI: https://doi.org/10.1080/19420676.2019.1624272

[166] Mormina, M. (2019), Science, Technology and Innovation as Social Goods for Development: Rethinking Research Capacity Building from Sens Capabilities Approach, Sci Eng Ethics, 25:671-692.

[167] Ibid.

[168] Ibid.

[169] Roslan, A., and Mustafa, M. (2006), Globalisation, Unemployment, and Poverty: The Need for a New Perspective on Social Protection in Malaysia, Malaysian Management Journal, 10, 1&2, pp. 49-65.

[170] Fia, M., and Sacconi, L. (2019), Justice and Corporate Governance: New Insights from Rawlsian Social Contract and Sens Capabilities Approach, Journal of Business Ethics, 160, pp. 937-960.

[171] Putnam, R., Leonardi, R., and Nanetti, R. (1993), Making democracy work: Civic tradition in modem Italy, Princeton University Press, Princeton.

with the organisation of economic activities. The efficiency of informal institutions with regard to the organisation of economic resources is due to the lower transaction costs associated with collecting information on the best ways to conduct business. Furthermore, such informal institutions have proved to be beneficial to China in its transition from a planned economy to a mixed-market economy after its 1978 incremental reforms, co-existing with formal institutions as these developed over time.[172] One study has found that even as China's economic reforms progressed and formal institutions such as regulated traditional banking developed, the informal social network of family and knowledge-based positive relationships remained important in the context of allowing for greater financial inclusion.[173] Furthermore, the same study has found that social networks co-exist with formal institutions as a mechanism for facilitating greater financial inclusion, especially because rent seeking is prevalent in China.[174] Therefore, 'formalising' informal institutions such as social networks and reducing the regulatory control and structural weakness of formal financial institutions is important for strengthening financial reforms in China.[175] This will only serve to improve the level of economic development in the country. And in the context of economic development, it has a negative inverse relationship with the level of corruption in a country.[176]

Microfinance is also important for economic development in developing countries. However, in Bangladesh it has been found that the decentralisation of decision making in the microfinance sector, in an institutional context, has led to the social mission of microfinance institutions not being completely realised.[177] In this case, the decentralisation of decision making has been due to 'practice drift' at local levels rather than 'mission drift'.[178] And in the case of small-business low-income clients of

[172] Allen, F., Qian, J., & Qian, M. (2005), Law, finance, and economic growth in China. Journal of Financial Economics, 77(1): 57–116.

[173] Chai, S., Chen, Y., Huang, B., Ye, D. (2019), Social Networks and Informal Financial Inclusion in China, Asia Pac J Manag, 36, pp. 529-563.

[174] Ibid.

[175] Ibid.

[176] Bajada, C., and Shashnov, M. (2019), The effects of economic development and the evolution of social institutions on the level of corruption: Comparing the Asia-Pacific with other regional blocs, Asia Pacific Business Review, 25:4.

[177] Maitrot, M. (2018), Understanding Social Performance: A 'practice drift' at the Frontline of Microfinance Institutions in Bangladesh, Development and Change, 50 (3), pp. 623-654.

[178] Ibid.

Micro-Finance Institutions (MFIs) in Zambia, it has been found that information and communication technologies are integrated into business models primarily to reduce costs rather than for the betterment of social good.[179]

Beyond HDI

Economic policy of countries and governments around the world after World War II was founded on the basis of national income accounting, with an emphasis on GDP growth as the macroeconomic policy objective.[180] Nevertheless, the deteriorating global environment due to climate change, especially after the mid-twentieth century due to an increase in human economic activity, has resulted in a rethinking of GDP growth as the objective of macroeconomic policy as well as its use in the context of improving economic welfare.[181] And in the case of GDP growth being the objective of macroeconomic policy, three specific challenges have been identified.[182] Firstly, the reach for unlimited economic growth has had and is having a devastating impact on the environment through climate change.[183] However, climate change is just one aspect of damage to the environment, there being many others, including species extinction and desertification.[184] Secondly, there is no causality between high levels of economic growth and a reduction in inequality in society.[185] Moreover, it is also open to question as to whether after a threshold level of economic growth has surpassed, the quality of life shows any further improvement.[186]

[179] Wakunuma, K., Siwale, J., and Beck, R. (2018), Computing for Social Good: Supporting microfinance institutions in Zambia, EJ Info Sys Dev Countries, 85;e12090.

[180] Malay, O. (2019), Do Beyond GDP indicators initiated by powerful stakeholders have a transformative potential? Ecological Economics, 162, pp. 100-107.

[181] Malay, O. (2019), Do Beyond GDP indicators initiated by powerful stakeholders have a transformative potential? Ecological Economics, 162, pp. 100-107.

[182] Cassiers, I., and Thiry, G. (2014), A high-stakes shift: Turning the tide from GDP to new prosperity indicators. In: Redefining Prosperity, Cassiers, I. (Ed), Routledge, London, pp. 22–40.

[183] Steffen, W., Richardson, K., Rockström, J., Cornell, S.E., Fetzer, I., Bennett, E.M., and Folke, C. (2015), Planetary boundaries: guiding human development on a changing planet. Science 347.

[184] Hosseini, S., and Gills, B. (2020): Beyond the critical: reinventing the radical imagination in transformative development and globalization studies, Globalization DOI: https://doi.org/10.1080/14747731.2020.1736852

[185] Piketty, T. (2014), Capital in the Twenty-First Century. Belknap, Cambridge, MA.

[186] Max-Neef, M. (1995), Economic growth and quality of life: a threshold hypothesis. Ecol. Econ. 15, 115-118.

It is only in the initial phases of a country's economic development that increases in income levels through increasing economic growth lead to an improvement in the living standards of citizens.[187] And it has been theoretically shown that as income levels rise, people have more options and this is what leads to an improvement in the quality of life of the individual. But as this happens, individuals' tastes and preferences change such that it may become impossible to place a monetary value on such tastes and preferences.[188]

The growing disparity in income levels between the rich and the poor in every country around the world has led international organisations to question the appropriateness of using the mechanism of maximising economic growth and GDP as a means of achieving intra-country and inter-country equality amongst people. In this case, it has been recognised that the maximisation of economic growth should only be one side of the coin of the strategy to bring about an equality of prosperity to all peoples—the other side of the coin being to focus on embracing policies which bring about an improvement in human well-being resulting from an improvement in the accessibility to all of nutrition, education, housing, sustainable development and healthcare.[189] These requirements may be termed as the beyond-GDP indicators of welfare, the quantification of which would allow an assessment of whether public policy initiatives have been successful or not. Furthermore, what is measured will have an impact on policy strategies.[190] Also, the quantification of the factors of welfare and well-being will have implications for the design of policy.[191] Similarly, if there are flaws in the quantification of welfare and well-being measures, this may lead to the design and execution of flawed policies.[192]

The maximisation of welfare and well-being should be the common objective of governments around the world. However, the effectiveness of

[187] Puglisi, S., and Serban, I. (2019). Beyond GDP: Which options to better represent modern socio-economic progress. Sociology and Social Work Review, 3(1), 17-32.

[188] Ibid.

[189] Stiglitz, J., Sen, A.K., Fitoussi, J.P. (2009), The Measurement of Economic Performance and Social Progress Revisited: Reflections and Overview, OFCE, Centre de recherche en economie de Sciences Po.

[190] Seaford, C. (2013), The multiple uses of subjective well-being indicators. Soc. Indic. Res. 114 (1), 29–43.

[191] Aitken, A. (2019), Measuring Welfare Beyond GDP, National Institute Economic Review, No. 249.

[192] Ibid.

the quantification of welfare improvements in a country is more debatable. Most often, the actual level of welfare in a country is measured in terms of GDP per capita.[193] Nevertheless, there are a few weaknesses to measuring welfare in the context of GDP per capita. This is because it considers only income in the context of welfare while ignoring other aspects of welfare associated with health, quality of life and education.[194] Moreover, GDP per capita as a welfare measure also does not consider the negative externalities associated with the impact on welfare of damage to the environment, which can result in social costs.[195] Perhaps, unsurprisingly, businesses which perform a social function such as the provision of renewable energy would be in favour of deprioritising economic growth as a central economic objective of governments, as these firms operate partly in the context of poverty alleviation and sustainable energy supply.[196] Furthermore, the quality-of-life indications associated with a work-life balance are not so evident when using GDP per capita as a welfare measure.[197] The deficiencies associated with GDP per capita as a measure of welfare has led to the development of new ways of evaluating and assessing the level of welfare in countries. These developments have tended to follow two paths.[198] The first path evaluates welfare in the context of the choices available to people in the context of the actual or potential supply of goods and services to individuals and the actual use to which the goods and services can be put.[199] If the choices available can help with the development of individual capabilities and these capabilities can be realised as functionings, then it is possible to say that human welfare has been furthered. The second pathway involves either amending GDP per capita so

[193] Kalimeris, P., Bithas, K., Richardson, C., and Nijkamp, P. (2020), Hidden Linkages between resources and economy: A 'Beyond-GDP' approach using alternative welfare indicators, Ecological Economics, 169.

[194] Ibid.

[195] Ibid.

[196] Gabriel, Cle-Anne., Nazar, S., Zhu, D., and Kirkwood, J. (2019), Performance Beyond Economic Growth: Alternatives from Growth-Averse Enterprises in the Global South, Alternatives, Global, Local, Political, Vol. 44, 2-4, pp. 119-137.

[197] Costanza, R., Kubiszewski, I., Giovannini, E., Lovins, H., McGlade, J., Pickett, K.E., et al. (2014), Development. Nature 505 (7483), 283–285.

[198] Kalimeris, P., Bithas, K., Richardson, C., and Nijkamp, P. (2020), Hidden Linkages between resources and economy: A 'Beyond-GDP' approach using alternative welfare indicators, Ecological Economics, 169.

[199] Sen, A., 2008. The economics of happiness and capability. In: Capability and Happiness, Bruni, L., Comim, F., Pugno, M. (Eds) Oxford University Press, New York.

that the impact of negative externalities on human welfare are quantified and accounted for[200] or redefining the quantification of welfare in terms of happiness or satisfaction.[201] An alternative to measuring the extent of well-being which has been proposed is the HDI or the Human Development Index.[202] However, several other indices have also been suggested. These include the Index of Sustainable Welfare (ISEW)[203] and the Quality-of-Life Index[204] as well as several others. These alternative measures of welfare and well-being assert the causal relationship between well-being and the availability of resources.[205] In the context of the causal relationship between GDP and energy, the former either has been replaced by the alternative measures of well-being or is compared to these.[206] However, the HDI has replaced GDP as an indicator in assessing the link between the inequality of income distribution and natural resource consumption.[207] This is also true in the context of climate change and the nature of its empirical analysis.[208] But there are also problems associated with using the HDI to measure improvements in welfare and human development.[209] Firstly, under the pretext that human development improves when individuals have more choices, the HDI uses life expectancy, literacy, enrolment and per capita income as the measures which facilitate this. However,

[200] Talberth, J., and Bohara, A.K. (2006), Economic openness and green GDP, Ecol. Econ. 58 (4), 743–758.

[201] Costanza, R., Kubiszewski, I., Giovannini, E., Lovins, H., McGlade, J., Pickett, K.E., et al. (2014), Development, Nature 505 (7483), 283–285.

[202] UNEP, 2014. In: von Weizsäcker, E.U., de Larderel, J., Hargroves, K., Hudson, C., Smith, M., Rodrigues, M. (Eds.), Decoupling 2: Technologies, Opportunities and Policy Options. A Report of the Working Group on Decoupling to the International Resource Panel. United Nations Environment Programme.

[203] Costanza, R., Kubiszewski, I., Giovannini, E., Lovins, H., McGlade, J., Pickett, K.E., et al. (2014), Development. Nature 505 (7483), 283–285.

[204] Maridal, J. (2016), A worldwide measure of societal quality of life. Soc. Indic. Res. 1–38.

[205] Kalimeris, P., Bithas, K., Richardson, C., and Nijkamp, P. (2020), Hidden Linkages between resources and economy: A 'Beyond-GDP' approach using alternative welfare indicators, Ecological Economics, 169.

[206] Ibid.

[207] Steinberger, J.K., and Roberts, J.T. (2010), From constraint to sufficiency: the decoupling of energy and carbon from human needs, 1975–2005. Ecol. Econ. 70 (2), 425–433.

[208] Van den Bergh, C.J.M., and Botzen, W.J.W. (2018), Global impact of a climate treaty if the Human Development Index replaces GDP as a welfare proxy. Clim. Policy 18 (1), 76–85. https://doi.org/10.1080/14693062.2016.1227954

[209] Crespo, C. (2010), Implicit Assumptions when Measuring in Economics: The Human Development Index (HDI) as a Case Study: Revista Cultura Economica, Ano XXVIII, No. 79.

the detail of how this happens is missing from the UNDP's Human Development Reports.[210] Nevertheless, the original Human Development Report acknowledged that literacy was the key factor in facilitating individuals to acquire knowledge through learning, while recognising that other variables may also have to be accounted for.[211] This deficiency was fixed in later reports to some extent by the inclusion of enrolment in addition to literacy.[212] Another limitation of the HDI is the assertion that income per capita is an accurate proxy for the command on resources an individual has in order to attain a decent living standard. However, one limitation of this is that goods, services and factors which are not exchanged for money are completely ignored. For example, the impact of childhood upbringing can have either a negative or a positive impact in adulthood, whether choices are available or not. And a positive childhood upbringing cannot be bought in most countries. However, the Human Development Report of 1990 does acknowledge the lack of a specific causation of income growth with human development.[213] Another limitation of using GDP per capita as a proxy is that the distorting effects of taxes and exchange rates make a legitimate comparison between countries difficult.[214] From a technical perspective, taking the logarithm of income implies that not only high income levels are not reflected in human development[215] but also the need to reflect equality is given greater weighting.[216] Finally, there is no clear indication of how the capabilities reflected either directly or indirectly by GDP per capita are related to those

[210] Ibid.

[211] UNDP (1990), Human Development Report 1990, Oxford University Press, Oxford. http://hdr.undp.org/sites/default/files/reports/219/hdr_1990_en_complete_nostats.pdf

[212] Crespo, C. (2010), Implicit Assumptions when Measuring in Economics: The Human Development Index (HDI) as a Case Study: Revista Cultura Economica, Ano XXVIII, No. 79.

[213] UNDP (1990), Human Development Report 1990, Oxford University Press, Oxford. http://hdr.undp.org/sites/default/files/reports/219/hdr_1990_en_complete_nostats.pdf

[214] UNDP (1990), Human Development Report 1990, Oxford University Press, Oxford. http://hdr.undp.org/sites/default/files/reports/219/hdr_1990_en_complete_nostats.pdf

[215] Anand, S., and Sen, A. (2000), "The Income Component of the Human Development Index", Journal of Human Development, 1/1, pp. 83-106.

[216] Anand, S., and Sen, A. (1994), "Human Development Index: Methodology and Measurement", Occasional Papers, 12, Human Development Report Office, New York.

capabilities reflected either directly or indirectly by longevity and education.[217] Furthermore, the selected components of the HDI may not be the ones which are most indicative of either welfare improvements or human development itself.[218] Similarly to the way in which the logarithm of income is considered in the HDI, the same is also true of how life expectancy is treated. In this case, the last years of life end up being less valuable than an individual's earlier years. However, living a long life may mean that in the later years more valuable knowledge from life experiences can be imparted to the younger generation. This is not accounted for in the HDI. Another flaw of the way in which the HDI is constructed is that equal weighting is given to each of its components. And there is no justification for this in the Human Development Reports.[219] Furthermore, cultural differences may also make the HDI as a measure of human progress to be less credible. For example, in some countries, closer family ties may take precedence over income, and religious faith may be more important than literacy.[220] And in the way in which the HDI is calculated, literacy is given greater weighting than enrolment. School enrolment is necessary for literacy in most countries, yet there is no justification in the Human Development Reports as to why literacy is weighted more than enrolment.[221] It is clearly evident that the HDI is only able to quantify the basic features of human progress and development.[222] In this case, it is evident that the HDI misses out the important factors associated with human development and progress such as female empowerment, cognitive development, the quality of child rearing, a safe and secure environment, and sustainable development.[223] And in the quantification of the basic features of human development, the HDI is susceptible to significant levels of

[217] Anand, S., and Sen, A. (2000), "The Income Component of the Human Development Index", Journal of Human Development, 1/1, pp. 83-106.

[218] Crespo, C. (2010), Implicit Assumptions when Measuring in Economics: The Human Development Index (HDI) as a Case Study: Revista Cultura Economica, Ano XXVIII, No. 79.

[219] Ibid.

[220] Ibid.

[221] Ibid.

[222] Stewart, F. (2019) The Human Development Approach: An Overview, Oxford Development Studies, 47:2, 135-153, DOI: https://doi.org/10.1080/13600818.2019.1585793

[223] Stewart, F. (2019) The Human Development Approach: An Overview, Oxford Development Studies, 47:2, 135-153, DOI: https://doi.org/10.1080/13600818.2019.1585793

measurement errors in each of its components.[224] But, of all the components of the HDI, the biggest measurement errors are to be found in GNI per capita, as it is only calculated periodically.[225] Nevertheless, it has been found that a dynamic construct of the HDI is better at being able to indicate changes in the trajectory of human development than the standard construct of the HDI.[226]

Conclusion

After the end of World War II, the consensus amongst policymakers with regard to how prosperity was to be created for all was to maximise economic growth and GDP. It was assumed that such an economic policy strategy would allow income levels to rise, and this would trickle down to all rungs of society. However, the trickle-down effect of wealth and income may not happen in countries at the later stages of economic development, although it may be true in countries at the initial stages of economic development. Moreover, over the last four decades, as globalisation took hold over the world it also became evident that economic prosperity was anything but trickling down through societies. In this case, it became evident that economic prosperity was becoming polarised such that a minority in countries were becoming richer while the majority remained poor. This could have been due to either a lack of opportunity or a lack of capability on the part of individuals. Nevertheless, following the realisation that economic growth was a necessary but not a sufficient policy objective to bring about economic prosperity for all, there was a shift in thinking to the view that policies which improved the well-being of the citizens of a country were also important. The dimensions of human well-being and development are associated with cognitive development as well as with physical and mental well-being, amongst others such as longevity, literacy, enforceable human rights, freedom of thought, the freedom of political

[224] Castles, Ian. (1998), The mis-measure of nations: A review essay on the Human Development Report 1998, Population and Development Review 24(4): 831–45. https://doi.org/10.2307/2808029

[225] Ghislandi, S., Sanderson, W., and Scherbov, S. (2018), A Simple Measure of Human Development: The Human Life Indicator, Population and Development Review 45 (1), pp. 219-233.

[226] Zirogiannis, N., Krutilla, K., Tripodis, Y., Fledderman, K. (2019), Human Development Over Time: An Empirical Comparison of a Dynamic Index and the Standard HDI, Soc Indic Res, 141, pp. 773-798.

preferences and the ability to respect oneself. The emphasis of development methodology towards the human development multidimensional approach reached a climax in 1990. In this case, economic activity was seen as a means of human development measured by the extent of the choices and the opportunities which were becoming available to individuals to improve their well-being. The multidimensional approach to economic development should focus on the use of policies to maximise economic growth and GDP as well as policies to enhance and improve the factors associated with human well-being and development. However, the research on the economic growth- human development nexus is varied. For example, in Nigeria it has been found that there is a one-way causation from economic growth to economic development. And in some countries, the increased public spending on female health and education tended to strengthen the link between economic growth and human development. In this case, the extent to which economic growth impacts on human development is very much dependent on the amount of public funds spent by a government as well as what the money is spent on. In Latin America it was found that public spending on health promoted economic growth through income generation, but in African countries it was found that the level of human capital stock was more important to economic growth than government spending on health and education. And in Eastern European countries it was found that early public policy emphasis on human development not only facilitated economic growth, but also sustained it. In India, it has been found that financial inclusion is important for the country's economic growth, whereas in Saudi Arabia, at least in the short run, it has been found that there is a negative relationship between financial inclusion and economic growth—although, in the long term, economic growth, financial inclusion and human development have a causal relationship. Also, it has been found that the political processes at the country level as well as in global institutions may act in such a way that welfare and human development either do not progress or do not progress fast enough. This is a specific area which needs reform.

Human development is not just an outcome of a preconfigured genetic programme a person is born with. But human development is unique to everyone, dependent on culture, relationships and the environment to which everyone is exposed, with adaptations taking place over a lifetime. This ideological emphasis stems from an integration of knowledge from the fields of biology, neuroscience, psychology and the social sciences. This integrated approach to childhood development leads to the idea that genes act only when stimulated by the environment, and as such genes are followers rather than prime movers. This, in the context of childhood upbringing, has not been factored into the human development policy framework, especially from the perspective that the roots of lifetime inequality may be found within the realms of childhood upbringing. A childhood upbringing which nurtures the qualities of resilience and adaptability in individuals may lead to a reduction in inequality. This is because as adults, people will be able to overcome obstacles while maintaining the integrity of their health. Furthermore, adopting socio-economic policies which foster the creation of an environment in which opportunities are available to activate an individual's cognitive capability is also important. Economic activity should be focused on the development of well-being. Thus, there is a nexus between human behaviour and economic activity. Economic activity should be focused on improving human well-being (by improving and toning resilience) as well as the development and enhancement of cognitive capacity. It is here that the nexus between human behaviour and economic development can be found.

References

Agogue, M., Berthet, E., Fredberg, T., Le Masson, P., Segrestin, B., Stoetzel, M., Wiener, M., & Ystrom, A. (2017). Explicating the Role of Innovation Intermediaries in the 'Unknown': A Contingency Approach. *Journal of Strategy and Management, 10*(1), 19–39. https://doi.org/10.1108/JSMA-01-2015-0005

Aitken, A. (2019). Measuring Welfare Beyond GDP. *National Institute Economic Review, No. 249.*

Alkire, S. (2002). Dimensions of Human Development. *World Development, 30*(2), 181–205.

Allen, F., Qian, J., & Qian, M. (2005). Law, Finance, and Economic Growth in China. *Journal of Financial Economics, 77*(1), 57–116.

Anand, S., & Sen, A. (1994). *Human Development Index: Methodology and Measurement, Occasional Papers, 12.* Human Development Report Office.

Anand, S., & Sen, A. (2000). The Income Component of the Human Development Index. *Journal of Human Development, 1*(1), 83–106.

Anning-Dorson, T. (2019). Complementary Capabilities Across Cultures. *Cross Cultural & Strategic Management, 26*(4), 567–586.

Asongu, S., & Odhiambo, N. (2019). Basic Formal Education Quality, Information Technology, and Inclusive Human Development in Sub-Saharan Africa. *Sustainable Development, 27*, 419–428.

Aust, V., Morais, A., & Pinto, I. (2020). How Does Foreign Direct Investment Contribute to Sustainable Development Goals? Evidence from African Countries. *Journal of Cleaner Production, 245*, 118823.

Bajada, C., & Shashnov, M. (2019). The Effects of Economic Development and the Evolution of Social Institutions on the Level of Corruption: Comparing the Asia-Pacific with Other Regional Blocs. *Asia Pacific Business Review, 25*, 4.

Bandura, A. (1977). Self-Efficacy: Toward a Unifying Theory of Behavioural Change. *Psychological Review, 84*, 191–215.

Barraket, J. (2019). The Role of Intermediaries in Social Innovation: The Case of Social Procurement in Australia. *Journal of Social Entrepreneurship*. https://doi.org/10.1080/19420676.2019.1624272

BEPA. (2011). *Empowering People, Driving Change: Social Innovation in the European Union* (p. 34). Retrieved from http://ec.europa.eu/bepa/pdf/publications_pdf/social_innovation.pdf

Bhayana, S., & Kakkar, A. (2019). Sustainable Development Goals, Going Beyond GDP: India's Case. *Indian Journal of Economics and Development, 7*(2), 1–8.

Bradford, E., Jentzsch, I., & Gomez, J. (2015). From Self to Social Cognition: Theory of Mind Mechanisms and Their Relation to Executive Functioning. *Cognition, 138*, 21–34.

Buchanan, N. S., & Ellis, H. S. (1955). *Approaches to Economic Development*. Twentieth Century Fund.

Camp, S., & Speidel, J. J. (1987). *The International Human Suffering Index*. Population Crisis Committee.

Cantor, P., Osher, D., Berg, J., Steyer, L., & Rose, T. (2019). Malleability, Plasticity, and Individuality: How Children Learn and Develop in Context. *Applied Developmental Science, 23*(4), 307–337. https://doi.org/10.1080/10888691.2017.1398649

Cascio, C., Moore, D., & McGlone, F. (2019). Social Touch and Human Development. *Developmental Cognitive Neuroscience, 35*, 5–11.

Cassiers, I., & Thiry, G. (2014). A High-Stakes Shift: Turning the Tide from GDP to New Prosperity Indicators. In I. Cassiers (Ed.), *Redefining Prosperity* (pp. 22–40). Routledge.

Castles, I. (1998). The Mis-measure of Nations: A Review Essay on the Human Development Report 1998. *Population and Development Review, 24*(4), 831–845. https://doi.org/10.2307/2808029

Chai, S., Chen, Y., Huang, B., & Ye, D. (2019). Social Networks and Informal Financial Inclusion in China. *Asia Pacific Journal of Management, 36*, 529–563.

Chakraborty, A. (2005). Kerala's Changing Development Narratives. *Economic and Political Weekly, 40*(6), 541–547.

Chikalipah, S., & Okafor, G. (2018). Dynamic Linkage Between Economic Growth and Human Development: Time Series Evidence from Nigeria. *Journal of International Development, 31*, 22–28.

Coleman, J. (1988). Social Capital in the Creation of Human Capital. *The American Journal of Sociology, 94*, 95–120.

Costantini, V., & Monni, S. (2008). Environment, Human Development and Economic Growth. *Ecological Economics, 64*, 867–880.

Costanza, R., Kubiszewski, I., Giovannini, E., Lovins, H., McGlade, J., Pickett, K. E., et al. (2014). Development. *Nature, 505*(7483), 283–285.

Cremin, L. (1980). *American Education: The National Experience*. Harper & Row.

Crespo, C. (2010). Implicit Assumptions When Measuring in Economics: The Human Development Index (HDI) as a Case Study. *Revista Cultura Economica, XXVIII*, 79.

Cunha, F., & Heckman, J. (2007). *The Evolution of Uncertainty in Labor Earnings in the US Economy, Working Paper*. University of Chicago.

Cunha, F., & Heckman, J. (2009). The Economics and Psychology of Inequality and Human Development. *Journal of the European Economic Association, 7*(2–3), 320–364.

Defourny, J., & Nyssens, M. (2008). Social Enterprise in Europe: Recent Trends and Developments. *Social Enterprise Journal, 4*(3).

Dholakia, R. (2003). Regional Disparity in Economic and Human Development in India. *Economic and Political Weekly, 38*(39), 4166–4172.

Eggoh, J., Houeninvo, H., & Sossou, G.-A. (2015). Education, Health and Economic Growth in African Countries. *Journal of Economic Development, 40*(1).

Fedyk, M. (2015). How (Not) to Bring Psychology and Biology Together. *Philosophical Studies, 172*(4), 949–967.

Fia, M., & Sacconi, L. (2019). Justice and Corporate Governance: New Insights from Rawlsian Social Contract and Sens Capabilities Approach. *Journal of Business Ethics, 160*, 937–960.

Fitzpatrick, S., & Watts, B. (2017). Competing Visions: Security of Tenure and the Welfarisation of English Social Housing. *Housing Studies, 32*(8), 1021–1038.

Fraser, J. (2020). *Social Institutions and International Human Rights Law Implementation*. Cambridge University Press.

Gabriel, C.-A., Nazar, S., Zhu, D., & Kirkwood, J. (2019). Performance Beyond Economic Growth: Alternatives from Growth-Averse Enterprises in the Global South. *Alternatives, Global, Local, Political, 44*(2–4), 119–137.

Ghislandi, S., Sanderson, W., & Scherbov, S. (2018). A Simple Measure of Human Development: The Human Life Indicator. *Population and Development Review, 45*(1), 219–233.

Ghosh, M. (2006). Economic Growth and Human Development in Indian States. *Economic and Political Weekly, 41*(30), 3321–3329.

Gidron, B., & Monnickendam-Givon, Y. (2017). A Social Welfare Perspective of Market-Oriented Social Enterprises. *International Journal of Social Welfare, 26*(2), 127–140.

Gim, C., Miler, C., & Hirt, P. (2019). The Resilience Work of Institutions. *Environmental Science and Policy, 97*, 36–43.

Glatzer, W. (2015). Monitoring and Analysing Quality of Life – An Introduction. In W. Glatzer, L. Camfield, V. Moller, & M. Rojas (Eds.), *Global Handbook of Quality of Life: Exploration of Well-Being of Nations and Continents.* Springer.

Greenfield, P. (2009). Linking Social Change and Developmental Change: Shifting Pathways of Human Development. *Developmental Psychology, 45*(2), 401–418.

Grisez, G., Boyle, J., & Finnis, J. (1987). Practical Principles, Moral Truth and Ultimate Ends. *American Journal of Jurisprudence, 32*, 99–151.

Hall, J. K., Daneke, G. A., & Lenox, M. J. (2010). Sustainable Development and Entrepreneurship: Past Contributions and Future Directions. *Journal of Business Venturing, 25*, 439–448.

Hathroubi, S. (2019). Inclusive Finance, Growth and Socio-Economic Development in Saudi Arabia: A Threshold Cointegration Approach. *Journal of Economic Development, 44*(2).

Hechter, M., Opp, K.-D., & Wippler, R. (2017). Introduction. In M. Hechter, K.-D. Opp, & R. Wippler (Eds.), *Social Institutions: Their Emergence, Maintenance and Effects.* Routledge.

Henderson, F., & Hall, K. (2019). Social Enterprise, Social Innovation, and Self-Directed Case: Lessons from Scotland. *Social Enterprise Journal, 15*(4), 438–456.

Henderson, F., Reilly, C., Moyes, D., & Whittam, G. (2018). From Charity to Social Enterprise: The Marketization of Social Care. *International Journal of Entrepreneurial Behavior and Research, 24*(3), 651–666.

Hickel, J. (2020). The Sustainable Development Index: Measuring the Ecological Efficiency of Human Development in the Anthropocene. *Ecological Economics, 167*, 106331.

Hosseini, S., & Gills, B. (2020). Beyond the Critical: Reinventing the Radical Imagination in Transformative Development and Globalization Studies. *Globalization.* https://doi.org/10.1080/14747731.2020.1736852

Ihsan, N., & Aziz, B. (2019). A Multidimensional Analysis of Quality of Life: Pakistan's Context. *Social Indicators Research, 142*, 201–227.

Jenner, P. (2016). The Role of the Intermediary in Social Enterprise Sustainability: An International Comparative Study. *Journal of New Business Ideas and Trends, 14*(1), 23–40.

Judrupa, I., & Pipare, A. (2019). Measurement of the Quality of Life in the Regions of Latvia. *Proceedings of the 2019 International Conference 'Economic Science for Rural Development', 51*, 152–159.

Kalimeris, P., Bithas, K., Richardson, C., & Nijkamp, P. (2020). Hidden Linkages Between Resources and Economy: A 'Beyond-GDP' Approach Using Alternative Welfare Indicators. *Ecological Economics, 169*, 106508.

Kaplan, S. (2018). *Huma Rights in Thick and Thin Societies: The Universal Declaration and Bridging the Gap.* Cambridge University Press.

Keating, D. P. (2016). Transformative Role of Epigenetics in Child Development Research: Commentary on the Special Section. *Child Development, 87*(1), 135–142. https://doi.org/10.1111/cdev.12488

Lamb, M., & Tamis-Lemonda, C. (2004). The Role of the Father: An Introduction. In M. Lamb (Ed.), *The Role of the Father in Childhood Development*. Wiley.

Majeed, M. T. (2019). Quality of Life and Globalization: Econometric Evidence from Asian Economies. *Journal of Quantitative Methods, 3*(1), 84–113.

Malay, O. (2019). Do Beyond GDP Indicators Initiated by Powerful Stakeholders Have a Transformative Potential? *Ecological Economics, 162*, 100–107.

Maridal, J. (2016). A Worldwide Measure of Societal Quality of Life. *Social Indicators Research, 2016*, 1–38.

Max-Neef, M. (1995). Economic Growth and Quality of life: A Threshold Hypothesis. *Ecological Economics, 15*, 115–118.

Mayer, D. (2001). The Long-Term Impact of Health on Economic Growth in Latin America. *World Development, 29*(6), 1025–1033.

Miller, L., Neupane, S., Neupane, S., Lohani, M., Joshi, N., Shrestha, M., & Thorne-Lyman, A. (2019). Diet Quality Over Time Is Associated with Better Development in Rural Nepali Children. *Maternal & Child Nutrition, 2020*, e12964. https://doi.org/10.1111/mcn.12964

Mincer, J. (1984). Human Capital and Economic Growth. *Economics of Education Review, 3*(3), 195–205.

Mormina, M. (2019). Science, Technology, and Innovation as Social Goods for Development: Rethinking Research Capacity Building from Sen's Capabilities Approach. *Science and Engineering Ethics, 25*, 671–692.

Nijnik, M., Secco, L., Miller, D., & Melnykovych, M. (2019). Can Social Innovation Make a Difference to Forest Dependent Communities? *Forest Policy and Economics, 100*, 207–213.

Nolan, B., & Whelan, C. T. (2007). On the Multidimensionality of Poverty and Social Exclusion. In J. Micklewright & S. Jenkins (Eds.), *Poverty and Inequality: New Directions*. Oxford University Press.

OECD. (2011a). *Compendium of OECD Well-Being Indicators*. OECD.

OECD. (2011b). *How's Life? Measuring Well-Being*. OECD. https://doi.org/10.1787/9789264121164-en

OECD. (2013). *OECD Guidelines on Measuring Subjective Well-Being*. OECD. https://doi.org/10.1787/9789264191655-en

Osher, D., Cantor, P., Berg, J., Steyer, L., & Rose, T. (2020). Drivers of Human Development: How Relationships and Context Shape Learning and Development. *Applied Developmental Science, 24*(1), 6–36.

Partzsch, L., & Ziegler, R. (2011). Social Entrepreneurs as Change Agents: A Case Study on Power and Authority in the Water Sector. *International Environmental Agreements: Politics, Law and Economics, 11*, 63–83.

Picciotti, A. (2017). Towards Sustainability: The Innovation Paths of Social Enterprise. *Annals of Public and Cooperative Economics, 88*, 233–256.

Piketty, T. (2014). *Capital in the Twenty-First Century.* Cambridge, MA.

Puglisi, S., & Serban, I. (2019). Beyond GDP: Which Options to Better Represent Modern Socio-Economic Progress. *Sociology and Social Work Review, 3*(1), 17–32.

Putnam, R., Leonardi, R., & Nanetti, R. (1993). *Making Democracy Work: Civic Tradition in Modem Italy.* Princeton University Press.

Ranis, G. (2004). *Human Development and Economic Growth, Center Discussion Paper No. 887.* Yale University.

Ranis, G., Stewart, F., & Ramirez, A. (2000). Economic Growth and Human Development. *World Development, 28*(2), 197–219.

Ratha, D. (2013). *The Impact of Remittances on Economic Growth and Poverty Reduction, Migration Policy Institute, Policy Brief No. 8.*

Robert, K., Parris, T., & Leiserowitz, A. (2005). What Is Sustainable Development? Goals, Indicators, Values and Practice. *Environment: Science and Policy for Sustainable Development, 47*(3), 8–21.

Roslan, A., & Mustafa, M. (2006). Globalisation, Unemployment, and Poverty: The Need for a New Perspective on Social Protection in Malaysia. *Malaysian Management Journal, 10*(1&2), 49–65.

Sachs, J. (2012). From Millennium Development Goals to Sustainable Development Goals. *Lancet, 379*, 2206–2211.

Saebi, T., Foss, N., & Linder, S. (2018). Social Entrepreneurship Research: Past Achievements and Future Promises. *Journal of Management, 45*(1), 70–95.

Sahasranamam, S., & Nandakumar, M. (2010). Individual Capital and Social Entrepreneurship: Role of Formal Institutions. *Journal of Business Research, 107*, 104–117.

Sandal, J.-U., Yakobchok, V., Lytvynchuk, I., & Plotnikova, M. (2019). Institutions for Forming Social Capital in Territorial Communities. *Management Theory and Studies for Rural Business and Infrastructure Development, 41*(1), 67–76.

Seaford, C. (2013). The Multiple Uses of Subjective Well-Being Indicators. *Social Indicators Research, 114*(1), 29–43.

Sears, R. (1957). Identification as a Form of Behavioural Development. In D. Harris (Ed.), *The Concept of Development.* University of Minnesota Press.

Sen, A. K. (1990). Development as Capability Expansion. In K. Griffin & J. Knight (Eds.), *Human Development and the International Development Strategy for the 1990s.* London.

Sen, A. (1992). *Inequality Re-examined.* Russell Sage Foundation.

Sen, A. (1993). Capability and Well-Being. In M. Nussbaum & A. Sen (Eds.), *The Quality of Life.* Clarendon Press.

Sen, A. (2008). The Economics of Happiness and Capability. In L. Bruni, F. Comim, & M. Pugno (Eds.), *Capability and Happiness*. Oxford University Press.
Seth, S., & Santos, M. E. (2020). Multidimensional Inequality and Human Development. In *Cambridge Handbook of the Capability Approach* (pp. 392–416). Cambridge University Press.
Sethi, D., & Sethy, S. (2017). Financial Inclusion Matters for Economic Growth in India. *International Journal of Social Economics, 46*(1), 132–151.
Shome, S., & Tondon, S. (2010). Balancing Human Development with Economic Growth: A Study of ASEAN 5. *Annals of University of Petrosani, Economics, 10*(1), 335–348.
Siddiqui, D., & Ahmed, Q. (2019). The Causal Relationship Between Institutions and Economic Growth: An Empirical Investigation for Pakistan Economy. *International Economics and Business, 5*(1).
Simón, F. J. G., González-Cruz, T., & Contreras-Pacheco, O. (2017). Policies to Enhance Social Development Through the Promotion of SME and Social Entrepreneurship: A Study in the Colombian Construction Industry. *Entrepreneurship and Regional Development, 29*, 51–70.
Singh, A. (2018). *The Process of Social Value Creation: A Multiple-Case Study on Social Entrepreneurship in India*. Springer.
Srinivasan, N. T. (1994). Human Development: A New Paradigm or Reinvention of the Wheel. *The American Economic Review, 84*(2).
Steffen, W., Richardson, K., Rockström, J., Cornell, S. E., Fetzer, I., Bennett, E. M., & Folke, C. (2015). Planetary Boundaries: Guiding Human Development on a Changing Planet. *Science, 347*, 6219.
Steinberger, J. K., & Roberts, J. T. (2010). From Constraint to Sufficiency: The Decoupling of Energy and Carbon from Human Needs, 1975–2005. *Ecological Economics, 70*(2), 425–433.
Stewart, F. (2019). The Human Development Approach: An Overview. *Oxford Development Studies, 47*(2), 135–153. https://doi.org/10.1080/13600818.2019.1585793
Stewart, F., Ranis, G., & Samman, E. (2018). *Advancing Human Development: Theory and Practice*. Oxford University Press.
Suddaby, R., Coraiola, D., Harvey, C., & Foster, W. (2020). History and the Micro-foundations of Dynamic Capabilities. *The Strategic Management Journal, 41*, 530–556.
Suri, T., Boozer, N., Ranis, G., & Stewart, F. (2010). Paths to Success: The Relationship Between Human Development and Economic Growth. *World Development, 39*(4), 506–522.
Talberth, J., & Bohara, A. K. (2006). Economic Openness and Green GDP. *Ecological Economics, 58*(4), 743–758.

Tamura, R., Dwyer, J., Devereux, J., & Baier, S. (2019). Economic Growth in the Long Run. *Journal of Development Economics, 137*, 1–35.

Theodorakopoulos, N., Ram, M., & Beckinsale, M. (2013). Human Resource Development for Inclusive Procurement by Intermediation: A Situated Learning Theory Application. *The International Journal of Human Resource Management, 24*(12), 2321–2338. https://doi.org/10.1080/09585192.2013.781433

Turner, J. (1997). *The Institutional Order: Economy, Kinship, Religion, Polity, Law and Education in Evolutionary and Comparative Perspective*. Longman.

Turner, J. (2010). *Theoretical Principles of Sociology, Volume 1: Macrodynamics*. Springer.

UNCTAD. (2014). *World Investment Report 2014 - Investing in the SDGs: An Action Plan*. Retrieved from https://unctad.org/en/PublicationsLibrary/wir2014_en.pdf

UNDP. (1990). *Human Development Report 1990*. Oxford University Press. Retrieved from http://hdr.undp.org/sites/default/files/reports/219/hdr_1990_en_complete_nostats.pdf

United Nations. (2015). *Transforming Our World: The 2030 Agenda for Sustainable Development*. Retrieved from https://www.un.org/ga/search/view_doc.asp?symbol¼A/RES/70/1&Lang¼E

US National Research Council, Policy Division, Board on Sustainable Development. (1999). *Our Common Journey: A Transition Toward Sustainability*. National Academy Press.

Van den Bergh, C. J. M., & Botzen, W. J. W. (2018). Global Impact of a Climate Treaty If the Human Development Index Replaces GDP as a Welfare Proxy. *Climate Policy, 18*(1), 76–85. https://doi.org/10.1080/14693062.2016.1227954

Wakunuma, K., Siwale, J., & Beck, R. (2018). Computing for Social Good: Supporting Microfinance Institutions in Zambia. *Electronic Journal of Information Systems in Developing Countries, 85*, e12090.

Wang, H., Zhao, Y., Dang, B., Han, P., & Shi, X. (2019). Network Centrality and Innovation Performance: The Role of Formal and Informal Institutions in Emerging Economies. *Journal of Business and Industrial Marketing, 34*(6), 1388–1400.

Watson, D., Whelan, C. T., & Maitre, B. (2017). Non-Monetary Indicators and Multiple Dimensions: The ESRI Approach to Poverty Measurement. *The Economic and Social Review, 48*(4), 369–392.

Weber, R., Schnell, S., & S. (2003). Contracting in: How a Business Intermediary Sought to Create Supplier Networks and Jobs in the Inner City. *Economic Development Quarterly, 17*(2), 148–164. https://doi.org/10.1177/0891242403017002003

Whelan, C., Watson, D., & Maitre, B. (2019). From Income Poverty to Multidimensional Quality of Life. *The Economic and Social Review, 50*(4), 683–705.

Yaya, S., Ghosh, S., & Ghose, B. (2019). Subjective Happiness, Health and Quality of Life and Their Sociocultural Correlates Among Younger Population in Malawi. *Social Sciences, 8*, 55.

Zirogiannis, N., Krutilla, K., Tripodis, Y., & Fledderman, K. (2019). Human Development Over Time: An Empirical Comparison of a Dynamic Index and the Standard HDI. *Social Indicators Research, 141*, 773–798.

CHAPTER 3

The Economics of Psychology

Introduction

In the previous chapter, the transition from a unilateral to a multilateral development philosophy was evaluated. This transition involved a shift in the strategy of economic policy moving away from the notion that economic prosperity would be available for all in the long term by pursuing the economic objective of maximising GDP or economic growth. However, this, accompanied with the emergence and dominance of globalisation over the last 40 years, has resulted in increasing the income disparities amongst people within countries as well as between countries. Wealth and income as become concentrated in the hands of the few while the many remain poor. This outcome as led to a growing belief that maximising GDP or economic growth is only one aspect of a multidimensional economic policy. The other aspects of economic policy should emphasise the development and enhancement of human well-being. These kinds of policies should begin even before a child is born, resulting in an adult who is cognitively developed as well as being both resilient and adaptable.

To better understand the economics of underdevelopment, it is necessary to better understand the sources of human inequality and how these

S. Ramesh, *The Political Economy of Human Behaviour and Economic Development*,
https://doi.org/10.1007/978-3-031-12666-6_3

can be optimally reduced.[1] The sources of lifetime inequality may be due to poor cognitive and non-cognitive development in the early years of a child's life. This may lead to difficulties in acquiring skills and abilities in later life, the foundation for which are laid in the early years of a child's life.[2] This could be due to either a lack of good parenting or to a lack of financial resources or a combination of both. However, an individual's genes may also play an overlapping part in the potential for the development of language ability, cognition, reading as well as mathematical ability.[3] But the extent to which these traits develop will be dependent on the differing levels of environmental factors to which individuals are exposed. This is specifically true in the context of human cognition, which needs to be seen as a process which is both continuous and complex rather than as a historically developing sequential logical capability.[4] Moreover, a cognitive system needs to be seen as one which is physical in the context that it is a complex system which is coupled with its environment, giving rise to its 'embodiment'.[5]

Ability and Human Development

Children who are good at reading, writing and arithmetic tend to grow up with a diverse range of intellectual abilities.[6] Moreover, intelligent children earned higher salaries in adulthood and were more likely to be able to move up the social hierarchy than children of lesser ability.[7] The ability to read, write and communicate using language is also important for cognitive development. In the context of the development of spoken language

[1] Cunha, F., and Heckman, J. (2009), The Economics and Psychology of Inequality and Human Development, Journal of the European Economic Association, 7 (2-3), pp. 320-364.

[2] Ibid.

[3] Haworth, C., Kovas, Y., Harlaar, N., Hayiou-Thomas, M., Petrill, S., Dale, P., and Plomin, R. (2009), Generalist Genes and Learning Disabilities: A Multivariate Genetic Analysis of Low Performance in Reading, Mathematics, Language and General Cognitive Ability in a Sample of 8000 12 Year Old Twins, Journal of Child Psychology and Psychiatry, 50:10, pp. 1318-1325.

[4] Riegler, A. (2002), When is a Cognitive System Embodied, Cognitive Systems Research 3, pp. 339-348.

[5] Ibid.

[6] Spearman, C. (1904), 'General intelligence' objectively determined and measured. Am. J. Psychol. 15, 201–293.

[7] Judge, T., Higgins, C., Thoresen, C., Barrick, M. (1999), The Big Five Personality Traits, General Mental Ability, and Career Success Across The Life Span, Personnel Psychology, 52.

there are two competing theories.[8] Firstly, the ability to construct logical sequences of spoken language is present in infancy and becomes functional over time because of metacognitive development.[9] And, secondly, the ability to construct logical sequences of sentences emerges over childhood as a child picks up words from its environment.[10]

Determining the neuroanatomical features which correlate with general intelligence especially in the growing and evolving brains of children and adolescents has proved to be difficult.[11] In this case, it has been found that the key to understanding intelligence in children and adolescents is not cortical thickness but the direction of change of cortical thickness.[12] Empirical studies have shown that whereas in late childhood and into adulthood the relationship between cortical thickness and intelligence is positive, in early childhood it is negative.[13] Furthermore, the development of the frontal cortical region of the brain correlates with the development of a child's cognitive ability.[14] Adolescence is also an important stage of cognitive development, during which there's a thinning of the lining of the cerebral cortex, the lining of the latter having shown an accelerated increase during childhood.[15] The changes in the lining of the cerebral cortex (motor, sensory and associative functionality) from childhood to adolescence to adulthood represents the physical manifestation of the changes taking place in cognitive capacity through the life cycle stages of a human being. If these changes can be positively impacted by economic activity, then this could have positive implications for human behaviour as well as economic development.

[8] Walley, A., Metsala, J., Garlock, V. (2003), Spoken Vocabulary growth: Its role in the development pf phoneme awareness and early reading ability, Reading and Writing: An Interdisciplinary Journal, 16.

[9] Kuhl, P.K., Williams, K.A., Lacerda, F., Stevens, K.N., and Lindblom, B. (1992), Linguistic experience alters phonetic perception in infants by 6 months of age. *Science, 255*, 606–608.

[10] Fowler, A.E. (1991), How early phonological development might set the stage for phoneme awareness. In S.A. Brady & D.P. Shankweiler (Eds.), Phonological processes in literacy: A tribute to Isabelle Y. Liberman (pp. 97–117), Erlbaum, New Jersey.

[11] Shaw, P., Greenstein, D., Lerch, J., Clasen, L., Lenroot, R., Gogtay, N., Evans, A., Rapoport, J., and Giedd, J. (2006), Intellectual Ability and Cortical Development in children and Adolescents, Nature, Vol. 440.

[12] Ibid.

[13] Ibid.

[14] Ibid.

[15] Ibid.

An important aspect of human development with regard to cognition is the concept of 'secondary altriciality'.[16] As *Homo sapiens* evolved, nature was confronted with two aspects of that evolution.

These were bipedalism and brain size. The former had the implication that human females could not give birth to infants with large brains, so they had to give birth to children with small brains, which then went through substantial post-natal growth.[17] The secondary effects of nature's evolutionary ingenuity is that human children need parental support and care for many years after birth. Thus, second altriciality has a direct impact on the development of cognitive abilities. Moreover, the development of a child's cognitive abilities is very much dependent on its interaction with the immediate external environment.[18] The development of linguistic ability may require not only the development of sensory-motor cortical areas but also the interaction of peripheral somatic areas.[19] In this case, it is evident that good motor development may be an essential pre-requisite for further cognitive development.[20] This is because the physical contact an infant engages with in its immediate environment will allow it to be able to perceive objects.[21] The nature of a child's relationships with peers in middle childhood (ages 6–12) will be impacted upon by the nature of the pre-school child-mother relationship.[22] Moreover, pre-adolescent anxiety levels were impacted by both mother and child attachment history and the temperament of the child.[23] And, the relationship between

[16] Coqueugniot, H., Hublin, J., Veillon, F., Houet, F., and Jacob, T. (2004), Early Brain Growth in Homo Erectus and Implications for Cognitive Ability, Nature, Vol. 431.

[17] Rosenberg, K. & Trevathan, W. (2002), Birth, obstetrics and human evolution. Br. J. Obstet. Gynaecol. 109, 1199–1206.

[18] Rosenzweig, M. R. & Bennett, E. L. (1996), Psychobiology of plasticity: effects of training and experience on brain and behavior. Behav. Brain Res. 78, 57–65.

[19] Coqueugniot, H., Hublin, J., Veillon, F., Houet, F., and Jacob, T. (2004), Early Brain Growth in Homo Erectus and Implications for Cognitive Ability, Nature, Vol. 431.

[20] Bushnell, E. W., & Boudreau, J. P. (1993), Motor development and the mind: The potential role of motor abilities as a determinant of aspects of perceptual development. Child Development, 64, 1005–1021.

[21] Piek, J., Dawson, L., Smith, L., and Gasson, N. (2008), The Role of early fine and gross motor development on later motor and cognitive ability, Human Movement Science 27, pp. 668-681.

[22] McElwain, N., Booth-La Force, C., Lansford, J., Wu, X., and Dyer, W. (2008), A Process Model of Attachment-Friend Linkages: Hostile Attribution Biases, Language Ability, and Mother-Child Affective Mutuality as Intervening Mechanisms, Child Development, Vol. 79, No. 6, pp. 1891-1906.

[23] Brumariu, L., and Kerns, K. (2013), Pathways to Anxiety; Contributions of Attachment History, Temperament, Peer Competence, and Ability to Manage Intense Emotions, Child Psychiatry Hum Dev, 44, pp. 504-515.

security and disorganisation with anxiety was due to the level of the children's peer competence.[24] The level of the child's personal security and levels of anxiety are dependent on the child's ability to manage its emotions.[25] The link between motor development and cognitive development has been noted as far back as the 1950s.[26] And birth before the full gestation period of nine months has been found to lead to a greater risk for the infant becoming disabled or experiencing delayed motor development.[27] Moreover, the consumption of alcohol by pregnant mothers in a quantity greater than one drink a day may impair the mental and cognitive development of the child.[28] Furthermore, infants who have been born pre-term have been shown to experience difficulties associated with muscle tone regulation, leading to trunk and neck hyperextension. And this may have an impact on other aspects of the infant's development, especially cognitive development. Further evidence for this has been found in the context of poor postural control in infants at the age of six months and deficient performance in problem reduction tasks, compared to infants of the same age with better postural control.[29]

It has been shown that the time taken by an infant to achieve specific developmental milestones can result in different developmental outcomes.[30] For example, infants who started to walk within the first 13 months of being born had different relationships with their mothers compared to infants who began to walk after this period.[31] Infants who began to walk earlier had positive relationships with their mothers. This may suggest that the development of motor skills may impact on the

[24] Ibid.

[25] Ibid.

[26] Piaget, J. (1953). The origin of the intelligence in the child, Routledge, London.

[27] Piek, J., Dawson, L., Smith, L., and Gasson, N. (2008), The Role of early fine and gross motor development on later motor and cognitive ability, Human Movement Science 27, pp. 668-681.

[28] O'Callaghan, F., O'Callaghan, M., Najman, J., Williams, G., and Bor, W. (2007), Prenatal alcohol exposure and attention, learning and intellectual ability at 14 years: A Prospective Longitudinal Study, Early Human Development, 83, pp. 115-123.

[29] Wijnroks, L., & van Veldhoven, N. (2003). Individual differences in postural control and cognitive development in preterm infants. Infant Behavior and Development, 26, 14–26.

[30] Campos, J. J., Anderson, D. I., Barbu-Roth, M. A., Hubbard, E. M., Hertenstein, M. J., & Witherington, D. (2000). Travel broadens the mind. Infancy, 1, 149–219.

[31] Biringen, Z., Emde, R. N., Campos, J. J., & Appelbaun, M. I. (1995). Affective reorganization in the infant, the mother, and the dyad: The role of upright locomotion and its timing. Child Development, 66, 499–512.

cognitive as well as the emotional capabilities of the infants.[32] Empirical studies have also shown the determinants of motivational ability may also differ by gender.[33] For example, there is a positive correlation between a boy's intellectual efforts and his expectations of intellectual success, and girls who want to succeed intellectually will spend more of their leisure in intellectual pursuits.[34] Moreover, in the case of children in general it has also been found that there is a strong positive correlation between the development of language ability and the theory of the mind.[35] The implications of the findings of studies which find a causative correlation between motor development in infants and later cognitive development are that governments should formulate early-stage education policies which take these findings into account. In the context of the development of mathematical ability, the accumulated knowledge of the child is important in determining the extent of the future learning of additional techniques and skills.[36] However, learning strategies which are varied is probably the best way in which to accumulate knowledge of arithmetic.[37] The area of the brain whose development is important for laying the neural foundations required for cognitively identifying and then representing quantities is the horizontal segment of the intraparietal sulcus.[38] This can be found on the lateral surface of the parietal lobe of the brain.

Although the study of time falls within the study of physics, it is a very important concept in the context of the psychological processes associated with human development.[39] However, whereas developmental psychology

[32] Piek, J., Dawson, L., Smith, L., and Gasson, N. (2008), The Role of early fine and gross motor development on later motor and cognitive ability, Human Movement Science 27, pp. 668-681.

[33] Crandall, V., Katkovsky, W., and Preston, A. (1962), Motivational and Ability Determinants of Young Children's Intellectual Achievement Behaviours, Child Development, Vol. 33, No. 3, pp. 643-661.

[34] Ibid.

[35] Pelletier, J., and Astington, J. (2004), Action, Consciousness and Theory of Mind: Children's Ability to Coordinate Story Characters' Actions and Thoughts, Early Education and Development, 15:1, 5-22, DOI: https://doi.org/10.1207/s15566935eed1501_1

[36] Blair, C., Knipe, H., and Gamson, D. (2008), Is There a Role for Executive Functions in the Development of Mathematics Ability, Mind, Brain and Education, Vol. 2, No. 2.

[37] Ibid.

[38] Dehaene, S., Piazza, M., Pinel, P., and Cohen, L, (2003), Three parietal circuits for number processing. Cognitive Neuropsychology, 2 0, 487 – 506.

[39] Carstensen, L. (2006), The Influence of a Sense of Time on Human Development, Science, Vl. 312.

is based on the idea of change over time, theoretical models of human development are centred on chronological age.[40] While at younger ages, the chronological age of an individual may be an imperfect predictor of cognitive development, at older ages it may be not.[41] This may be because over a life time, people are exposed to different environments and therefore experiences, causing them to develop in different ways.[42] These different environments are associated with exposure to differing levels of stress, socio-economic status, health status and social and family relationships. Cumulative differences in these factors over time will lead to differing development trajectories.[43] Thus, although chronological age may provide a better insight into cognitive development at a young age, at older ages this insight becomes less and less relevant.[44] In this case, as individuals get older the time horizon becomes more and more important, as the less and less time available as one approaches old age and death incentivises prioritisation of life's objectives.[45] Furthermore, it has been found that as people get older there is a tendency to process negative news less deeply than positive news.[46] In other words positive news is processed more deeply than negative news. This is reflected in the increased amygdala activation seen through brain scans when older people are shown positive images. On the other hand, increased amygdala activation does not occur in older people when they are shown negative images. However, amygdala activation is seen in younger people when they are shown negative as well as positive images.[47] The implication of the differences is that the desensitisation of older people to negative news may lead them to be less critical and therefore more susceptible to scams.[48] However, it may also be the case that whether old or young, those who by nature consider time from the perspective of limited horizons may be more willing to take risks than those who do not. Nevertheless, in younger individuals the brain systems associated with cognitive control and emotional regulation may not have

[40] Ibid.

[41] Ibid.

[42] Baltes, P. (1987), Dev. Psychol. 23, 611.

[43] House, J., and Health, J. (2002), Soc. Behav. 43, 125.

[44] Carstensen, L. (2006), The Influence of a Sense of Time on Human Development, Science, Vl. 312.

[45] Ibid.

[46] Mather, M., et al. (2004), Psychol. Sci. 15, 259.

[47] Carstensen, L. (2006), The Influence of a Sense of Time on Human Development, Science, Vl. 312.

[48] Ibid.

developed sufficiently enough to counterbalance the emotions which dictate what actions are taken.[49] In this case, emotions may affect not only how new information is integrated into existing beliefs but also the contextual way in which specific actions are selected in response to various environmental stimulations.[50] And in the context of the dynamic nature of the relationship between ability measures and performance, it was found that in younger adults fluency abilities were more indicative of performance, while in older adults memory abilities were more indicative of performance[51]—although intellectual performance can be stimulated across the adult life span through relevant cognitive interventions.[52]

The Nature of Ability

Abilities are unique to an individual with a characteristic structure.[53] This structure may be associated with inherited genes and developing cognition through the development of the brain. This is affected by the external environment. In fact, this must have a big impact on the development of human cognition, as a significant amount of human brain growth occurs in the post-natal stage, when the infant is interacting with its parental environment.[54] An important synergy between brain development at this stage and the interaction of the infant with the environment is that this facilitates the ability to learn languages.[55] The nature of an individual's cognitive and non-cognitive ability will be determined by the nature and composition of the individual's brain. In general, the area of the brain which determines the cognitive and non-cognitive capacity of any individual is the cerebral cortex. In this part of the brain are sited the sensory,

[49] Luna B, et al. (2001), Maturation of widely distributed brain function subserves cognitive development. Neuroimage 13(5):786–793.

[50] Moutsiana, C., Garrett, N., Clarke, R., Lotto, R., Blakemore, S., Sharot, T. (2013), Human development of the ability to learn from bad news, PNAS, Vol. 110, No. 41.

[51] Hultsch, D., Nesselroade, J., and Plemons, J. (1976), Learning-Ability Relations in Adulthood, Hum. Dev, 19, pp. 234-247.

[52] Blieszner, R., Willis, S., and Baltes, P. (1981), Training Research in Aging on the Fluid Ability of Inductive Reasoning, Journal of Applied Developmental Psychology, 2, pp. 247-265.

[53] Greco, J. (2007), The Nature of Ability and the Purpose of Knowledge, Philosophical Issues, Vol. 17, The Metaphysics of Epistemology, pp. 57-69.

[54] Coqueugniot, H., Hublin, J., Veillon, F., Houet, F., and Jacob, T. (2004), Early Brain Growth in Homo Erectus and Implications for Cognitive Ability, Nature, Volume 431.

[55] Mayberry, R., Lock, E., and Kazmi, H. (2002), Linguistic Ability and Early Language Exposure, Nature, Vol. 417.

motor and associative functions of human behaviour. Moreover, as previously stated, changes in the cortical thickness dictate how intelligence develops over the human life cycle.[56] In early childhood, the relationship between cortical thickness and intelligence is negative.[57] But in late childhood, defined as being in the age range 6–12, a positive correlation exists between the level of intelligence and the extent of cortical thickness.[58] Changes in the levels of intelligence are associated with cortical development in the cerebral cortex's frontal regions. The changes in the cortical thickness from childhood to adolescence, increasing and then decreasing respectively, suggest that the development of cognitive ability is a dynamic process.[59] The implication is that if a child or an adolescent is suitably mentally stimulated, this may have a positive impact on the development of intelligence due to changes in cortical thickness. While intelligence has only been interpreted as being cognitive in nature, it may also be represented in an emotional capacity with regard to an individual's capability to perceive and regulate his/her emotions.[60] However, the extent of an individual's emotional intelligence can be determined by emotional congruence, the extent of emotional empathy with others and the level of social perceptiveness.[61] Emotional congruence is independent of cognitive ability. However, the extent of social perceptiveness is dependent on the extent of verbal communication and inductive reasoning.[62]

Aside from the environmental stimulation a child or an adolescent receives, impacting on the physiological development of the brain, inherited genes may also play a role. In this case, some genes may play a role in the production of specific proteins required by the brain for its development, especially with regard to the cerebral cortex and its composition.[63] It is important to consider the physiology, composition and structure of

[56] Shaw, P., Greenstein, D., Lerch, J., Clasen, L., Lenroot, R., Gogtay, N., Evans, A., Rapoport, J., and Giedd, J. (2006), Intellectual ability and cortical development in children and adolescents, Nature, Vol. 440.

[57] Ibid.

[58] Ibid.

[59] Shaw, P., Greenstein, D., Lerch, J., Clasen, L., Lenroot, R., Gogtay, N., Evans, A., Rapoport, J., and Giedd, J. (2006), Intellectual ability and cortical development in children and adolescents, Nature, Vol. 440.

[60] Barchard, K., and Hakstian, A. (2004), The Nature and Measurement of Emotional Intelligence Abilities; Basic Dimensions and Their Relationships with Other Cognitive Ability and Personality Variables, Educational and Psychological Measurement, Vol. 64, No. 3, pp. 437-462.

[61] Ibid.

[62] Ibid.

[63] Plomin, R. (1999), Genetics and General Cognitive Ability, Nature, Vol. 402.

the cerebral cortex because it is this part of the brain which is important for the development of cognitive functions.[64] General cognitive ability and its development are dependent upon the extent of the interaction of four features of cognition.[65] The latter includes information processing speed, capacity of the memory, the extent of verbal communication as well as the ability to identify and comprehend the spatial relations between objects.[66] An empirical study has found that some types of spatial ability can be dependent on gender.[67] In this case, large gender differences can be found in the context of mental rotation but only small gender differences in the context of spatial perception.[68]

The analysis of general cognitive intelligence has allowed for its quantification in the context of a variable g. The value of this variable is considered to be a good indicator of an individual's ultimate educational and occupational levels, and it is considered to be both a reliable and a stable measure.[69] The level of general cognitive intelligence as measured by the value of g may depend on an individual's genetic inheritance from its parents.[70] The results of empirical studies strongly suggest that the value of g is dependent on an individual's inherited genes.[71] More specifically, the results suggest that an individual's inherited genes are responsible for at least 50% of the variation in g.[72] Furthermore, the impact of genes on an individual extends over his/her lifetime. Inherited genetic propensities will cause individuals to create a personalised environment which they will seek to sustain.[73] It has also been found that the effects of an individual's genes on his/her development tend to be cumulative rather than interactive with regard to any genetic variance in g which can be identified.[74] The cumulative impact of genes on the variation of g may be because of the

[64] Caplan, D. (2014), Cognitive Functions and the Cerebral Cortex, IN Dementia: Comprehensive Principals and Practices, Dickerson, B., and Atri, A. (Eds), Oxford University Press.

[65] Plomin, R. (1999), Genetics and General Cognitive Ability, Nature, Vol. 402.

[66] Ibid.

[67] Linn, M., and Petersen, A. (1985), Emergence and Characterisation of Sex Differences in Spatial Ability: A meta-Analysis, Child Development, Vol. 56, No. 6, pp. 1479-1498.

[68] Ibid.

[69] Gottfredson, L. S. (1997), Intelligence 24, 13-23.

[70] Mackintosh, N. J. (1998), IQ and Human Intelligence, Oxford University Press, Oxford.

[71] Bouchard, T. J. Jr. and McGue, M. (1981), Science 212, 1055–1059.

[72] Plomin, R. (1999), Genetics and General Cognitive Ability, Nature, Vol. 402.

[73] Ibid.

[74] Ibid.

deliberate nature of the selection of mates.[75] In other words, individuals of the same socio-economic status tend to mate while avoiding selecting mates from a dissimilar socio-economic status. The implication is that well-off people, better educated and on higher incomes, would tend to produce offspring who would have similar tendencies.[76] Nevertheless, the environmental conditions in which an adolescent/child may live and learn will also be important in changing g. Reforms in higher education and improvements in teaching methods are evidence for this because the educational attainment of children has improved over time.[77] Further evidence for this is provided by the cases of children who have moved from families who have been abusive to families who have been more accommodating to their needs.[78] But with regard to developing cognitive skills in mathematics, it has been found that a good socio-economic environment is not enough. In this case, individual temperament and personality are also important.[79]

The extent to which individual differences in genes give rise to variations in the value of g is no longer the focus of empirical analysis and research.[80] This is perhaps because of the growing empirical evidence of the importance of both nature (genes) and nurture (nature of family environment) on g.[81] The empirical evidence gained was because of observing the behaviours and development of twins in a bad family environment as well as in a good family environment. The development of g has also been evaluated based on gender differences. For example, when girls can learn in a less pressurised environment, a conducive environment, they can achieve elevated levels of g.[82] It has also been found that a shared environment results in siblings achieving a similar level of g.[83] However, this only

[75] Ibid.

[76] Plomin, R. (1999), Genetics and General Cognitive Ability, Nature, Vol. 402.

[77] Flynn, J. (1999), Am. Psychol. 54, 5–20.

[78] Duyme, M., Dumaret, A.-C. and Tomkiewicz, S. (1999), Proc. Natl Acad. Sci. USA **96,** 8790–8794.

[79] Aiken, L. (1973), Ability and Creativity in Mathematics, Review of Educational Research, Vol. 45, No. 4.

[80] Plomin, R. (1999), Genetics and General Cognitive Ability, Nature, Vol. 402.

[81] Ibid.

[82] Casey, M. (1996), Understanding Individual Differences in Spatial Ability within Females: A Nature/Nurture Interactionist Framework, Development Review, 16, pp. 241-260.

[83] Harris, J. R. (1998), The Nurture Assumption: Why Children Turn Out the Way They Do, New York, The Free Press.

accounts for 25% of the variation in g between individuals, with childhood shared environmental factors having less impact on g after adolescence. But even within the context of a shared environment there may be differences in upbringing which children may experience. These differences could arise due to differences in the ways in which parents treat siblings and siblings' experiences at school may also contribute to differences in g, especially overall. It may be the case then that the role of nurture on the development of g is underestimated and further research should be conducted in this area.[84] It may be the case that the nature of a child's interaction with its environment may depend upon its inherited genes, with genes contributing positively to the development of a child's g.[85] However, a poor socio-economic environment may overcome this effect with an entirely negative outcome.[86] Government policy can overcome this effect by providing opportunities for children to overcome the circumstances of their birth.

Contemporary theories about how the brain functions may be impacted upon by the results of empirical work currently being conducted on the effects on the development of human cognition of either nature, nurture or both. For example, according to one such theory, the brain functions on a modular basis. The implication is that while various parts of the brain may be responsible for the distinctive features of cognitive functioning, this is activated by the interaction of all parts of the brain working together. For example, the artistic and design abilities of an individual result from the specialisation of the right hemisphere of the brain in this ability.[87] It is due to the genetic bottom-up reductionist perspective that the modular functioning of the brain results.[88] However, this contrasts with empirical studies which suggests that genetic effects directly impact on g. But this does not mean that a single cognitive process may be associated with genetic effects, with different genes impacting on various aspects of cognitive abilities. Neuroimaging techniques may be used to determine whether

[84] Ibid.

[85] Rowe, D. C. & van den Oord, E. J. C. G. (1999), Genetic and environmental influences on vocabulary IQ: Parental education level as moderator Child Dev. Vol. 70, No. 5.

[86] Plomin, R. (1994), Genetics and Experience: The Interplay Between Nature and Nurture, Sage Publications, Thousand Oaks, CA.

[87] Cross, N. (1990), The nature and nurture of design ability, Design Studies, Vol. 11, No. 3.

[88] Plomin, R. (1994), Genetics and Experience: The Interplay Between Nature and Nurture, Sage Publications, Thousand Oaks, CA.

the correlation between genetic inheritance and modular processes can be defined as being close to 1.[89] It may be through modular and genetic correlations that the brain functions holistically by accumulating knowledge based on the senses[90]—although the focus of current research should be on determining if the genetic effect on g is with regard to a single, specific cognitive function or if cognitive processes are modular. If research does eventually lead to the identification of specific genes for g, then there will be significant implications for society as well as for science. In this case, if an individual's cognitive functions do not develop fully, then this may be due to a malfunction in one or more of the genes which have been identified as having an impact on the development of cognitive functions, valued by g. Mutations may arise in genes because of changes in the amino acid base pair during the replication of genes. The result is that a different version of the protein is produced when the gene is switched on and off. It is taken for granted that genes may affect brain and cognitive development and therefore g. However, with 30,000 genes known to be expressed in the human brain, it is difficult to pinpoint just more than a handful of genes which may impact on behaviour.[91] In this case, the association of specific genes with the cognitive decline in dementia has been confirmed as well as the association of the genes responsible for reading disability.[92] Research is leading to the identification of specific DNA segments and the relationship of these with g.[93] In the case of science, the knowledge of which genes impact on g will allow for greater integration of various disciplines, including psychology, economics and sociology, for example, with DNA as the common factor determining human behaviour.[94] And in the case of society, knowledge of which genes impact on brain and cognitive development and individual variation in these genes may allow for personalised educational study plans, which could allow individuals to learn and study more effectively. In this case, it has been found that the way in which

[89] Kosslyn, S. & Plomin, R. (1998), Towards neuro-cognitive genetics: goals and issues in Dougherty, D., Rauch, S. L. & Rosenbaum, J. F. (Eds) Psychiatric Neuroimaging Strategies: Research and Clinical Applications, American Psychiatric Press, Washington, DC.

[90] Plomin, R. (1994), Genetics and Experience: The Interplay Between Nature and Nurture, Sage Publications, Thousand Oaks, CA.

[91] Plomin, R. (1994), Genetics and Experience: The Interplay Between Nature and Nurture, Sage Publications, Thousand Oaks, CA.

[92] Ibid.

[93] Ibid.

[94] Ibid.

a student's learning activities are organised and structured has a significant impact on how students perceive their own ability.[95]

Cognitive and Non-cognitive Capabilities: Early and Persistent Gaps

Individual capabilities can be defined as either cognitive or non-cognitive capabilities. The cognitive capacity of an individual relates to how well he/she can perform in a test, exam or any other summative assessment requirement.[96] Cognition should not be seen as a human characteristic but one that spans the range of creatures, from the 'mindful to the mindless'.[97] Nevertheless, the non-cognitive intelligence of an individual encompass a wide range of skills and behaviours which interplay with cognitive capabilities to achieve academic performance, which in turn cannot quantify or measure the magnitude of non-cognitive intelligence.[98] The extent and depth of the non-cognitive skills, especially the team-building and interpersonal skills, of an individual are contextually important to the promotion to leadership positions.[99] Non-cognitive intelligence features include the individual character traits, the level of self-belief and motivation to achieve.[100] And some non-cognitive skills such as tenacity and the ability to self-control may be entirely dependent on personality traits and may not be malleable as are other traits.[101] It is the non-cognitive contribution

[95] Simpson, C. (1981), Classroom Structure and the Organisation of Ability, Sociology of Education, Vol. 54, No. 2, pp. 120-132.

[96] Beckmann, E., and Minnaert, A. (2018), Non-cognitive Characteristics of Gifted Students With Learning Disabilities: An In-depth Systematic Review, Frontiers in Psychology, Volume 9, Article 504.

[97] Duijn, M., Keijzer, F., and Franken, D. (2006), Principles of Minimal Cognition: Casting Cognitions as Sensorimotor Coordination, Adaptive Behaviour, Vol. 14 (2), pp. 157-170.

[98] Farrington, C. A., Roderick, M., Allensworth, E., Nagaoka, J., Keyes, T. S., Johnson, D. W., et al. (2012). Teaching Adolescents to Become Learners: The Role of Noncognitive Factors in Shaping School Performance. Chicago, IL: University of Chicago Consortium on Chicago School Research.

[99] Edin, P., Nybom, M., Fredriksson, P., and Ockert, B. (2017), The Rising Return to Non-Cognitive Skill, IZA DP No. 10914, IZA Institute of Labor Economics.

[100] Gutman, L. M., and Schoon, I. (2013). The Impact of Non-Cognitive Skills on Outcomes for Young People, Education Endowment Foundation, London.

[101] Gutman, L., and Schoon, I. (2013), The Impact of Non-Cognitive Skills on Outcomes of Young People, Education Foundation, Cabinet Office, https://educationendowmentfoundation.org.uk/evidence-summaries/evidence-reviews/essential-life-skills/

of motivation and focus on achievement which allows individuals to succeed in their cognitive endeavours through academic performance.[102] It has been noted that gifted children may be unable to achieve their full potential due to a lack of non-cognitive capacity. One model which integrates the cognitive and non-cognitive pathways' contribution towards academic performance through intelligence, task focus and creativity is the Three Ring Model associated with ability.[103] This model has been expanded to allow for the possible outcomes of giftedness with regard to the socio-economic background of the family.[104] If this is supportive in the positive development of non-cognitive skills which are supportive of the giftedness of the individual, then the potential for achievement can be realised.[105] However, when the family socio-economic environment is not conducive to the development of supportive non-cognitive skills, then gifted students may not be able to achieve their full potential.[106] This is because when gifted students are in a learning environment, their learning will be impacted by negative behavioural pathways which have evolved according to the socio-economic environment in which they grew up.[107] In other words a socio-economic environment which degrades the development of a child's non-cognitive skills may as a consequence also constrain the development of the child's cognitive capacity. The features of the negative behavioural pathways experienced by gifted students will vary from one student to another to varying degrees of heterogeneity.[108] It is the latter

[102] Schneider, W. (2000), Giftedness, expertise, and (exceptional) performance: a developmental perspective, IN International Handbook of Giftedness and Talent, Heller, K.A., Mönks, F.J., Sternberg, R.J., and Subotnik, R.F. (Eds), Elsevier, Amsterdam.

[103] Renzulli, J. S. (1978), What makes giftedness? Re-examining a definition. Phi Delta, Kappan 60, 180–184.

[104] Mönks, F. J., and Mason, E. J. (2000), Developmental psychology and giftedness: theories and research, IN International Handbook of Giftedness and Talent, Heller, K.A., Mönks, F.J., Sternberg, R.J., and Subotnik, R.F. (Eds), Elsevier, Amsterdam, 141–157.

[105] Ibid.

[106] Peters, W. A. M., Grager-Loidl, H., and Supplee, P. (2000), Underachievement in gifted children and adolescents: theory and practice, IN International Handbook of Giftedness and Talent, Heller, K.A., Mönks, F.J., Sternberg, R.J., and Subotnik, R.F. (Eds), Elsevier, Amsterdam, 609–621.

[107] Coleman, L. J., and Cross, T. L. (2000), Social-emotional development and the personal experience of giftedness, IN International Handbook of Giftedness and Talent, Heller, K.A., Mönks, F.J., Sternberg, R.J., and Subotnik, R.F. (Eds), Elsevier, Amsterdam, 203–213.

[108] Yoo, J. E., and Moon, S.M. (2006), Counselling needs of gifted students: an analysis of intake forms at a university-based counselling center, Gifted Child Q. 50, 52–61. doi: https://doi.org/10.1177/001698620605000106

which allows for the development and provision of tailored support to gifted students, allowing them to overcome the difficulties they may face and ultimately achieving their full potential.[109] However, in the case of students with learning difficulties, it has been found that a higher proportion are males,[110] and in general such students have problems associated with both working memory and short-term memory.[111] Both types of memory problems are associated with cognitive problems of the learner. However, in contrast, the deficiencies in the non-cognitive characteristics of students with learning difficulties are associated with an inability to schedule and assess their own learning and its mechanisms.[112] Furthermore, students with learning difficulties are more likely to suffer from psychological problems associated with low self-worth as well as a lack of motivation to learn.[113] The development of the non-cognitive skills of students may be denigrated even further by the segregation of the student cohort into classes based on the level of ability in a particular subject. This denigration of non-cognitive skills upon segregation into classes based on ability is particularly evidenced in males.[114] Such segregation is done on the basis that the cognitive skills of the students can be improved through targeted teaching.

In general, both gifted students and those with learning disabilities are frustrated in a school environment.[115] Moreover, such students also exhibit a duality in their cognitive and non-cognitive skills. For example, students

[109] Freeman, J. (2000), Families: the essential context for gifts and talents, IN International Handbook of Giftedness and Talent, Heller, K.A., Mönks, F.J., Sternberg, R.J., and Subotnik, R.F.(Eds), Elsevier, Amsterdam, 573–587.

[110] Morrison, G. M., and Cosden, M. (1997), Risk, resilience, and adjustment of individuals with learning disabilities, Learn. Disabil. Q. 20, 43–60. doi: https://doi.org/10.2307/1511092

[111] Trainin, G., and Swanson, H. L. (2005), Cognition, metacognition, and achievement of college students with learning disabilities, Learn. Disabil. Q. 28, 261–272. doi: https://doi.org/10.2307/4126965

[112] Hallahan, D. P., and Kauffman, J.M. (2006), Exceptional Learners: An Introduction to Special Education, Pearson, Boston, MA.

[113] Galway, T. M., and Metsala, J. L. (2011), Social cognition and its relation to psychosocial adjustment in children with nonverbal learning disabilities J. Learn. Disabil. 44, 33–49. doi: https://doi.org/10.1177/0022219410371680

[114] McDool, E. (2019): Ability grouping and children's non-cognitive outcomes, Applied Economics, DOI: https://doi.org/10.1080/00036846.2019.1705239

[115] Beckmann, E., and Minnaert, A. (2018), Non-cognitive Characteristics of Gifted Students with Learning Disabilities: An In-depth Systematic Review, Frontiers in Psychology, Volume 9, Article 504.

with cognitive skills suggesting high ability may perform less well than expected because they have negative non-cognitive skills such as low self-esteem and poor interpersonal skills despite being highly motivated.[116] These findings highlight the fact that the development of a child's non-cognitive skills is just as important as the development of his/her cognitive skills—in which case the development of the full potential of a child's cognitive performance depends to a great extent on his/her self-belief, levels of motivation to study and the ability to plan and assess his/her own learning. And because the development of non-cognitive skills is dependent on the child's socio-economic environment, directed government policy to improve that environment may be justified by a child's improved cognitive performance.[117] The importance of a suitable environment for the development of non-cognitive skills even in the late teens has also been established in the literature. In this case, it has been found that a university education facilitates the development of individual extrovert characteristics not due to the curriculum or the subject but because of the university experience itself.[118] In this case, a statistically significant relationship has been found between peers' ability and the development of non-cognitive skills by classmates.[119] This effect was stronger in the case of males, rather than females.[120] However, interactive teaching will help to improve the capabilities of both boys and girls.[121]

The number of working females in the labour force in OECD countries has increased over the last few decades.[122] As increased women go to work, the child will miss the nurturing role of the mother, and this may impact on the child's cognitive and non-cognitive development. Therefore, the results of the research which explores the relationship between childcare and the impact on childhood development are important to both parents

[116] Ibid.

[117] Ibid.

[118] Kassenboehmer, S.C., Leung, F., and Schurer, S. (2018), University Education and Non-Cognitive Skill Development, Oxford Economic Papers, 70(2), pp. 538-562.

[119] Comi, S., Origo, F. and Pagani, L. (2017). Peer effects on non-cognitive skills. Available at: http://www.aiel.it/cms/cms-files/submission/all20170615160133.pdf

[120] Ibid.

[121] Addabbo, T., Tommaso, M., and Maccagnan, A. (2016), education Capability: A Focus on Gender and Science, Soc Indic Res, 128:793-812.

[122] McDonnell, T. (2016), Non-Cognitive Development in Early Childhood: The Influence of Maternal Employment and the Mediating Role of Childcare, The Economic and Social Review, Vol. 47, No. 4, pp. 499-541.

and policymakers[123]—important to the former, as they can best decide how often they should go to work and/or to decide the nature of the childcare to provide for their child, and important to policymakers because they can then formulate the optimal childcare provision policies to offer to families. Indeed, it has been found that there has been an increase in the provision of childcare facilities by the state because of increasing numbers of working mothers and this has in turn encouraged more women to go to work.[124] And in turn, maternal employment and the quality of childcare alternatives may have an impact on the non-cognitive skills development of toddlers and infants. In this case, it may be concluded that non-cognitive skills are correlated with a quantification of intelligence. And perhaps non-cognitive skills are as equally important as cognitive skills for the personal development of individuals.[125] In this case, it has been found that the nature of a non-cognitive skill such as attitude towards learning, in conjunction with good parenting, can have a significant impact on the cognitive development of individuals.[126] More specifically, a negative attitude towards learning held by an individual will lower the chances of high-level qualifications being achieved.[127] Furthermore, good child rearing practices of parents in terms of setting rules at home for their children to follow also facilitate higher-level learning and foster academic achievement.[128] However, performance goals or academic achievement may be thwarted if the children's working memory is limited.[129] This finding is in contrast to other studies which have established a positive correlation between achievement goals and working memory on academic performance, although it has not been clearly established whether these factors have a

[123] Ibid.

[124] Thévenon, O. (2013), Drivers of Female Labour Force Participation in the OECD, OECD Social, Employment and Migration Working Papers, No. 145, OECD Publishing.

[125] Brunello, G. and Schlotter, M. (2011), Non-Cognitive Skills and Personality Traits: Labour Market Relevance and their Development in Education and Training Systems, IZA DP No. 5743.

[126] Tavares, L. (2007) Non-cognitive skills, parenting practices and academic success. Paper presented at British Household Panel Survey conference, Institute for Social and Economic Research, University of Essex, Colchester, July.

[127] Ibid.

[128] Ibid.

[129] Lee, K., Ning, F., and Goh, H. (2014), Interaction between cognitive and non-cognitive factors: the influences of academic goal orientation and working memory on mathematical performance, Educational Psychology, Vol. 34, No. 1, pp. 73-91.

joint impact.[130] But in this case, the finding may suggest that a poor short-term working memory may have a negative impact on academic performance even when the performance motivation of the child is very high.[131] When a child is under stress due to environmental factors, the use of its cognitive capacity to deal with such a situation my impact negatively on its short-term memory.[132] In this case, there is a link between a child's environmental conditions in the context of poverty and the extent of the level of the development of the brain[133]—the implication being that a child's environment associated with poverty may lead to under-development of the brain.[134] And while schooling may enhance a child's cognitive development, good parenting will help to enhance both cognitive and non-cognitive skills.[135] And such development is more conducive in the early years of a child's life, whether in a bad or in a good environment.[136] This under-development is so drastic that the effects on behaviour, cognitive and non-cognitive development carry over into adulthood.[137] In the transition from childhood to adulthood, the human brain becomes less and less malleable as it develops, and so it is not difficult to see why poverty in childhood may have long-lasting lifetime impacts—perhaps even leading to the impairment of an individual's cognitive and non-cognitive capabilities over a lifetime. Therefore, it becomes evident that as brain

[130] Ibid.

[131] Lee, K., Ning, F., and Goh, H. (2014), Interaction between cognitive and non-cognitive factors: the influences of academic goal orientation and working memory on mathematical performance, Educational Psychology, Vol. 34, No. 1, pp. 73-91.

[132] Shrimpton, S., Oates, K., and Hayes, S. (1998), Children's Memory of Events: Effects of Stress, age, Time Delay and Location of Interview, Applied Cognitive Psychology, Vol. 12, pp. 133-143.

[133] McColloch, C. (2013). Mindfulness Intervention in Education: Can we address cognitive and non-cognitive deficits of children in poverty at school. Psychological Inquiry, 18, 211237.

[134] Schamberg, M.A., and Evans, G.W, (2009), Childhood poverty, chronic stress, and Adult working memory, National Academy of Sciences, Vol. 106, No. 13.

[135] Masten, A.S., and Shaffer, A. (2006), How families matter in child development: reflections from research on risk and resilience. In: Families count: Effects on child and adolescent development, Clarke-Stewart A, and Dunn, J. (Eds) Cambridge University Press, New York, pp. 5-25.

[136] Heckman, J.J., and Kautz, T.D. (2012), Hard Evidence on Soft Skills, Working Paper 18121 National Bureau of Economic Research http://www.nber.org/papers/w18121

[137] Duncan, G.J., Kalil, A., and Ziol-Guest, K, Early-Childhood Poverty and Adult Attainment, Behavior, and Health, Child Development, Jan/Feb 2010, Vol 81, no. 1 p 206-325.

development is malleable in childhood, then it becomes possible for the right level of directed policy intervention to have a positive impact on the development of the child. Such direct intervention is needed because of the significant empirical evidence which corroborates the negative impact of childhood poverty on brain development.[138] Research suggests that the conditions of poverty under which a child grows under will lead to not only low levels of educational attainment but also behavioural and mental health problems later in life.[139] Thus, schooling may be the environment which either increases or decreases the differences in abilities amongst pupils.[140] And children growing up in an environment of poverty, coupled with having parents of low educational attainment, experience lower levels of achievement at school in comparison to their well-off peers with more educated parents.[141] As a result the former group of children may experience lower levels of lifetime productivity as well as lower standards of living[142]—although families which are at a material disadvantage can make up for this by better parenting.[143] This underlines the importance of targeted interventionist policies which allow children to develop thinking strategies which allow for better brain development, leading to enhanced development of cognitive and non-cognitive skills. One such interventionist strategy is that of mindfulness. This is a programme of behaviour control which allows children to develop the skill of attentiveness or paying attention.[144] The development of such a skill would allow children to be better able to deal with adverse environmental circumstances and develop

[138] McColloch, C. (2013). Mindfulness Intervention in Education: Can we address cognitive and non-cognitive deficits of children in poverty at school. Psychological Inquiry, 18, 211237.

[139] Magnuson, K., and Votruba-Drzal, E. (2009), Enduring Influences of Childhood Poverty, Changing Poverty: Changing Policies, Cancian, M., and Danziger, S. (Eds), Russell Sage Foundation, New York.

[140] Hartog, J. (2001), On Human Capital and Individual Capabilities, Review of Income and Wealth, Series 47, No. 4.

[141] McColloch, C. (2013). Mindfulness Intervention in Education: Can we address cognitive and non-cognitive deficits of children in poverty at school. Psychological Inquiry, 18, 211237.

[142] Ibid.

[143] Joshi, H. (2014), 'Non-Cognitive' Skills: What are they and how can they be measured in the British cohort Studies, CLS Working Paper 2014/6.

[144] McColloch, C. (2013). Mindfulness Intervention in Education: Can we address cognitive and non-cognitive deficits of children in poverty at school. Psychological Inquiry, 18, 211237.

avoidance strategies rather than to blame themselves. The development of mindfulness skills would allow children to escape the inhibited learning which results from growing up in a poverty-stricken environment.[145] Associated with this environment are a range of factors such as the structure of the family, the level of parental education, racial discrimination and the family's financial stability.[146] However, more specifically ethnicity, class size, mother's level of education and the family income level can be associated with the low educational attainment of children.[147] This may result because the stress and emotional distress the children suffer as a result of living in a non-conducive environment means that they use their cognitive power not for learning but to find ways in which to survive and anticipate future crises. The result is that the child's learning is constrained, resulting in poor academic achievement. Therefore, it is self-evident that teaching a child ways in which stress and emotional distress can be overcome, by facilitating better emotional regulation and empathy,[148] may result in more effective learning and higher levels of academic achievement. Childhood development should therefore embrace greater public investment such that the impacts of poverty on brain development are mitigated. Investment in childhood programmes to foster mindfulness may allow a child to be better at emotional regulation and separating self from circumstance and thus enhancing their own academic achievement and allowing for subsequent additional skill formation in the future.[149]

Upbringing: Family Investments and Endowments

The literature on childhood development is indicative of the fact that the level of cognitive capacity is affected not only by the environment in which a child grows up but also by the external environment sensed by an unborn

[145] Cunha, F., and Heckman, J. (2007), The technology of Skill Formation, American Economic Review, 97(2), 31-47.

[146] Hart, B., and Risley, T. R. (1995), Meaningful differences in the everyday experience of young American children, Paul H Brookes Publishing.

[147] Krueger, A.B, (1999), Experimental Estimates of Education Production Functions, The Quarterly Journal of Economics, Vol. 114, No. 2. pp. 497-532.

[148] McColloch, C. (2013). Mindfulness Intervention in Education: Can we address cognitive and non-cognitive deficits of children in poverty at school. Psychological Inquiry, 18, 211237.

[149] Heckman, J.J. (2009), Integrating Personality Psychology into Economics. National Bureau of Economic Research. Cambridge MA, 2011. http://www.nber.org/papers/w17378

child in its mother's womb. Moreover, the lifetime level of cognitive ability is effectively determined within the first several years of a child's life. This is typically before the child reaches the age of 10 and after this age it would be extremely difficult to change the IQ of the child. However, while the development of a child's non-cognitive skills, such as those associated with working as a team, showing leadership and showing initiative and restraint, is also affected by the environmental conditions faced by a developing child, these tend to get changed and altered by experience even when the child has reached adulthood. Furthermore, while non-cognitive skills may be in demand in the real world, for example, in the context of entrepreneurship, these skills may also impact on the development of cognitive and social skills—for example, through the ability to socially interact with others. It has only been recognised within the last 30 years that investments made to facilitate the development of cognitive and non-cognitive skills are complementary and tend to support each other in a dynamic self-sustaining manner.[150] However, all human beings have limited cognitive capacity, as our brains and mental processing powers are not suitable and capable of exponential rates of processing power upon the receipt of added information. This would suggest that all investments in developing the cognitive and non-cognitive capacities of individuals should be made on an equal, per-person basis. Nevertheless, the fact is that investment in young people from disadvantaged backgrounds, with regard to education and vocational training, will result in lower rates of return in contrast to the investment in the education and vocational training of young people from advantaged backgrounds. This is because young people from disadvantaged backgrounds will have less well-developed cognitive and non-cognitive skills in comparison to their peers from more advantaged backgrounds. Therefore, it must follow that investment in developing the cognitive and non-cognitive skills of young adults may be prohibitively expensive. It must follow from a public policy point of view that the equalisation of investment in the development of the cognitive and non-cognitive skills of all children under the age of 10, whether from advantaged or disadvantaged backgrounds, will ensure that the returns per individual as well as to society will be much greater than investments made during the teenage years. Moreover, the environment in which a child

[150] Heckman, J. J., Lochner, L., and Taber, C, (1998), Explaining Rising Wage In-equality: Explorations with a Dynamic General Equilibrium Model of Earnings with Heterogeneous Agents, Review of Economic Dynamics 1, no. 1: 1-58.

experiences during the early years of its life is important. This is because the environmental upbringing faced by a young child has an impact on the expression of its genes. However, while ability may result from an interaction of a child's environment and its genes, government intervention programmes should be designed such that the result is the development of a child's cognitive abilities specifically. However, given the link between a child's cognitive and non-cognitive abilities, programmes should be designed to improve both types of abilities. This is specifically in the context of a deprived childhood environment in which a lower level of parental income may lead to children not having access to education and other resources required for his/her cognitive and non-cognitive development. Such circumstances may lead to the non-optimal expression of a child's genes. Empirical evidence suggests that programmes designed to permanently increase parental incomes have a more significant impact on alleviating the effects of low parental incomes on childhood development than programmes designed to alter schooling choices.[151]

Some empirical studies have shown that more than 33% of differences in the educational achievement of children is due to the family background.[152] Furthermore, the level of correlation of achievements amongst siblings is very much dependent on the socio-economic background of the parents.[153] Although it has been found that educational constraints to a child's education caused by low parental incomes may be more effectively overcome by increasing parental permanent incomes then by altering educational opportunities, early investment in childhood education would also help a child develop its cognitive and non-cognitive abilities compared to investments made at a later stage.[154] However, the context of intergenerational transfers amongst group of countries may perhaps need to be better understood because of the outcome on economic growth.[155]

[151] Chevalier, A., Harmon, C., O'Sullivan, V., and Walker, I. (2013), The Impact of Parental Income and Education on the Schooling of their Children, IZA Journal of Labor Economics 2, Article Number 8.

[152] Bredtmann, J., and Smith, N. (2018), Inequalities in Educational Outcomes: How Important is The Family? Oxford Bulletin of Economics and Statistics, 80, 6.

[153] Ibid.

[154] Heckman, J. (2011), The Economics of Inequality: The Value of Early Childhood Education, American Educator, v 35, No. 1, pp. 31-35.

[155] Cox, D., and Fachamps, M. (2008), Extended Family and Kinship Networks: Economic Insights and Evolutionary Directions, IN Handbook of Development Economics, Vol. 4, Schultz, T., and Strauss, J. (Eds), North-Holland.

For example, in some countries intergenerational transfers are to the elderly, whereas in other countries the transfers are to the young.[156] Obviously, the latter will have a bigger impact on economic growth than the former, as younger people will live longer and so will be able to contribute more in helping the economy of the country grow. However, with regard to educational attainment, it has been found that educational parent-child correlations reflect 16.67% genetic transmission and 83.33% social inheritance.[157] Moreover, a child's educational attainment, dependent on the quality of its genes, is not impacted upon significantly by the makeup or composition of parental genes[158]—although a child's educational attainment is affected jointly by a combination of genetic inheritance (random) and social inheritance. The latter can be selected to an extent by the individual, whereas with the former an individual's genes may not have been his/her choice. Social inheritance can also be improved not only with parental involvement at the community level but also with groups associated with children's extracurricular activities. Moreover, such parental involvement also causes the behaviour of children at school to improve.[159]

Education not only improves the earnings of an individual over his/her life[160] but also results in individuals acting in the best interests of society.[161] However, many real-world educational investment decisions seem to diverge from those which would result from an economic model.[162] In reality, girls tend to perform less well than boys in a competitive

[156] Ibid.

[157] Conley, D., Domingue, B., Cesarini, D., Dawes, C., Rietveld, C., and Boardman, J. (2015), Is the Effect of Parental Education on Offspring Biased or Moderated by Genotype, Sociological Science, 2:82-105.

[158] Ibid.

[159] Neymotin, F. (2014), How Parental Involvement Affects Childhood Behavioral Outcomes, J Fam Econ, ISS. 35, pp. 433-451.

[160] Heckman, J.J., Lochner, L.J., and Todd, P.E. (2006), Earnings functions, rates of return and treatment effects: The Mincer equation and beyond. Handbook of the Economics of Education, vol. 1. Elsevier B.V. North Holland, Amsterdam.

[161] Lochner, L. (2011), Nonproduction benefits of education: crime, health, and good citizenship. Handbook of the Economics of Education, vol. 4. Elsevier B. V. North Holland, Amsterdam.

[162] Koch, A., Nafziger, J., Nielsen, H. (2015), Behavioral Economics of Education, Journal of Economic Behavior & Organisation, 115.

environment in numerical tests,[163] and students give up on education before reaching their potential.[164] In both cases, the returns would be higher if the contrary were the case. A better understanding of why real-world investments fall short of the predictions of standard economic models can be gained through a behavioural economics approach which integrates psychological and sociological findings into standard economic theory.[165] In the context of the economics of education, the specialism of behavioural economics is strongly associated with the study of an individual's non-cognitive skills. These non-cognitive skills are strongly associated with an individual's objectives, personal characteristics, motivation and choices. Typically, in empirical analyses, these variables are difficult to control for, resulting in biases in the results.[166] These non-cognitive skills are of importance in the economic, educational and leisure activities of individuals.[167] However, perhaps for too long, the non-cognitive skills associated with transitioning from an array of individualised inputs (time, financial resources, personal characteristics) into the outputs of educational insights seem not to have been really understood.[168] But insights from behavioural economics may help to explain the real-world divergences of personal investments from the predictions of theoretical economic models. The main drawback of using insights from behavioural economics is that these insights are based on the results of experiments in the real world—the implication being that data may be limited compared to the panel data sets of traditional econometric analysis, and the environment artificial[169]—in which case, the results of such experiments may not be as realistic as if the evaluation were based on a real-life case study. The other constraints of using behavioural/experimental economics to explain real-life investments in education include the use of adapted standard economic models as well as the inability to explain the long-run effects of

[163] Niederle, M., and Vesterlund, L. (2010), Explaining the gender gap in math test scores: the role of competition. J. Econ. Perspect. 24, 129–144.

[164] Oreopoulos, P. (2007), Do dropouts drop out too soon? Wealth, health and happiness from compulsory schooling. J. Public Econ. 97, 2213–2229.

[165] Koch, A., Nafziger, J., Nielsen, H. (2015), Behavioral Economics of Education, Journal of Economic Behaviour & Organisation, 115.

[166] Behrman, J., and Wolfe, B. (1984), The Socioeconomic Impact of Schooling in a Developing Economy, The Review of Economics and Statistics, Vol. 66, No. 2, pp. 296-303.

[167] Heckman, J.J., and Kautz, T. (2012), Hard evidence on soft skills. Labour Econ. 19(4).

[168] Koch, A., Nafziger, J., Nielsen, H. (2015), Behavioral Economics of Education, Journal of Economic Behaviour & Organisation, 115.

[169] Ibid.

human behaviour[170]—although the short-term effects of given incentives on human motivation can be observed through field experiments. The implication of the constraints is that research into behavioural/experimental economics needs to evolve over time to provide solutions to the constraints.

Following years of research and statistical analysis by scholars starting in 1966,[171] the education process consisting of inputs and outputs was formalised into a mathematical relationship.[172] In this mathematical relationship, the level of student achievement is the dependent variable, and the independent variables are associated with peer, school, family and early-stage ability factors. However, one of the factors not explicitly included in the education function is the role of nutrition and diet in children's education. In this case, it has been found that poor families in rural parts of China are only able to provide a poor nutritional environment for their children compared to families in urban centres, who tend to have higher incomes.[173] Thus, children from poor families in rural China will tend to underperform academically, especially during the early primary years, which are crucial for the development of a child's lifelong adulthood cognitive powers. The family plays a critical role in shaping the future of the young child into adulthood, and being born into a poor dysfunctional family environment may contribute to heightened inequality in adulthood.[174] However, society can only benefit if policymakers are able to devise policy such that poor children's development will not be hindered by a lack of financial resources.[175] Nevertheless, removing the financial constraints faced by disadvantage children may not necessarily improve either their educational or social mobility because the transfer of ability

[170] Ibid.

[171] Coleman, J.S. (1966), Equality of educational opportunity. U.S. Govt. Print. Off, Washington, Summary report.

[172] Todd, P., and Wolpin, K. (2003), On the specification and estimation of the production function for cognitive achievement. Econ. J. 113, 3–33.

[173] Yu, S., and Hannum, E. (2007), Food for Thought: Poverty, Family Nutritional Environment, And Children's Educational Performance in Rural China, Sociological Perspectives, Vol. 50, Issue 4, pp. 53-77.

[174] Heckman, J.J. (2008), Schools, skills, and synapses. Econ. Inq. 4 (3), 289–324.

[175] Plug, E., and Vijverberg, W. (2005), Does Family Income Matter for Schooling Outcomes? Using Adoptees as a Natural Experiment, The Economic Journal, 115, pp. 879-906.

from one generation to the next is 50% determined by genes.[176] Moreover, a large family size also impacts negatively on a child's achievements at school, where additional restrictions on parental investment also already exist.[177] Furthermore, differences in income and in genetic traits which help to optimise academic achievement may help to explain the prevalence of inequality in society.[178] In this case, it can be said that the chances of a child achieving academic and social status later in life are dependent not only on the personal traits inherited from his/her parents but also on the level of human capital investment made by the parents on the child and random events.[179] Nevertheless, even in cases where children have been adopted, the educational levels of the biological parents are important, as this will determine the extent of the educational achievement of the children.[180] It follows that to some extent the ability of an individual is a genetically transmitted characteristic.[181] Empirically, it has been found that 55%–60% of the parent's academic ability is transmitted through genes to the children.[182] Currently, the mechanism by which this takes place is indeterminate.[183] However, although the parents may be educated, this may not always lead to the optimal development of a child's cognitive abilities. In developing countries, the extent and level of maternal education may have a positive impact on the nutrition and overall health of a child.[184] However, this relationship becomes less strong when maternal capital such as health status, abilities and habits according to the background of the family are taken into account.[185] On the other hand, it has

[176] Plug, E.J.S. and Vijverberg, W.P.M. (2003), Schooling, family background, and adoption: is it nature or is it nurture? Journal of Political Economy, vol. 111, pp. 611–41.

[177] Aslund, O., and Gronquist, H. (2010), Family Size and Child Outcomes: Is there really no trade off? Labour Economics 17, pp. 130-139.

[178] Andergassen, R., and Nardini, F. (2019), Intergenerational Mobility and Social Status in a model with Human Capital Investments and Trait Inheritance, Macroeconomic Dynamics, doi: https://doi.org/10.1017/51365100519000427

[179] Ibid.

[180] Lochner, L. (2008), Intergenerational Transmission, IN New Palgrave Dictionary of Economics, Durlauf, S., and Blume, L. (Eds), Palgrave Macmillan, 2nd Edition.

[181] Ibid.

[182] Plug, E., and Vijverberg, W. (2003), Schooling, Family Background and Adoption: Is it Nature or Nurture? Journal of Political Economy, Vol. 111, No. 3.

[183] Ibid.

[184] Behrman, J., and Wolfe, B. (1987), How Does Mothers Schooling Affect Family Health, Nutrition, Medical Care Usage and Household Sanitation, Journal of Econometrics, 36, pp. 185-204.

[185] Ibid.

been found that in Africa, schools foster the development of children's cognitive skills and this is a primary determinant of wage levels in adulthood.[186] However, the African primary school system is neither efficient nor effective at fostering the development of either mathematical or computational skills in children.[187] This should indicate to policymakers that more teaching and school resources should be deployed to facilitate the development of mathematical and computational skills of children.[188]

A child growing up in a functional family with an educated mother may be able to develop higher levels of cognitive and non-cognitive capacity in adulthood and thereby reduced lifetime inequality by being able to make better decisions. A child's education may benefit if the mother is educated, as this may allow her to have selected the best partner amongst the pool of available men.[189] Moreover, highly educated parents are more likely than less-educated counterparts to invest more resources in the education and upbringing of their young child, facilitating a better development of the child's non-cognitive skills.[190] While empirical analysis has shown that the intergenerational impact of parental education on childhood development is positive and causal,[191] what is not clear are the factors which may arise from a good parental education which may more specifically contribute to better childhood upbringing. Moreover, parental resources such as income and time are important not only in the positive upbringing of a child, but also in the transmission of positive qualities such as self-control, motivation, tenacity and a desire for success, for example.[192] The values received by a child from its parents can be broken down into attitudes (trusting nature, preferences associated with time and risk) and outcomes

[186] Moll, P. (1996), Primary Schooling, Cognitive Skills and Wages in South Africa, Economica, 65, 263-84.

[187] Ibid.

[188] Ibid.

[189] Plug, E. (2002), How Do Parents Raise the Educational Attainment of Future Generations? IZA Discussion Paper No. 652.

[190] Sepahuand, M., and Shahbazian, R., and Swain, R. (2013), Time Investment by parents in cognitive and non-cognitive childcare activities, Working Paper No;2013;10, Uppsala University, Department of Economics.

[191] Holmlund, H., Lindahl, M., and Plug, E. (2011), The causal effect of parents' schooling on children' schooling: a comparison of estimation methods. J. Econ. Lit. 49(3), 615–651.

[192] Koch, A., Nafziger, J., Nielsen, H. (2015), Behavioral Economics of Education, Journal of Economic Behaviour & Organisation, 115.

(willingness to work, willingness to have children, becoming an entrepreneur).[193] As the child grows into adulthood and old age, these values will change and become adapted to the environment the individual faces.[194] Empirically, it has been found that if a mother's working hours increase, this will have a negative impact on the child's achievements.[195] Moreover, the additional income earned which contributes to the well-being of the child is only partial compensation.[196] With regard to school resources, empirical research suggests that small class sizes help to develop children's non-cognitive skills,[197] and that some teachers help children develop better cognitive skills whilst other teachers help children develop their non-cognitive skills.[198] Nevertheless, empirically it has been found that the explanatory power of teaching qualifications and teaching experience in the context of what constitutes a good teacher is very little.[199] However, in order to understand the impact of soft skills on the educational achievement of children, it is important to understand the impact of class size and the nature of the teacher in the context of soft skill development. The behaviour of children is also impacted by their peer groups, which is why this is also a component of the educational production function. It follows that peer groups which are disruptive, drug taking for example, can have a negative impact on educational achievement, which can be quantified by exam grades.[200] Moreover, an ethnic background in conjunction with religious beliefs has less impact on educational outcomes when the effect of location on economic mobility is considered.[201] For

[193] Albanese, G., De Blasio, G., and Sestito, P. (2016), My Parents Taught Me. Evidence on the Family Transmission of Values, J. Popol Econ, 29, pp. 571-592.

[194] Albanese, G., De Blasio, G., and Sestito, P. (2016), My Parents Taught Me. Evidence on the Family Transmission of Values, J. Popol Econ, 29, pp. 571-592.

[195] Hill, M., and O'Neill, J. (1994), Family Endowments and the Achievement of Young Children with Special Reference to the Underclass, The Journal of Human Resources, Vol. 29, No. 4.

[196] Ibid.

[197] Fredriksson, P., Oosterbeek, H., and Ockert, B. (2013), Long-term effects of class size. Q. J. Econ. 128 (1), 249–285.

[198] Jackson, C.K. (2013), Non-cognitive ability, test scores, and teacher quality: evidence from 9th grade teachers in North Carolina. NBER Discussion Paper No. 18624.

[199] Hanushek, E.A., and Rivkin, S.G. (2006), Teacher quality. Handbook of the Economics of Education, vol. 2. Elsevier B.V. North Holland, Amsterdam, pp. 1051–1078.

[200] Eriksen, T.L.M., Nielsen, H.S., and Simonsen, M. (2014), Bullying in elementary school. J. Hum. Resour. 49 (4), 839–871.

[201] Sander, W. (1992), The Effects of Ethnicity and Religion on Educational Attainment, Economics of Education Review, Vol. 11, No. 2, pp. 119-135.

example, rural children's education will be more disadvantaged than will the education of urban children, as the former will have access to fewer resources.

For many years it was thought that the lifetime achievement of adults was only dependent on their cognitive skill formation in childhood. This could be, for example, a higher level of educational attainment, leading to higher income earnings.[202] Nevertheless, after the end of the 1990s, it became evident that non-cognitive skills such as self-control[203] and motivation[204] are also important contributors to educational achievement. This is because without either or both, it would be possible for children, adolescents and even adults to drop out of studies. Moreover, while the non-cognitive skills of a child may impact on its educational attainment, it is also the case that the educational environment will also impact on the evolution and development of a child's cognitive skills.[205] In conjunction with peer and family influences, the school environment is also important for the development of the non-cognitive skills of children.[206] However, whereas traditional economic approaches to evaluating the impact of investment in education to educational outcomes allow for a multidimensional approach to modelling inputs to outputs in the context of cognitive and non-cognitive skill formation, the latter remains less understood than the former. This is particularly in the context of the relationship between non-cognitive and cognitive skills. The former is required for the latter. Non-cognitive skills such as tenacity and self-control are required to overcome fatigue and boredom to optimise educational attainment, for example.[207] However, in the absence of individual self-control mechanisms, a commitment mechanism such as coursework deadlines can

[202] Cunha, F., and Heckman, J. (2007), The technology of skill formation. Am. Econ. Rev. 97 (2), 31–47.

[203] Eckstein, Z., and Wolpin, K.I. (1999), Why youths drop out of high school: the impact of preferences, opportunities and abilities. Econometrica 67 (6), 1295–1339.

[204] Oreopoulos, P. (2007), Do dropouts drop out too soon? Wealth, health and happiness from compulsory schooling. J. Public Econ. 97, 2213–2229.

[205] Koch, A., Nafziger, J., Nielsen, H. (2015), Behavioral Economics of Education, Journal of Economic Behaviour & Organisation, 115.

[206] Gupta, N.D., and Simonsen, M. (2010), Non-cognitive child outcomes and universal high-quality childcare, J. Public Econ. 94 (1), 30–43.

[207] Steel, P. (2007), The nature of procrastination: a meta-analytic and theoretical review of quintessential self-regulatory failure. Psychol. Bull. 133 (1), 65.

overcome the lack of self-control, especially in adult learners.[208] This is an insight from behavioural economics. Self-confidence is also a crucial factor in achieving academic success. This is because it motivates effort, which will lead to the latter.[209] It follows, therefore, that teachers and tutors can act strategically by teaching in such a way that the self-confidence of students may be boosted. For example, a teacher can instruct students at a higher level than required by the syllabus and then set an exam which the students may find easy. Empirical analysis has shown that even small differences between students in terms of the levels of self-confidence can have big impacts on learning and knowledge accumulation.[210] The socio-economic background of a child can also influence his/her level of self-confidence.[211] In this case, giving students' feedback on their performance at an early stage can only boost their confidence.[212] Nevertheless, a child's confidence levels as well as other attributes such as tenacity, the ability to take risks and to trust others can also result from the immediate parental environment.[213] Moreover, the genetic impact on the values of parents and children brought up in a conducive parental environment seems to be negligible.[214] Nevertheless, in addition to the transmission of parental values and behaviours through the parental environment, the non-cognitive abilities of a child can also develop and be enhanced by the school environment he/she may face. This is particularly with regard to class size and

[208] Koch, A., Nafziger, J., Nielsen, H. (2015), Behavioral Economics of Education, Journal of Economic Behaviour & Organisation, 115.

[209] Benabou, R., and Tirole, J. (2002), Self-confidence and personal motivation. Q. J. Econ. 117 (3), 871–916.

[210] Filippin, A., and Paccagnella, M. (2012), Family background, self-confidence and economic outcomes. Econ. Educ. Rev. 31, 824–834.

[211] Chowdry, H., Crawford, C., and Goodman, A. (2011), The role of attitudes and behaviours in explaining socio-economic differences in attainment at age 16. Longit. Life Course Stud. 2, 5–76.

[212] Koch, A., Nafziger, J., Nielsen, H. (2015), Behavioral Economics of Education, Journal of Economic Behaviour & Organisation, 115.

[213] Zumbuehl, M., Dohmen, T., and Pfann, G. (2013), Parental investment and the intergenerational transmission of economic preferences and attitudes. SOEP Discussion Paper No. 570.

[214] Benjamin, D.J., Cesarini, D., Chabris, C.F., Glaeser, E.L., Laibson, D.L., Guðnason, V., Harris, T.B., Launer, L.J., Purcell, S., Smith, A.V., Johannesson, M., Magnusson, P.K.E., Beauchamp, J.P., Christakis, N.A., Atwood, C.S., Herbert, B., Freese, J., Hauser, R.M., Hauser, T.S., Grankvist, A., Hultman, C.M., and Lichtenstein, P. (2012), The promises and pitfalls of genoeconomics. Annu. Rev. Econ. 4, 627–662.

teacher quality.[215] However, one of the puzzles associated with the relationship between these two factors and student achievement is that there is no directly causal relationship between the two. One of the reasons for this is that the child's cultural values and identity may not match those of the school, resulting in a lack of motivation on the part of the child to academically achieve.[216] The implication of this assertion is that schools should maintain a range of values which are broad enough to accommodate the diverse range of socio-economic and cultural values so that many children can be embraced in the schools' vision. This will lower the probability that children will lack the motivation to succeed academically because their values are not matched by those of the school. In addition to parental and school environment, peer environment is also crucial to the development of children's cognitive skills. In the context of peer interaction amongst children and how their non-cognitive abilities develop relies to a certain extent on the minimum level of self-confidence amongst the children in the group. It has been found that the development of all children's non-cognitive skills will benefit if there is such a minimum level of confidence amongst the children in the peer group.[217] Moreover, children's self-control problems are made worse when the level of self-confidence of the children in the group is low.[218] Nevertheless, an individual child's self-control problem is reduced when he/she is amongst a peer group in which the level of patience is extremely high. In this case, being part of such a peer group will allow the child with self-control problems to adapt his/her motivation to achieve higher levels of educational outcomes.[219] The nature of the sibling environment also has an impact on the development of a child's cognitive and non-cognitive skills. In this case, it has been found that childhood environments characterised by brotherly rivalry or chauvinistic attitudes towards women hinder the development of

[215] Koch, A., Nafziger, J., Nielsen, H. (2015), Behavioral Economics of Education, Journal of Economic Behaviour & Organisation, 115.

[216] Akerlof, G.A., and Kranton, R.E. (2002), Identity and schooling: some lessons for the economics of education. J. Econ. Lit. 40 (4), 1167–1201.

[217] Battaglini, M., Benabou, R., and Tirole, J. (2005), Self-control in peer groups. J. Econ. Theory 123, 105–134.

[218] Ibid.

[219] Hsiaw, A. (2010), Goal setting, social comparison, and self-control, mimeo, Harvard University.

a child's cognitive and non-cognitive skills.[220] From the preceding discussion, it is evident that not only are the genes[221] of a child important in the context of his/her non-cognitive skills, but so are the environmental factors[222] faced by the child. This knowledge will be useful to policymakers such that they are able to design policies which can change the environmental factors (parental, school and peer) to better facilitate the development of a child's non-cognitive skills. In the short run, policymakers should focus on removing the constraints and barriers children from poor, disadvantaged backgrounds face such as ease of access to financing higher education and nepotism in the jobs market.[223] In the long term, policymakers should focus on intervening in the first eight years of a child's life to balance socio-economic inequalities.[224] This could, for example, be associated with free school meals, free access to library books and focused, teacher-led mentoring for children from poor backgrounds.

Modelling Human Capability Formation

Traditional economic theory regresses the human contribution to economic activity in the context of labour and rationality. With regard to the latter, there are two approaches to constructing a rational choice theory.[225] Firstly, the construction of specific criteria centred on the behaviour of indifference curves allows for a preference ordering, which is indicative of self-interest, to result. Such a logical ordering of preferences will be the driving force behind actual behaviour of individuals and their rational

[220] Rao, N., and Chatterjee, T. (2018), Sibling Gender and Wage Differences, Applied Economics, 50:15, pp. 1725-1745.

[221] Benjamin, D.J., Cesarini, D., Chabris, C.F., Glaeser, E.L., Laibson, D.L., Guðnason, V., Harris, T.B., Launer, L.J., Purcell, S., Smith, A.V., Johannesson, M., Magnusson, P.K.E., Beauchamp, J.P., Christakis, N.A., Atwood, C.S., Herbert, B., Freese, J., Hauser, R.M., Hauser, T.S., Grankvist, A., Hultman, C.M., and Lichtenstein, P. (2012), The promises and pitfalls of genoeconomics. Annu. Rev. Econ. 4, 627–662.

[222] Zumbuehl, M., Dohmen, T., and Pfann, G. (2013), Parental investment and the intergenerational transmission of economic preferences and attitudes. SOEP Discussion Paper No. 570.

[223] Galiani, S. (2008), Social Mobility: What is it and why does it matter? 7th Social Equity Forum, Inter-American Development Bank.

[224] David, P. (2001), Knowledge, Capabilities and Human Capital Formation in Economic Growth, New Zealand Treasury Working Paper No. 01/13.

[225] Martins, N. (2011), Can neuroscience inform economics? Rationality, emotions and preference formation, Cambridge Journal of Economics, 35, pp. 251-267.

choices.[226] The second approach depends on the preference ordering to be based on observed choices. Both approaches lead to the conclusion that there is a single ordering of preferences which contextualises actual behaviour with regard to rational behaviour.[227] Moreover, such a singular preference ordering based on complete information is deemed to be an indicator of the well-being of the individual making choices based on such an ordering.[228] The depiction of rationality, permissible by singular, complete preference ordering, allows for the prediction of events in the context of neoclassical economics.[229] However, the latter's main goal is the prediction of events, with rationality playing a secondary underpinning goal.[230] The methodology used by neoclassical economists to derive a framework of analysis to predict events based on rationality is founded on an assumption that the social context is a closed system.[231] A feature of analysis of such a system is that conjunctions are both consistent and consecutive.[232] For example, if the weather is cold, I will switch on the heating system in my house. Moreover, the modelling of rational activity based on either a set of axioms or the observation of actual choices allows for the existence of closed systems, without which the predictability of actual behaviour would not be possible.[233] Models which rely upon 'closed systems' can be defined as 'deductivist'.[234] These models allow for one rational choice which allows for the predictability of events.[235] Moreover, such predictability results only if the assumption of 'perfect knowledge' made by neoclassical economists holds to allow for a certain world. Furthermore, another critique of neoclassical economic theory is that different theorists

[226] Ibid.

[227] Sen, A. K. (2002), Rationality and Freedom, Cambridge, MA, The Belknap Press of Harvard University Press.

[228] Sen, A. K. (1982), Choice, Welfare and Measurement, Oxford, Blackwell; Cambridge, MA, MIT Press.

[229] Sen, A. K. (2002), Rationality and Freedom, Cambridge, MA, The Belknap Press of Harvard University Press.

[230] Ibid.

[231] Martins, N. (2011), Can neuroscience inform economics? Rationality, emotions and preference formation, Cambridge Journal of Economics, 35, pp. 251-267.

[232] Lawson, T. (1997), Economics and Reality, Routledge, London.

[233] Martins, N. (2011), Can neuroscience inform economics? Rationality, emotions and preference formation, Cambridge Journal of Economics, 35, pp. 251-267.

[234] Ibid.

[235] Sen, A. K. (2002), Rationality and Freedom, Cambridge, MA, The Belknap Press of Harvard University Press.

may understand a specific human action in many ways thus allowing for different interpretations.[236] The implication is that economic models based on different interpretations of human action may give rise to different results, creating difficulties for policy design. However, whatever the interpretation of human actions, all neoclassical economic approaches are based on closed system modelling, which is characterised by a complete set of ordered preferences which can be mathematically represented by a utility function.[237] In this context, constrained optimisation techniques allow for the prediction of the behaviour of economic agents.[238] Furthermore, even when choice under uncertainty is considered, economic modelling relies on the assertion that the probability distributions of the various outcomes are known by the economic agents.[239] However, in the real world, human behaviour is anything but predictable, and the state of knowledge is anything but perfect.

Neuroeconomics is an emerging field, which is reliant on the findings of neuroscience, and aims to better understand the actions of an economic agent based on human motivation. In this case, more specifically, neuroscience seeks to amend existing economic theory by using research findings on the human brain and emotions to construct more realistic models of human behaviour.[240] These models of human behaviour tend to be more realistic because they allow for the fact that varying states of the brain may facilitate differences in preference ordering according to the varying emotions and motivations of economic agents.[241] However, neoclassical economics has dominated neuroeconomics such that the models being constructed are still deductivist.[242] In other words, each brain state still allows for a complete ordering of preferences and therefore for the predictability of the actions of an economic agent. A characteristic feature of economic models which are deductivist constructive in nature is the assumption that there can be a complete ordering of preferences, in the context of states of the brain, and that these can be represented by a utility

[236] Martins, N. (2011), Can neuroscience inform economics? Rationality, emotions and preference formation, Cambridge Journal of Economics, 35, pp. 251-267.

[237] Ibid.

[238] Ibid.

[239] Ibid.

[240] Ibid.

[241] Martins, N. (2011), Can neuroscience inform economics? Rationality, emotions and preference formation, Cambridge Journal of Economics, 35, pp. 251-267.

[242] Ibid.

function.[243] Nevertheless, models which are a more realistic representation of human behaviour should be constructed. These models should be able to link non-cognitive factors such as beliefs and attitudes with an individual's working environment, more effectively. This will allow researchers to better understand an individual's productivity in the context of performance.[244]

The Somatic Marker Hypothesis (SMH) allows for the conceptualisation of decision making.[245] SMH relies upon the assertion that decision making is a complex process which is reliant upon the interaction of a number of layers of neural connections as well as through the interaction of cognitive and non-cognitive abilities of individuals.[246] Moreover, SMH also allows for a more consistent representation of human behaviour by more effectively integrating the empirical findings of both neuroeconomics and neuroscience into a coherent framework.[247] The SMH framework also shows that lower-order biological, non-cognitive factors such as emotions have an impact on higher-level cognitive activities such as reasoning and decision making.[248]

The structure of the brain is also a representation of various levels of biological regulatory processes. Furthermore, lower-level regulatory processes such as emotions are evolutionary and simpler in terms of the interaction of psychological functions than is the reasoning, which involves the more complex interaction of physiological functions. The different states of the mind which may result at any specific time involve the complex interaction of many different biological regulatory processes, in which case it may not be possible to represent these states in the context of the deductivist approach in terms of a unique preference ordering. In this case, it is evident that any theory of human behaviour should be reflective

[243] Romero, A., Bellas, F., Becerra, J., and Duro, R. (2019), Bootstrapping Autonomous Skill Learning in the MDB Cognitive Architecture IN Understanding the brain function and emotions, Vicente, J., et al. (Eds), Springer Nature Switzerland.

[244] Baines, T., and Kay, J. (2002), Human Performance Modelling as An Aid in the Process of Manufacturing System Design: A Pilot Study, International Journal of Production Research, 40:10, pp. 2321-2334.

[245] Martins, N. (2011), Can neuroscience inform economics? Rationality, emotions and preference formation, Cambridge Journal of Economics, 35, pp. 251-267.

[246] Bechara, A., Damasio, H. and Damasio, A. R. (2000), Emotion, decision making and the orbifrontal cortex, Cerebral Cortex, vol. 10, 295–307.

[247] Martins, N. (2011), Can neuroscience inform economics? Rationality, emotions and preference formation, Cambridge Journal of Economics, 35, pp. 251-267.

[248] Ibid.

of a better understanding of the physical physiological structures of the human brain and body which gives rise to lower-level emotions as well as more complex reasoning processes. Nevertheless, while emotions are a representation of a lower-level of human behaviour, these emotions can be categorised as being either primary or secondary in nature.[249] Primary emotions are more instinctive and the display of such behaviours such as fear and anger is more likely to occur in situations involving the very survival of an individual in comparison to the display of emotions such as sympathy and jealousy.[250] The display of primary survival behaviours such as anger and fear occurs when the amygdala or the cingulated cortex of the brain is stimulated, by sensory perceptions. The stimulation of the amygdala and/or the cingulated cortex will in turn lead to the stimulation of the hypothalamus, the basal forebrain and the brain stem.[251] The areas of the brain which need to be stimulated and activated for the expression of primary emotions are also the ones required for the display of primary emotions. However, the difference is that when secondary emotions occur, the ventromedial prefrontal cortex of the brain is stimulated and activated first, resulting in physical responses. It is only after the stimulation of the ventromedial prefrontal cortex that the areas stimulated by primary emotions, the hypothalamus, the basal forebrain and the brain stem, are activated.[252] Therefore, it is evident that while secondary emotions are required for the display of complex behaviours such as reasoning and decision making, the emergence of these are also dependent upon the stimulation and activation of the areas of the brain required for the display of primary emotions.[253,254] Nevertheless, in addition to the ventromedial prefrontal cortex, hypothalamus, basal forebrain and brain stem, the prefrontal cortex is also an important contributor to the processing of primary and secondary emotions. This is because objective memory is stored in the inferior part of the dorsolateral region of the prefrontal cortex, while dimensionless memory is stored in the superior part of the

[249] Damasio, A. R. (2003), Looking for Spinoza: Joy, Sorrow, and the Feeling Brain, Harcourt Brace and Company, New York.

[250] Martins, N. (2011), Can neuroscience inform economics? Rationality, emotions, and preference formation, Cambridge Journal of Economics, 35, pp. 251-267.

[251] Ibid.

[252] Ibid.

[253] Ibid.

[254] Ibid.

dorsolateral region.[255] Memories stored in these regions are known as primary inducers and are responsible for allowing for the capability to recognise a scenario in the environment and stimulate the amygdala accordingly.[256] Nevertheless, in addition to memories, specific biochemical molecules may also be responsible for specific behaviours—for example, traditional Game Theory, which suggests that cooperation may result due rational strategic moves. However, results from neuroeconomics studies indicate that cooperative behaviour amongst humans actually results when oxytocin is released by the pituitary gland into the hypothalamus.[257] Nevertheless, cooperation and its effectiveness may be a learned behaviour which not only develops individually but also facilitates the survival of the group in the long term as well[258]—although the consensus as to whether such cooperative behaviour would lead to a higher probability for the long-term survival of the group will be culturally determined.[259]

Human capital has several characteristics.[260] Firstly, it involves the capability to assimilate and interpret data, to interact with others as well as the environment at large, received from sensory organs such as the eyes, nose, ears and skin through physical contact. Secondly, human capital can be thought of in terms of the provision of labour for the real sector of the economy. Thirdly, human capital can be associated with the skills required by an individual to undertake entrepreneurial activities. And lastly, human capital can be associated with the development of innovative ideas and knowledge which may result in innovations. An effective knowledge-transfer-promoting organisation should be able to invest in developing its

[255] Bechara, A., Damasio, H. and Damasio, A. R. (2000), Emotion, decision making and the orbifrontal cortex, Cerebral Cortex, vol. 10, 295–307.

[256] Bechara, A., Damasio, H. and Damasio, A. R. (2000), Emotion, decision making and the orbifrontal cortex, Cerebral Cortex, vol. 10, 295–307.

[257] Kosfeld, M., Heinrichs, M., Zak, P. J., Fischbacher, U. and Fehr, E. (2005), Oxytocin increases trust in humans, Nature, vol. 435, 473–6.

[258] Yu, C., Tan, G., Lu, H., Wang, Z., Meng, J., Hao, J., and Ren, F. (2016), Modelling Adaptive Learning Behaviours For Consensus Formation in Human Societies, Scientific Reports, 6, 27626, DOI: https://doi.org/10.1038/srep27626

[259] Hodgson, A., Siemieniuch, C., Hubbard, E., and Sinclair, M. (2010), Modelling the human components of complex systems, 5th International Conference on System of Systems Engineering.

[260] David, P. (2001), Knowledge, Capabilities and Human Capital Formation in Economic Growth, New Zealand Treasury Working Paper No. 01/13.

knowledge-accumulating ability, particularly with regard to how customer needs are spread in the market.[261]

Human capital can be associated with the tangible and intangible characteristics of individuals.[262] The tangible characteristics of individuals are more usually associated with height, weight, physical endurance and strength. On the other hand, the intangible characteristics of an individual are often associated with cognitive ability as well as non-cognitive ability. The former is often associated with an individual's capacity for abstract thinking to find solutions to real-world problems. On the other hand, an individual's non-cognitive ability is often associated with motivation, tenacity, leadership and the ability to interact with others, for example. Economists usually associate the term 'human capital' with the intangible qualities of an individual, nominally his/her cognitive and non-cognitive skills.[263] The nature of these skills means that they can only be acquired through academic or vocational education or a combination of both. However, an individual's mood will have an impact on an individual's cognition while his/her emotions will dictate the actions which will be taken by an individual in each specific circumstance.[264] This may be because moods last longer than emotions and are not triggered by specific environmental conditions[265]—although the mood will dictate the extent to which the individual will interpret his/her environment. And this will determine the extent of the emotional reaction.[266] However, emotions can also cause moods to change, following the evaluation of an individual's immediate environment.[267] Moreover, personality is like moods in that it is a long-term personal condition which is not dependent on a specific circumstance.[268]

[261] David, P. (2001), Knowledge, Capabilities and Human Capital Formation in Economic Growth, New Zealand Treasury Working Paper, No. 01/13, New Zealand Government, The Treasury, Wellington.

[262] Ibid.

[263] Ibid.

[264] Thalmann-Magnenat, N., and Kasap, Z. (2009), Modelling Socially Intelligent Virtual Humans, Conference Paper, Nanyang Technological University, Singapore.

[265] Ibid.

[266] Ibid.

[267] Ibid.

[268] Vinayagamoorthy, V., Gillies, M., Steed, A., Tanguy, E., Pan, X., Loscos, C., and Slater, M. (2006), Building expression into virtual characters, IN Eurographics Conference State of the Art Reports.

The need to acquire both an education and skills would mean that either a private or a public cost would be incurred in acquiring these skills. The ability of a country to meet the public cost of educating and training its citizens to a satisfactory level would depend upon its level of economic growth. However, while the economic growth of a country has been the policy focus of most, if not all, countries since the end of the Second World War, there has been in recent years a shift amongst policymakers to recognising the importance of economic welfare of citizens. While economic growth often associates individuals with market-based activities, economic welfare also associates individuals with non-market-based activities such as the pursuit of leisure activities and strengthening family association. These activities may either directly or indirectly contribute towards the development of human capital.[269] Knowledge can also be thought of as a form of human capital which links economic welfare with economic growth. In this case, when knowledge becomes codified, it becomes generic information, which allows tasks to be performed more efficiently, leading to an increase in productivity and thus economic growth.[270] However, social capital such as the relationships within families and amongst peers across society at differing levels cannot be used for the pursuit of private interests as it is considered to be a public good.[271] Furthermore, whereas the formation of social capital requires the presence of groups, the formation of human capital is individually driven. An individual's characteristics are dependent upon a combination of tangible inputs and intangible inputs.[272]

The nature of the tangible inputs which may impact on the individual includes the quality of parental care given to the child as well as the quality of the education and nutrition he/she receives. The development and nature of social capital, however, represent the extent of the intangible inputs a child receives. It is the extent of the interaction between these tangible and intangible inputs which dictates the extent of the development of human capital, which itself can be divided into tangible as well as intangible assets.[273] The tangible assets of an individual are his/her non-cognitive abilities, while the intangible assets of the individual are

[269] David, P. (2001), Knowledge, Capabilities and Human Capital Formation in Economic Growth, New Zealand Treasury Working Paper No. 01/13.

[270] Ibid.

[271] Ibid.

[272] Ibid.

[273] Ibid.

represented by his/her cognitive skills.[274] While education is important for the development of an individual's cognitive ability, it only acts as a signal to employers of the suitability of an individual for a job.[275] However, on-the-job training schemes and programmes are also important for the development of human capital development and its contribution to increasing individual productivity and the economic growth of a country. This contrasts with neoclassical economic theory, which asserts that economic growth occurs due to the accumulation of capital.[276] However, the rate of economic growth will decline over time as additional capital is used to replace capital which is no longer productive, economic growth eventually reaching a steady state.

Following the discussion above, it has become evident that in order to model human capability formation successfully, it is important to capture the integrated impact of different types of human capital on macroeconomic performance.[277] In this case, it is not just sufficient to understand the individual processes which lead to the formation of the tangible and intangible aspects of human capital, but also at the aggregate level in the context of the capabilities and qualities of each population sample.[278] In this case, demographic shifts in the age of the population may, for example, affect the quality of tangible human capital at the aggregate level. If the workforce becomes older, then the workers at an aggregate level will become less productive, indicating a fall in the quality of tangible human capital. Moreover, the tangible elements of human capital may also be impacted by an individual's environmental conditions such as access to sufficient nutrition and the capacity to become unwell.[279] The tangible elements of human capital may be improved and strengthened with public expenditure on nutrition (free meals for those on low incomes) and suitable information on how well-being can be protected. However, the codification of various levels of knowledge and information is important with regard to the development of intangible capital.[280] The extent of

[274] David, P. (2001), Knowledge, Capabilities and Human Capital Formation in Economic Growth, New Zealand Treasury Working Paper No. 01/13.

[275] Ibid.

[276] Ibid.

[277] Ibid.

[278] Ibid.

[279] Ibid.

[280] David, P. (2001), Knowledge, Capabilities and Human Capital Formation in Economic Growth, New Zealand Treasury Working Paper No. 01/13.

codification is dependent on the level of technological development. The extent of the level of technological will thus have an impact on the strength of economic activities due to its impact on the extent of the codification of knowledge and information.[281] However, the extent of the impact of the codification of knowledge and information on economic activity will be dependent upon the costs of knowledge transfer and the extent of the relevance of economic information to the relevant economic stakeholders.[282]

Conclusion

The source of inequality in adulthood may lie in the poor development of the cognitive and non-cognitive features of brain development in the early years of a child's life. This may be because of an individual having inferior-quality genes, a poor upbringing or poor access to resources due to the low incomes of parents. Therefore, it is critical to better understand brain development in the early years of a child's life so that governments can devise policies which allow for the optimal development of the cognitive and non-cognitive abilities of a child. And, in the context of brain development, the area of the evolving brain of children solely responsible for general intelligence is the frontal cortical region. However, the key to understanding intelligence in children and adults is not cortical thickness but the direction of change in cortical thickness. The relationship between cortical thickness and intelligence in childhood is a negative one, but becomes positive in late childhood and beyond. In intelligent children there is an initial accelerated phase of cortical increase, followed by a period of rapid cortical thinning during early adolescence. The implication of this is that the physical representation of intelligence in the brain is a dynamic process in the transition from infant to adolescence and thence from adolescence to adulthood. The link between motor development and cognitive development has been noted as far back as the 1950s. Moreover, motor development may also help facilitate the acquisition and use of language by the child. Furthermore, empirical studies have also established a positive correlation between the development of self-awareness and the awareness of others, Theory of Mind (ToM), in and by

[281] Ibid.

[282] Ibid.

children with the extent of their ability to talk.[283] The implication of the findings of studies which find a causative link between motor development in infants and later cognitive development is that governments should formulate early-stage education policies which take these findings into account.

The development of a child's abilities is not only dependent on its genes but also on the development of cognition through the development of the brain. The external environment has a significant impact on the development of human cognition, as a significant amount of human brain growth occurs in the post-natal stage, when the infant is interacting with its external environment, which also encompasses parenting. The level of intelligence is mostly associated with the level of change in cortical development mostly associated with the frontal regions of the cerebral cortex. Cortical thickness also varies with age, increasing in childhood but decreasing during adolescence—with the former reflecting growing intelligence while the latter reflecting declining intelligence. But critical to the development of a child's brain are the genes it inherits from its parents. In this case, genes play a key role in the body's production of specific proteins. Genes which produce brain-specific proteins are therefore critical to the development of the cerebral cortex. The structure and function of the cerebral cortex support human cognitive functions. There are four main aspects of cognitive ability which all interact in the development of general cognitive ability. These aspects of cognitive ability include the speed associated with processing information, memory capacity, verbal ability and spatial ability. General cognitive ability is usually quantified in the context of a variable g. The shared environmental factors of siblings only accounts for 25% of the variation in g. However, in any case, after adolescence the impact of childhood environmental factors on g becomes less and less relevant to the individual's development. Nevertheless, shared environmental differences such as parental treatment, experiences at school and experiences with peers contribute to the long-term development of g. But no matter what the nature of the external environment faced by a child, it is the genetic makeup of an individual which determines the nature of the interaction, with regard to personal preferences in design, selection and construction, with the external environment.

[283] Grazzani, I., Ornagha, V., Conte, E., Pepe, A., and Caprin, C. (2018), The Relation Between Emotion Understanding and the Theory of Mind in Children Aged 3-8: The Key Role of Language, Front. Psychol. https://doi.org/10.3389/fpsyg.2018.00724

The cognitive capacity of an individual relates to how well he/she can perform in a test, exam or any other summative assessment. However, cognition is not a human characteristic but one that spans all creatures. And in addition to cognitive intelligence, humans are also endowed with non-cognitive intelligence. The non-cognitive intelligence of an individual encompasses a wide range of skills and behaviours which interplay with cognitive capabilities to facilitate academic performance. But this is in no way a quantification of non-cognitive intelligence. The features of non-cognitive intelligence include the individual character traits, the level of self-belief as well as the motivation to achieve. It is the non-cognitive contribution of motivation and focus on achievement which allows individuals to succeed in their cognitive endeavours, as evidenced by academic achievement. Moreover, some non-cognitive skills such as tenacity and the ability to self-control may be entirely dependent on personality traits and may not be malleable like other traits—although a socio-economic environment which degrades the development of a child's non-cognitive skills may constrain the development of a child's cognitive ability. Moreover, a child's short-term memory may be strained and limited when the child is using its cognitive capacity to deal with stress and emotions caused by environmental factors. The implication is that there is a link between a child's environmental conditions in the context of poverty and the extent of the level of development of the brain—in which case a child's external environment associated with poverty may lead to the under-development of the brain. Nevertheless, while schooling may enhance a child's cognitive development, good parenting will help to enhance both cognitive and non-cognitive skills. Such development is more conducive in the early years of a child's life, whether growing up in a poor or a good environment. In the transition from childhood to adulthood, the human brain becomes less and less malleable as it develops. Therefore, it is not difficult to see why poverty in childhood may have long-lasting lifetime impacts. Empirical research suggests that the conditions of poverty under which a child grows will lead to not only low levels of educational attainment but also behavioural and mental health problems later in life. A poor environmental upbringing may lead to poor control of emotions, leading to stress and a negative impact on cognition. Therefore, investment in childhood programmes to foster mindfulness may allow a child to be better at emotional regulation and separating self from circumstance and thus enhancing its own academic achievement as well as additional skill formation in the future.

The lifetime level of cognitive ability is effectively determined within the first several years of a child's life. The implication is that investments in childhood development either by parents or by the state will facilitate the development of cognitive as well as non-cognitive skills of young children. And these investments will be more effective when made in the early years of a child's life than in later years. Behavioural economics is the study of an individual's non-cognitive skills. These skills are strongly associated with an individual's objectives, personal characteristics, motivation and choices. Well-developed non-cognitive skills contribute to optimising the development of cognitive skills. Moreover, the chances of a child achieving academic and social status later in life are dependent not only on personal traits inherited from parents but also on the level of human capital investment made by the parents on the child—although sibling rivalry and chauvinistic attitudes may reduce the impact of parental investments on the development of a child's cognitive and non-cognitive skills. Nevertheless, random events may also play a part. In association with parental investment, genes also play a part in the development of a child's academic ability. However, more directly associated with a child's inherited genes is a better-educated mother. The latter would be able to select the best male from a pool of potential suitors. A better education leads to better decisions. The extent of school resources also impacts on the development of a child's cognitive and non-cognitive skills. Empirical research suggests that small class sizes help to develop a child's non-cognitive skills. And while some teachers are better than others at facilitating the development of a child's cognitive skills, still other teachers may be better at developing a child's non-cognitive skills.

Traditional economic theory reduces the human contribution to economic activity with regard to just identifying the role of labour and rationality. The latter has been accomplished in two ways. Firstly, the construction of specific criteria centred on the behaviour of indifference curves allows for a preference ordering. This allows for the theoretical formalisation of self-interest. Secondly, preference orderings can be constructed based on observed choices. Neuroeconomics is an emerging field of study which depends on the empirical findings of neuroscience. The aim is to better understand the actions of an economic agent based on human motivation. In this case, neuroscience seeks to amend existing economic theory by using research findings on the human brain and emotions to construct more realistic models of human behaviour. This is because these models allow for the fact that the varying states of the brain may allow for differences in the ordering of preferences. For example, the state of the brain is different when we are hungry compared to when we are full. As a result, an individual's preference ordering will be different according to each condition. Still the assumption that each brain state can be categorised in the context of a complete ordering of preferences is made. This leads to the possibility of mathematically modelling utility in the context of a utility function. This is a closure condition, which is a feature of the deductivist school of economic modelling. In this case, it is evident that more realistic models of human behaviour should be constructed which are better able to link non-cognitive factors such as beliefs and attitudes with an individual's working environment to better understand an individual's productivity in the context of performance.

An analytical framework which allows decision making to be conceptualised is the Somatic Marker Hypothesis (SMH). This recognises that reasoning as a decision-making process is reliant upon several layers of neural operations which are dependent on non-cognitive factors (emotions, attention) as well as cognitive factors (processing of stored information). The framework of analysis provided by the Somatic Marker Hypothesis represents a starting point for integrating the research results of neuroscience and neuroeconomics in a consistent way by which human behaviour and motivation can be integrated and explained. According to SMH, higher-level states such as reasoning and decision making rely upon lower-level bio-regulatory processes such as emotions. Thus, a theory of actual human behaviour must be based on physical structures which make up the human physiology and the resulting bio-regulatory processes which give rise to the complex reasoning and decision-making processes which human beings are capable of. Underlying the bio-regulatory processes are primary and secondary emotions. Primary emotions are associated with survival and include fear and anger, for example. The pathway for brain stimulation for the activation of primary emotions encompasses, in consecutive order, the hypothalamus, the basal forebrain and the brain stem. Secondary emotions include sympathy and jealousy, for example, and rely upon the areas of the brain activated for the facilitation of primary emotions. Secondary emotions are more complex and are required for activities such as reasoning and planning. In addition to the triggering of the areas of the brain required for the activation of primary emotions, secondary emotions are triggered by the activation of the ventromedial prefrontal cortex.

Human capital can be associated with the tangible and intangible characteristics of an individual. The tangible characteristics include height, weight, physical endurance and strength, for example. The intangible characteristics include the cognitive and non-cognitive abilities of an individual. To model human capability formation successfully, it is important to capture the integrated impact of diverse types of human capital on macroeconomic performance. In this case, it is not sufficient to understand the individual processes which lead to the formation of the tangible and intangible aspects of human capital but also at the aggregate level in the context of the capabilities and qualities of each population sample. For example, demographic shifts in the age of the population sample may affect the quality of tangible human capital at the aggregate level. Moreover, the tangible elements of human capital may be affected by an individual's environmental conditions such as access to nutrition, warmth and shelter. The intangible aspects of human capital are associated with parental resources, access to schools as well as the quality of teaching.

References

Addabbo, T., Tommaso, M., & Maccagnan, A. (2016). Education Capability: A Focus on Gender and Science. *Social Indicators Research, 128*, 793–812.

Aiken, L. (1973). Ability and Creativity in Mathematics. *Review of Educational Research, 45*(4).

Akerlof, G. A., & Kranton, R. E. (2002). Identity and Schooling: Some Lessons for the Economics of Education. *Journal of Economic Literature, 40*(4), 1167–1201.

Albanese, G., De Blasio, G., & Sestito, P. (2016). My Parents Taught Me. Evidence on the Family Transmission of Values. *Journal of Population Economics, 29*, 571–592.

Andergassen, R., & Nardini, F. (2019). Intergenerational Mobility and Social Status in a Model with Human Capital Investments and Trait Inheritance. *Macroeconomic Dynamics*. https://doi.org/10.1017/S1365100519000427

Aslund, O., & Gronquist, H. (2010). Family Size and Child Outcomes: Is There Really No Trade Off? *Labour Economics, 17*, 130–139.

Baines, T., & Kay, J. (2002). Human Performance Modelling as an Aid in the Process of Manufacturing System Design: A Pilot Study. *International Journal of Production Research, 40*(10), 2321–2334.

Baltes, P. (1987). Theoretical Propositions of Life-Span. *Developmental Psychology, 23*, 611.

Barchard, K., & Hakstian, A. (2004). The Nature and Measurement of Emotional Intelligence Abilities: Basic Dimensions and Their Relationships with Other

Cognitive Ability and Personality Variables. *Educational and Psychological Measurement, 64*(3), 437–462.
Battaglini, M., Benabou, R., & Tirole, J. (2005). Self-Control in Peer Groups. *Journal of Economic Theory, 123*, 105–134.
Bechara, A., Damasio, H., & Damasio, A. R. (2000). Emotion, Decision Making and the Orbifrontal Cortex. *Cerebral Cortex, 10*, 295–307.
Beckmann, E., & Minnaert, A. (2018). Non-cognitive Characteristics of Gifted Students with Learning Disabilities: An In-depth Systematic Review. *Frontiers in Psychology, 9*, 504.
Behrman, J., & Wolfe, B. (1984). The Socioeconomic Impact of Schooling in a Developing Economy. *The Review of Economics and Statistics, 66*(2), 296–303.
Behrman, J., & Wolfe, B. (1987). How Does Mothers Schooling Affect Family Health, Nutrition, Medical Care Usage and Household Sanitation. *Journal of Econometrics, 36*, 185–204.
Benabou, R., & Tirole, J. (2002). Self-Confidence and Personal Motivation. *Quarterly Journal of Economics, 117*(3), 871–916.
Benjamin, D. J., Cesarini, D., Chabris, C. F., Glaeser, E. L., Laibson, D. L., Guðnason, V., Harris, T. B., Launer, L. J., Purcell, S., Smith, A. V., Johannesson, M., Magnusson, P. K. E., Beauchamp, J. P., Christakis, N. A., Atwood, C. S., Herbert, B., Freese, J., Hauser, R. M., Hauser, T. S., Grankvist, A., Hultman, C. M., & Lichtenstein, P. (2012). The Promises and Pitfalls of Genoeconomics. *Annual Review of Economics, 4*, 627–662.
Biringen, Z., Emde, R. N., Campos, J. J., & Appelbaun, M. I. (1995). Affective Reorganization in the Infant, the Mother, and the Dyad: The Role of Upright Locomotion and Its Timing. *Child Development, 66*, 499–512.
Blair, C., Knipe, H., & Gamson, D. (2008). Is There a Role for Executive Functions in the Development of Mathematics Ability. *Mind, Brain and Education, 2*(2), 80–89.
Blieszner, R., Willis, S., & Baltes, P. (1981). Training Research in Aging on the Fluid Ability of Inductive Reasoning. *Journal of Applied Developmental Psychology, 2*, 247–265.
Bouchard, T. J., Jr., & McGue, M. (1981). Familial Studies of Intelligence: A Review. *Science, 212*, 1055–1059.
Bredtmann, J., & Smith, N. (2018). Inequalities in Educational Outcomes: How Important Is the Family? *Oxford Bulletin of Economics and Statistics, 80*, 6.
Brumariu, L., & Kerns, K. (2013). Pathways to Anxiety: Contributions of Attachment History, Temperament, Peer Competence, and Ability to Manage Intense Emotions. *Child Psychiatry & Human Development, 44*, 504–515.
Brunello, G., & Schlotter, M. (2011). *Non-cognitive Skills and Personality Traits: Labour Market Relevance and Their Development in Education and Training Systems, IZA DP No. 5743.*

Bushnell, E. W., & Boudreau, J. P. (1993). Motor Development and the Mind: The Potential Role of Motor Abilities as a Determinant of Aspects of Perceptual Development. *Child Development, 64*, 1005–1021.

Campos, J. J., Anderson, D. I., Barbu-Roth, M. A., Hubbard, E. M., Hertenstein, M. J., & Witherington, D. (2000). Travel Broadens the Mind. *Infancy, 1*, 149–219.

Caplan, D. (2014). Cognitive Functions and the Cerebral Cortex. In B. Dickerson & A. Atri (Eds.), *Dementia: Comprehensive Principles and Practices*. Oxford University Press.

Carstensen, L. (2006). *The Influence of a Sense of Time on Human Development* (p. 312). Science.

Casey, M. (1996). Understanding Individual Differences in Spatial Ability Within Females: A Nature/Nurture Interactionist Framework. *Development Review, 16*, 241–260.

Chevalier, A., Harmon, C., O'Sullivan, V., & Walker, I. (2013). The Impact of Parental Income and Education on the Schooling of Their Children. *IZA Journal of Labor Economics, 2*, 8.

Chowdry, H., Crawford, C., & Goodman, A. (2011). The Role of Attitudes and Behaviours in Explaining Socio-Economic Differences in Attainment at Age 16. *Longitudinal and Life Course Studies, 2*, 5–76.

Coleman, J. S. (1966). *Equality of Educational Opportunity*. United States Government Printing Office, Washington, Summary Report.

Coleman, L. J., & Cross, T. L. (2000). Social-Emotional Development and the Personal Experience of Giftedness. In K. A. Heller, F. J. Mönks, R. J. Sternberg, & R. F. Subotnik (Eds.), *International Handbook of Giftedness and Talent* (pp. 203–213). Elsevier.

Comi, S., Origo, F., & Pagani, L. (2017). *Peer Effects on Non-cognitive Skills*. Retrieved from http://www.aiel.it/cms/cms-files/submission/all20170615160133.pdf

Conley, D., Domingue, B., Cesarini, D., Dawes, C., Rietveld, C., & Boardman, J. (2015). Is the Effect of Parental Education on Offspring Biased or Moderated by Genotype. *Sociological Science, 2*, 82–105.

Coqueugniot, H., Hublin, J., Veillon, F., Houet, F., & Jacob, T. (2004). Early Brain Growth in Homo Erectus and Implications for Cognitive Ability. *Nature, 431*, 299.

Cox, D., & Fachamps, M. (2008). Extended Family and Kinship Networks: Economic Insights and Evolutionary Directions. In T. Schultz & J. Strauss (Eds.), *Handbook of development economics* (Vol. 4). Elsevier.

Crandall, V., Katkovsky, W., & Preston, A. (1962). Motivational and Ability Determinants of Young Children's Intellectual Achievement Behaviours. *Child Development, 33*(3), 643–661.

Cross, N. (1990). The Nature and Nurture of Design Ability. *Design Studies, 11*(3).

Cunha, F., & Heckman, J. (2007). The Technology of Skill Formation. *American Economic Review, 97*(2), 31–47.
Cunha, F., & Heckman, J. (2009). The Economics and Psychology of Inequality and Human Development. *Journal of the European Economic Association, 7*(2–3), 320–364.
Damasio, A. R. (2003). *Looking for Spinoza: Joy, Sorrow, and the Feeling Brain.* Harcourt, Brace and Company.
David, P. (2001). *Knowledge, Capabilities and Human Capital Formation in Economic Growth, New Zealand Treasury Working Paper No. 01/13.*
Dehaene, S., Piazza, M., Pinel, P., & Cohen, L. (2003). Three Parietal Circuits for Number Processing. *Cognitive Neuropsychology, 20*, 487–506.
Duijn, M., Keijzer, F., & Franken, D. (2006). Principles of Minimal Cognition: Casting Cognitions as Sensorimotor Co-ordination. *Adaptive Behaviour, 14*(2), 157–170.
Duncan, G. J., Kalil, A., & Ziol-Guest, K. (2010). Early-Childhood Poverty and Adult Attainment, Behavior, and Health. *Child Development, 81*(1), 206–325.
Duyme, M., Dumaret, A.-C., & Tomkiewicz, S. (1999). How Can We Boost IQs of "Dull Children"?: A Late Adoption Study. *Proceedings of the National Academy of Sciences, 96*, 8790–8794.
Eckstein, Z., & Wolpin, K. I. (1999). Why Youths Drop Out of High School: The Impact of Preferences, Opportunities, and Abilities. *Econometrica, 67*(6), 1295–1339.
Edin, P., Nybom, M., Fredriksson, P., & Ockert, B. (2017). *The Rising Return to Non-cognitive Skill, IZA DP No. 10914.* IZA Institute of Labor Economics.
Eriksen, T. L. M., Nielsen, H. S., & Simonsen, M. (2014). Bullying in Elementary School. *The Journal of Human Resources, 49*(4), 839–871.
Farrington, C. A., Roderick, M., Allensworth, E., Nagaoka, J., Keyes, T. S., Johnson, D. W., et al. (2012). *Teaching Adolescents to Become Learners: The Role of Noncognitive Factors in Shaping School Performance.* University of Chicago Consortium on Chicago School Research.
Filippin, A., & Paccagnella, M. (2012). Family Background, Self-Confidence and Economic Outcomes. *Economics of Education Review, 31*, 824–834.
Flynn, J. (1999). Searching for Justice: The Discovery of IQ Gains Over Time. *The American Psychologist, 54*, 5–20.
Fowler, A. E. (1991). How Early Phonological Development Might Set the Stage for Phoneme Awareness. In S. A. Brady & D. P. Shankweiler (Eds.), *Phonological Processes in Literacy: A Tribute to Isabelle Y. Liberman* (pp. 97–117). Erlbaum.
Fredriksson, P., Oosterbeek, H., & Ockert, B. (2013). Long-Term Effects of Class Size. *Quarterly Journal of Economics, 128*(1), 249–285.
Freeman, J. (2000). Families: The Essential Context for Gifts and Talents. In K. A. Heller, F. J. Mönks, R. J. Sternberg, & R. F. Subotnik (Eds.), *International Handbook of Giftedness and Talent* (pp. 573–587). Elsevier.

Galiani, S. (2008). *Social Mobility: What Is It and Why Does It Matter? 7th Social Equity Forum*. Inter-American Development Bank.

Galway, T. M., & Metsala, J. L. (2011). Social Cognition and Its Relation to Psychosocial Adjustment in Children with Nonverbal Learning Disabilities. *Journal of Learning Disabilities, 44*, 33–49. https://doi.org/10.1177/0022219410371680

Grazzani, I., Ornagha, V., Conte, E., Pepe, A., & Caprin, C. (2018). The Relation Between Emotion Understanding and the Theory of Mind in Children Aged 3-8: The Key Role of Language. *Frontiers in Psychology*. https://doi.org/10.3389/fpsyg.2018.00724

Greco, J. (2007). The Nature of Ability and the Purpose of Knowledge. *Philosophical Issues, 17*, 57–69.

Gupta, N. D., & Simonsen, M. (2010). Non-cognitive Child Outcomes and Universal High Quality Childcare. *Journal of Public Economics, 94*(1), 30–43.

Gutman, L. M., & Schoon, I. (2013). *The Impact of Non-cognitive Skills on Outcomes for Young People*. Education Endowment Foundation.

Hallahan, D. P., & Kauffman, J. M. (2006). *Exceptional Learners: An Introduction to Special Education*. Pearson.

Hanushek, E. A., & Rivkin, S. G. (2006). Teacher Quality. In *Handbook of the Economics of Education* (Vol. 2, pp. 1051–1078). Elsevier.

Harris, J. R. (1998). *The Nurture Assumption: Why Children Turn Out the Way They Do*. The Free Press.

Hart, B., & Risley, T. R. (1995). *Meaningful Differences in the Everyday Experience of Young American Children*. Paul H. Brookes Publishing.

Hartog, J. (2001). On Human Capital and Individual Capabilities. *Review of Income and Wealth, Series, 47*(4).

Haworth, C., Kovas, Y., Harlaar, N., Hayiou-Thomas, M., Petrill, S., Dale, P., & Plomin, R. (2009). Generalist Genes and Learning Disabilities: A Multivariate Genetic Analysis of Low Performance in Reading, Mathematics, Language and General Cognitive Ability in a Sample of 8000 12-Year-Old Twins. *Journal of Child Psychology and Psychiatry, 50*(10), 1318–1325.

Heckman, J. J. (2008). Schools, Skills, and Synapses. *Economic Inquiry, 4*(3), 289–324.

Heckman, J. J. (2009). *Integrating Personality Psychology into Economics*. National Bureau of Economic Research, 2011. Retrieved from http://www.nber.org/papers/w17378

Heckman, J. (2011). The Economics of Inequality: The Value of Early Childhood Education. *American Educator, 35*(1), 31–35.

Heckman, J. J., & Kautz, T. (2012a). Hard Evidence on Soft Skills. *Labour Economics, 19*(4), 451.

Heckman, J. J., & Kautz, T. D. (2012b). *Hard Evidence on Soft Skills, Working Paper 18121*. National Bureau of Economic Research. Retrieved from http://www.nber.org/papers/w18121

Heckman, J. J., Lochner, L., & Taber, C. (1998). Explaining Rising Wage Inequality: Explorations with a Dynamic General Equilibrium Model of Earnings with Heterogeneous Agents. *Review of Economic Dynamics, 1*(1), 1–58.

Heckman, J. J., Lochner, L. J., & Todd, P. E. (2006). Earnings Functions, Rates of Return and Treatment Effects: The Mincer Equation and Beyond. In *Handbook of the Economics of Education* (Vol. 1). Elsevier.

Hill, M., & O'Neill, J. (1994). Family Endowments and the Achievement of Young Children with Special Reference to the Underclass. *The Journal of Human Resources, 29*, 4.

Hodgson, A., Siemieniuch, C., Hubbard, E., & Sinclair, M. (2010). Modelling the Human Components of Complex Systems. In *5th International Conference on System of Systems Engineering*.

Holmlund, H., Lindahl, M., & Plug, E. (2011). The Causal Effect of Parents' Schooling on Children' Schooling: A Comparison of Estimation Methods. *Journal of Economic Literature, 49*(3), 615–651.

House, J., & Health, J. (2002). *Social Behaviour, 43*, 125.

Hsiaw, A. (2010). *Goal Setting, Social Comparison, and Self-Control, Mimeo*. Harvard University.

Hultsch, D., Nesselroade, J., & Plemons, J. (1976). Learning-Ability Relations in Adulthood. *Human Development, 19*, 234–247.

Jackson, C. K. (2013). *Non-cognitive Ability, Test Scores, and Teacher Quality: Evidence from 9th Grade Teachers in North Carolina. NBER Discussion Paper No. 18624.*

Joshi, H. (2014). *'Non-cognitive' Skills: What Are They and How Can They Be Measured in the British Cohort Studies, CLS Working Paper 2014/6.*

Judge, T., Higgins, C., Thoresen, C., & Barrick, M. (1999). The Big Five Personality Traits, General Mental Ability, and Career Success Across the Life Span. *Personnel Psychology, 52*(3), 621–665.

Kassenboehmer, S. C., Leung, F., & Schurer, S. (2018). University Education and Non-cognitive Skill Development. *Oxford Economic Papers, 70*(2), 538–562.

Koch, A., Nafziger, J., & Nielsen, H. (2015). Behavioral Economics of Education. *Journal of Economic Behavior & Organisation, 115*, 3.

Kosfeld, M., Heinrichs, M., Zak, P. J., Fischbacher, U., & Fehr, E. (2005). Oxytocin Increases Trust in Humans. *Nature, 435*, 473–476.

Kosslyn, S., & Plomin, R. (1998). Towards Neuro-Cognitive Genetics: Goals and Issues. In D. Dougherty, S. L. Rauch, & J. F. Rosenbaum (Eds.), *Psychiatric Neuroimaging Strategies: Research and Clinical Applications*. American Psychiatric Press.

Krueger, A. B. (1999). Experimental Estimates of Education Production Functions. *The Quarterly Journal of Economics, 114*(2), 497–532.

Kuhl, P. K., Williams, K. A., Lacerda, F., Stevens, K. N., & Lindblom, B. (1992). Linguistic Experience Alters Phonetic Perception in Infants by 6 Months of Age. *Science, 255*, 606–608.

Lawson, T. (1997). *Economics and Reality*. Routledge.

Lee, K., Ning, F., & Goh, H. (2014). Interaction Between Cognitive and Non-cognitive Factors: The Influences of Academic Goal Orientation and Working Memory on Mathematical Performance. *Educational Psychology, 34*(1), 73–91.

Linn, M., & Petersen, A. (1985). Emergence and Characterisation of Sex Differences in Spatial Ability: A Meta-Analysis. *Child Development, 56*(6), 1479–1498.

Lochner, L. (2008). Intergenerational Transmission. In S. Durlauf & L. Blume (Eds.), *New Palgrave Dictionary of Economics* (2nd ed.). Palgrave Macmillan.

Lochner, L. (2011). *Nonproduction Benefits of Education: Crime, Health, and Good Citizenship. Handbook of the Economics of Education* (Vol. 4). Elsevier.

Luna, B., et al. (2001). Maturation of Widely Distributed Brain Function Subserves Cognitive Development. *NeuroImage, 13*(5), 786–793.

Mackintosh, N. J. (1998). *IQ and Human Intelligence*. Oxford University Press.

Magnuson, K., & Votruba-Drzal, E. (2009). *Enduring Influences of Childhood Poverty, Changing Poverty: Changing Policies*. Russell Sage Foundation.

Martins, N. (2011). Can Neuroscience Inform Economics? Rationality, Emotions and Preference Formation. *Cambridge Journal of Economics, 35*, 251–267.

Masten, A. S., & Shaffer, A. (2006). How Families Matter in Child Development: Reflections from Research on Risk and Resilience. In A. Clarke-Stewart & J. Dunn (Eds.), *Families Count: Effects on Child and Adolescent Development* (pp. 5–25). Cambridge University Press.

Mather, M., et al. (2004). Amygdala Responses to Emotionally Valenced Stimuli in Older and Younger Adults. *Psychological Science, 15*, 259.

Mayberry, R., Lock, E., & Kazmi, H. (2002). Linguistic Ability and Early Language Exposure. *Nature, 417*, 38.

McColloch, C. (2013). Mindfulness Intervention in Education: Can We Address Cognitive and Non-cognitive Deficits of Children in Poverty at School. *Psychological Inquiry, 18*, 211237.

McDonnell, T. (2016). Non-cognitive Development in Early Childhood: The Influence of Maternal Employment and the Mediating Role of Childcare. *The Economic and Social Review, 47*(4), 499–541.

McDool, E. (2019). Ability Grouping and Children's Non-cognitive Outcomes. *Applied Economics*. https://doi.org/10.1080/00036846.2019.1705239

McElwain, N., Booth-La Force, C., Lansford, J., Wu, X., & Dyer, W. (2008). A Process Model of Attachment-Friend Linkages: Hostile Attribution Biases,

Language Ability, and Mother-Child Affective Mutuality as Intervening Mechanisms. *Child Development, 79*(6), 1891–1906.
Moll, P. (1996). Primary Schooling, Cognitive Skills and Wages in South Africa. *Economica, 65*, 263–284.
Mönks, F. J., & Mason, E. J. (2000). Developmental Psychology and Giftedness: Theories and Research. In K. A. Heller, F. J. Mönks, R. J. Sternberg, & R. F. Subotnik (Eds.), *International Handbook of Giftedness and Talent* (pp. 141–157). Elsevier.
Morrison, G. M., & Cosden, M. (1997). Risk, Resilience, and Adjustment of Individuals with Learning Disabilities. *Learning Disability Quarterly, 20*, 43–60. https://doi.org/10.2307/1511092
Moutsiana, C., Garrett, N., Clarke, R., Lotto, R., Blakemore, S., & Sharot, T. (2013). Human Development of the Ability to Learn from Bad News. *PNAS, 110*(41).
Neymotin, F. (2014). How Parental Involvement Affects Childhood Behavioral Outcomes. *Journal of Family and Economic Issues, 35*, 433–451.
Niederle, M., & Vesterlund, L. (2010). Explaining the Gender Gap in Math Test Scores: The Role of Competition. *The Journal of Economic Perspectives, 24*, 129–144.
O'Callaghan, F., O'Callaghan, M., Najman, J., Williams, G., & Bor, W. (2007). Prenatal Alcohol Exposure and Attention, Learning and Intellectual Ability at 14 Years: A Prospective Longitudinal Study. *Early Human Development, 83*, 115–123.
Oreopoulos, P. (2007). Do Dropouts Drop Out too Soon? Wealth, Health, and Happiness from Compulsory Schooling. *Journal of Public Economics, 97*, 2213–2229.
Pelletier, J., & Astington, J. (2004). Action, Consciousness and Theory of Mind: Children's Ability to Coordinate Story Characters' Actions and Thoughts. *Early Education and Development, 15*(1), 5–22. https://doi.org/10.1207/s15566935eed1501_1
Peters, W. A. M., Grager-Loidl, H., & Supplee, P. (2000). Underachievement in Gifted Children and Adolescents: Theory and Practice. In K. A. Heller, F. J. Mönks, R. J. Sternberg, & R. F. Subotnik (Eds.), *International Handbook of Giftedness and Talent* (pp. 609–621). Elsevier.
Piaget, J. (1953). *The Origin of the Intelligence in the Child*. Routledge.
Piek, J., Dawson, L., Smith, L., & Gasson, N. (2008). The Role of Early Fine and Gross Motor Development on Later Motor and Cognitive Ability. *Human Movement Science, 27*, 668–681.
Plomin, R. (1999). Genetics and General Cognitive Ability. *Nature, 402*, C25.
Plug, E. (2002). *How Do Parents Raise the Educational Attainment of Future Generations? IZA Discussion Paper No. 652.*

Plug, E. J. S., & Vijverberg, W. P. M. (2003). Schooling, Family Background, and Adoption: Is It Nature or Is It Nurture? *Journal of Political Economy, 111*, 611–641.

Plug, E., & Vijverberg, W. (2005). Does Family Income Matter for Schooling Outcomes? Using Adoptees as a Natural Experiment. *The Economic Journal, 115*, 879–906.

Rao, N., & Chatterjee, T. (2018). Sibling Gender and Wage Differences. *Applied Economics, 50*(15), 1725–1745.

Renzulli, J. S. (1978). What Makes Giftedness? Re-examining a Definition. *Phi Delta Kappan, 60*, 180–184.

Riegler, A. (2002). When Is a Cognitive System Embodied. *Cognitive Systems Research, 3*, 339–348.

Romero, A., Bellas, F., Becerra, J., & Duro, R. (2019). Bootstrapping Autonomous Skill Learning in the MDB Cognitive Architecture. In J. Vicente et al. (Eds.), *Understanding the Brain Function and Emotions.*

Rosenberg, K., & Trevathan, W. (2002). Birth, Obstetrics and Human Evolution. *British Journal of Obstetrics and Gynaecology, 109*, 1199–1206.

Rosenzweig, M. R., & Bennett, E. L. (1996). Psychobiology of Plasticity: Effects of Training and Experience on Brain and Behaviour. *Behavioural Brain Research, 78*, 57–65.

Rowe, D. C., & van den Oord, E. J. C. G. (1999). Genetic and Environmental Influences on Vocabulary IQ: Parental Education Level as Moderator. *Child Development, 70*(5).

Sander, W. (1992). The Effects of Ethnicity and Religion on Educational Attainment. *Economics of Education Review, 11*(2), 119–135.

Schamberg, M. A., & Evans, G. W. (2009). *Childhood Poverty, Chronic Stress, and Adult Working Memory* (Vol. 106, p. 13). National Academy of Sciences.

Schneider, W. (2000). Giftedness, Expertise, and (Exceptional) Performance: A Developmental Perspective. In K. A. Heller, F. J. Mönks, R. J. Sternberg, & R. F. Subotnik (Eds.), *International Handbook of Giftedness and Talent.* Elsevier.

Sen, A. K. (1982). *Choice, Welfare and Measurement.* Blackwell.

Sen, A. K. (2002). *Rationality and Freedom.* The Belknap Press of Harvard University Press.

Sepahuand, M., Shahbazian, R., & Swain, R. (2013). *Time Investment by Parents in Cognitive and Non-cognitive Childcare Activities, Working Paper No. 2013, 10.* Uppsala University, Department of Economics.

Shaw, P., Greenstein, D., Lerch, J., Clasen, L., Lenroot, R., Gogtay, N., Evans, A., Rapoport, J., & Giedd, J. (2006). Intellectual Ability and Cortical Development in Children and Adolescents. *Nature, 440.*

Shrimpton, S., Oates, K., & Hayes, S. (1998). Children's Memory of Events: Effects of Stress, Age, Time Delay and Location of Interview. *Applied Cognitive Psychology, 12*, 133–143.

Simpson, C. (1981). Classroom Structure and the Organisation of Ability. *Sociology of Education, 54*(2), 120–132.

Spearman, C. (1904). 'General Intelligence' Objectively Determined and Measured. *The American Journal of Psychology, 15*, 201–293.

Steel, P. (2007). The Nature of Procrastination: A Meta-Analytic and Theoretical Review of Quintessential Self-Regulatory Failure. *Psychological Bulletin, 133*(1), 65.

Tavares, L. (2007, July). Non-cognitive Skills, Parenting Practices and Academic Success. In *Paper Presented at British Household Panel Survey Conference*. Institute for Social and Economic Research, University of Essex.

Thalmann-Magnenat, N., & Kasap, Z. (2009). *Modelling Socially Intelligent Virtual Humans, Conference Paper*. Nanyang Technological University.

Thévenon, O. (2013). *Drivers of Female Labour force Participation in the OECD, OECD Social, Employment and Migration Working Papers, No. 145*. OECD.

Todd, P., & Wolpin, K. (2003). On the Specification and Estimation of the Production Function for Cognitive Achievement. *The Econometrics Journal, 113*, 3–33.

Trainin, G., & Swanson, H. L. (2005). Cognition, Metacognition, and Achievement of College Students with Learning Disabilities. *Learning Disability Quarterly, 28*, 261–272. https://doi.org/10.2307/4126965

Vinayagamoorthy, V., Gillies, M., Steed, A., Tanguy, E., Pan, X., Loscos, C., & Slater, M. (2006). Building Expression into Virtual Characters. In *Eurographics Conference State of the Art Reports*.

Walley, A., Metsala, J., & Garlock, V. (2003). Spoken Vocabulary Growth: Its Role in the Development of Phoneme Awareness and Early Reading Ability. *Reading and Writing: An Interdisciplinary Journal, 16*.

Wijnroks, L., & Van Veldhoven, N. (2003). Individual Differences in Postural Control and Cognitive Development in Preterm Infants. *Infant Behavior and Development, 26*, 14–26.

Yoo, J. E., & Moon, S. M. (2006). Counselling Needs of Gifted Students: An Analysis of Intake Forms at a University-Based Counselling Center. *Gifted Child Quarterly, 50*, 52–61. https://doi.org/10.1177/001698620605000106

Yu, S., & Hannum, E. (2007). Food for Thought: Poverty, Family Nutritional Environment, and Children's Educational Performance in Rural China. *Sociological Perspectives, 50*(4), 53–77.

Yu, C., Tan, G., Lu, H., Wang, Z., Meng, J., Hao, J., & Ren, F. (2016). Modelling Adaptive Learning Behaviours for Consensus Formation in Human Societies. *Scientific Reports, 6*, 27626. https://doi.org/10.1038/srep27626

Zumbuehl, M., Dohmen, T., & Pfann, G. (2013). *Parental Investment and the Intergenerational Transmission of Economic Preferences and Attitudes. SOEP Discussion Paper No. 570.*

CHAPTER 4

The Theories of Cognitive Development

Introduction

As discussed in the previous chapter the first few years of a child's life are important for its mental and physical development.[1] This is because it is in the early years of a child's life that there is the most significant lifetime growth of the brain and the nervous system. This is specifically with regard to new neural connections and the strengthening of existing connections.[2] Furthermore, the early years of a child's life are also important with regard to overall motor development.[3] This is due to the fact that in the early years of a child's life the roots of the advanced motor responses, such as being able to jump up in the air and land on two feet, of later life are put down due to the physical interactions of the infant with its external environment.[4] Imaging of the brain suggests that motor activity and the completion of cognitive tasks co-activate both the neo-cerebellum and the

[1] Gabbard, C. (2008), Lifelong Motor Development, 5th ed., Pearson Education, San Francisco.

[2] Shonkoff, J., and Phillips, D. (2000), From Neurons to Neighbourhoods: The Science of Early Childhood Development, National Academy Press, Washington.

[3] Veldman, S., Santos, R., Jones, R., Sousa-Sa, E., and Okely, A. (2019), Associations between gross motor skills and cognitive development in toddlers, Early Human Development, 132, pp. 39-44.

[4] Gallahue, D., and Ozmun, J., (2002), Understanding Motor Development: Infants, Children, Adolescents, Adults, fifth edition, McGraw-Hill, New York.

S. Ramesh, *The Political Economy of Human Behaviour and Economic Development*,
https://doi.org/10.1007/978-3-031-12666-6_4

dorsolateral prefrontal cortex.[5] This causality is also supported by the experiences of psychologists and educationalists specialising in childhood development.[6] Moreover, the theories associated with childhood development rely upon the causality between motor and cognitive development. Piaget's theory on the childhood development of cognition is associated with the actualisation of the brain associated with thinking due to physical movements.[7] Similarly, Systems Theory proposes that the movement of body parts such as the limbs and eyes is caused by the joint action of cognitive and motor processes.[8] Moreover, the theory of the Ecological Perspective suggests that infants can draw upon and process visual information so as to produce physical movements.[9] Those motor skills more closely associated with interaction with cognition were those associated with picking up and holding objects as well as the timing of the associated movements, these effects being stronger in the pre-teenage years of a child than in its teenage years.[10] A bi-directionality has also been detected with regard to the cognition-academic nexus.[11] In other words, consistent exposure to high-quality schooling will aid the development of a child's cognitive and academic ability. Pre-school education is also important, as it is at this stage of development that a child acquires the beginnings of the Theory of Mind concepts, perpetual awareness and the start of inductive and deductive reasoning.[12] The pre-school enrolment will help the child develop his/her language and mathematics skills.[13] It has also been found that early pre-school enrolment will have a positive impact on a child's

[5] Diamond, A. (2007), Interrelated and interdependent, Dev. Sci. 10, 152–158.

[6] Bowman, B., Donovan, S., and Bums, S. (2001), (Eds.), Committee on Early Childhood Pedagogy, National Academy Press: National Research Institute, Washington, DC.

[7] Piaget, J., and Cook, M. (1952), The Origins of Intelligence in Children, International Universities Press, New York.

[8] Thelen, E., and Smith, L. (1994), A Dynamic Systems Approach to the Development of Cognition and Action, MIT press, Cambridge, MA.

[9] Gibson, J. (1979), The Ecological Approach to Visual Perception, Lawrence Erlbaum, Hillsdale, NJ.

[10] Veldman, S., Santos, R., Jones, R., Sousa-Sa, E., and Okely, A. (2019), Associations between gross motor skills and cognitive development in toddlers, Early Human Development, 132, pp. 39-44.

[11] Peng, P., and Kievit, R. (2020), The Development of Academic Achievement and Cognitive Abilities: A Bidirectional Perspective, Child Development Perspectives, Vol. 14, No. 1, pp. 15-20.

[12] Kazi, S., Kazali, E., Makris, N., Spanoudis, G., and Demetriou, A. (2019), Cognizance in Cognitive Development: A Longitudinal Study, Cognitive Development, 52, 100805.

[13] Drange, N., and Havnes, T. (2019), Early Childcare and Cognitive Development: Evidence from an Assignment Lottery, Journal of Labour Economics, Vol. 37, No. 2.

cognitive development from an age of 6 to late adolescence, aged 18.[14] The level of development accessible to a child in the first three years of its life will have a lifetime impact.[15] However, it is at this stage that parents struggle with balancing work with childcare—more free time for the parents may allow them to give quality parenting to their child. Families would benefit from the public provision of in-kind quality child care, in this case.[16] Although it is only in late childhood that children acquire or complete the development of inferential awareness, relational and deductive reasoning and the awareness of cognitive processes.[17] The link between the development of cognitive abilities in children and specific parts of the brain has been established by such programmes as the Adolescent Brain Cognitive Development (ABCD) study, which makes available baseline data on the brain development of over 11,000 US children.[18] The data associated with brain development is acquired using magnetic resonance imaging. Other studies have shown that the causality between motor skills and cognitive activity is strongest in infants.[19] In the study of cognition in infants, executive functions such the ability to concentrate, working memory and mental agility have been used as measures of cognition.[20] The level of development of executive functions in infants is seen as an efficient indicator of a child's school academic performance.[21] This has been specifically associated with the level of working memory.[22] The development of working memory will also allow young children to develop the ability

[14] Dhuey, E., Figlio, D., Karbownik, K., and Roth, J. (2019), School Starting Age and Cognitive Development, Journal of Policy Analysis and Management, Vol. 38, No. 3, pp. 538-578.

[15] Chaparro, J., Sojourner, A., and Wiswall, M. (2020), Early Childhood Care and Cognitive Development, National Bureau of Economic research, Working Paper 26813.

[16] Ibid.

[17] Kazi, S., Kazali, E., Makris, N., Spanoudis, G., and Demetriou, A. (2019), Cognizance in Cognitive Development: A Longitudinal Study, Cognitive Development, 52, 100805.

[18] Compton, W., Dowling, G., and Garavan, H. (2019), Ensuring the Best Use of Data: The Adolescent Brain Cognitive Development Study, JAMA Paediatrics, Vol. 173, No. 9.

[19] Pereira, K., Valentini, N., and Saccani, R. (2016), Brazilian infant motor and cognitive development: longitudinal influence of risk factors, Pediatr. Int. 58, 1297–1306.

[20] Diamond, A. (2013), Executive functions, Annu. Rev. Psychol. 64, 135–168.

[21] Best, J., Miller, P., Naglieri, J. (2011), Relations between executive function and academic achievement from ages 5 to 17 in a large, representative national sample, Learn. Individ. Differ. 21, 327–336.

[22] Veldman, S., Santos, R., Jones, R., Sousa-Sa, E., and Okely, A. (2019), Associations between gross motor skills and cognitive development in toddlers, Early Human Development, 132, pp. 39-44.

to order events.[23] The lateral prefrontal cortex of the brain is associated with the development of behaviour, language and cognition.[24] Some studies have also shown a strong connection between the level of agility and working memory as well as between the level of agility and the depth of concentration.[25] However, although the inter-relatedness of motor development and cognitive ability has been recognised through research, the emotional development of the child is also important in facilitating the development of learning in a child's early years.[26] Nevertheless, the motor development of a child up to the age of 4 will have a positive impact on the child's cognitive capacity in terms of working memory capacity and the ability to solve problems from the age of 6 to the age of 11.[27] But the facilitation of the development of the motor skills of very young children will also facilitate the lifelong development of cognitive ability.[28] There is therefore the possibility that the development of cognition from a very young age to adulthood and beyond may follow in sequential stages.[29]

Piaget's Theory of Cognitive Development

Piaget's theory of cognitive development is based on the notion of 'constructivism', that is, complex cognitive processes emerge from the incremental moulding of psychological changes in the brain with environmental experiences.[30] Although the hierarchical development of cognitive thought

[23] Gelman, R. (1978), Cognitive Development, Ann. Rev. Psychol, 29, pp. 297-332.

[24] Fuster, J. (2002), Frontal Lobe and Cognitive Development, Journal of Neurocytology, 31, pp. 373-385.

[25] Niederer, I., Kriemler, S., Gut, J., Hartmann, T., Schindler, C., Barral, J et al. (2011), Relationship of aerobic fitness and motor skills with memory and attention in preschoolers (Ballabeina): a cross-sectional and longitudinal study, BMC Pediatr. 11, 34.

[26] Veldman, S., Santos, R., Jones, R., Sousa-Sa, E., and Okely, A. (2019), Associations between gross motor skills and cognitive development in toddlers, Early Human Development, 132, pp. 39-44.

[27] Piek, J., Dawson, L., Smith, L., Gasson, N. (2008), The role of early fine and gross motor development on later motor and cognitive ability, Hum. Mov. Sci. 27 (2008) 668–681.

[28] Veldman, S., Santos, R., Jones, R., Sousa-Sa, E., and Okely, A. (2019), Associations between gross motor skills and cognitive development in toddlers, Early Human Development, 132, pp. 39-44.

[29] Flavell, J. (1982), On Cognitive Development, Child Development, Vol. 53, No. 1, pp. 1-10.

[30] Johnson, S. (2003), The Nature of Cognitive Development, TRENDS in Cognitive Science, Vol. 7, No. 3.

and its physiological structures is universal to all of humanity, the way in which these structures or basic cognitive processes interact with the environment is dependent on the culture of the individual.[31] The roots of Piaget's work lay in his search for how knowledge developed in a child.[32] Indeed, Piaget's focus of analysis was with a human development and genetics emphasis.[33] Much of the research Piaget conducted was by observing the reactions of his own children to differently presented scenarios as they grew up.[34] The scenario-induced reactions of children were used to observe their reasoning processes across different states of development.[35] This kind of analysis of childhood responses and behaviours allowed Piaget to put forward the idea that there was a state of correlation between the brain development of children and their behavioural development.[36] However, during Piaget's time, the technology was not available in order to fully explore this correlation and evaluate its truthfulness or its falsehood[37]—although, in recent times, with the development of scanning, techniques the stages of the brain development of a child can be technologically assessed and correlations made with changes in behaviour during the process of ageing. While Piaget's work and theory were developed in the 1920s, they did not become widely available until the 1950s and the 1960s when English translations of his books became widely available.[38]

[31] Dasen, P. R. (1994), Culture and cognitive development from a Piagetian perspective. In W. J. Lonner & R. Malpass (Eds.), Psychology and culture (pp. 145-149). Boston: Allyn & Bacon.

[32] Mayer, S. J. (2005), The early evolution of Jean Piaget's clinical method. History of Psychology, 8(4), 362–382.

[33] Duveen, G. (2000), Piaget ethnographer. Social Science Information, 39(1), 79–97.

[34] Lefmann, T., and Combs-Orme, T. (2013), Early Brain Development for Social Work Practice: Integrating Neuroscience with Piaget's Theory of Cognitive Development, Journal of Human Behaviour in the Social Environment, 23, pp. 640-647.

[35] Mayer, S. J. (2005), The early evolution of Jean Piaget's clinical method. History of Psychology, 8(4), 362–382.

[36] Lefmann, T., and Combs-Orme, T. (2013), Early Brain Development for Social Work Practice: Integrating Neuroscience with Piaget's Theory of Cognitive Development, Journal of Human Behaviour in the Social Environment, 23, pp. 640-647.

[37] Kolb, B., & Fantie, B. D. (2009), Development of the child's brain and behavior, IN C. R. Reynolds & E. Fletcher-Janzen (Eds.), Handbook of clinical child neuropsychology (3rd ed., pp. 19–46). Springer, New York, NY.

[38] Silverthorn, P. (1999), Jean Piaget' s theory of development. Available from:http://chd.gse.gmu.edu/immersion/knowledgebase/theorists/constructivism/Piaget.htm

In any case, Piaget identified four major stages of development in childhood, the success of each successive stage being dependent on the success of the previous stage of development.[39] The first sub-stage is the Sensorimotor Period, which lasted from birth to the age of 2. The second stage of development is the Preoperational Thought period, which lasted from the age of 2 to the age of 7. The third stage of development is the Concrete Operations Period, from the age of 7 to the age of 11. And finally, the last stage is the Formal Operations Period, from the age of 11 to the age of 15. The results of neuroscience research suggest that the infant's experiences and environment in the Sensorimotor Period will set the trajectory of development for an entire lifetime.[40] The development of the brain from birth to the age of 2 is probably the most dynamic compared to the other years in the life of a human being.[41] During this period of brain development, the experiences and activities of the infant will influence the emergence of the foundations of cognitive framework upon which abstract thinking, reasoning and planning abilities will be developed.[42] So complex is the Sensorimotor Period from birth to the age of 2 that Piaget was able to sub-divide this stage into six sub-stages across which an infant's learning was based on the use of its five senses as well as being dependent upon the movement of its limbs.[43] The six sub-stages of development in the Sensorimotor Period included birth to 1 month, 1–4 months, 4–8 months, 8–12 months, 12–18 months and 18–24 months.[44] During sub-stage 1, the brain, which at birth only weighs 25% of the adult weight,[45] develops

[39] Piaget, J. (1973), The child and reality: Problems of genetic psychology, Penguin Books, New York, NY.

[40] Shonkoff, J. P., & Phillips, D. (2000), From neurons to neighbourhoods: The science of early childhood development. National Academy Press, Washington, DC.

[41] Knickmeyer, R. C. et al. (2008). A structural MRI study of human brain development from birth to 2 years. The Journal of Neuroscience, 28(47), 12176–12182.

[42] Levin, H. S., Culhane, K. A., Hartmann, J., Evankovich, K., & Mattson, A. J. (1991), Developmental changes in performance on tests of purported frontal lobe functioning, Developmental Neuropsychology, 7, 377–395.

[43] Lefmann, T., and Combs-Orme, T. (2013), Early Brain Development for Social Work Practice: Integrating Neuroscience with Piaget's Theory of Cognitive Development, Journal of Human Behaviour in the Social Environment, 23, pp. 640-647.

[44] Ibid.

[45] DiPietro, J. A, (2000), Baby and the brain: Advances in child development. Annual Review of Public Health, 21, 455–471.

through three development processes.[46] Through the first process, Dendritic Arborisation, more and more neurons become interconnected through the branching out of dendrites. The communication between the neurons because of activation or firing as a result of stimulation by neurotransmitters is at the heart of the functioning of the brain.[47] The repeated firing of neurons strengthens their connections and it is in this process that the roots of learning are to be found.[48] The activities of the infant responsible for brain development in the first sub-stage of the Sensorimotor Period include the stimulus received visually as well as the stimulation of muscles and the movement of the limbs.[49] Through this kind of stimulus, up to 40,000 synapses a second are formed in the brain of an infant in the first 12 months of its life.[50] It is therefore apparent that during the first sub-stage, the infant is becoming acquainted with and acquiring knowledge about its environment by using its senses.[51] Like all animals, human infants are also born with reflexes. However, whereas in other animals these reflexes act to determine their behaviour, in human infants these reflexes allow for learning from the environment, which facilitates the incremental development of physiological neural pathways and structures in the brain.[52] Furthermore, Piaget associated two processes with a human infant's ability to adapt to its environment.[53] These processes included the assimilation of information and knowledge from the infant's external environment through a reflexive strategy and the accommodation of

[46] Lefmann, T., and Combs-Orme, T. (2013), Early Brain Development for Social Work Practice: Integrating Neuroscience with Piaget's Theory of Cognitive Development, Journal of Human Behaviour in the Social Environment, 23, pp. 640-647.

[47] Webb, S. J., Monk, C. S., & Nelson, C. A. (2001), Mechanisms of postnatal neurobiological development: Implications for human development, Developmental Neuropsychology, 19(2), 147–171.

[48] Lefmann, T., and Combs-Orme, T. (2013), Early Brain Development for Social Work Practice: Integrating Neuroscience with Piaget's Theory of Cognitive Development, Journal of Human Behaviour in the Social Environment, 23, pp. 640-647.

[49] Piaget, J., & Inhelder, B. (1969), The Psychology of the Child, Basic Books, New York, NY.

[50] Tau, G. Z., & Peterson, G. S. (2010), Normal development of brain circuits. Neuropsychopharmacology Reviews, 35, 147–168.

[51] Lefmann, T., and Combs-Orme, T. (2013), Early Brain Development for Social Work Practice: Integrating Neuroscience with Piaget's Theory of Cognitive Development, Journal of Human Behaviour in the Social Environment, 23, pp. 640-647.

[52] Huitt, W., and Hummel, J. (2003), Piaget's Theory of Cognitive Development, Educational Psychology Interactive, Valdosta, GA: Valdosta State University.

[53] Ibid.

physiological structures in the brain according to these interactive inputs.[54] However, the processes of accommodation and assimilation are not limited to use in a human's infant stage but are also applicable throughout life, during which adaptation to an ever-changing complex environment takes place.

After birth, the primary motor cortex of the infant's brain encompassing the brainstem, the thalamus, the sensorimotor cortex and the cerebellar vermis experiences rapid development.[55] Moreover, as the infant consumes more food, the metabolic rate[56] of the brain is at its highest level in these regions[57] in comparison to other regions of the brain. In the first sub-stage, the myelin sheath which encapsulates the axons also develops and thickens.[58] And as this process occurs, the speed of transmission of stimuli between the neurons begins to increase as well. The more efficient the development of the myelin sheath, the process of myelination, the better the co-ordination of the visual tracking and limb movements of the infant.[59] The second sub-stage of the Sensorimotor Period, aged 1–4 months, involves the infant developing habits as well as improved co-ordination due to learning. An example of this would be that the infant sucking its thumb is no longer a matter of chance but a deliberate act of co-ordination between the thumb and the mouth.[60] Furthermore, communication in the infant's brain improves in the first four months of its life as white matter, myelinated axons, develops.[61] The level of integration of motor, sensory and cognitive information by the infant is very

[54] Ibid.

[55] Terumitsu, M., Ikeda, K., Kwee, I. L., & Nakada, T. (2009), Participation of primary motor cortex area 4a in complex sensory processing: 3.0-T fMRI study, Neuroreport, 20(7), 679–683.

[56] Chugani, H. T., Phelps, M. E., & Mazziotta, J. C. (1987), Positron emission tomography study of human brain functional Development, Annals of Neurology, 22, 487–497.

[57] Johnson, M. H. (2001), Functional brain development in humans, Nature, 2, 475–483.

[58] Webb, S. J., Monk, C. S., & Nelson, C. A. (2001), Mechanisms of postnatal neurobiological development: Implications for human development, Developmental Neuropsychology, 19(2), 147–171.

[59] Deoni, S. C. et al. (2011). Mapping infant brain myelination with magnetic resonance imaging. Journal of Neuroscience, 31(2), 784–791. doi: https://doi.org/10.1523/JNEUROSCI.2106-10.2011

[60] Lefmann, T., and Combs-Orme, T. (2013), Early Brain Development for Social Work Practice: Integrating Neuroscience with Piaget's Theory of Cognitive Development, Journal of Human Behaviour in the Social Environment, 23, pp. 640-647.

[61] Barkovich, J. A., Kjos, B. O., Jackson, D. E., & Norman, D. (1988), Normal maturation of the neonatal and infant brain: MR imaging at 1.5 T1. Neuroradiology, 166, 173–180.

much dependent on the state of development of communication in the brain itself.[62] The development of the ability of the infant to tell its self apart from its environment forms the third sub-stage of the Sensorimotor Period, when the infant is aged between 4 and 8 months. At this stage connections in the hippocampus region of the brain are rapidly laid down, facilitating greater learning and memory.[63] This type of brain development at this stage may help to explain why the infant is engaged in a repetitive learning process, during which it identifies specific actions it takes with specific results.[64] The infant also shows greater balance and motor co-ordination during this stage because the cerebellum, the part of the brain responsible for this type of activity, doubles in size.[65] This period marks a transition in the behaviour of the infant from an unintentional impact on its environment to an intentional one.[66] The fourth sub-stage of Piaget's Sensorimotor Period, during which the infant is aged 8–12 months, shows the infant developing planning skills at a foundation level. Furthermore, at this age, the infant's cognitive development allows it to combine interactions with real world objects and dialogue with others to articulate meaningful statements.[67] The emergence of planning at this stage of the infant's life is accompanied by the development of the frontal cortex, which increases in synaptic density,[68] which is instrumental in enabling higher-order cognitive functions.[69] Furthermore, as the number of connections

[62] Lefmann, T., and Combs-Orme, T. (2013), Early Brain Development for Social Work Practice: Integrating Neuroscience with Piaget's Theory of Cognitive Development, Journal of Human Behaviour in the Social Environment, 23, pp. 640-647.

[63] Paldino, A., & Purpura, D. (1979), Quantitative analysis of the spatial distribution of axonal and dendritic terminals of hippocampal pyramidal neurons in immature human brain. Experimental Neurology, 64, 604–619.

[64] Lefmann, T., and Combs-Orme, T. (2013), Early Brain Development for Social Work Practice: Integrating Neuroscience with Piaget's Theory of Cognitive Development, Journal of Human Behaviour in the Social Environment, 23, pp. 640-647.

[65] Knickmeyer, R. C., et al. (2008). A structural MRI study of human brain development from birth to 2 years. The Journal of Neuroscience, 28(47), 12176–12182.

[66] Lefmann, T., and Combs-Orme, T. (2013), Early Brain Development for Social Work Practice: Integrating Neuroscience with Piaget's Theory of Cognitive Development, Journal of Human Behaviour in the Social Environment, 23, pp. 640-647.

[67] Smillie, D. (1982), Rethinking Piaget's Theory of Infancy, Human Development, 25, pp. 282-294.

[68] Huttenlocher, P. R. (1990), Morphometric study of human cerebral cortex development. Neuropsychologia, 28, 517–527.

[69] Luna, B., et al. (2001), Maturation of widely distributed brain function subserves cognitive development. NeuroImage, 13, 786–793.

increases in the hippocampus, neuromuscular functioning also increases such that the actions of the infant become more and more intentional. This is particularly because the extent and quality of the outer sheathing of the corticospinal tract in the brain stem are at a very advanced state within the first 12 months from birth, and that of the spinal cord within 28 months.[70] The ability of the infant to engage in conscious thought and sensory perception[71] also develops during the fourth sub-stage of the Sensorimotor Period. This will result in the improved physical articulation of thoughts by the infant, resulting in a more effective planning of its actions.[72] This is primarily because of the increased sheathing of three lobes of the brain, the parietal, the occipital as well as the frontal.[73] In stage 5, 12–18 months, the infant will begin to experiment with its actions in order to determine if an action taken in different ways will produce the same or a similar result.[74] At this stage of development, the infant is able to develop the ability to visualise not only its relationship with other objects in the world but also the relationship between objects.[75] The infant also develops the ability to visualise and think about an object even when it cannot be seem, perceiving that it is located out of sight.[76] The perception that objects exist even if they cannot be seen is a big stride in the development of the cognition of the infant.[77] The cognitive skills associated with the retrieval of objects by the infant are related to the

[70] Brody, B., Kinney, H., Kloman, A., & Gilles, F. (1987), Sequence of central nervous system myelination in human infancy: I. An autopsy study of myelination. Journal of Neuropathology & Experimental Neurology, 46, 283–301.

[71] Paterson, S. J., Heim, S., Friedman, J. T., Choudhury, N., & Benasich, A. A. (2006), Development of structure and function in the infant brain: Implications for cognition, language and social behavior. Neuroscience and Biobehavioral Reviews, 30, 1087–1105.

[72] Lefmann, T., and Combs-Orme, T. (2013), Early Brain Development for Social Work Practice: Integrating Neuroscience with Piaget's Theory of Cognitive Development, Journal of Human Behaviour in the Social Environment, 23, pp. 640-647.

[73] Paterson, S. J., Heim, S., Friedman, J. T., Choudhury, N., & Benasich, A. A. (2006), Development of structure and function in the infant brain: Implications for cognition, language and social behavior. Neuroscience and Bio-Behavioral Reviews, 30, 1087–1105.

[74] Lefmann, T., and Combs-Orme, T. (2013), Early Brain Development for Social Work Practice: Integrating Neuroscience with Piaget's Theory of Cognitive Development, Journal of Human Behaviour in the Social Environment, 23, pp. 640-647.

[75] Thomas, R. M. (1996), Comparing theories of child development, Brooks/Cole Publishing Company, Pacific Grove, CA.

[76] Ibid.

[77] Piaget, J., & Cook, M. (Trans.) (1954), The development of object construct. In The construction of reality in the child (pp. 3–96). New York, NY: Basic Books.

development of the dorsolateral prefrontal cortex (DPC) of the brain.[78] The DPC region of the brain is responsible for the organisation and regulation of motor responses as well as the planning of these responses by the infant.[79] During this stage, the basal ganglia caudate nucleus also develops in volume, and this correlates with the motor development of the infant.[80] The developments in the brain during this period can be associated with the infant gaining the ability to walk and crawl to different locations by facilitating muscle co-ordination. The sixth and final sub-stage (18–24 months) of the Sensorimotor Period is associated with the development of the infant's creativity and insight, leading the path to Piaget's pre-functional thought period.[81] During this stage, the infant can use symbols to pretend that a horse can be represented by a stick, for example.[82] By interacting with objects, infants at this stage of development can develop their own techniques in dealing with objects. This is intelligence acquired through reflective learning.[83] Nevertheless, there is some evidence to suggest that cognitive development and adaptation to the environment are dependent on social structures.[84] For example, cognitive development may be more favourable in environments and cultures in which education is valued. In the sixth and final stage of development, the infant is also able to control its behaviour, initiating actions and then curtailing these as required by the environment. This behavioural control is associated with the development of connections in the cerebellum, thalamus, striatum and neocortex regions of the infant's brain.[85] By the end of the first 24 months from birth, an infant's brain size, and development with regard to the

[78] Diamond, A. (1990), The development and neural bases of memory functions as indexed by the AB and delayed response tasks in human infants and infant monkeys. Annals of the New York Academy of Sciences, 60, 231–267.

[79] Johnson, M. H. (2001), Functional brain development in humans. Nature, 2, 475–483.

[80] Herrero, M. T., Barcia, C., & Navarro, J. M. (2002), Functional anatomy of thalamus and basal ganglia. Child's Nervous System, 18, 386–404.

[81] Thomas, R. M. (1996), Comparing theories of child development. Pacific Grove, CA: Brooks/Cole Publishing Company.

[82] Lefmann, T., and Combs-Orme, T. (2013), Early Brain Development for Social Work Practice: Integrating Neuroscience with Piaget's Theory of Cognitive Development, Journal of Human Behaviour in the Social Environment, 23, pp. 640-647.

[83] Piaget, J. (1963), The origins of intelligence in children, W.W. Norton & Company, Inc., New York, NY.

[84] Buck-Morss, S. (1975), Socio-Economic Bias in Piaget's Theory and Its Implications for Cross-Cultural Studies, Hum. Dev 18, pp. 35-49.

[85] Luna, B., et al., (2001). Maturation of widely distributed brain function subserves cognitive development. NeuroImage, 13, 786–793.

density of neurons, glia, axons and dendritic connections, is just over 80% of the adult size.[86] It is estimated that the brain of the infant grows in capacity over the first 12 months of its life by just over 100% and by 15% in the subsequent 12 months.[87] However, in addition to the increase in the size of the brain of the infant in the first 12 months of its life, the ongoing efficient organisation of synaptic connections to allow for a more effective transmission of information through the different regions of the brain is also important.[88] Thus, rather than increasing cognitive capacity being associated with increasing synaptic connections, the loss of weak synaptic connections and the strengthening of stronger (reinforced), important connections is an important feature of brain development during early childhood.[89] Moreover, as the physiological structures develop and become used more often, the better these perform with regard to cognitive thinking.[90] Therefore, it follows intuitively that as people get older, the better they are at solving problems and tasks with practice.[91] While Piaget's theory of cognitive development may explain how the interactions of an infant may facilitate the development of physiological cognitive structures in the brain, it may not fully explain the creativity and emotions of human adulthood.[92]

Knowledge of the development of the brain of an infant in the very first years of its life will allow policymakers to devise public policies that will

[86] Knickmeyer, R. C. et al. (2008). A structural MRI study of human brain development from birth to 2 years. The Journal of Neuroscience, 28(47), 12176–12182.

[87] Webb, S. J., Monk, C. S., & Nelson, C. A. (2001). Mechanisms of postnatal neurobiological development: Implications for human development. Developmental Neuropsychology, 19(2), 147–171.

[88] Luna, B., et al., (2001). Maturation of widely distributed brain function subserves cognitive development. NeuroImage, 13, 786–793.

[89] Casey, B. J., Giedd, J. N., & Thomas, K. M. (2000), Structural and functional brain development and its relation to cognitive development. Biological Psychology, 54, 241–257.

[90] Larsen, R. (1973), Levels of Conceptual Development in Melodic Permutations Concepts Based on Piaget's Theory, Journal of Research in Music Education, Vol. 21, No. 3, pp. 256-263.

[91] Larsen, R. (1973), Levels of Conceptual Development in Melodic Permutations Concepts Based on Piaget's Theory, Journal of Research in Music Education, Vol. 21, No. 3, pp. 256-263.

[92] Riegel, K. (1973), Dialectic Operations: The Final Period of Cognitive Development, Human Develop, 16, pp. 346-370.

facilitate more effective brain development.[93] State-led interventions on how infants are nurtured will thus have a positive effect on their entire life. It is also self-evident that there is a causal relationship between the development of axons, neurons and dendritic connections and the environment in which a child is nurtured.[94] It therefore follows that if the environment in which an infant is nurtured is changed, then the neural pathways or connections between neurons in its brain will also change.[95] In this case, it is evident that maturation by itself is not enough to explain the cognitive development of an individual, but that the social and cultural influences in the environment of an infant are also important.[96] Moreover, the time each infants spends developing in the context of Piaget's sub-stages of the Sensorimotor Period will vary.[97] This may suggest that teachers should devise individual student teaching plans and not use a generic teaching plan for all students.[98] Suitable individual teaching plans may help to accelerate the cognitive development of each student.[99] The more teachers are able to ascertain and understand the state of cognitive development of each student, the more productive the teaching will be in facilitating learning.[100] Moreover, teaching and learning techniques which facilitate a higher level of thinking in learners will in turn facilitate greater levels of intellectual development, and the generation of new knowledge.[101]

[93] Egan, M., Neely-Barnes, S., & Combs-Orme, T. (2011), Integrating neuroscience into the lifespan. Journal of Social Work Education, 47(2), 269–282.

[94] Schore, A. N. (2001), Effects of a secure attachment relationship on right brain development, affect regulation, and infant mental health. Infant Mental Health Journal, 22(1–2), 7–66.

[95] Clark, D. A., & Beck, A. T. (2010), Cognitive theory and therapy of anxiety and depression: Convergence with neurobiological findings. Trends in Cognitive Sciences, 14(9), 418–424.

[96] Driver, R. (1978), When is a stage not a stage? A Critique of Piaget's theory of cognitive development and its application to science education, Educational Research, 21;1, 54-61.

[97] Kamii, C. (1982), Number in preschool and kindergarten: Educational implications of Piaget's theory. National Association for the Education of Young Children, Washington, DC.

[98] Driver, R. (1978), When is a stage not a stage? A Critique of Piaget's theory of cognitive development and its application to science education, Educational Research, 21; 1, 54-61.

[99] Zimmerman, B. J., & Whitehurst, G. J. (1979). Structure and function: A comparison of two views of the development of language and cognition. In G. J. Whitehurst and B. J. Zimmerman (Eds.), *The functions of language and cognition*, Academic Press, New York.

[100] Ojose, B. (2008), Applying Piaget's Theory of Cognitive Development to Mathematics Instruction, The Mathematics Educator, Vol. 18, No. 1, pp. 26-30.

[101] Wach, H. (1981), Visual Implications of Piaget's Theory of Cognitive Development, Journal of Learning Disabilities, Vol. 14, No. 10.

Therefore, a better understanding of human behaviour can only be achieved through a biological approach.[102] Thus, an appreciation of the biology of human beings is important for devising interventionist strategies.[103]

Vygotsky's Theory of Cognitive Development

Vygotsky was a psychologist based in the former USSR. His analysis of human psychological functioning was based not on a modular approach but on a systems approach.[104] The implication of this is that Vygotsky did not believe that psychological functions such as the development of memory should be studied separately from the development of the psychological system itself.[105] Moreover, Vygotsky believed that the focus of research should be on the changing nature of the relationships between the different psychological functions.[106] This, therefore emphasises a systems approach to the analysis of psychological functions rather than a modular one. The systemic approach to the analysis of psychological functions views these functions as arising from a synergy of biological and psychological processes. This is in contrast to the reductionist view in psychological research, encompassing Cartesian thinking, which views a divergence between biological and psychological processes.[107] However, Vygotsky believed that an individual could not be separated from either its social or its biological environment.[108] The implication is that an analysis of both is

[102] Combs-Orme, T. (2013), Epigenesis and the social work imperative. Social Work, 58(1), 23–30.

[103] Lefmann, T., and Combs-Orme, T. (2013), Early Brain Development for Social Work Practice: Integrating Neuroscience with Piaget's Theory of Cognitive Development, Journal of Human Behaviour in the Social Environment, 23, pp. 640-647.

[104] Vasileva, O., and Balyasnikova, N. (2019), (Re) Introducing Vygotsky's Thought: From Historical Overview to Contemporary Psychology, Frontiers in Psychology, Volume 10, Article 1515.

[105] Ibid.

[106] Luria, A. R., and Vygotsky, L. S. (1930/1992), Ape, primitive man and child, 1930/1992, Harvester Wheatsheaf: Great Britain.

[107] Toomela, A. (2015), Vygotsky's theory on the Procrustes' bed of linear thinking: looking for structural–systemic Theseus to save the idea of 'social formation of mind, Cult. Psychol. 21, 318–339. doi: https://doi.org/10.1177/1354067X15570490

[108] Vasileva, O., and Balyasnikova, N. (2019), (Re) Introducing Vygotsky's Thought: From Historical Overview to Contemporary Psychology, Frontiers in Psychology, Volume 10, Article 1515.

important for reaching a better understanding of the cognitive and psychological development of the individual. Nevertheless, although Vygotsky believed in the robustness of the systemic analysis of psychological functions, he also believed a single unique psychological system is made up of many interdependent components.[109] Each of the elements of the psychological system contributes to the functioning of the system as a whole, and if one element changes, then the whole system will be affected.[110] Similarly, when an element of the psychological system becomes one of its constituents, then the element also changes. Analogously, if the human mind can be a psychological system, then the elements which make it a whole functioning system must have developed from earlier basic elements. However, as the human mind becomes as one through the fusion of its elements, then the way in which psychological functioning behaves acquires new features. For example, decision making is affected by emotional states.[111] Nevertheless, the organisation of elements in a psychological system will follow a hierarchical structure. The implication is that some elements may be functionally below those above them.[112] With regard to the human mind, Vygotsky may have held the view that its elements were also structured in a hierarchical manner. For example, higher-level psychological functions such as decision making and the transmission of knowledge via language and speech are dependent on lower-level psychological functions such as the formation of concepts and memory.[113] It was Vygotsky's contention that isolated elements of cognition such as memory would 'merge' with higher-order psychological functions which developed much earlier, for example, speech.[114] However, it is not clear how lower-level psychological functions may affect higher-level psychological functions, especially in development.[115] Nevertheless, the system approach to the development of psychological functions led Vygotsky to acknowledge that the

[109] Toomela, A. (2015), Vygotsky's theory on the Procrustes' bed of linear thinking: looking for structural–systemic Theseus to save the idea of 'social formation of mind. Cult. Psychol. 21, 318–339. doi: https://doi.org/10.1177/1354067X15570490

[110] Vasileva, O., and Balyasnikova, N. (2019), (Re) Introducing Vygotsky's Thought: From Historical Overview to Contemporary Psychology, Frontiers in Psychology, Volume 10, Article 1515.

[111] Ibid.

[112] Ibid.

[113] Ibid.

[114] Ibid.

[115] Wertsch, J. V., and Tulviste, P. (1992), L. S. Vygotsky and contemporary developmental psychology. Dev. Psychol. 28, 548–557. doi: https://doi.org/10.1037/0012-1649.28.4.548

hierarchical organisation of psychological functions into systems would mean that a better understanding of the developmental processes an individual is subject to then increases the chances of achieving a better understanding of the human mind.[116] Moreover, when a component of a psychological system becomes fully integrated with the system, then the properties of both the system and the component change.[117] Once a child acquires the ability to speak and to understand language, this then acts as a medium of transmission of information between the mind of the child and its environment. This is in addition to the other ways in which a child can acquire information about its environment, for example, through its eyes, ears, touch and smell. However, language has the biggest impact on shifting psychological functions to a higher level as the newborn baby transits into childhood and then adulthood.[118] Furthermore, from Vygotsky's perspective to understand how human cognition develops, it is not enough to study the mind of an adult, which typically represents the final product of several years of psychological development. In this case, the development of cognition and the human mind can only be better understood through the study of how the brain of a newborn develops subject to the environment. This is specifically in the context of psychological processes which promote the development of a hierarchical psychological system and its functionality. Moreover, over time, as the child has new experiences using physical activity and verbal communications, neural connections in the brain will reorganise to form new psychological functional systems.[119] Thus, the first few years of a child's life are accompanied by a recurring series of rewiring of the brain.[120] Both disorders arising from brain damage and disorders which affect brain development can be better understood by considering the brain as a hierarchical

[116] Vasileva, O., and Balyasnikova, N. (2019), (Re) Introducing Vygotsky's Thought: From Historical Overview to Contemporary Psychology, Frontiers in Psychology, Volume 10, Article 1515.

[117] Kohler, W. (1947). Gestalt psychology, Liveright, New York.

[118] Vasileva, O., and Balyasnikova, N. (2019), (Re) Introducing Vygotsky's Thought: From Historical Overview to Contemporary Psychology, Frontiers in Psychology, Volume 10, Article 1515.

[119] Ibid.

[120] De Graaf-Peters, V. B., and Hadders-Algra, M. (2006), Ontogeny of the human central nervous system: what is happening when? Early Hum. Dev. 82, 257–266. doi: https://doi.org/10.1016/j.earlhumdev.2005.10.013

structure.[121] In this hierarchical ordering of psychological functions, damage to lower-level sub-systems will affect higher-level functions and damage to higher-level sub-systems may affect lower-level functions.

A systemic analysis of psychological functions can also benefit from cultural knowledge.[122] This is in the context of a search by psychological researchers in the last century for a universal theory of the development of the human brain and mind.[123] However, research in the first decade of the twenty-first century has indicated that culture does matter in affecting psychological functions and abilities.[124] In this case, whereas human beings are born with the same psychological mechanisms, processes and systems, cultural differences may result in the development of varying levels of psychological functions. Furthermore, differences in language complexity between diverse cultures may also facilitate differences in the development of not only psychological functions but also brain development. And in the context of language development and the mind, Vygotsky believed that the age of 2 is an important point for cognitive development because it is at this age speech and thought processes begin to integrate.[125] Moreover, according to Vygotsky, it is at the age of 2 that a child's knowledge of vocabulary increases rapidly, and it is able to associate the extent of the use of language with behaviours, actions and the immediate environment.[126] As a result, the developing child is able to use language and thought processes not only for communication but also for problem solving. In the development of human cognition, language therefore plays numerous roles.[127] Firstly, language allows an infant not only to acquire

[121] Vasileva, O., and Balyasnikova, N. (2019), (Re) Introducing Vygotsky's Thought: From Historical Overview to Contemporary Psychology, Frontiers in Psychology, Volume 10, Article 1515.

[122] Ibid.

[123] Vasileva, O., and Balyasnikova, N. (2019), (Re) Introducing Vygotsky's Thought: From Historical Overview to Contemporary Psychology, Frontiers in Psychology, Volume 10, Article 1515.

[124] Benson, J. E., and Sabbagh, M. A. (2010), Theory of mind and executive functioning: a developmental neuropsychological approach, IN Developmental social cognitive neuroscience, Zelazo, P., Chandler, M., and Crone, E.(eds), Psychology Press, New York.

[125] Vasileva, O., and Balyasnikova, N. (2019), (Re) Introducing Vygotsky's Thought: From Historical Overview to Contemporary Psychology, Frontiers in Psychology, Volume 10, Article 1515.

[126] Ibid.

[127] Mahmoodi-Shahrebabaki, M. (2019). Vygotsky, Education, and Literacy. Unpublished manuscript, Department of Literacy Studies, Middle Tennessee State University.

knowledge, but over time, to construct distinct pieces of knowledge into a coherent framework. Secondly, language is required for the acquisition of knowledge and knowledge is required for the acquisition of language. Thirdly, the thoughts of children will be evident in the language they use. Lastly, the use of language allows children not only to solve problems but also to reflect on their own behaviours.

In terms of Vygotsky's thinking, the environment faced by a human being is one that is affected by both social and cultural factors.[128] Moreover, the environment is most immediately created by humans and the space between humans is integrated through communication using language. It was the connection of a human environment and the use of language which were most important for Vygotsky, especially from the perspective of the development of cognition, a process he referred to as internalisation.[129] The latter could also be thought of as the process of generating and organising thoughts, which Vygotsky referred to as inner speech, using language by the child.[130] Inner speech facilitates not only the organisation of thoughts but also the exchange of thoughts through language and the use of speech. However, in addition to the environment and the use of language in mediating the environment, the development of human cognition is dependent on more knowledgeable others (MKOs) and zone proximal development (ZPD).[131] The former represents individuals who are more cognitively developed than the learner is, a parent in the eyes of a child. While the 'child' represents the gap between potential cognitive development and actual cognitive development as measured through the problem-solving ability.[132] Learners can internalise skills and increase their ZPD in the process by gaining knowledge from the MKOs.[133] An analytical framework, for studying the development of cognitive processes, which encompasses the acquisition and use of language by an infant in its socio-

[128] Stetsenko, A., and Arievitch, I. M. (2010), Cultural-historical activity theory: foundational worldview and major principles, IN The sociocultural turn in psychology: The contextual emergence of mind and self, Martin, J., and Kirschner, S. (Eds), Columbia University Press, New York.

[129] Vasileva, O., and Balyasnikova, N. (2019), (Re) Introducing Vygotsky's Thought: From Historical Overview to Contemporary Psychology, Frontiers in Psychology, Volume 10, Article 1515.

[130] Lewis, C. (2019), Vygotsky and Moral Education: A Response to and expansion of Tappan, Educational Philosophy and Theory, 51:1, 41-50.

[131] Ibid.

[132] Ibid.

[133] Ibid.

economic environment is crucial to understanding that such processes are non-individualistic.[134]

The Development of Measured Intelligence

Intelligence can be defined from three perspectives.[135] These include measured intelligence, social intelligence and biological intelligence. Measured intelligence is a composite of three features, error checking, persistence and mental processing speed. Eysenck's model of measured intelligence arises from the feature of tests that different individuals may achieve the same result while at the same time getting different questions wrong.

The relationship between intelligence and personality has been empirically evaluated by using three different methodologies.[136] The first method involves analysing correlations between measured indicators of personality and intelligence.[137] The second approach considers that intelligence is a composite part of personality, involving the development of measures of intelligence as a personality trait.[138] The third approach to investigating the link between intelligence and personality involves analysing the links between the dimensions of intelligence and the dimensions of personality.[139] This third approach has been used to evaluate the relationship between intelligence and personality using achievement requirements as a personality trait.[140] The findings of this empirical research used Eysenck's model of intelligence[141] in order to evaluate the relationship between personality

[134] Kontopodis, M. (2019) Transformative activist stance and pedagogy of daring: Moving beyond Lev Vygotsky in dialogue with Anna Stetsenko, Pedagogy, Culture & Society, 27:2, 301-304, DOI: https://doi.org/10.1080/14681366.2018.1475890

[135] Eysenck, H. J. (1992). Intelligence: the one and the many? IN Detterman, D.K (Ed.), Current topics in human intelligence, Vol. 2: is mind modular or unitary? (pp. 83–116). Ablex, Norwood, NJ.

[136] Harris, J. (2004), Measured Intelligence, achievement, openness to experience and creativity, Personality and Individual Differences, 36, pp. 913-929.

[137] Zeidner, M. (1995). Personality and trait correlates of intelligence IN Saklofske, D.H and Zeidner, M. (Eds.), International handbook of personality and intelligence (pp. 299–319). New York: Plenum Press.

[138] Ackerman, P. L. (1997). Personality, self-concept, interests and intelligence: which construct doesn't fit? Journal of Personality, 65, 171–204.

[139] Raad, B., and Schouwenburg, H. (1996), Personality in Learning and Education: A Review, European Journal of Personality, Vol. 10, Issue 5.

[140] Harris, J. (2004), Measured Intelligence, achievement, openness to experience and creativity, Personality and Individual Differences, 36, pp. 913-929.

[141] Eysenck, H. J. (1982), A model for intelligence, Springer-Verlag, New York.

traits and intelligence. In this case, error checking and persistence, behavioural features specified by Eysenck (1982) in his model, contributors to intelligence, were taken to be personality traits. The resulting analysis indicated that there was a positive relationship between intelligence and these personality traits. The idea that intelligence may be a composite of an individual's personality may also be rooted in the link associated with 'openness to experience'.[142] The latter is associated with the creative aspects of an individual.[143] It has also been empirically found that there is a positive correlation between 'openness to experience' and intelligence.[144] The link between 'openness to experience' and intelligence may be better understood by evaluating the differences in verbal reasoning scores between twins and single births.[145] In this case, the verbal reasoning scores of twins were much lower than those of single births.[146] The reason for this may be that differences in the post-natal environment favoured the cognitive development of the single-birth child compared to that of twins, and that both pre-birth and birth experiences had no impact on the cognitive development of either single births or twins.[147] The difference between the measured intelligence of twins and that of single births highlights the importance of the quality of a child's post-natal environment for its cognitive development.

There are two types of processes associated with human cognition.[148] The first is a sub-conscious emotional response which does not involve a 'cognitive' assessment of the situation, and is therefore automatic. The second is a measured response based on a cognitive assessment of the situation. This second response may be comparable with the axioms of

[142] McCrae, R. R., and Costa, P. T. Jr., (1997), Conceptions and correlates of openness to experience IN Hogan, R., Johnson, J.A and Briggs, S. R (Eds.), Handbook of personality psychology (pp. 825–847), Academic Press, San Diego, CA.

[143] McCrae, R. R. (1987), Creativity, divergent thinking, and openness to experience. Journal of Personality and Social Psychology, 52, 1258–1265.

[144] Harris, J. (2004), Measured Intelligence, achievement, openness to experience and creativity, Personality and Individual Differences, 36, pp. 913-929.

[145] Record, R.G., McKeown, T., and Edwards, J. (1970), An Investigation of the difference in measured intelligence between twins and single births, Ann. Hum. Genet., Lond, 34, 11.

[146] Ibid.

[147] Ibid.

[148] Kahneman, D. (2011), Thinking, fast and slow, Macmillan, London.

probability theory.[149] The former can be defined as emotional intelligence. Emotional intelligence (EI) is the ability to recognise, show, appreciate, control and utilise human emotions.[150] Some researchers believe that EI is different from features of measured intelligence associated with personality and intelligence, playing an important role in the development of an individual.[151] Moreover, empirical findings suggest that the quality of such an ability will have positive feedback effects on performance at work, in relationships as well as on health and academic performance.[152] For example, the development of team emotional intelligence has a positive feedback effect on separating relationship conflict and task conflict.[153] Therefore, if constructive ways can be found to improve emotional intelligence, then the effects on individual psychological well-being can only be positive.[154] But in order to improve the level of an individual's emotional intelligence, it is first necessary to measure it. This is achievable using a competency-based measure based upon which a questionnaire can be derived.[155] Nevertheless, perhaps further empirical work is required to confirm whether policies to develop emotional intelligence will have a positive impact on work performance, both academic and non-academic[156]—although it has been empirically found that in an organisation context, emotional intelligence is a contributing factor towards individual success.[157] However, emotional intelligence falls within the con-

[149] Dellermann, D., Ebel, P., Sollner, M., and Leimeister, J. (2019), Hybrid Intelligence, Bus Inf Syst Eng 61 (5), pp. 637-643.

[150] Petrides, K. V., and Furnham, A. (2003). Trait emotional intelligence: Behavioural validation in two studies of emotion recognition and reactivity to mood induction. European Journal of Personality, 17, 39–57. doi: https://doi.org/10.1002/per.466

[151] Ciarrachi, J., Chan, A., and Bajgar, J. (2001), measuring emotional intelligence in adolescents, Personality and Individual Differences, 31, pp. 1105-1119.

[152] Martins, A., Ramalho, N., & Morin, E. (2010). A comprehensive meta-analysis of the relationship between emotional intelligence and health. Personality and Individual Differences, 49, 554–564. doi: https://doi.org/10.1016/j.paid.2010.05.029

[153] Lee, C., and Wang, C. (2017), The Effect of Team Emotional Intelligence on Team Process and Effectiveness, Journal of Management and Organisation, 25:6, pp. 844-859.

[154] Kotsou, I., Mikolajczak, M., Heeren, A., Gregoire, J., and Leys, C. (2019), Improving Emotional Intelligence: A Systematic Review of Existing Work and Future Challenges, Emotion Review, Vol. 11, No. 2, pp. 151-165.

[155] Dulewicz, V., and Higgs, M. (1999), Can emotional intelligence be measured and developed, Leadership & Organisation. Development Journal 20/5, pp. 242-252.

[156] Ibid.

[157] Dulewicz, S.V. and Higgs, M.J. (1998a), Emotional intelligence: managerial fad or valid construct?', Henley Working. Paper 9813, Henley Management College.

text of 'multiples intelligences', which also includes cognitive abilities.[158] The latter is dependent on the environment in which an individual lives and works. Therefore, if the work environment is not sufficiently conducive, then it may be the case that not only does cognitive intelligence fail to develop but so does emotional intelligence.[159] In the context of the nature versus nurture debate, it has been found that both intelligence and practice are important for the lifelong development of complex cognitive skills.[160] And while IQ is a measure of general cognitive ability, it should be a measure of an evolutionary formative construct.[161]

Cognitive ability may be difficult to compare because current tests provide a range of scores which do not have any basis in psychometric theory.[162] The dearth of test scores available commercially may be due the need of the test publishers to generate revenues.[163] Studies into the impact of training on the development of emotional intelligence also have flaws, although it is evident that such training does positively impact on emotional intelligence.[164] For example, a study has found that following emotional intelligence training, optimal performance was reached in decision-making tasks which involved emotions.[165] Nevertheless, there are a number of reasons as to why the impact of training on improving emotional intelligence may be inconclusive. Firstly, the emotional intelligence conceptual model may be devised incorrectly with the result that measurement problems may emerge. Secondly, there could be information asym-

[158] Gardner, H. (1983), Frames of Mind, Harper-Collins, New York, NY.

[159] Dulewicz, S.V. and Higgs, M.J. (1998a), Emotional intelligence: managerial fad or valid construct?', Henley Working. Paper 9813, Henley Management College.

[160] Vaci, N., Edelsbrunner, P., Stern, E., Neubauer, A., Bilalic, M., and Grabner, R. (2019), The Joint Influence of Intelligence and Practice on Skill Development Throughout the Life Span, PNAS, Vol. 116, No. 37.

[161] Kovacs, K., and Conway, A. (2019), What is IQ? Life Beyond 'General Intelligence,' Current Directions in Psychological Science, Vol. 28(2), pp. 189-194.

[162] Beaujean, A., and Benson, N. (2019), Theoretically Consistent Cognitive Ability Test Development and Score Interpretation, Contemporary School Psychology, 23, pp. 126-137.

[163] Frazier, T. W., and Youngstrom, E. A. (2007), Historical increase in the number of factors measured by commercial tests of cognitive ability: are we over factoring? Intelligence, 35, 169–182. https://doi.org/10.1016/j.intell.2006.07.002

[164] Groves, K., McEnrue, M., and Shen, W. (2006), Developing and Measuring the emotional intelligence of Leaders, Journal of Management Development, Vol. 27, No. 2, pp. 225-250.

[165] Alkazei, A. et al. (2009), Increases in Emotional Intelligence After an Online Training Program Are Associated with Better Decision Making On the Iowa Gambling Task, Psychological Reports, Vol. 122 (3), pp. 853-879.

metry regarding the treatment, especially with regard to the duration of the treatment as well as the nature of the training involved. And lastly the lack of a control group may have prevented a viable analysis of the success or failure of the study to be concluded. Nevertheless, self-report measures may be developed which allow EI in adolescents to be reliably measured while controlling for the personality and cognitive measures of intelligence.[166] This would allow for training programmes to be developed which would facilitate skills development in adolescents, enabling them to manage the emotional difficulties they may encounter in their daily lives.[167] The need for adolescents to develop skills associated with emotion management acknowledges, to a certain extent, the emotional and mental health challenges faced by adolescents in today's world.[168]

The Development of Moral Understanding

Moral reasoning from a Piagetian perspective is to see the moral value of actions and decisions from the perspective of another person.[169] As a transition from childhood to adulthood, adolescence is representative of a period in one's life during which there is a conscious search for an identity of the self.[170] It may also be a period in one's life during which there may be a range of negative behaviours in evidence, primarily due to a lack of moral reasoning ability. In this case, it would seem appropriate if some form of moral reasoning training could be developed by reorganising cognitive thinking so that the development of moral reasoning is facilitated.[171] One way in which this can be achieved is by using cognitive behavioural therapy to restructure cognitive processes such that thinking will allow for negative behaviours to become 'overruled' by positive behaviours through improved moral reasoning.

[166] Ciarrachi, J., Chan, A., and Bajgar, J. (2001), measuring emotional intelligence in adolescents, Personality and Individual Differences, 31, pp. 1105-1119.

[167] Salovey, P., and Sluyter, D. J. (1997), Emotional Development and emotional intelligence: Educational Implications, Basic Books, New York.

[168] Asher, S.R., and Rose, A.J. (1997), Promoting children's social-emotional adjustment with peers IN Emotional development and emotional intelligence: Educational Implications, Basic Books, New York.

[169] Siregar, R., Taufik, A., and Yustiana, Y. (2020), Development of Moral Reasoning Using Cognitive Behavioral Therapy, The 2nd International Conference on Elementary Education, Vol. 2, Nomor 1.

[170] Ibid.

[171] Ibid.

Piaget believed that according to the level of the maturity of development, the state of a child's moral reasoning could be defined in two diverse ways. These included heteronomous morality and autonomous morality.[172] Nevertheless, children between the age of 7 and 10 are in a state of transition between heteronomous morality and autonomous morality, exhibiting features of both states, and are said to be in a semi-autonomous state. And it is the transition from heteronomous to autonomous moral reasoning which defines a child's development. In this case, it becomes evident from a Piagetian perspective that individuals who can think autonomously in the presence of laws and regulations and in the context of the difference between right and wrong have a well-developed sense of moral reasoning. In contrast to the Piagetian perspective, Kohlberg defines moral reasoning with regard to the structuring of thought rather than content and the difference between right and wrong.[173] Therefore, moral reasoning should not be an automatic ability to distinguish between good and bad behaviours but the cognitive processes which result in the making of that distinction. Thus, Kohlberg's theory of moral reasoning is one which is based on structure (thought processes) rather than content (innate ability to determine if an action is good or bad).[174] There are six stages to Kohlberg's theory of moral development.[175] These include punishment and obedience, actions satisfying self and others, behaviours allowing for peer approval, behaviour towards authority, behaviours according to acceptable societal standards and, finally, universal ethical principles.[176] These stages suggest a consistency in reasoning, although Kohlberg emphasises perspective, taking in the context of moral reasoning.[177] Reasoning may become inconsistent in the case of different perspectives. Another critique of Kohlberg's theory of moral development is that it may not be possible to

[172] Ibid.

[173] Kohlberg, L. (1976), Moral Stages and Moralization IN Lickona, T. (Ed.), Moral Development and Behavior: Theory, Research and Social Issues, Hot, Rinehart and Winston, New York.

[174] Siregar, R., Taufik, A., and Yustiana, Y. (2020), Development of Moral Reasoning Using Cognitive Behavioral Therapy, The 2nd International Conference on Elementary Education, Vol. 2, Nomor 1.

[175] Sullivan, E. (1977), A Study of Kohlberg's Structural Theory of Moral Development: A Critique of Liberal Social Science Ideology, Hum. Dev, 20, pp. 352-376.

[176] Ibid.

[177] Carpendale, J. (2000), Kohlberg and Piaget on Stages and Moral Reasoning, Developmental Review, 20, pp. 181-205.

apply it cross-culturally.[178] This is particularly because in Western tradition man is seen as a rational agent, whereas in Confucian tradition, for example, man is seen as an integral component of the universe.

It may also be considered that moral reasoning is a process which is guided by a framework of moral rules and responsibilities but based on individual circumstances as well as an understanding of social circumstances.[179] Although Kohlberg and Piaget focus on developing a theory of moral development based on the development of cognitive ability, there are differences between the work of the two.[180] In this context, there is a difference between the theories of moral development of Kohlberg and of Piaget. On the one hand, Piaget emphasises problems which are physical and logical. But Kohlberg emphasises problems which are associated with reasoning as well as with society. Therefore, Kohlberg's theory of moral development has been more broadly developed than that of Piaget. Kohlberg's theory of moral reasoning breaks down the process of reasoning into three levels, the pre-conventional, the conventional and the post-conventional.[181] However, according to Piaget, moral development relies upon the interaction with others, which in his view also stimulates the structures of cognitive development in the brain. Therefore, from the Piagetian perspective, there is a line of causation from the development of cognitive abilities of an individual to his/her moral development. Moreover, according to Piaget, moral reasoning can be developed in children through their education. Nevertheless, Kohlberg suggests that the development of moral reasoning may be dependent on three factors, opportunities to take specific roles, a particular moral situation and cognitive moral conflicts.[182] In the case of opportunities to take specific roles, the development of moral reasoning may be facilitated when circumstances expose individuals to other viewpoints. Contextually, this may occur when parents morally educate their children on the rights and

[178] Dien, D. (1982), A Chinese Perspective on Kohlberg's Theory of Moral Development, Developmental Review, 2, pp. 331-341.

[179] Kurtines, M. W and Gerwitz, J. L. (1992), Morality, Moral Behavior & Moral Development, Universitas Indonesia Press, Jakarta.

[180] Siregar, R., Taufik, A., and Yustiana, Y. (2020), Development of Moral Reasoning Using Cognitive Behavioral Therapy, The 2nd International Conference on Elementary Education, Vol. 2, Nomor 1.

[181] Ibid.

[182] Janssens, J and Geris, J. (1992), Child Rearing: Influence on Prosocial and Moral Development. University of Nijimegen, Netherlands.

wrongs of actions. For example, if a child is caught cheating in an exam at school, the parents of the child may be summoned to school by its headmaster—in which case, the child may be further reprimanded at home that it is morally wrong to cheat. Secondly, moral reasoning may develop in the context of a moral situation. For example, if a child witnesses a bullying incident at school, he/she may decide to report it to teachers out of a moral responsibility for the person(s) being bullied. Lastly, moral reasoning may develop because of differences in the moral reasoning between individuals with higher and lower reasoning abilities. In this context, when children conflict with others with higher-level moral reasoning skills, it is evident that such children will themselves develop higher-level moral reasoning skills. It has been found contextually that moral reasoning can also develop either through cultural factors[183] or by being emphasised in a family environment. In this case, the parents define the norms and boundaries of what they perceive to be morally correct, and this may facilitate the development of moral reasoning in the child.[184] Nevertheless, as discussed previously, the level of the development of moral reasoning is also dependent on the extent of cognitive development according to Kohlberg. In this case, the state of the level of education has an impact on the level of cognitive development and thus indirectly on the level of development of moral reasoning.[185] In other words, the higher the level of education, the more likely that a higher level of moral reasoning will develop. The positive correlation of higher levels of education with higher levels of moral reasoning may suggest that a programme of education to 'rewire' cognitive thinking towards improved moral reasoning may be beneficial for children and young adolescents. This rewiring of cognitive thinking processes is the emphasis of cognitive behavioural therapy.[186] However, Kohlberg's stages of moral development, moral development evolves to higher stages

[183] Zhang, Z. (2013), Children's Moral Reasoning: Influence of Culture and Collaborative Discussion. Thesis, Publication: University of Illinois at Urbana-Champaign.

[184] Janssens, J and Geris, J. (1992), Child Rearing: Influence on Prosocial and Moral Development, University of Nijimegen, Netherlands.

[185] Mayhew, M.J., Seifert, T.A., Pascarella, E.T. et al., (2012), Going Deep into Mechanisms for Moral Reasoning Growth: How Deep Learning Approaches Affect Moral Reasoning Development for First-year Students. Res High Educ **53,** 26–46. https://doi.org/10.1007/s11162-011-9226-3

[186] Siregar, R., Taufik, A., and Yustiana, Y. (2020), Development of Moral Reasoning Using Cognitive Behavioral Therapy, The 2nd International Conference on Elementary Education, Vol. 2, Nomor 1.

over a six-stage sequence,[187] maybe of no significant value to educators in assessing the extent of moral development in children because it relies upon knowing the effects of an individual's environment on the development of moral reasoning[188]—although the emphasis is on the rational thought of the individual rather than the impact of the environment.[189] However, it is important to understand the processes which lead to the effects. In contrast to Kohlberg's stage theory of moral development,[190] Vygotsky (1978) proposed a zone of proximal development theory for better understanding the context of learning situations.[191] This zone of proximal development allows for researchers to gain better insights into the development of moral reasoning not only through processes which have already occurred but also through processes which are in formation.[192] The Vygotskian approach to moral development allows for an analysis which combines the study of the development of self-awareness of moral values as well as those which result due to the moral intervention of elders, such as the parents of the child.[193] In fact research evidence suggests that there is a positive causative relationship between relevant parental behaviours, especially the level of moral reasoning when interacting with children and the development of moral reasoning in a child.[194] This is also dependent on the state of the attitude of the child to its environment as well as its behaviour. These are developed by the age of 7, increas-

[187] Tappan, M., and Brown, L. (1989), Toward a Narrative Approach to Moral Development and Moral Education, Harvard Educational Review, Vol. 59, No. 2.

[188] Crawford, P. (2001), Educating for Moral Ability: Reflections on Moral Development based on Vygotsky's Theory of Concept Formation, Journal of Moral Education, 30, 2, pp. 113-129.

[189] Nokes, K. (1989), Rethinking Moral Reasoning Theory, Journal of Nursing Scholarship, Vol. 21, No. 3.

[190] Kohlberg, L. (1976) Moral stages and moralization: the cognitive developmental approach, IN: Moral Development and Behaviour: theory, research, and social issues, Lickona, T. (Eds), Holt, Rinehart and Winston, New York.

[191] Vygotsky, L.S. (1978), Mind in Society: the development of higher psychological processes, Cole, M., John-Steiner, S., Scribner, S., and Souberman, E. (Eds), Harvard University Press, Cambridge.

[192] Crawford, P. (2001), Educating for Moral Ability: Reflections on Moral Development based on Vygotsky's Theory of Concept Formation, Journal of Moral Education, 30, 2, pp. 113-129.

[193] Tappan, M. (1998), Moral education in the zone of proximal development, Journal of Moral Education, 27, pp. 141–160.

[194] Walker, L., and Hennig, K. (1999), Parenting Style and the Development of Moral Reasoning, Journal of Moral Education, 28, 3, pp. 359-374.

ing to the age of 10, then with no change until the age of 14, showing a progressive decline thereafter.[195] However, in the development of moral judgement in children, this is characterised by a conceptual continuity rather than a discontinuity.[196] In the context of a child's environmental attitude, parental behaviour will also impact upon the emotional and social competence of the child. More specifically, when a child expresses emotions and a parent(s) responds negatively, then this will facilitate the development of low social competence and negative emotions on the part of the child.[197] Therefore, it is evident that the embedding of moral values within the psyche of adolescents in particular is very much dependent upon good parenting.[198] Therefore, parents should be guided towards crafting a parenting style which allows for a positive enriching and nourishing environment for children to grow.[199] Research suggests that the emotional development of a child also contributes to its moral development.[200] Emotional dispositions are common to all animals.[201] But in humans a level of rationality is able to control emotions such that moral development evolves. Moral development is also important for effective cooperation amongst individual, who as they age recognise the importance of moral norms and social norms, such as loyalty to the group, for such cooperation.[202] Furthermore, in the context of the development of moral reasoning, younger children are more likely to make moral

[195] Otto, S., Evans, G., Moon, M., and Kaiser, F. (2019), The Development of Children's Environmental Attitude and Behaviour, Global Environmental Change, 58.

[196] Margoni, F., and Sunan, L. (2020), Conceptual Continuity in the Development of Intent-Based Moral Judgement, Journal of Experimental Child Psychology, 194.

[197] Eisenberg, N., Cumberland, A., and Spinrad, T. (1998), Parental Socialisation of Emotion, Psychological Inquiry, 9, 4.

[198] Fatima, S., Dawood, S., and Munir, M. (2020), Parenting Styles, Moral Identity and Prosocial Behaviours in Adolescents, Current Psychology, https://doi.org/10.1007/s12144-020-00609-3

[199] Ibid.

[200] Eisenberg, N. (2000), Emotion, Regulation and Moral Development, Annu. Rev. Psychol, 51, pp. 665-697.

[201] Pipatti, O. (2019), Morality Mae Visible: Edward Westermarck's Moral and Social Theory, Routledge, New York.

[202] McGuire, L., Rizzo, M., Killen, M., and Rutland, A. (2019), The Role of Competitive and Cooperative Norms in the Development of Deviant Evaluations, Child Development, Vol. 90, No. 6.

judgements of other based on their intentions rather than on the outcomes of their actions, while in older children the case is not so clear cut.[203]

Conclusion

The first few years of a child's life are ones in which there is significant development of the brain, the nervous system as well as motor development. This is specifically in the context of not only the addition of new connections but also the strengthening of existing connections. Moreover, it has been found through neuroimaging techniques that movement (motor activity) and the completion of tasks which require thinking processes serve to simultaneously activate two regions of the brain—the dorsolateral prefrontal cortex as well as the neo-cerebellum. The simultaneous motor activity and the completion of tasks requiring thinking and the stimulation of brain areas is not a coincidence. In this case, theories associated with cognitive development rely upon this causality. Piaget's theory of cognitive development is dependent upon the causality between simultaneous thinking and physical movement and the actuation of areas of the brain. Therefore, it is evident that Piaget's theory promotes the idea that as incremental psychological changes occur in the brain, leading to a change in its overall structure, cognitive processes develop as a result. Piaget's theory is based on four stages of psychological development. These include the Sensorimotor Period (birth to the age of 2), the Preoperational Thought Period (age 2 to age 7), the Concrete Operations Period (age 7 to age 11) and the Formal Operations Period (age 11 to age 15). Research suggests that the environment and experiences faced by an infant in the Sensorimotor Period will set the foundations for a lifetime of development. Furthermore, during this period much of an infant's brain development takes place due to the stimulation of the brain via movement of limbs and muscles as well as through its senses. The latter allows the infant to become more aware of its environment. As a result of mental and physical stimulation, over 2.4 million synapses are formed every minute in the brain of an infant in its first 12 months. And within the first 24 months of the life of an infant, its brain has already reached 80% of an adult's brain size. Typical measures of cognition in infants have been identified as the level of working memory, the level of concentration and the ability to

[203] Hilton, B., and Kuhlmeior, V. (2019), Intention Attribution and the Development of Moral Evaluation, Frontiers in Psychology, Vol. 9.

multi-task. These measures are also indicators of executive function. The level of development of this in infants is seen as a predictor of future academic performance.

In contrast to Piaget's theory of cognitive development, which emphasises modular changes in the psychological cognitive system, Vygotsky places greater emphasis on the development of the entire psychological system. In this case, according to Vygotsky, the development of one component in a psychological system changes the functionality of the entire system. Thus, the development of memory may change the way in which the brain functions because it will be able to 'store' more information. Therefore, it may be the case that with more information, the functioning of the brain can lead to better decisions. Furthermore, when a child acquires the ability to speak, then information in the mind of the child about its thoughts, feelings and the environment can be exchanged with others. It has also been found through research that the nature of the post-natal environment of a child is especially important for the extent of its potential for cognitive development. As a child develops, however, in adapting to its environment, the intelligent control of its emotions (emotional intelligence) may be important to its overall development.

Moral reasoning, the ability to discern good from bad behaviour, may also be important for the development of a child into adulthood. The ability to discern the content of one's own actions and the action of others, good actions or bad actions, is a typical Piagetian perspective. In contrast, according to the Kohlberg perspective, the structure of thought is more important than content awareness for the development of moral reasoning. Therefore, according to Kohlberg, the cognitive processes which lead to content awareness are more important than the automatic recognition of content awareness with regard to the development of moral reasoning. However, the automatic recognition of content awareness of behaviours, one which arises from an increasing self-awareness and that instilled by peers and elders, represents the Vygotskian approach to moral development.

References

Ackerman, P. L. (1997). Personality, Self-Concept, Interests and Intelligence: Which Construct Doesn't Fit? *Journal of Personality, 65*, 171–204.

Alkazei, A., et al. (2009). Increases in Emotional Intelligence After an Online Training Program Are Associated with Better Decision Making on the Iowa Gambling Task. *Psychological Reports, 122*(3), 853–879.

Asher, S. R., & Rose, A. J. (1997). *Promoting Children's Social-Emotional Adjustment with Peers in Emotional Development and Emotional Intelligence: Educational Implications*. Basic Books.

Barkovich, J. A., Kjos, B. O., Jackson, D. E., & Norman, D. (1988). Normal Maturation of the Neonatal and Infant Brain: MR Imaging at 1.5 T. *Neuroradiology, 166*, 173–180.

Beaujean, A., & Benson, N. (2019). Theoretically Consistent Cognitive Ability Test Development and Score Interpretation. *Contemporary School Psychology, 23*, 126–137.

Benson, J. E., & Sabbagh, M. A. (2010). Theory of Mind and Executive Functioning: A Developmental Neuropsychological Approach. In P. Zelazo, M. Chandler, & E. Crone (Eds.), *Developmental Social Cognitive Neuroscience*. Psychology Press.

Best, J., Miller, P., & Naglieri, J. (2011). Relations Between Executive Function and Academic Achievement from Ages 5 to 17 in a Large, Representative National Sample. *Learning and Individual Differences, 21*, 327–336.

Bowman, B., Donovan, S., & Bums, S. (Eds.). (2001). *Committee on Early Childhood Pedagogy*. National Academy Press, National Research Institute.

Brody, B., Kinney, H., Kloman, A., & Gilles, F. (1987). Sequence of Central Nervous System Myelination in Human; Infancy: I. An Autopsy Study of Myelination. *Journal of Neuropathology & Experimental Neurology, 46*, 283–301.

Buck-Morss, S. (1975). Socio-Economic Bias in Piaget's Theory and Its Implications for Cross-Cultural Studies. *Human Development, 18*, 35–49.

Carpendale, J. (2000). Kohlberg and Piaget on Stages and Moral Reasoning. *Developmental Review, 20*, 181–205.

Casey, B. J., Giedd, J. N., & Thomas, K. M. (2000). Structural and Functional Brain Development and Its Relation to Cognitive Development. *Biological Psychology, 54*, 241–257.

Chaparro, J., Sojourner, A., & Wiswall, M. (2020). *Early Childhood Care and Cognitive Development, National Bureau of Economic research, Working Paper 26813.*

Chugani, H. T., Phelps, M. E., & Mazziotta, J. C. (1987). Positron Emission Tomography Study of Human Brain Functional Development. *Annals of Neurology, 22*, 487–497.

Ciarrachi, J., Chan, A., & Bajgar, J. (2001). Measuring Emotional Intelligence in Adolescents. *Personality and Individual Differences, 31*, 1105–1119.

Clark, D. A., & Beck, A. T. (2010). Cognitive Theory and Therapy of Anxiety and Depression: Convergence with Neurobiological Findings. *Trends in Cognitive Sciences, 14*(9), 418–424.

Combs-Orme, T. (2013). Epigenesis and the Social Work Imperative. *Social Work, 58*(1), 23–30.

Compton, W., Dowling, G., & Garavan, H. (2019). Ensuring the Best Use of Data: The Adolescent Brain Cognitive Development Study. *JAMA Paediatrics, 173*(9).

Crawford, P. (2001). Educating for Moral Ability: Reflections on Moral Development Based on Vygotsky's Theory of Concept Formation. *Journal of Moral Education, 30*(2), 113–129.

Dasen, P. R. (1994). Culture and Cognitive Development from a Piagetian Perspective. In W. J. Lonner & R. Malpass (Eds.), *Psychology and Culture* (pp. 145–149). Allyn & Bacon.

De Graaf-Peters, V. B., & Hadders-Algra, M. (2006). Ontogeny of the Human Central Nervous System: What Is Happening When? *Early Human Development, 82*, 257–266. https://doi.org/10.1016/j.earlhumdev.2005.10.013

Dellermann, D., Ebel, P., Sollner, M., & Leimeister, J. (2019). Hybrid Intelligence. *Business and Information Systems Engineering, 61*(5), 637–643.

Deoni, S. C., et al. (2011). Mapping Infant Brain Myelination with Magnetic Resonance Imaging. *Journal of Neuroscience, 31*(2), 784–791. https://doi.org/10.1523/JNEUROSCI.2106-10.2011

Dhuey, E., Figlio, D., Karbownik, K., & Roth, J. (2019). School Starting Age and Cognitive Development. *Journal of Policy Analysis and Management, 38*(3), 538–578.

Diamond, A. (1990). The Development and Neural Bases of Memory Functions as Indexed by the AB and Delayed Response Tasks in Human Infants and Infant Monkeys. *Annals of the New York Academy of Sciences, 60*, 231–267.

Diamond, A. (2007). Interrelated and Interdependent. *Developmental Science, 10*, 152–158.

Diamond, A. (2013). Executive Functions. *Annual Review of Psychology, 64*, 135–168.

Dien, D. (1982). A Chinese Perspective on Kohlberg's Theory of Moral Development. *Developmental Review, 2*, 331–341.

DiPietro, J. A. (2000). Baby and the Brain: Advances in Child Development. *Annual Review of Public Health, 21*, 455–471.

Drange, N., & Havnes, T. (2019). Early Childcare and Cognitive Development: Evidence from an Assignment Lottery. *Journal of Labour Economics, 37*(2).

Driver, R. (1978). When Is a Stage Not a Stage? A Critique of Piaget's Theory of Cognitive Development and Its Application to Science Education. *Educational Research, 21*(1), 54–61.

Dulewicz, S.V., & Higgs, M. J. (1998). *Emotional Intelligence: Managerial Fad or Valid Construct?, Henley Working Paper 9813*. Henley Management College.

Dulewicz, V., & Higgs, M. (1999). Can Emotional Intelligence Be Measured and Developed. *Leadership & Organisation Development Journal, 20*(5), 242–252.

Duveen, G. (2000). Piaget Ethnographer. *Social Science Information, 39*(1), 79–97.

Egan, M., Neely-Barnes, S., & Combs-Orme, T. (2011). Integrating Neuroscience into the Lifespan. *Journal of Social Work Education, 47*(2), 269–282.

Eisenberg, N. (2000). Emotion, Regulation and Moral Development. *Annual Review of Psychology, 51*, 665–697.

Eisenberg, N., Cumberland, A., & Spinrad, T. (1998). Parental Socialisation of Emotion. *Psychological Inquiry, 9*, 4.

Eysenck, H. J. (1982). *A Model for Intelligence*. Springer.

Eysenck, H. J. (1992). Intelligence: The One and the Many? In D. K. Detterman (Ed.), *Current Topics in Human Intelligence, Vol. 2: Is Mind Modular or Unitary?* (pp. 83–116). Ablex.

Fatima, S., Dawood, S., & Munir, M. (2020). Parenting Styles, Moral Identity and Prosocial Behaviours in Adolescents. *Current Psychology*. https://doi.org/10.1007/s12144-020-00609-3

Flavell, J. (1982). On Cognitive Development. *Child Development, 53*(1), 1–10.

Frazier, T. W., & Youngstrom, E. A. (2007). Historical Increase in the Number of Factors Measured by Commercial Tests of Cognitive Ability: Are We Over Factoring? *Intelligence, 35*, 169–182. https://doi.org/10.1016/j.intell.2006.07.002

Fuster, J. (2002). Frontal Lobe and Cognitive Development. *Journal of Neurocytology, 31*, 373–385.

Gabbard, C. (2008). *Lifelong Motor Development* (5th ed.). Pearson Education.

Gallahue, D., & Ozmun, J. (2002). *Understanding Motor Development: Infants, Children, Adolescents, Adults* (5th ed.). McGraw Hill.

Gardner, H. (1983). *Frames of Mind*. HarperCollins.

Gelman, R. (1978). Cognitive Development. *Annual Review of Psychology, 29*, 297–332.

Gibson, J. (1979). *The Ecological Approach to Visual Perception*. Lawrence Erlbaum.

Groves, K., McEnrue, M., & Shen, W. (2006). Developing and Measuring the Emotional Intelligence of Leaders. *Journal of Management Development, 27*(2), 225–250.

Harris, J. (2004). Measured Intelligence, Achievement, Openness to Experience and Creativity. *Personality and Individual Differences, 36*, 913–929.

Herrero, M. T., Barcia, C., & Navarro, J. M. (2002). Functional Anatomy of Thalamus and Basal Ganglia. *Child's Nervous System, 18*, 386–404.

Hilton, B., & Kuhlmeior, V. (2019). Intention Attribution and the Development of Moral Evaluation. *Frontiers in Psychology, 9*.

Huitt, W., & Hummel, J. (2003). *Piaget's Theory of Cognitive development, Educational Psychology Interactive*. Valdosta State University.

Huttenlocher, P. R. (1990). Morphometric Study of Human Cerebral Cortex Development. *Neuropsychologia, 28*, 517–527.

Janssens, J., & Geris, J. (1992). *Child Rearing: Influence on Prosocial and Moral Development*. University of Nijimegen.

Johnson, M. H. (2001). Functional Brain Development in Humans. *Nature, 2*, 475–483.

Johnson, S. (2003). The Nature of Cognitive Development. *Trends in Cognitive Science, 7*(3).

Kahneman, D. (2011). *Thinking, Fast and Slow*. Macmillan.

Kamii, C. (1982). *Number in Preschool and Kindergarten: Educational Implications of Piaget's Theory*. National Association for the Education of Young Children.

Kazi, S., Kazali, E., Makris, N., Spanoudis, G., & Demetriou, A. (2019). Cognizance in Cognitive Development: A Longitudinal Study. *Cognitive Development, 52*, 100805.

Knickmeyer, R. C., et al. (2008). A Structural MRI Study of Human Brain Development from Birth to 2 Years. *The Journal of Neuroscience, 28*(47), 12176–12182.

Kohlberg, L. (1976). Moral Stages and Moralization: The Cognitive Developmental Approach. In T. Lickona (Ed.), *Moral Development and Behaviour: Theory, Research, and Social Issues*. Holt, Rinehart and Winston.

Kohler, W. (1947). *Gestalt Psychology*. Liveright.

Kolb, B., & Fantie, B. D. (2009). Development of the Child's Brain and Behavior. In C. R. Reynolds & E. Fletcher-Janzen (Eds.), *Handbook of Clinical Child Neuropsychology* (3rd ed., pp. 19–46). Springer.

Kontopodis, M. (2019). Transformative Activist Stance and Pedagogy of Daring: Moving Beyond Lev Vygotsky in Dialogue with Anna Stetsenko. *Pedagogy, Culture & Society, 27*(2), 301–304. https://doi.org/10.1080/14681366.2018.1475890

Kotsou, I., Mikolajczak, M., Heeren, A., Gregoire, J., & Leys, C. (2019). Improving Emotional Intelligence: A Systematic Review of Existing Work and Future Challenges. *Emotion Review, 11*(2), 151–165.

Kovacs, K., & Conway, A. (2019). What Is IQ? Life Beyond 'General Intelligence'. *Current Directions in Psychological Science, 28*(2), 189–194.

Kurtines, M. W., & Gerwitz, J. L. (1992). *Morality, Moral Behavior & Moral Development*. Universitas Indonesia Press.

Larsen, R. (1973). Levels of Conceptual Development in Melodic Permutations Concepts Based on Piagets Theory. *Journal of Research in Music Education, 21*(3), 256–263.

Lee, C., & Wang, C. (2017). The Effect of Team Emotional Intelligence on Team Process and Effectiveness. *Journal of Management and Organisation, 25*(6), 844–859.

Lefmann, T., & Combs-Orme, T. (2013). Early Brain Development for Social Work Practice: Integrating Neuroscience with Piaget's Theory of Cognitive Development. *Journal of Human Behaviour in the Social Environment, 23*, 640–647.

Levin, H. S., Culhane, K. A., Hartmann, J., Evankovich, K., & Mattson, A. J. (1991). Developmental Changes in Performance on Tests of Purported Frontal Lobe Functioning. *Developmental Neuropsychology, 7*, 377–395.

Lewis, C. (2019). Vygotsky and Moral Education: A Response to and Expansion of Tappan. *Educational Philosophy and Theory, 51*(1), 41–50.

Luna, B., et al. (2001). Maturation of Widely Distributed Brain Function Subserves Cognitive Development. *NeuroImage, 13*, 786–793.

Luria, A. R., & Vygotsky, L. S. (1930/1992). *Ape, Primitive Man and Child, 1930/1992*. Harvester Wheatsheaf.

Mahmoodi-Shahrebabaki, M. (2019). *Vygotsky, Education, and Literacy. Unpublished Manuscript*, Department of Literacy Studies, Middle Tennessee State University.

Margoni, F., & Sunan, L. (2020). Conceptual Continuity in the Development of Intent-Based Moral Judgement. *Journal of Experimental Child Psychology, 194*.

Martins, A., Ramalho, N., & Morin, E. (2010). A Comprehensive Meta-Analysis of the Relationship Between Emotional Intelligence and Health. *Personality and Individual Differences, 49*, 554–564. https://doi.org/10.1016/j.paid.2010.05.029

Mayer, S. J. (2005). The Early Evolution of Jean Piaget's Clinical Method. *History of Psychology, 8*(4), 362–382.

Mayhew, M. J., Seifert, T. A., Pascarella, E. T., et al. (2012). Going Deep into Mechanisms for Moral Reasoning Growth: How Deep Learning Approaches Affect Moral Reasoning Development for First-Year Students. *Research in Higher Education, 53*, 26–46. https://doi.org/10.1007/s11162-011-9226-3

McCrae, R. R. (1987). Creativity, Divergent Thinking, and Openness to Experience. *Journal of Personality and Social Psychology, 52*, 1258–1265.

McCrae, R. R., & Costa, P. T., Jr. (1997). Conceptions and Correlates of Openness to Experience. In R. Hogan, J. A. Johnson, & S. R. Briggs (Eds.), *Handbook of Personality Psychology* (pp. 825–847). Academic Press.

McGuire, L., Rizzo, M., Killen, M., & Rutland, A. (2019). The Role of Competitive and Cooperative Norms in the Development of Deviant Evaluations. *Child Development, 90*(6).

Niederer, I., Kriemler, S., Gut, J., Hartmann, T., Schindler, C., Barral, J., et al. (2011). Relationship of Aerobic Fitness and Motor Skills with Memory and Attention in Preschoolers (Ballabeina): A Cross-Sectional and Longitudinal Study. *BMC Pediatrics, 11*, 34.

Nokes, K. (1989). Rethinking Moral Reasoning Theory. *Journal of Nursing Scholarship, 21*(3).

Ojose, B. (2008). Applying Piaget's Theory of Cognitive Development to Mathematics Instruction. *The Mathematics Educator, 18*(1), 26–30.

Otto, S., Evans, G., Moon, M., & Kaiser, F. (2019). The Development of Children's Environmental Attitude and Behaviour. *Global Environmental Change, 58*, 101947.

Paldino, A., & Purpura, D. (1979). Quantitative Analysis of the Spatial Distribution of Axonal and Dendritic Terminals of Hippocampal Pyramidal Neurons in Immature Human Brain. *Experimental Neurology, 64*, 604–619.

Paterson, S. J., Heim, S., Friedman, J. T., Choudhury, N., & Benasich, A. A. (2006). Development of Structure and Function in the Infant Brain: Implications for Cognition, Language and Social Behavior. *Neuroscience and Biobehavioural Reviews, 30*, 1087–1105.

Peng, P., & Kievit, R. (2020). The Development of Academic Achievement and Cognitive Abilities: A Bidirectional Perspective. *Child Development Perspectives, 14*(1), 15–20.

Pereira, K., Valentini, N., & Saccani, R. (2016). Brazilian Infant Motor and Cognitive Development: Longitudinal Influence of Risk Factors. *Pediatrics International, 58*, 1297–1306.

Petrides, K. V., & Furnham, A. (2003). Trait Emotional Intelligence: Behavioural Validation in Two Studies of Emotion Recognition and Reactivity to Mood Induction. *European Journal of Personality, 17*, 39–57. https://doi.org/10.1002/per.466

Piaget, J. (1963). *The Origins of Intelligence in Children*. W.W. Norton & Company.

Piaget, J. (1973). *The Child and Reality: Problems of Genetic Psychology*. Penguin Books.

Piaget, J., & Cook, M. (1952). *The Origins of Intelligence in Children*. International Universities Press.

Piaget, J., & Cook, M. (1954). The Development of Object Construct. In *The Construction of Reality in the Child* (pp. 3–96). Basic Books.

Piaget, J., & Inhelder, B. (1969). *The Psychology of the Child*. Basic Books.

Piek, J., Dawson, L., Smith, L., & Gasson, N. (2008). The Role of Early Fine and Gross Motor Development on Later Motor and Cognitive Ability. *Human Movement Science, 27*(2008), 668–681.

Pipatti, O. (2019). *Morality Mae Visible: Edward Westermarck's Moral and Social Theory*. Routledge.

Raad, B., & Schouwenburg, H. (1996). Personality in Learning and Education: A Review. *European Journal of Personality, 10*, 5.

Record, R. G., McKeown, T., & Edwards, J. (1970). An Investigation of the Difference in Measured Intelligence Between Twins and Single Births. *Annals of Human Genetics, 34*, 11.

Riegel, K. (1973). Dialectic Operations: The Final Period of Cognitive Development. *Human Development, 16*, 346–370.

Salovey, P., & Sluyter, D. J. (1997). *Emotional Development and Emotional Intelligence: Educational Implications*. Basic Books.

Schore, A. N. (2001). Effects of a Secure Attachment Relationship on Right Brain Development, Affect Regulation, and Infant Mental Health. *Infant Mental Health Journal, 22*(1–2), 7–66.

Shonkoff, J., & Phillips, D. (2000). *From Neurons to Neighbourhoods: The Science of Early Childhood Development.* National Academy Press.

Silverthorn, P. (1999). *Jean Piaget's Theory of Development.* Retrieved from http://chd.gse.gmu.edu/immersion/knowledgebase/theorists/constructivism/Piaget.htm

Siregar, R., Taufik, A., & Yustiana, Y. (2020). Development of Moral Reasoning Using Cognitive Behavioral Therapy. In *The 2nd International Conference on Elementary Education* (Vol. 2).

Smillie, D. (1982). Rethinking Piaget's Theory of Infancy. *Human Development, 25,* 282–294.

Stetsenko, A., & Arievitch, I. M. (2010). Cultural-Historical Activity Theory: Foundational Worldview and Major Principles. In J. Martin & S. Kirschner (Eds.), *The Sociocultural Turn in Psychology: The Contextual Emergence of Mind and Self.* Columbia University Press.

Sullivan, E. (1977). A Study of Kohlberg's Structural Theory of Moral Development: A Critique of liberal Social Science Ideology. *Human Development, 20,* 352–376.

Tappan, M. (1998). Moral Education in the Zone of Proximal Development. *Journal of Moral Education, 27,* 141–160.

Tappan, M., and Brown, L. (1989), Toward a Narrative Approach to Moral Development and Moral Education, Harvard Educational Review, 59 2

Tau, G. Z., & Peterson, G. S. (2010). Normal Development of Brain Circuits. *Neuropsychopharmacology Reviews, 35,* 147–168.

Terumitsu, M., Ikeda, K., Kwee, I. L., & Nakada, T. (2009). Participation of Primary Motor Cortex area 4a in Complex Sensory Processing: 3.0-T fMRI Study. *Neuroreport, 20*(7), 679–683.

Thelen, E., & Smith, L. (1994). *A Dynamic Systems Approach to the Development of Cognition and Action.* MIT Press.

Thomas, R. M. (1996). *Comparing Theories of Child Development.* Brooks/Cole Publishing Company.

Toomela, A. (2015). Vygotsky's Theory on the Procrustes' Bed of Linear Thinking: Looking for Structural–Systemic Theseus to Save the Idea of 'Social Formation of Mind'. *Culture & Psychology, 21,* 318–339. https://doi.org/10.1177/1354067X15570490

Vaci, N., Edelsbrunner, P., Stern, E., Neubauer, A., Bilalic, M., & Grabner, R. (2019). The Joint Influence of Intelligence and Practice on skill Development Throughout the Life Span. *PNAS, 116*(37).

Vasileva, O., & Balyasnikova, N. (2019). (Re)introducing Vygotsky's Thought: From Historical Overview to Contemporary Psychology. *Frontiers in Psychology, 10*, 1515.

Veldman, S., Santos, R., Jones, R., Sousa-Sa, E., & Okely, A. (2019). Associations Between Gross Motor Skills and Cognitive Development in Toddlers. *Early Human Development, 132*, 39–44.

Vygotsky, L. S. (1978). *Mind in Society: The Development of Higher Psychological Processes.* Harvard University Press.

Wach, H. (1981). Visual Implications of Piagets Theory of Cognitive Development. *Journal of Learning Disabilities, 14*(10).

Walker, L., & Hennig, K. (1999). Parenting Style and the Development of Moral Reasoning. *Journal of Moral Education, 28*(3), 359–374.

Webb, S. J., Monk, C. S., & Nelson, C. A. (2001). Mechanisms of Postnatal Neurobiological Development: Implications for Human Development. *Developmental Neuropsychology, 19*(2), 147–171.

Wertsch, J. V., & Tulviste, P. (1992). L. S. Vygotsky and Contemporary Developmental Psychology. *Developmental Psychology, 28*, 548–557. https://doi.org/10.1037/0012-1649.28.4.548

Zeidner, M. (1995). Personality and Trait Correlates of Intelligence. In D. H. Saklofske & M. Zeidner (Eds.), *International Handbook of Personality and Intelligence* (pp. 299–319). Plenum Press.

Zhang, Z. (2013). *Children's Moral Reasoning: Influence of Culture and Collaborative Discussion.* Thesis, Publication, University of Illinois at Urbana-Champaign.

Zimmerman, B. J., & Whitehurst, G. J. (1979). Structure and Function: A Comparison of Two Views of the Development of Language and Cognition. In G. J. Whitehurst & B. J. Zimmerman (Eds.), *The Functions of Language and Cognition.* Academic Press.

CHAPTER 5

Cognitive Development and Childhood Learning

Introduction

The human brain experiences significant growth in the first 2 years of life, laying the foundations for its structural and connective development through childhood, adolescence as well as adulthood. These foundations are dependent upon and shaped by the characteristics as well as the features of the family into which the child is born, but also the characteristics and features of the wider environment in which the family itself exists. In the case of the family, the child may have to compete with siblings for the limited material and psychological resources which the parents may have to offer. For example, the level of the parents' income may only allow them access to food sources of varying quality and nutritional content. Moreover, the level of parental income will also dictate the frequency with which the children will eat—although the nutritional value of the food that is eaten may have a greater positive impact on brain development than the frequency with which meals are eaten. However, while the nutritional content of food gives the potential for the physiological structures of the brain to develop, it is the infants pre- and post-natal environment which will provide the stimuli to alter the infant's genes through epigenetic mechanisms to various levels depending on the nature of the stimuli. These altered genes will then determine the quality of the brain structures as well as the quality of neuronal connections within the brain. The altered

S. Ramesh, *The Political Economy of Human Behaviour and Economic Development*,
https://doi.org/10.1007/978-3-031-12666-6_5

genes may produce diverse types of proteins, changing the genes themselves, which form the building blocks of all living tissue, including those required to form the structures of the brain. A poor childhood experience may inhibit and constrain gene expression in later life. The result of this may be that the proteins produced later in life may not be of optimal quality and may not be of the correct type.[1] Proteins may also be produced which 'switch on' genes which emphasise character weaknesses rather than character strengths. Brain development is optimised when the number of neural connections increases exponentially. This only occurs when the quality of proteins produced is both optimal and high in number.[2] This in turn will affect the level of development of cognitive capacity of the brain development of the infant. It is also at this stage of development that the brain is at its most malleable to change in the external environment; the resulting stimuli allows the infant to acquire new skills and abilities. Furthermore, in late infancy, at the toddler stage, the infant also develops emotional regulation mechanisms because of the amygdala forming connections with other parts of the brain. The development by the infant of mechanisms to emotionally regulate itself is also central to the development of its cognitive ability. However, key to cognitive advancement is the acquisition of language by the infant. As vocabulary expands, the infant's cognitive capacity develops even further because it can physically construct its thoughts in words through vocal expression. Furthermore, as the infant grows through childhood and adolescence into an adult the parts of the brain may become increasingly specialised in function. It would therefore seem that the first 24 months of life of a human being contribute most towards its lifelong accomplishments. Therefore, the implication is that governments should foster economic and social policies which allow for the development of a conducive environment for an infant to optimally develop its cognitive capacity. Moreover, such economic and social policies should be promoted throughout society on a universal basis regardless of either parental or household income. Such policies may include the provision of either free or subsidised nutritional meals, milk and childcare by the state.

[1] Shah et al. (2014), Genetic and environmental exposures constrain epigenetic drift over the human life course, Genome Res, 24, pp. 1725–1733.

[2] Zhang, Y.E., Landback, P., Vibranovski, M.D., Long, M. (2011), Accelerated Recruitment of New Brain Development Genes into the Human Genome, PLoS Biol 9(10): e1001179. https://doi.org/10.1371/journal.pbio.1001179.

Neuroscience of Learning and Development

The study of the impact on the brain development of an infant nurtured in an environment characterised by poverty has become possible through the development of new techniques and processes.[3] These include epigenetics, neuroimaging, cognitive psychophysiology and neuroendocrinology, for example.[4] These techniques will help to shed light on how the physiology of the brain develops and changes over time as a child grows up, whether in poverty, in prosperity or in between the two. Contrasting studies of the brain development of children in these groups will allow policymakers to formulate educational, nutritional and parenting policies which will facilitate the optimum brain development of children such that they can benefit themselves and the whole of society in adulthood. In this case, children who grow up in an educationally, nutritionally and parentally impoverished environment are likely to suffer non-optimal brain development, resulting in poor memory, learning difficulties and lacking in concentration. As a result, they will develop few skills and enter a life of crime, unemployment or employment in low-skilled jobs. These scenarios are likely to incur costs on society. It is from this perspective that neuroscience can contribute through the results of studies to help policymakers develop suitable educational, nutritional and parenting policies which will facilitate the optimal development of the brain during childhood and beyond. Education allows for the development of cognition through the rewiring of the brain as learning takes place and new skills and experiences are acquired.[5] A better understanding of this process will allow for the development of optimal educational policies to suit both the young and the old. Neuroscience is a specialism which seeks to better understand the biological changes and mechanisms which take place in the development of cognitive skills. Educational neuroscience is a specialism which seeks to optimise the results of neuroscience research with educational policy.[6]

The purpose of education in society is often seen as facilitating the development of skills, knowledge and cognition of the incredibly young in

[3] Pollak, S., and Wolfe, B. (2020), How Developmental Neuroscience can help address the problem of child poverty, National Bureau of Economic Research, Working Paper No. 26842.

[4] Ibid.

[5] Knowland, V., and Thomas, M. (2014), Educating the adult brain: How the neuroscience of learning can inform educational policy, Int. Rev. Educ, 60, pp. 99–122.

[6] Mareschal, D., Tolmie, A., and Butterworth, B. (2013), Educational neuroscience, Wiley-Blackwell, Oxford.

preparation for the adult world.[7] However, in the contemporary world the work regimes have gone through systematic change due to developments in technology as well as due to changes in culture and lifestyles. In this case, whereas one might have expected to have a job for life 50 years ago, in today's world it can be expected that an individual may have had multiple careers and jobs over the span of a working life to retirement age. Moreover, structural unemployment, whether regional or technological, may mean that workers losing their jobs will have to retrain and acquire new skills to allow them to accept new roles and jobs. This is also true in the case of cyclical unemployment. Furthermore, in developing countries, education may not be available to children, with the implication that they may have to acquire skills through educational opportunities later in life, in adulthood.[8] It is also true that in developing countries, lack of educational opportunities to women contributes to gender inequality, especially in the context of illiteracy.[9] A positive correlation exists between higher levels of literacy and employability.[10] Therefore, it is evident that even without a basic level of literacy, women and men may only be able to get 'blue-collar' work in agriculture and/or in manufacturing, excluding them from the knowledge economy. The effect of the lack of literacy on the employability of women may be greater than that on men, especially in developing countries. The impact will be reduced access to jobs with high salaries. In developing countries, families tend to be of a larger size than in developed countries. Often such large families will be saddled with loans taken out from local pawnbrokers or landowners with extortionate interest rates. A lack of literacy, leading to lack of access to jobs with large salaries, large families and indebtedness, contributes to poverty and inequality in developing countries.

The physical and the social environment which surrounds us from the very moment we are born to the moment we die has a profound impact

[7] Knowland, V., and Thomas, M. (2014), Educating the adult brain: How the neuroscience of learning can inform educational policy, Int. Rev. Educ, 60, pp. 99–122.

[8] Ibid.

[9] UNESCO (United Nations Educational, Scientific and Cultural Organisation). (2004). The plurality of literacy and its implications for policies and programmes. Paris: UNESCO Education Sector.

[10] BIS (Department for Business Innovation and Skills). (2009). Skills for life: Changing lives. London, UK: BIS.

on the development of the human brain.[11] Moreover, neuroimaging techniques can be used to determine the extent to which individual brain development is shaped by interactions of the individual with specific social and physical environments.[12] In this case, the Lewin equation can be used to quantify a functional relationship between the behaviour of an individual as a function of the individual's genetics, neurobiology and psychology and the environment, perhaps using methods associated with computational modelling.[13] However, at a biological level, the influence of the environment may lead to physiological changes in the brain due to epigenetic mechanisms.[14] But there may also be bodily functions, such as blood sugar regulation, maintenance of an adequate body temperature as well as the need to maintain a minimum oxygen level, which the brain must also be involved with.[15] The accomplishment of these objective functions could result automatically through reinforcement learning, in the same way that dopamine is released in the brain during the experiencing of pleasure.[16] Empirical studies of the relationship between brain function and behaviour have shown that epigenetic mechanisms have changed brain physiology as a result of childhood experiences.[17] The latter could lead to the bodily production of proteins which alter the functions of genes, although there are no changes to the individual's DNA sequences.[18] Moreover, exposure to certain influential environments can impact critically on the physiology of brain development in all species. However, brain development is most flexible to environmental changes during periods known as sensitive periods. Moreover, the rate of brain development is not the same for different individuals.[19] The brain is most malleable to the acquisition of

[11] Berman, M., Kardan, O., Kotabe, H., Nusbaum, H., and London, S. (2019), The Promise of Environmental Neuroscience, Nature Human Behaviour, Vol. 3, pp. 414–417.

[12] Ibid.

[13] Lewin, K. (1936), Principles of Topological Psychology. 4–7, McGraw-Hill, New York.

[14] Berman, M., Kardan, O., Kotabe, H., Nusbaum, H., and London, S. (2019), The Promise of Environmental Neuroscience, Nature Human Behaviour, Vol. 3, pp. 414–417.

[15] Richards, B., et al. (2019), A Deep Learning Framework for Neuroscience, Nature Neuroscience, Vol. 22, pp. 1761–1770.

[16] Schultz, W., Dayan, P., and Montague, P.R. (1997), A Neural Substrate of Production and Reward, Science, 275, 1593-1599.

[17] Essex, M. J. et al. (2013), Child Dev. 84, 58–75.

[18] Berman, M., Kardan, O., Kotabe, H., Nusbaum, H., and London, S. (2019), The Promise of Environmental Neuroscience, Nature Human Behaviour, Vol. 3, pp. 414–417.

[19] Huttenlocher, P. R. (2002), Neural plasticity: The effects of the environment on the development of the cerebral cortex, Harvard University Press, Cambridge, MA.

certain skills compared to others at different time periods. For example, babies are capable of learning aspects of spoken language far earlier than the written aspects of the language.[20] The implication is that educational policies can be designed and implemented for specific age ranges.[21] However, empirical research supports the idea that the biggest boost to brain development occurs in the first few years of a child's life, when the number of synapses grows exponentially—although this is followed by a period of consolidation during which some synaptic connections become stronger while others become weaker, depending on the extent to which they are in use. However, in some individuals the brain shows substantial development all the way to adolescence.[22] The development of the emotional brain is heightened at this stage and coincides with changes in the physiological brain structures associated with both limbic and cognitive control.[23] The former is associated with structures which are to be found on either side of the thalamus and below the medial temporal lobe of the cerebrum. The latter is to be found in the forebrain. The specific changes to the limbic and cognitive structures in the forebrain may be hierarchical in nature.[24] Moreover, these hierarchical changes may be gradual and consequential in nature, with former changes necessary for later changes to be possible.[25] The development of the emotional brain is heightened during adolescence because it is at this stage of development that there is an urgent need for individual self-regulation between emotion and action. In this case, the cerebellum has a role in controlling cognition, emotion and motor control.[26] Moreover, the transition from a childhood to an adult environment may necessitate the need for greater self-regulation.[27]

[20] Neville, H. J., Mills, D. L., and Lawson, D. S. (1992), Fractionating language: Different neural subsystems with different sensitive periods. Cerebral Cortex, 2(3), 244–258.

[21] Thomas, M. S. C. (2012), Brain plasticity and education. British Journal of Educational Psychology—Monograph Series II: Educational Neuroscience, 8, 142–156.

[22] Knowland, V., and Thomas, M. (2014), Educating the adult brain: How the neuroscience of learning can inform educational policy, Int. Rev. Educ, 60, pp. 99–122.

[23] Casey, B.J., Heller, A., Gee, D., and Cohen, A. (2019), Development of the Emotional Brain, Neuroscience letters, 693, pp. 29–34.

[24] Casey, B.J., Heller, A., Gee, D., and Cohen, A. (2019), Development of the Emotional Brain, Neuroscience letters, 693, pp. 29–34.

[25] Ibid.

[26] Schmahmann. J., Guell, X., Stoodley, C., and Halko, M. (2019), The Theory and Neuroscience of Cerebellar Cognition, Annu. Rev. Neurosci, 42.

[27] Casey, B.J., Heller, A., Gee, D., and Cohen, A. (2019), Development of the Emotional Brain, Neuroscience letters, 693, pp. 29–34.

Nevertheless, this process also coincides with the decreasing malleability of the brain to the external environment; perhaps the brain becomes more specialised for use in adult life.[28] The enduring impact of the environment on brain development, even after childhood and adolescence into adulthood, is seen in the hippocampus, where new neurons form as perhaps a response to new memories.[29] Nevertheless, in general the brain is more malleable at younger ages, during which the environment may be contrastingly different from that which an adult brain would face. Therefore, one of the objectives of educational neuroscience is to determine ways, perhaps through assessment development, as to how the malleability of the brain can be improved in adulthood.[30] Evidence that the brain can be malleable to development later in life comes from observations on brain trauma patients having to relearn how to walk and talk, and individuals born in deprived backgrounds and exposed to more favourable environments later in life experiencing new learning.[31] The level of the body's physiological stress response at a young age may impact on the development of brain cognitive function. If the stress response due to a negative external environment cannot be effectively managed, it may lead to epigenetic mechanisms altering brain physiology such that later learning is inhibited in a child's path to adulthood.[32] For example, if a child experiences violence and physical abuse, this may cause epigenetic mechanisms to reduce the development of the hippocampus and so the development of associative memory.[33] However, if a child receives the emotional and physical support of a caregiver, it may be possible that the stress response is effectively managed, leading to a reduction in the capacity of the

[28] Thomas, M. S. C., & Johnson, M. H. (2008), New advances in understanding sensitive periods in brain development. Current Directions in Psychological Science, 17(1), 1–5.

[29] Knowland, V., and Thomas, M. (2014), Educating the adult brain: How the neuroscience of learning can inform educational policy, Int. Rev. Educ, 60, pp. 99–122.

[30] Ibid.

[31] Ibid.

[32] Blair, C., & Raver, C. C. (2012), Child development in the context of adversity: Experiential canalization of brain and Behavior, American Psychologist, 67(4), 309–318. https://doi.org/10.1037/a0027493.

[33] Lambert, H., Peverill, M., Sambrook, K., Rosen, M., Shendan, M., and McLaughlin, K. (2019), Altered Development of Hippocampus-Dependent Associative Learning Following Early Life Adversity, Developmental Cognitive Neuroscience, 38.

epigenetic mechanism to damage the physiology of development of the brain.[34] The ability to concentrate on the matter at hand and to ignore distractions is also an important contributor to an individual's learning, whether it is in childhood or in adulthood.[35] Therefore, individual effort, the non-cognitive skills of an individual, may impact on brain malleability, and so without this, individual effort learning may not be possible in adulthood.

Gene-Environment Interplay and Development

The genetic differences between individuals may explain the differences in lifetime attainment in the context of differing environments.[36]The implication is that government-engineered social and equitable policies will help to facilitate the transmissibility of genetic propensities associated with education.[37] However, it is difficult to pinpoint the causal mechanisms which give rise to life outcomes because this is the result of the dynamic interplay of genes, quality of parenting and socio-economic background, which can be associated with the level of access to education, health, housing and nutrition.[38] Therefore, it becomes evident that unlike traditional econometric analysis where statistics can be used to determine the causality between variables and the importance of specific variables, statistics cannot be used to determine causation between genes and the environment.[39] While the specific nature of the differences in genes which may give rise to success or failure in life is difficult to pinpoint and quantify, the level of inequality can be quantified using the Gini coefficient.[40]

[34] Magnuson, K., and Schindler, H. (2019), Supporting Children's Early Development by Building Caregivers Capacities and Skills: A Theoretical Approach Informed by New Neuroscience Research, Journal of Family Theory and Review, 11, pp. 59–78.

[35] Zelazo, P. D. (2004). The development of conscious control in childhood. Trends in Cognitive Sciences, 8(1), 12–17.

[36] Selita, F., and Kovas, Y. (2019), Genes and Gini: What Inequality Means for Heritability, J. Biosoc. Sci, 51, pp. 18–47.

[37] Ibid.

[38] Plomin, R., DeFries, J. C., Knopik, V. S. and Neiderhiser, J. M. (2016), Top 10 replicated findings from Behavioral genetics, Perspectives on Psychological Science 11(1), 3–23.

[39] Van Barell, C., Weiss, A., and Penke, L. (2019), Developing Individual Differences in Primate Behaviour: The Role of Genes, Environment and their interplay, Behavioral Ecology and Sociobiology, Vol. 73, 20.

[40] Selita, F., and Kovas, Y. (2019), Genes and Gini: What Inequality Means for Heritability, J. Biosoc. Sci, 51, pp. 18–47.

Nevertheless, the Gini is only a measure of the level of inequality in a country, not a measure of its wealth.[41] Therefore, it may easily be the case that both a developed economy and a developing economy may have the same Gini value, between 0 and 1.[42] If Gini has a value of 0, then this indicates a situation of perfect equality, whereas a value of 1 would indicate perfect inequality. The value of the Gini is determined from the Lorenz curve, with the poorest to the richest proportion of the population represented on the *Y*-axis, and the successive proportion of income on the *X*-axis. So, a point (0.7, 0.3) would suggest that the lower 70% of a country's population earns 30% of a country's total income. And, if for a country the value of the Gini coefficient is 0.8, it would mean that there is 80% inequality and only 20% equality. However, the wealth Gini and the income Gini of a country need to be carefully evaluated. For example, in a country with a high-wealth Gini and a low-income Gini, resources may not be so unequally distributed in society.[43] However, in a country with a high-income Gini and a low-wealth Gini, the opposite may be the case and the level of inequality due to a focused distribution of the country's resources may be high.[44] The Gini coefficient is indicative of the extent to which resources are distributed in a specific country. Inevitably, there may be a link between the Gini and the gene in determining life's outcomes. This causal relationship can be represented from two perspectives.[45] Firstly, the genetic aspect of an individual's success or failure is dependent on individual environmental circumstances. If a child inherits good genes from its parents, its resulting characteristics may help it overcome the constraints of developing in a poor socio-economic environment and allow it to achieve academic and professional success through hard work.[46] Programmes and an upbringing which help to contribute positively towards a child's development may also be important in helping a child

[41] Ibid.

[42] Ibid.

[43] Selita, F., and Kovas, Y. (2019), Genes and Gini: What Inequality Means for Heritability, J. Biosoc. Sci, 51, pp. 18–47.

[44] World Bank (2017a) The World Bank GINI Report. URL: http://data.worldbank.org/indicator/SI.POV.GINI.

[45] Selita, F., and Kovas, Y. (2019), Genes and Gini: What Inequality Means for Heritability, J. Biosoc. Sci, 51, pp. 18–47.

[46] Stumm, S., Smith-Woolley, E., Ayorech, Z., McMillan, A., Rimfield, K., Dale, P., and Plomin, R. (2019), Predicting Educational Achievement from genomic measures and socio-economic status, Development Science, DOI: https://doi.org/10.1111/desc.12925.

build character and resilience. Secondly, the latter may either facilitate or constrain the expression of the former in either a negative or a positive manner. For example, if an individual's genes make the individual conducive to addiction, then a stressful environment may lead to drug, alcohol and/or even cigarette addiction. If it is possible to analyse an individual's genetic disposition, then addiction-enhancing genes can be identified and an individual advised to find themselves an environment in which they are less vulnerable to their genetic disposition.

The unequal distribution of income and resources in a society will give rise to inequality. It may also lead to the uneven development of biological and cognitive mechanisms. This may have a direct impact on the well-being of parents and, in particular, mothers going through pregnancy.[47] However, it has been found that the occurrence of mental illness amongst parents is not highly prevalent in societies with the highest levels of poverty but those in which there is the highest level of societal disarray[48]—for example, single-parent families or children home alone while both parents are at work with no one to look after them. Nevertheless, whether or not parents experience mental health problems due to the stress brought on by poverty or societal disarray, the inevitable result may be the poor parenting of children.[49] However, this does not give rise to behavioural variation in young children, as in humans this only occurs during and after adolescence.[50] Moreover, the level of parenting may also be moulded by the personality of the child.[51] The nature of the socio-economic environment in which a child grows up may have an impact on the quality of gene expression later in life. This may impact on the quality and type of proteins produced, affecting brain development either positively (good

[47] Selita, F., and Kovas, Y. (2019), Genes and Gini: What Inequality Means for Heritability, J. Biosoc. Sci, 51, pp. 18–47.

[48] Pinto, R., Ashworth, M. and Jones, R. (2008), Schizophrenia in black Caribbeans living in the UK: an exploration of underlying causes of the high incidence rate, British Journal of General Practice 58(551), 429–434.

[49] Johnson, S. L., Wibbels, E. and Wilkinson, R. (2015), Economic inequality is related to cross-national prevalence of psychotic symptoms. Social Psychiatry and Psychiatric Epidemiology 50(12), 1799–1807.

[50] Van Barell, C., Weiss, A., and Penke, L. (2019), Developing Individual Differences in Primate Behaviour: The Role of Genes, Environment and their interplay, Behavioral Ecology and Sociobiology, Vol. 73, 20.

[51] Ayoub, M. et al. (2019), Genetic and Environmental Associations Between Child Personality and Parenting, Social Psychological and Personality Science, Vol. 10 (6), pp. 711–721.

socio-economic background) or negatively (poor socio-economic background).[52] It is therefore evident that epigenetic mechanisms may arise due to a child's environmental circumstances.[53] More specifically, it can be stated that the assumption that psychological phenotypes, the nature of gene expression due to environmental circumstances, develop due to the interaction of genes and the environment is rooted in all behavioural genetic models.[54] Furthermore, children born to stressed mothers in an environment characterised by poverty and a lack of socio-economic equity may also find that gene expression is inhibited or enhanced.[55] In any case, it is evident that the efficient functioning of genes will have a profound impact on the development of an individual.[56] Therefore, it is important that both the pre-birth and the post-birth environment of a child are stress-free for the mother and the child so as to favour an environment which is conducive to the optimal expression of a child's genes. Governments could, for example, facilitate policies which will facilitate this outcome. Moreover, it has been found that genetic factors may also contribute to a child's educational attainment, for example, by influencing the child's cognitive and non-cognitive development.[57]

[52] Bick, J., Naumova, O., Hunter, S., Barbot, B., Lee, M., Luthar, S. S. and Grigorenko, E. L. (2012), Childhood adversity and DNA methylation of genes involved in the hypothalamus-pituitary adrenal axis and immune system: whole-genome and candidate-gene associations. Development and Psychopathology 24(4), 1417–1425.

[53] Palladino, V., McNeill, R., Reif, A., and Kittel-Schneider, S. (2019), genetic Risk Factors and Gene-Environment Interactions in Adult and Childhood Attention-Deficit/Hyperactivity Disorder, Psychiatric Genetics, Vol. 29, No. 3.

[54] Briley, D., Livengood, J., Derringer, J., Tucker-Drob, E., Fraley, R., and Roberts, B. (2017), Interpreting Behaviour Genetic Models: Seven Developmental Processes to Understand, Behaviour Genetics, 49, pp. 196–210.

[55] Kovas, Y., Henry, J., Feklicheva, I., Soldatova, E. and Malykh, S. (2016), Early environment and development: epigenetic mechanisms. In Behavioural Genomics: Child Development and Education, Malykh, S. B. et al. (Eds) Publishing House of Tomsk State University, Tomsk.

[56] Plomin, R., DeFries, J. C., Knopik, V. S. and Neiderhiser, J. M. (2016) Top 10 replicated findings from behavioral genetics. Perspectives on Psychological Science 11(1), 3–23.

[57] Krapohl, E., Rimfeld, K., Nicholas, G., Shakeshaft, N., Trzaskowski, M., McMillan, A. et al. (2014), The high heritability of educational achievement reflects many genetically influenced traits, not just intelligence. PNAS. URL: www.pnas.org/cgi/doi/10.1073/pnas.1408777111.

Developmental Time

The months following the birth of a child are ones of rapid change with regard to its cognition, physical physiology and socio-emotional outlook.[58] The individual developmental differences which occur in these factors during infancy give rise to the differences which emerge through adolescence and then into adulthood.[59] The extent of the development of attention and concentration in infants is also a good indicator of the extent of cognitive development, especially executive functioning, later in life.[60] An infant's observation and looking behaviours are often associated with attention, whose development is dependent on the extent of the development of a specific neural network called an orienting network. The latter allows the infant to use its attention flexibly and to refocus as and when required.[61] Until the infants brain develops, attention is the way in which the infant's behaviour is controlled exogenously. However, once the infant's brain and cognitive functions develop sufficiently, these work hand in hand with the infant's attention to become a mode of endogenous behavioural control and self-regulation.[62] At this stage the infant's cognitive control of its behaviour is optimised by the executive functions of the brain, representing the interaction of several interlinked processes.[63] The development of processes which enable and facilitate the development of attention in infants is important because it lays the mechanisms which underpin the extent of self-regulation as the child becomes an

[58] Blankenship, T., Slough, M., Calkins, S., Deater-Deckard, K., Kim-Spoon, J., and Bell, M. (2018), Attention and Executive Functioning in Infancy: Links to Childhood Executive Function and Reading Achievement, Developmental Science, 22, https://doi.org/10.1111/desc.12824.

[59] Bornstein, M. H., & Leventhal, T. (2015), Children in bioecological landscapes of development. In R. IN Handbook of child psychology and developmental science: Vol. 4. Ecological settings and processes (7th ed., pp. 1–5), Lerner. M. (Ed.), Wiley, Hoboken, NJ.

[60] Cuevas, K., and Bell, M. A. (2014), Infant attention and early childhood executive function. *Child Development*, *85*, 397–404. https://doi.org/10.1111/cdev.12126.

[61] Frick, J. E., Colombo, J., and Saxon, T. F. (1999). Individual and developmental differences in disengagement of fixation in early infancy, Child Development, 70, 537–548. https://doi.org/10.1111/1467-8624.00039.

[62] Blair, C. (2016). Developmental science and executive function. Current directions in psychological science, 25(1), 3–7. https://doi.org/10.1177/0963721415622634.

[63] Diamond, A. (2013). Executive functions. Annual Review of Psychology, 64, 35–168. https://doi.org/10.1146/annurev-psych-113011-143750.

adolescent.[64] The characteristics of an infant's attention, at 5 months of age, can be associated with his/her 'look' or 'shift of look'.[65] The infant utilises an instinctive orientational attentional network prior to the development of the physiological structures and networks of the brain associated with working memory, mental flexibility and self-control, the executive functions of the brain required for cognitive control.[66] The executive control of an infant develops between the ages of 2 and 3[67], and in childhood between the ages of 5 and 12.[68] Although, the infant will rely on instinctive attention until the physiological networks of the brain associated with executive function develop, the start of the development of these networks begins after the first 6 months of an infant's life as the prefrontal cortex develops.[69] The facilitation of the proper development of executive functions in the infant is important, as this will have a consequential impact on its development in childhood, affecting both the extent of learning at school and the extent of self-regulation as an adolescent.[70] The development of reading ability is also important for academic achievement. In this case, it has been found that there is a causal link between the development of reading ability and the extent of the development of

[64] Blair, C. (2016), Developmental science and executive function, Current directions in psychological science, 25(1), 3–7. https://doi.org/10.1177/0963721415622634.

[65] Blankenship, T., Slough, M., Calkins, S., Deater-Deckard, K., Kim-Spoon, J., and Bell, M. (2018), Attention and Executive Functioning in Infancy: Links to Childhood Executive Function and Reading Achievement, Developmental Science, 22, https://doi.org/10.1111/desc.12824.

[66] Posner, M. I., and Rothbart, M. K. (2007), Research on attention networks as a model for the integration of psychological science, Annual Review of Psychology, 58, 1–3. https://doi.org/10.1146/annurev.psych.58.110405.085516.

[67] Carlson, S. M., Mandell, D. J., and Williams, L. (2004), Executive function and theory of mind: Stability and prediction from ages 2 to 3. Developmental Psychology, 40, 1105. https://doi.org/10.1037/0012-1649.40.6.1105.

[68] Polderman, T. J., Posthuma, D., De Sonneville, L. M., Stins, J. F., Verhulst, F. C., and Boomsma, D. I. (2007), Genetic analyses of the stability of executive functioning during childhood. *Biological Psychology*, *76*(1), 11–20. https://doi.org/10.1016/j.biopsycho.2007.05.002.

[69] Diamond, A. (2013), Executive functions. Annual Review of Psychology, 64, 135–168. https://doi.org/10.1146/annurev-psych-113011-143750.

[70] Toll, S. W., Van der Ven, S. H., Kroesbergen, E. H., and Van Luit, J. E. (2011), Executive functions as predictors of math learning disabilities, Journal of Learning Disabilities, 44, 521–532. https://doi.org/10.1177/0022219410387302.

attention control and executive control.[71] Poor attention will lead to poor concentration, which in turn will have a negative impact on the development of reading skills. It is for this reason that the development of attention control and executive control is important for academic success. The development of optimal executive function control, and subsequently optimal reading ability, in the child is dependent on the development of optimal attention control in the infant.[72] In this case, governments should put in place programmes at early years' schools to allow infants to develop attention control skills. This would benefit the infant's long-term development of its cognitive skills through childhood, adolescence and beyond. Of the possible policies which could realistically impact positively on infant and childhood development are those which would improve parent-infant/child interactions.[73] For example, parents could be given more time to spend with their children to read them books or to sing them lullabies and songs, as these kinds of interactions have been found to have a positive impact on the development of reading ability of children.[74] Empirical research has suggested that higher levels of cognitive development in the first 2 years of a child's life will have a big impact on future educational attainment, and as a result on future salaries which can be commanded in adulthood.[75] However, it is also the case that divergences in the cognitive development of children from low-income families and high-income families occur as early as 1 year of age.[76] Even before birth

[71] McVay, J. C., and Kane, M. J. (2012), Why does working memory capacity predict variation in reading comprehension? On the influence of mind wandering and executive attention. Journal of Experimental Psychology: General, 141, 302. https://doi.org/10.1037/a0025250.

[72] Arrington, C. N., Kulesz, P. A., Francis, D. J., Fletcher, J. M., and Barnes, M. A. (2014), The contribution of attentional control and working memory to reading comprehension and decoding. Scientific Studies of Reading, 18(5), 325–346. https://doi.org/10.1080/10888438.2014.902461.

[73] Jenkins, J., and Handa, S. (2009), Parenting Skills and Early Childhood Development: Production Function Estimates from Longitudinal Data, Rev. Econ Household, 17, pp. 121–147.

[74] Ibid.

[75] Case, A., and Paxson, C. (2006). Stature and status: Height, ability and labor market outcomes. NBER, Working Paper No. 12466.

[76] Reardon, S. F. (2011), The widening academic achievement gap between the rich and the poor: New evidence and possible explanations. In Whither opportunity, Duncan, G.J., and Murnane, R.J. (Eds.), Russell Sage Foundation, New York, NY.

brain development is susceptible to external stimuli,[77] but perhaps more so after the birth of the infant in the first 24 months of life.[78] Therefore, to address the divergences in the cognitive development between children born into low-income environments and those born into higher-income environments, greater equality in adult life for the two cohorts can be ensued from the implementation of early intervention programmes.[79] This could perhaps involve higher transfer payments to low-income families so that parents can work less and spend more time with their children. Alternatively, public funds could be used to ensure that schools stay open longer so that children from low-income families can be given more classes and greater personal tutoring. In addition, parents can be taught the best ways in which to bring up children, especially in the context of engagement with children and a sensitivity to their needs,[80] as well as access to public resources such as the additional teaching resources mentioned earlier.[81] These kinds of interventionist early-stage programmes are important because the higher the level of cognitive development at an early stage, the greater will be the productivity returns of investments in human capital undertaken at later stages, in adolescence and adulthood[82]—although specific interventionist programmes may only be effective at specific stages of

[77] Sari, I. N., and Nugrahani, A. (2022), Level of Knowledge, Attitude, and Behavior of Pregnant Women in Giving Stimulation to the Fetus, Open Access Indonesian Journal of Medical Reviews, 2(3), 234–238. https://doi.org/10.37275/oaijmr.v2i3.192.

[78] Fox, S. E., Levitt, P., and Nelson, C. A. (2010), How the timing and quality of early experiences influence the development of brain architecture. Child Development, 81(1), 28–40. doi:https://doi.org/10.1111/j.1467-8624.2009.01380.x.

[79] Heckman, J. J., and Mosso, S. (2014), The economics of human development and social mobility, Annual Review of Economics, 6(1), 689–733. doi:https://doi.org/10.1146/annurev-economics-080213-040753.

[80] Hackman, D. A., Martha, J. F., and Michael, J. M. (2010), Socioeconomic status and the brain: Mechanistic insights from human and animal research, Nature Reviews Neuroscience, 11(9), 651–659.

[81] Love, J. M., Kisker, E. E., Ross, C., Raikes, H., Constantine, J., Boller, K., Brooks-Gunn, J., Chazan-Cohen, R., Banks Tarullo, L., Brady-Smith, C., Sidle Fuligni, A., Schochet, P. Z., Paulsell, D., and Vogel, C. (2005), The effectiveness of early head start for 3-year-old children and their parents: Lessons for policy and programs, Developmental Psychology, 41(6), 885–901.

[82] Jenkins, J., and Handa, S. (2009), Parenting Skills and Early Childhood Development: Production Function Estimates from Longitudinal Data, Rev. Econ Household, 17, pp. 121–147.

development and not at others.[83] Moreover, such early-stage programmes have been found to improve the quality of the interactions between the infant and its mother.[84] Furthermore, early-stage educational programmes will in the long run have a positive impact on a child's early development.[85] Nevertheless, a stressful environment may lead to a gene-environment interaction resulting in HT_{2A} activation in early life, leading to the development of anti-social behaviours in childhood and in later life.[86] As a child moves into adolescence, differences in personality become more pronounced due to the interaction between its genes and its environment.[87]

The level of parental engagement with children as well as the level of sensitivity to their needs is important because it may act to reduce the negative impact on upbringing and childhood development, which may result from growing up in a low-income environment.[88] The relationships that children have with their parents and their peers are also important in determining the extent of cognitive, emotional, social as well as personal development.[89] Cognitive, emotional, social and personal development are all interlinked, and these depend on the development of the physiological structures of the brain, which in turn has a positive link with good

[83] Hill, P., Edmonds, G., and Jackson, J. (2019), Pathways Linking Childhood Personality to Late Life Outcomes, Childhood Development Perspectives, Vol. 13, No. 2, pp. 116–120.

[84] Luthar, S. S., Crossman, E. J., and Small, P. J. (2015), Resilience and adversity. In R. M. Lerner (Ed.), Handbook of child psychology and developmental science: Vol. 3. Socioemotional processes (7th ed., pp. 247–286). Hoboken, Wiley, NJ.

[85] Rao, N., Richards, B., Sun, J., Weber, A., and Sincovich, A. (2019), Early Childhood Education and Child Development in Four Countries in East Asia and the Pacific, Early Childhood Research Quarterly, 47, pp. 169–181.

[86] Godar, S., et al. (2019), Gene-environment interactions in anti-social; behaviour are mediated by early life 5-HT_{2A} receptor activation, Neuropharmacology, 159.

[87] Kandler, C., Waaktaar, T., Mattus, R., Riemann, R and Torgersen, S. (2019), Unravelling the Interplay Between Genetic and Environmental Contributions in the Unfolding of Personality Differences from Early Adolescence to Young Adulthood, European Journal of Personality, Eur, J. Pers, 33, 221–244.

[88] Gershoff, E. T., Raver, C. C., Aber, J. L., and Lennon, M. C. (2007), Income is not enough: Incorporating material hardship into models of income associations with parenting and child development, Child Development, 78(1), 70–95.

[89] Osher, D., Cantor, P., Berg, J., Steyer, L., and Rose, T. (2020), Drivers of Human Development: How Relationships and Context Shape Learning and Development, Applied Developmental Science, 24:1, 6–36.

relationships.[90] Therefore, optimal brain development can be enhanced by the design and implementation of interventionist programmes which promote the development of good relationships between infants and children.[91] Research also suggests that interventionist programmes targeted at 4 year olds is inconsequential in terms of affecting cognitive development and life outcomes.[92] Nevertheless, despite the importance of engagement and sensitivity, the level of parental education may also contribute to the cognitive development of children.[93] This is especially true with regard to the level of maternal education as opposed to the level of paternal education. Better-educated mothers may be able to make better decisions with regard to the allocation of available resources to their children's needs. Mothers will also often decide what their children are allowed to do. For example, should the children be allowed to play with other children? And if a mother has two children of nursery school age, should both attend or only the eldest due to limited financial resources?

Biological Consequences of Psychosocial Adversities in Early Life

The past 40 years have witnessed the completion of empirical investigations into the parental impact of either stimulating positive media effects or reducing negative media effects on their children's development.[94] The emphasis of these studies shifted with the different types of media

[90] Jones, S., McGarrah, M., and Khan, J. (2019), Social and Emotional Learning: A Principled Science of Human Development in Context, Educational Psychologist, 54, 3, 129–143.

[91] Ibid.

[92] Lipsey, M. W., Kerry, G. H., Dong, N., Farran, D. C., and Bilbrey, C. (2013), Evaluation of the Tennessee voluntary prekindergarten program: Kindergarten and first grade follow-up results from the randomized control design, Vanderbilt University, Peabody Research Institute, Nashville, TN.

[93] Jenkins, J., and Handa, S. (2009), Parenting Skills and Early Childhood Development: Production Function Estimates from Longitudinal Data, Rev. Econ Household, 17, pp. 121–147.

[94] Nathanson, A. I. (1999), Identifying and explaining the relationship between parental mediation and children's aggression, Communication Research, 26, 124–143. doi:https://doi.org/10.1177/009365099026002002.

technologies as these developed over time.[95] Parental constraints on their children accessing different types of media technologies may have a positive impact on promoting social behaviours[96] while reducing aggressive tendencies.[97] However, while these earlier studies provided some indicative results of the effects of parental mediation on the behaviours of children with regard to having either access to or no access to specific media technologies, there has been a lack of analysis of this in a dynamic context across and between different age groups.[98] Moreover, there also seems to be a lack of scholarly attention on the differences in the development of parental mediation over time, particularly in the transition from early to middle childhood.[99] This is particularly in the context of empirical findings which show differences amongst parents in the use of active and restrictive mediation.[100] These differences could originate from the differences associated with parental gender, level of parental education as well as the age of the child.[101] In the case of the levels of parental education, parents who are more educated are much more likely to engage in parental mediation than parents who have a lower level of education.[102] But there is no real understanding as to how these differences may contribute to differentiating between parental behaviours associated with restrictive or active

[95] Beyens, I., Volkenburg, P., and Piotrowski, J. (2019), Development Trajectories of Parental Mediation Across Early and Middle Childhood, Human Communication Research, 45, pp. 226–250.

[96] Coyne, S. M., Padilla-Walker, L. M., Stockdale, L., & Day, R. D. (2011). Game on ... girls: Associations between co-playing video games and adolescent behavioral and family outcomes. Journal of Adolescent Health, 49, 160–165. doi: https://doi.org/10.1016/j.jadohealth.2010.11.249.

[97] Nathanson, A. I. (1999), Identifying and explaining the relationship between parental mediation and children's aggression, Communication Research, 26, 124–143. doi: https://doi.org/10.1177/009365099026002002.

[98] Beyens, I., Volkenburg, P., and Piotrowski, J. (2019), Development Trajectories of Parental Mediation Across Early and Middle Childhood, Human Communication Research, 45, pp. 226–250.

[99] Ibid.

[100] Nikken, P., & Schols, M. (2015). How and why parents' guide the media use of young children. Journal of Child and Family Studies, 24, 3423–3435. doi: https://doi.org/10.1007/s10826-015-0144-4.

[101] Beyens, I., Volkenburg, P., and Piotrowski, J. (2019), Development Trajectories of Parental Mediation Across Early and Middle Childhood, Human Communication Research, 45, pp. 226–250.

[102] Böcking, S., & Böcking, T. (2009). Parental mediation of television. Journal of Children and Media, 3, 286–302. doi: https://doi.org/10.1080/17482790902999959.

mediation.[103] Moreover, in order to better understand the differences between parental mediation strategies across families, it is necessary to move away from purely demographic factors.[104] In which case, the parenting style and parental responsiveness may be more important for the development of parental mediation strategies than purely demographic factors.[105] Parents who were prone to an autonomy-restricting parenting style were more likely to engage in active autonomy-restricting strategies.[106] On the other hand, parents who tended to be more responsive to their children's needs were characterised has having a mediation strategy which was both active and restrictive.[107] However, it may also be the case that parental mediation strategies are pre-determined by the levels of stress which parents may experience.[108] In any case, it may be best to recognise that parental mediation behaviour is based on a developmental process and therefore its very nature may change over time. For example, parental behaviours may be associated with less restrictive mediation when the child is more autonomous, in middle childhood circa ten years old, than when the child is immature and more prone to naughty behaviours.[109] Therefore, it may be better to consider parental mediation as a developmental theory, in which case it is likely to change as a child's

[103] Beyens, I., Volkenburg, P., and Piotrowski, J. (2019), Development Trajectories of Parental Mediation Across Early and Middle Childhood, Human Communication Research, 45, pp. 226–250.

[104] Shin, W., & Li, B. (2017), Parental mediation of children's digital technology use in Singapore. Journal of Children and Media, 11, 1–19. doi: https://doi.org/10.1080/17482798.2016.1203807.

[105] Ibid.

[106] Valkenburg, P. M., Piotrowski, J. T., Hermanns, J., & de Leeuw, R. (2013). Developing and validating the perceived parental media mediation scale: A self-determination perspective. Human Communication Research, 39, 445–469.. doi: https://doi.org/10.1111/hcre.12010.

[107] Shin, W., & Li, B. (2017), Parental mediation of children's digital technology use in Singapore. Journal of Children and Media, 11, 1–19. doi: https://doi.org/10.1080/17482798.2016.1203807.

[108] Evans, C. A., Jordan, A. B., & Horner, J. (2011). Only 2 h?: A qualitative study of the challenges parents perceive in restricting child television time. Journal of Family Issues, 32, 1223–1244. doi: https://doi.org/10.1177/0192513x11400558.

[109] Collins, W. A., Madsen, S. D., & Susman-Stillman, A. (2002). Parenting during middle childhood. In M. Bornstein (Ed.), Handbook of parenting (2nd ed., Vol. 1, pp. 73–101). Mahwah, NJ: Lawrence Erlbaum Associates.

developmental skills also change.[110] Contextually, as children mature, their cognitive skills develop[111] and therefore their interest in media content becomes more educational.[112] Therefore, parents will have a greater incentive to engage positively with their child's academic and educational interest and so contribute via positive mediation.[113] Moreover, as children mature in middle childhood, parents are more likely to give them greater autonomy in viewing media content which would likely result in the decreased use of parental mediation strategies.[114] Furthermore, younger children are more likely not to be able to discern between fact and fiction, and so are more likely to be scared by media content in contrast to children who are older.[115] So, children between the ages of 1 and 6 are more likely to face restrictive and active mediation parental strategies.[116] Therefore, the transition from the end of early childhood to middle childhood, between the ages of 5 and 7, may illicit the combined use of negative mediation and positive mediation efforts by parents in the development of their children.[117] The negative mediation would be required to prevent children accessing media detrimental to their development. On the other hand, the positive mediation would be required to facilitate the child's

[110] Padilla-Walker, L. M., Coyne, S. M., Fraser, A. M., Dyer, W. J., & Yorgason, J. B. (2012). Parents and adolescents growing up in the digital age: Latent growth curve analysis of proactive media monitoring. Journal of Adolescence, 35, 1153–1165. doi: https://doi.org/10.1016/j.adolescence.2012.03.005.

[111] Thomas, R. M. (1992). Comparing theories of child development (3rd ed.). Belmont, CA: Wadsworth.

[112] Wright, J. C., et al. (2001). American children's use of electronic media in 1997: A national survey. Journal of Applied Developmental Psychology, 22, 31–47. doi:https://doi.org/10.1016/S0193-3973(00)00064-2250.

[113] Beyens, I., Volkenburg, P., and Piotrowski, J. (2019), Development Trajectories of Parental Mediation Across Early and Middle Childhood, Human Communication Research, 45, pp. 226–250.

[114] Davies, J. J., & Gentile, D. A. (2012). Responses to children's media use in families with and without siblings: A family development perspective. Family Relations, 61, 410–425. doi: https://doi.org/10.1111/j.1741-3729.2012.00703.x.

[115] Cantor, J. (2002), Fright reactions to mass media. In Media effects (pp. 287–306), J. Bryant & D. Zillmann (Eds.), Hillsdale, NJ: Lawrence Erlbaum Associates.

[116] Warren, R. (2003). Parental mediation of preschool children's television viewing. Journal of Broadcasting & Electronic Media, 47, 394–417. doi:https://doi.org/10.1207/s15506878jobem4703.

[117] Beyens, I., Volkenburg, P., and Piotrowski, J. (2019), Development Trajectories of Parental Mediation Across Early and Middle Childhood, Human Communication Research, 45, pp. 226–250.

access to media which would be beneficial to their cognitive development. Therefore, negative, positive and restrictive mediation would tend to increase in early childhood according to the developmental aspects of parental mediation theory[118]—although there is a tendency for parental mediation to decrease during middle childhood. However, although these studies are indicative of the differences in mediation strategies between parents with children of different age groups, they are not indicative of how parental mediation strategies develop over time within the context of differing parental strategies.[119] In this case, the development of parental mediation strategies may evolve over time to meet the changing requirements of the child's development needs. This can only be better understood by following one family at a time over time rather than using cross-sectional studies. However, a child's behaviour may result in specific parental behaviours.[120] These behaviours could include specific mediation strategies.[121] In particular, negative behaviours exhibited by children may lead parents to adopt mediation strategies which constrain the negative behaviours of a child.[122] Therefore, it would seem likely that a combination of demographic factors and the causality between the behaviour of a child and the development of parental mediation strategies may explain the evolution of such strategies over the transition from early to middle childhood.[123] However, empirical studies which have explored the link between these variables only do so at a point in time. Therefore, such studies provide less insight into the evolutionary development of parental mediation strategies as the child develops from early to middle childhood.

[118] Ibid.

[119] Ibid.

[120] Kuczynski, L., & Parkin, M. (2007). Agency and bidirectionality in socialization: Interactions, transactions, and relational dialectics. In Handbook of Socialization (pp. 259–283), J. E. Grusec & P. Hastings (Eds.), Guilford, New York, NY.

[121] Van den Bulck, J., Custers, K., & Nelissen, S. (2016), The child-effect in the new media environment: Challenges and opportunities for communication research. Journal of Children and Media, 10, 30–38. doi:https://doi.org/10.1080/17482798.2015.1121897.

[122] Beyens, I., & Eggermont, S. (2016). Dark climates and media use in the family: The associations among child temperament, maternal mental well-being, and the frequency of mothers' use of television viewing to soothe their children. In The darker side of family communication: The harmful, the morally suspect, and the socially inappropriate L. N. Olson & M. A. Fine (Eds.), Peter Lang, New York, NY.

[123] Beyens, I., Volkenburg, P., and Piotrowski, J. (2019), Development Trajectories of Parental Mediation Across Early and Middle Childhood, Human Communication Research, 45, pp. 226–250.

Nevertheless, as children mature and develop, parental mediation becomes less active and restrictive.[124] This could perhaps be due to less interaction between the parents and the child as it becomes more autonomous as it gets older[125]—although, over time, restrictive mediation is less common than active mediation in early and middle childhood, reaching a zenith before the age of 9.[126] Furthermore, empirical analysis suggests that parental mediation strategies are different according to specific families and these differences cannot be explained just on the basis of differences in demographic factors.[127] Parental mediation strategies are important, in that if this is too restrictive it may have a negative impact on a child's development. In this case, the child may grow up and develop lacking confidence and self-esteem. On the other hand, an overtly unrestrictive mediation strategy may mean that the child is overconfident and tuned into negative habits, which may lead to conflict with others, leading to a lower integration into society later in life. However, parental mediation strategies represent just one of a number of factors which shapes the life outcomes of children as they develop over time.[128] The other factors which should be taken into account are those associated with the social and economic environment in which the child grows up.[129] Socio-economic factors and parental mediation strategies a child faces may give rise to negative and positive well-being effects later in life as an adolescent, depending on the development of the child's willpower and tenacity.[130] However, early childhood crises due to the environment into which the child is born and develops may in turn trigger the emergence and development of psychosocial and biological pathways which may or not may cause psychological

[124] Beyens, I., Volkenburg, P., and Piotrowski, J. (2019), Development Trajectories of Parental Mediation Across Early and Middle Childhood, Human Communication Research, 45, pp. 226–250.

[125] Collins, W. A., Madsen, S. D., & Susman-Stillman, A. (2002), Parenting during middle childhood. In M. Bornstein (Ed.), Handbook of parenting (2nd ed., Vol. 1, pp. 73–101), Bornstein, M. (Ed.), Lawrence Erlbaum Associates, Mahwah, NJ.

[126] Beyens, I., Volkenburg, P., and Piotrowski, J. (2019), Development Trajectories of Parental Mediation Across Early and Middle Childhood, Human Communication Research, 45, pp. 226–250.

[127] Ibid.

[128] Carr, D. (2019), Early-Life Influences on Later Life Well-Being: Innovations and Explorations, J Gerontol B Psychol Sci Soc Sci, Vol. 74, No. 5, pp. 829–831.

[129] Ibid.

[130] Ibid.

issues in later life.[131] Nevertheless, a tenacious and resilient character in adulthood may lead to overcoming the pathways associated with biological and psychosocial mechanism triggered by early stress, which may lead to ill health later in life. The factors of the external environment which may trigger these mechanisms include the unemployment of parents, mistreatment as a child and living in a stressful neighbourhood.[132] The unemployment of parents may lead a child to experience a poor socio-economic environment in early childhood. This could in turn lead to poor nutrition and a lack of social contact development, both limited by parental incomes, which could lead to mental health problems later in life.[133] Parental habits such as smoking may also lead to damaged health of a child in adulthood.[134] The detrimental health effects a child faces in adulthood are amplified if he or she also prone to the smoking habit in adulthood.[135] The level and extent of a child's socio-economic environment also has an impact on the level of development of its cognitive functioning later in life.[136] The implication is, if a child grows up in an environment in which there is a high level of disposable income, then it's chances of having access to a better level of education are higher and this will enhance the development of its cognitive abilities as it develops into adulthood. Moreover, because of better cognitive functioning, the child in adulthood will also be able to make better decisions and choices, which will ensure that it can optimise its socio-economic environment not for itself but also for its immediate family. Empirical studies have also established the likelihood of ill health in a child later in life because of having to climb a

[131] Carr, D. (2019), Early-Life Influences on Later Life Well-Being: Innovations and Explorations, J Gerontol B Psychol Sci Soc Sci, Vol. 74, No. 5, pp. 829–831.

[132] Ibid.

[133] Lam, J., & Ambrey, C. L. (2019), The scarring effects of father's unemployment? Job-security satisfaction and mental health at midlife. The Journals of Gerontology, Series B: Psychological Sciences and Social Sciences, 74, 105–112. doi:https://doi.org/10.1093/geronb/gbx117.

[134] Williams, M. M., Kemp, B. R., Ferraro, K. F., & Mustillo, S. A. (2019). Avoiding the major causes of death: Does childhood misfortune reduce the likelihood of being disease free in later life, The Journals of Gerontology, Series B:Psychological Sciences and Social Sciences, 74, 170–180. doi:https://doi.org/10.1093/geronb/gby039.

[135] Ibid.

[136] Scott, A. B., Reed, R. G., Garcia-Willingham, N. E., Lawrence, K. A., & Segerstrom, S. C. (2019). Lifespan socioeconomic context: Associations with cognitive functioning in later life. The Journals of Gerontology, Series B:Psychological Sciences and Social Sciences, 74, 113–125. doi:https://doi.org/10.1093/geronb/gby071.

mountain of adversity due to a deprived childhood. For example, a combination of a child experiencing both parental unemployment and parental bullying may contribute to a greater probability to ill health later in life.[137] Furthermore, a poor socio-economic environment in childhood may also lead to an early exposure to stress, which may also cumulatively lead to poor health over time in adulthood.[138] Stress may cause the body to produce proteins which negatively impact on gene expression in later life. [139] As a result as the child develops, it may not be able to cope with successive adversities it encounters in life, leading to more stress and to greater damage to health in later life.[140] The results of contemporary studies which have provided insights into the impact of a child's environmental circumstances on its health later in life have evaluated new data sources.[141] These include biomarker data, census-spatial data, intergenerational data and studies of ageing based on the population.[142] Studies using biomarker data have established the link between childhood adversity and ill health in adulthood by identifying the specific physiological pathways.[143] Moreover, the results of a study using census data reveal the impact on adult health due changes in parental income over time as an adult as well as the income

[137] Laditka, S. B., & Laditka, J. N. (2019). An enduring health risk of childhood adversity: Earlier, more severe, and longer lasting work disability in adult life. The Journals of Gerontology, Series B: Psychological Sciences and Social Sciences, 74, 136–147. doi: https://doi.org/10.1093/geronb/gby018.

[138] Surachman, A., Wardecker, B., Chow, S. M., & Almeida, D. (2019). Life course socio-economic status, daily stressors, and daily well-being: Examining chain of risk models. The Journals of Gerontology, Series B: Psychological Sciences and Social Sciences, 74, 126–135. doi: https://doi.org/10.1093/geronb/gby014.

[139] Meaney, M. (2001), Maternal Care, Gene Expression, and the Transmission of Individual Differences in Stress Reactivity Across Generations, Annual Review of Neuroscience 2001 24:1, 1161–1192.

[140] Dannefer, D. (2003), Cumulative advantage/disadvantage and the life course: Cross-fertilizing age and social science theory. The Journals of Gerontology, Series B: Psychological Sciences and Social Sciences, 58, S327–S337. doi: https://doi.org/10.1093/geronb/58.6.S327.

[141] Carr, D. (2019), Early-Life Influences on Later Life Well-Being: Innovations and Explorations, J Gerontol B Psychol Sci Soc Sci, Vol. 74, No. 5, pp. 829–831.

[142] Ibid.

[143] Karlamangla, A. S., Merkin, S. S., Almeida, D. M., Friedman, E. M., Mogle, J. A., & Seeman, T. E. (2019). Early-life adversity and dysregulation of adult diurnal cortisol rhythm. The Journals of Gerontology, Series B: Psychological Sciences and Social Sciences, 74, 160–169. doi: https://doi.org/10.1093/geronb/gby097.

level of the neighbourhood in which the child grows up.[144] Furthermore, studies which have analysed and evaluated intergenerational data suggest that a child growing up in a deprived environment, whether due to psychological or socio-economic circumstances, may overcome ill health as an adult through social mobility, which facilitates the development of resilience[145]—although this will also depend on the strength of character, which may be undermined by any type of abuse in childhood, leading to lack of confidence in adulthood, thus increasing the susceptibility to victimisation.[146] In addition, psychological and economic deprivation in childhood may reduce the effectiveness of being a parent in adulthood. Thus, inequality may become embedded in society in an intertemporal context. This leads to the idea that the effectiveness of intergenerational interactions as well as the cohesiveness of society may depend upon the life-changing nature of the impact of the environment in which a child grows up.[147] Therefore, at a policy level it is evident that educational and social policies should be introduced which mitigate the intertemporal transmission of the effects of childhood deprivation from one generation to the next.[148]

[144] Kail, B. L., Spring, A., & Gayman, M. (2019). A conceptual matrix of the temporal and spatial dimensions of socioeconomic status and their relationship with health. The Journals of Gerontology, Series B: Psychological Sciences and Social Sciences, 74, 148–159. doi: https://doi.org/10.1093/geronb/gby025.

[145] Willson, A. E., & Shuey, K. M. (2019). A longitudinal analysis of the intergenerational transmission of health inequality. The Journals of Gerontology, Series B: Psychological Sciences and Social Sciences, 74, 181–191. doi: https://doi.org/10.1093/geronb/gby059.

[146] Easton, S. D., Kong, J., Gregas, M. C., Shen, C., and Shafer, K. (2019), Child sexual abuse and depression in late life for men: A population-based, longitudinal analysis. The Journals of Gerontology, Series B: Psychological Sciences and Social Sciences. doi: https://doi.org/10.1093/geronb/gbx114.

[147] Lin, I. F., & Wu, H. S. (2019). Early-life parent–child relationships and adult children's support of unpartnered parents in later life. The Journals of Gerontology, Series B: Psychological Sciences and Social Sciences. doi: https://doi.org/10.1093/geronb/gby020.

[148] Carr, D. (2019), Early-Life Influences on Later Life Well-Being: Innovations and Explorations, J Gerontol B Psychol Sci Soc Sci, Vol. 74, No. 5, pp. 829–831.

Cognitive Development

The brain's emotional processing circuitry is centred in the amygdala.[149] Indeed, the structural features of the amygdala develop into their adult stage even before the birth of the infant.[150] The identification of the amygdala as the core of the brain's emotional processing circuitry was made possible due to the use of functional magnetic resonance imaging (FMRI).[151] Furthermore, studies associated with the connectivity of the amygdala with other areas of the brain indicate both positive and negative relationships.[152] For example, the amygdala shows positive connectivity with the medial prefrontal cortices and with the inula. These areas of the brain typically assess the nature of the emotional stimuli. On the other hand, the dorsal parietal and lateral prefrontal regions of the brain exhibit a negative connectivity with the amygdala. These regions of the brain associated with negative connectivity with the amygdala are associated with the regulation of both the emotional and the cognitive processes of the individual.[153] The optimal development of the amygdala is mandatory for the development of normal behaviour as well as the mental health wellbeing of a child.[154] The non-optimal development of the amygdala will lead to the development of psychiatric as well as mood disorders.[155] However, the development of the functional connectivity of the amygdala during adolescence is not so well understood and perhaps is an area in which there have not been many significant breakthroughs. Such breakthroughs would allow deeper insights into the early emergence and development of a child's capabilities associated with processing emotional

[149] Salzwedel, A., Stephens, R., Goldman, B., Lin, W., Gilmore, J., and Gao, W. (2019), Development of Amygdala Functional Connectivity During Infancy and its Relationship with 4-year Behavioural Outcomes, Biological Psychiatry CNNI, Volume 4, Issue 1, pp. 62–71.

[150] Ulfig N., Setzer, M., Bohl, J. (2003): Ontogeny of the human amygdala., Ann N Y Acad Sci 985:22–33.

[151] Salzwedel, A., Stephens, R., Goldman, B., Lin, W., Gilmore, J., and Gao, W. (2019), Development of Amygdala Functional Connectivity During Infancy and its Relationship with 4-year Behavioural Outcomes, Biological Psychiatry CNNI, Volume 4, Issue 1, pp. 62–71.

[152] Ibid.

[153] Ibid.

[154] Ibid.

[155] Ibid.

feelings.[156] This would facilitate the development of policies and interventions which would allow changes in a child's environment which may favour the optimal development of the amygdala. Moreover, the period of development of the amygdala associated with later infancy, the toddler stage of development,[157] is better associated with the emergence and development of self-emotional regulation mechanisms.[158] While later-stage infants such as toddlers have developed self-regulating emotional strategies such as self-referencing and self-comforting,[159] this is not developed in early-stage infants, who are very much dependent on their carers for emotional regulation and response stimuli.[160] Therefore, the policies and interventions should target the environment of the infant. The development of suitable policies and interventions to facilitate the creation of an optimal environment for the development of the amygdala of the infant will have implications. Specifically, the potential for the development of psychiatric as well as mood disorders during adolescence and later in life will be significantly reduced. Furthermore, the development of emotional regulatory mechanisms and strategies during late infancy has had enduring impacts on the development of not just cognition[161] but, sequentially, on an individual's quality of life.[162] Both are causally linked in that the development of higher levels of cognition will allow for better judgement, leading to optimal decisions about life choices, creating an environment which facilitates a better quality of life. It is perhaps because of the interconnectedness of the level of development of cognition and the quality of life that it is important to better understand the factors and mechanisms which

[156] Ibid.

[157] Cole, P, M., and Deater-Deckard, K. (2009), Emotion regulation, risk, and psychopathology. J Child Psychol Psychiatry 50:1327–1330.

[158] Posne, M.I., and Rothbart, M.K. (2000), Developing mechanisms of self-regulation, Dev Psychopathol 12:427–441.

[159] Salzwedel, A., Stephens, R., Goldman, B., Lin, W., Gilmore, J., and Gao, W. (2019), Development of Amygdala Functional Connectivity During Infancy and its Relationship with 4-year Behavioural Outcomes, Biological Psychiatry CNNI, Volume 4, Issue 1, pp. 62–71.

[160] Cole, P.M., Martin, S.E., and Dennis, T.A. (2004). Emotion regulation as a scientific construct: Methodological challenges and directions for child development research. Child Dev 75:317–333.

[161] Sarason, I.G. (1984), Stress, anxiety, and cognitive interference: Reactions to tests. J Pers Soc Psychol 46:929–938.

[162] Cole, P.M., Michel, M.K., and Teti, L, O. (1994), The development of emotion regulation and dysregulation: A clinical perspective. Monogr Soc Res Child Dev 59:73–100.

lead to the emergence and formation of the connections of the amygdala with other parts of the brain.[163] In this case, policy mechanisms can be put in place which enhance positive factors and mechanisms while reducing the impact of negative factors and mechanisms. However, it remains the case that the way in which the amygdala forms connections with other parts of the brain on its way to becoming central to the emotional regulatory system of the mind remains little understood.[164] Nevertheless, empirical analysis has shown that the level and state of development of the connections of the amygdala in the first 2 years of a child's life have a significant impact on its emotional and cognitive development to age 4 and beyond.[165] Specifically, in cases in which the amygdala formed connections with the sensorimotor cortices, 4 year olds did not become anxious in certain situations.[166] However, in cases where clusters formed in either the cuneus or the precuneus in the superior parietal lobule of each hemisphere of the brain in connection with the growth of the amygdala connections, it was found that the 4 year olds tended to be anxious.[167] Nevertheless, in its first year, the infant's amygdala connectivity is positively correlated with the medial prefrontal areas and negatively correlated with both the lateral parietal and the prefrontal regions. There were also regressive tendencies with regard to amygdala connectivity with the primary sensory cortices associated with behaviours such as kicking and crying.[168] It would seem, therefore, that by the end of the first year of a child's life, the brain-related network connectivity of the amygdala had reached an adult stage. This is characterised by positive connections with the prefrontal areas (subcortical and ventral medial) and negative connectivity with the parietal

[163] Salzwedel, A., Stephens, R., Goldman, B., Lin, W., Gilmore, J., and Gao, W. (2019), Development of Amygdala Functional Connectivity During Infancy and its Relationship with 4-year Behavioural Outcomes, Biological Psychiatry CNNI, Volume 4, Issue 1, pp. 62–71.

[164] Salzwedel, A., Stephens, R., Goldman, B., Lin, W., Gilmore, J., and Gao, W. (2019), Development of Amygdala Functional Connectivity During Infancy and its Relationship with 4-year Behavioural Outcomes, Biological Psychiatry CNNI, Volume 4, Issue 1, pp. 62–71.

[165] Ibid.

[166] Ibid.

[167] Ibid.

[168] Ibid.

regions (prefrontal and dorsal).[169] Furthermore, the shift of the amygdala connectivity away from the sensorimotor areas of the brain towards the medial prefrontal areas is evidenced by behaviour which is less physical and more cognitive in the context of emotional regulation in the first year of a child's life. However, while the physical aspects of emotional regulation develop in the first year, the development of emotional regulation in the second year of a child's life is characterised as being one dominated by cognitive processes, leading to the infant developing strategies for emotional regulation rather than merely acting by instinct.[170] In terms of policy, the implications are that the infant should be provided with stimuli especially in the first 2 years of its life, as well as beyond, in order to foster the optimal emotional brain connectivity in the first year and the development of cognitive emotional regulation processes in the second year. Sleep loss may also affect an infant's cognitive development by degrading several overlapping mechanisms associated with early cognitive development.[171] In this case, the development of amygdala connectivity may be negatively affected due to the loss of neural plasticity as a result of the infant losing sleep.[172] Moreover, the latter will also negatively impact on learning by degrading the ability to store knowledge through the consolidation of memories.[173] Sleep deprivation in children may also lead to depression due to the non-optimal formation of brain connections and structures as neural plasticity may be lost.[174] The emotional regulatory infrastructural development of the brain may also be impacted by the nature of the care

[169] Stein, J.L., Wiedholz, L.M., Bassett, D.S., Weinberger, D.R., Zink, C.F., Mattay, V.S., et al. (2007): A validated network of effective amygdala connectivity. NeuroImage 36:736–745

[170] Parritz, R.H. (1996): A descriptive analysis of toddler coping in challenging circumstances. Infant Behav Dev 19:171–180.

[171] Rudasill, K., Molfese, D., and Molfese, V. (2019), Child Sleep and Socioeconomic Context in the Development of Cognitive Abilities in Early Childhood, Child Development, Vol. 90, No. 5, pp. 1718–1737.

[172] Tononi, G., and Cirelli, C. (2014), Sleep and the price of plasticity: From synaptic and cellular homeostasis to memory consolidation and integration. Neuron, 81, 12–34. 10.1016/j.neuron.2013.12.025.

[173] Diekelmann, S., and Born, J. (2010), The memory function of sleep. Nature Reviews Neuroscience, 11, 114–126. https://doi.org/10.1038/nrn2762.

[174] Cheng, W., Rolls, E., Gong, W., Du, J., Zhang, J., Zhang, Xiao-Yang., Li, F., and Feng, J. (2020), Sleep Duration, Brain Structure and Psychiatric Cognitive Problems in Children, Molecular Psychiatry. https://doi.org/10.1038/s41380-020-0663-2.

giving in the first few years of a child's life and this may vary by culture.[175] Furthermore, the development of the brain will also be affected by the availability as well as the quality of food nutrients.[176]

Conclusion

Poverty and inequality are inextricably linked. This may be because poverty gives rise to poor nutrition, a lack of educational opportunities and stressed parents. As a result of these factors, an infant may therefore not be able to develop his or her cognitive ability because the full functionality of the brain will not be optimised. Newly emerging fields such as neuroimaging, epigenetics, neuroendocrinology and cognitive psychophysiology are giving researchers insights into the brain development of infants and how this may be affected by their socio-economic environment. The results of such studies will allow policymakers to optimally formulate educational, nutritional and parenting policies to facilitate the optimal brain development of infants. Children who grow up in an environment which is impoverished with regard to nutrition, education and care giving (parenting) are likely to suffer non-optimal brain development, resulting in poor memory, poor concentration and learning difficulties beyond childhood. As a result, individuals will not be able to acquire the knowledge and skills which would enable them to find jobs with good salaries. Instead, individuals may only be able to find jobs of a menial nature with low wages, which will not allow them to climb the ladders of prosperity. The ready availability of educational opportunities will facilitate the development of a child's cognitive ability, as the neuronal connections in the brain are rewired as learning takes place and new skills and experiences are acquired. The lack of educational opportunities is more likely to be widespread in developing countries, leading to greater levels of gender inequality with women being denied the right to even basic levels of literacy. Mental stimulation is particularly important during the infant stage of a child's development, as it is during this period that there is the most significant development of the brain and thus cognitive ability due to the exponential growth of synaptic

[175] Molitor, A., and Hsu, Hui-Chin(2019), Child Development Across Cultures, IN Cross-Cultural Psychology: Contemporary Themes and Perspectives, Keith, K. (Ed), John Wiley and Sons Ltd.

[176] Mattei, D., and Pietrobelli, A. (2019), Micronutrients and Brain Development, Current Nutrition Reports, 8, pp. 99–107.

connections. The brain is most malleable at younger ages, during which the environment faced by a child is quite different from the world faced by an adult brain. However, observational evidence supports the claim that the brain can be more malleable to development later in life when trauma patients may need to relearn speech and even how to walk. The level of the body's physiological stress response at an early age may impact on the development of brain cognitive function. If the stress response due to a negative external environment cannot be effectively managed, it may lead to epigenetic mechanisms which alter the brain's physiology such that later learning is inhibited in a child's path to adulthood. This may be because stress-induced epigenetic mechanisms may act to reduce the development of the hippocampus, thus degrading the development of associative memory. Stress-induced epigenetic mechanisms may cause the body to produce proteins which affect gene expression related to character development, which emphasises weakness. In this case, the optimal development of the amygdala is mandatory for the development of normal behaviour as well as the mental well-being of the child. This is specifically because the development of the amygdala is associated with the emergence and development of self-emotional regulation mechanisms.

References

Arrington, C. N., Kulesz, P. A., Francis, D. J., Fletcher, J. M., & Barnes, M. A. (2014). The contribution of attentional control and working memory to reading comprehension and decoding. *Scientific Studies of Reading, 18*(5), 325–346. https://doi.org/10.1080/10888438.2014.902461

Ayoub, M., et al. (2019). Genetic and environmental associations between child personality and parenting. *Social Psychological and Personality Science, 10*(6), 711–721.

Berman, M., Kardan, O., Kotabe, H., Nusbaum, H., & London, S. (2019). The promise of environmental neuroscience. *Nature Human Behaviour, 3*, 414–417.

Beyens, I., & Eggermont, S. (2016). Dark climates and media use in the family: The associations among child temperament, maternal mental well-being, and the frequency of mothers' use of television viewing to soothe their children. In N. Olson & M. A. Fine (Eds.), *The Darker Side of Family Communication: The Harmful, the Morally Suspect, and the Socially Inappropriate L.* Peter Lang.

Beyens, I., Volkenburg, P., & Piotrowski, J. (2019). Development trajectories of parental mediation across early and middle childhood. *Human Communication Research, 45*, 226–250.

Bick, J., Naumova, O., Hunter, S., Barbot, B., Lee, M., Luthar, S. S., & Grigorenko, E. L. (2012). Childhood adversity and DNA methylation of genes involved in the hypothalamus-pituitary adrenal axis and immune system: Whole-genome and candidate-gene associations. *Development and Psychopathology, 24*(4), 1417–1425.

BIS (Department for Business Innovation and Skills). (2009). *Skills for Life: Changing Lives*. BIS.

Blair, C. (2016). Developmental science and executive function. *Current Directions in Psychological Science, 25*(1), 3–7. https://doi.org/10.1177/0963721415622634

Blair, C., & Raver, C. C. (2012). Child development in the context of adversity: Experiential canalization of brain and behavior. *American Psychologist, 67*(4), 309–318. https://doi.org/10.1037/a0027493

Blankenship, T., Slough, M., Calkins, S., Deater-Deckard, K., Kim-Spoon, J., & Bell, M. (2018). Attention and executive functioning in infancy: Links to childhood executive function and reading achievement. *Developmental Science, 22*, e12824. https://doi.org/10.1111/desc.12824

Böcking, S., & Böcking, T. (2009). Parental mediation of television. *Journal of Children and Media, 3*, 286–302. https://doi.org/10.1080/17482790902999959

Bornstein, M. H. (2014). Human infancy… and the rest of the lifespan. *Annual Review of Psychology, 65*, 121–158. https://doi.org/10.1146/annurevpsych-120710-100359

Briley, D., Livengood, J., Derringer, J., Tucker-Drob, E., Fraley, R., & Roberts, B. (2017). Interpreting behaviour genetic models: Seven developmental processes to understand. *Behaviour Genetics, 49*, 196–210.

Cantor, J. (2002). Fright reactions to mass media. In J. Bryant & D. Zillmann (Eds.), *Media Effects* (pp. 287–306). Lawrence Erlbaum Associates.

Carlson, S. M., Mandell, D. J., & Williams, L. (2004). Executive function and theory of mind: Stability and prediction from ages 2 to 3. *Developmental Psychology, 40*, 1105. https://doi.org/10.1037/0012-1649.40.6.1105

Carr, D. (2019). Early-life influences on later life well-being: Innovations and explorations. *The Journals of Gerontology. Series B, Psychological Sciences and Social Sciences, 74*(5), 829–831.

Case, A., & Paxson, C. (2006). Stature and status: Height, ability and labor market outcomes. NBER, Working Paper No. 12466.

Casey, B. J., Heller, A., Gee, D., & Cohen, A. (2019). Development of the emotional brain. *Neuroscience Letters, 693*, 29–34.

Cheng, W., Rolls, E., Gong, W., Du, J., Zhang, J., Zhang, X.-Y., Li, F., & Feng, J. (2020). Sleep duration, brain structure and psychiatric cognitive problems in children. *Molecular Psychiatry*. https://doi.org/10.1038/s41380-020-0663-2

Cole, P. M., & Deater-Deckard, K. (2009). Emotion regulation, risk, and psychopathology. *Journal of Child Psychology and Psychiatry, 50*, 1327–1330.

Cole, P. M., Martin, S. E., & Dennis, T. A. (2004). Emotion regulation as a scientific construct: Methodological challenges and directions for child development research. *Child Development, 75*, 317–333.

Cole, P. M., Michel, M. K., & Teti, L. O. (1994). The development of emotion regulation and dysregulation: A clinical perspective. *Monographs of the Society for Research in Child Development, 59*, 73–100.

Collins, W. A., Madsen, S. D., & Susman-Stillman, A. (2002). Parenting during middle childhood. In M. Bornstein (Ed.), *Handbook of Parenting* (Vol. 1, 2nd ed., pp. 73–101). Lawrence Erlbaum Associates.

Coyne, S. M., Padilla-Walker, L. M., Stockdale, L., & Day, R. D. (2011). Game on … girls: Associations between co-playing video games and adolescent behavioral and family outcomes. *Journal of Adolescent Health, 49*, 160–165. https://doi.org/10.1016/j.jadohealth.2010.11.249

Cuevas, K., & Bell, M. A. (2014). Infant attention and early childhood executive function. *Child Development, 85*, 397–404. https://doi.org/10.1111/cdev.12126

Dannefer, D. (2003). Cumulative advantage/disadvantage and the life course: Cross-fertilizing age and social science theory. *The Journals of Gerontology, Series B: Psychological Sciences and Social Sciences, 58*, S327–S337. https://doi.org/10.1093/geronb/58.6.S327

Davies, J. J., & Gentile, D. A. (2012). Responses to children's media use in families with and without siblings: A family development perspective. *Family Relations, 61*, 410–425. https://doi.org/10.1111/j.1741-3729.2012.00703.x

Diamond, A. (2013). Executive functions. *Annual Review of Psychology, 64*, 35–168. https://doi.org/10.1146/annurev-psych-113011-143750

Diekelmann, S., & Born, J. (2010). The memory function of sleep. *Nature Reviews Neuroscience, 11*, 114–126. https://doi.org/10.1038/nrn2762

Easton, S. D., Kong, J., Gregas, M. C., Shen, C., & Shafer, K. (2019). Child sexual abuse and depression in late life for men: A population-based, longitudinal analysis. *The Journals of Gerontology, Series B: Psychological Sciences and Social Sciences*. https://doi.org/10.1093/geronb/gbx114

Essex, M. J., et al. (2013). *Child Development, 84*, 58–75.

Evans, C. A., Jordan, A. B., & Horner, J. (2011). Only two hours?: A qualitative study of the challenges parents perceive in restricting child television time. *Journal of Family Issues, 32*, 1223–1244. https://doi.org/10.1177/0192513x11400558

Fox, S. E., Levitt, P., & Nelson, C. A. (2010). How the timing and quality of early experiences influence the development of brain architecture. *Child Development, 81*(1), 28–40. https://doi.org/10.1111/j.1467-8624.2009.01380.x

Frick, J. E., Colombo, J., & Saxon, T. F. (1999). Individual and developmental differences in disengagement of fixation in early infancy. *Child Development, 70*, 537–548. https://doi.org/10.1111/1467-8624.00039

Gershoff, E. T., Raver, C. C., Aber, J. L., & Lennon, M. C. (2007). Income is not enough: Incorporating material hardship into models of income associations with parenting and child development. *Child Development, 78*(1), 70–95.

Godar, S., et al. (2019). Gene-environment interactions in anti-social behaviour are mediated by early life 5-HT_{2A} receptor activation. *Neuropharmacology, 159*.

Hackman, D. A., Martha, J. F., & Michael, J. M. (2010). Socioeconomic status and the brain: Mechanistic insights from human and animal research. *Nature Reviews Neuroscience, 11*(9), 651–659.

Heckman, J. J., & Mosso, S. (2014). The economics of human development and social mobility. *Annual Review of Economics, 6*(1), 689–733. https://doi.org/10.1146/annurev-economics-080213-040753

Hill, P., Edmonds, G., & Jackson, J. (2019). Pathways linking childhood personality to late life outcomes. *Childhood Development Perspectives, 13*(2), 116–120.

Huttenlocher, P. R. (2002). *Neural Plasticity: The Effects of the Environment on the Development of the Cerebral Cortex*. Harvard University Press.

Jenkins, J., & Handa, S. (2009). Parenting skills and early childhood development: Production function estimates from longitudinal data. *Review of Economics of the Household, 17*, 121–147.

Johnson, S. L., Wibbels, E., & Wilkinson, R. (2015). Economic inequality is related to cross-national prevalence of psychotic symptoms. *Social Psychiatry and Psychiatric Epidemiology, 50*(12), 1799–1807.

Jones, S., McGarrah, M., & Khan, J. (2019). Social and emotional learning: A principled science of human development in context. *Educational Psychologist, 54*(3), 129–143.

Kail, B. L., Spring, A., & Gayman, M. (2019). A conceptual matrix of the temporal and spatial dimensions of socioeconomic status and their relationship with health. *The Journals of Gerontology, Series B: Psychological Sciences and Social Sciences, 74*, 148–159. https://doi.org/10.1093/geronb/gby025

Kandler, C., Waaktaar, T., Mattus, R., Riemann, R., & Torgersen, S. (2019). Unravelling the interplay between genetic and environmental contributions in the unfolding of personality differences from early adolescence to young adulthood. *European Journal of Personality, 33*, 221–244.

Karlamangla, A. S., Merkin, S. S., Almeida, D. M., Friedman, E. M., Mogle, J. A., & Seeman, T. E. (2019). Early-life adversity and dysregulation of adult diurnal cortisol rhythm. *The Journals of Gerontology, Series B: Psychological Sciences and Social Sciences, 74*, 160–169. https://doi.org/10.1093/geronb/gby097

Knowland, V., & Thomas, M. (2014). Educating the adult brain: How the neuroscience of learning can inform educational policy. *International Review of Education, 60*, 99–122.

Kovas, Y., Henry, J., Feklicheva, I., Soldatova, E., & Malykh, S. (2016). Early environment and development: Epigenetic mechanisms. In S. B. Malykh et al. (Eds.), *Behavioural Genomics: Child Development and Education*. Publishing House of Tomsk State University.

Krapohl, E., Rimfeld, K., Nicholas, G., Shakeshaft, N., Trzaskowski, M., McMillan, A., et al. (2014). The high heritability of educational achievement reflects many genetically influenced traits, not just intelligence. *Proceedings of the National Academy of Sciences of the United States of America*. www.pnas.org. https://doi.org/10.1073/pnas.1408777111

Kuczynski, L., & Parkin, M. (2007). Agency and bidirectionality in socialization: Interactions, transactions, and relational dialectics. In J. E. Grusec & P. Hastings (Eds.), *Handbook of Socialization* (pp. 259–283). Guilford.

Laditka, S. B., & Laditka, J. N. (2019). An enduring health risk of childhood adversity: Earlier, more severe, and longer lasting work disability in adult life. *The Journals of Gerontology, Series B: Psychological Sciences and Social Sciences, 74*, 136–147. https://doi.org/10.1093/geronb/gby018

Lam, J., & Ambrey, C. L. (2019). The scarring effects of father's unemployment? Job-security satisfaction and mental health at midlife. *The Journals of Gerontology, Series B: Psychological Sciences and Social Sciences, 74*, 105–112. https://doi.org/10.1093/geronb/gbx117

Lambert, H., Peverill, M., Sambrook, K., Rosen, M., Shendan, M., & McLaughlin, K. (2019). Altered development of hippocampus-dependent associative learning following early life adversity. *Developmental Cognitive Neuroscience, 38*.

Lewin, K. (1936). *Principles of Topological Psychology* (pp. 4–7). McGraw-Hill.

Lin, I. F., & Wu, H. S. (2019). Early-life parent–child relationships and adult children's support of unpartnered parents in later life. *The Journals of Gerontology, Series B: Psychological Sciences and Social Sciences*. https://doi.org/10.1093/geronb/gby020

Lipsey, M. W., Kerry, G. H., Dong, N., Farran, D. C., & Bilbrey, C. (2013). *Evaluation of the Tennessee Voluntary Prekindergarten Program: Kindergarten and First Grade Follow-Up Results from the Randomized Control Design*. Vanderbilt University, Peabody Research Institute.

Love, J. M., Kisker, E. E., Ross, C., Raikes, H., Constantine, J., Boller, K., Brooks-Gunn, J., Chazan-Cohen, R., Banks Tarullo, L., Brady-Smith, C., Sidle Fuligni, A., Schochet, P. Z., Paulsell, D., & Vogel, C. (2005). The effectiveness of early head start for 3-year-old children and their parents: Lessons for policy and programs. *Developmental Psychology, 41*(6), 885–901.

Luthar, S. S., Crossman, E. J., & Small, P. J. (2015). Resilience and adversity. In R. M. Lerner (Ed.), *Handbook of Child Psychology and Developmental Science: Vol. 3. Socioemotional Processes* (7th ed., pp. 247–286). Wiley.

Magnuson, K., & Schindler, H. (2019). Supporting children's early development by building caregivers capacities and skills: A theoretical approach informed by new neuroscience research. *Journal of Family Theory and Review, 11*, 59–78.

Mareschal, D., Tolmie, A., & Butterworth, B. (2013). *Educational Neuroscience*. Wiley-Blackwell.

Mattei, D., & Pietrobelli, A. (2019). Micronutrients and brain development. *Current Nutrition Reports, 8*, 99–107.

McVay, J. C., & Kane, M. J. (2012). Why does working memory capacity predict variation in reading comprehension? On the influence of mind wandering and executive attention. *Journal of Experimental Psychology: General, 141*, 302. https://doi.org/10.1037/a0025250

Meaney, M. (2001). Maternal care, gene expression, and the transmission of individual differences in stress reactivity across generations. *Annual Review of Neuroscience, 24*(1), 1161–1192.

Molitor, A., & Hsu, H.-C. (2019). Child development across cultures. In K. Keith (Ed.), *Cross-Cultural Psychology: Contemporary Themes and Perspectives*. Wiley.

Nathanson, A. I. (1999). Identifying and explaining the relationship between parental mediation and children's aggression. *Communication Research, 26*, 124–143. https://doi.org/10.1177/009365099026002002

Neville, H. J., Mills, D. L., & Lawson, D. S. (1992). Fractionating language: Different neural subsystems with different sensitive periods. *Cerebral Cortex, 2*(3), 244–258.

Nikken, P., & Schols, M. (2015). How and why parents' guide the media use of young children. *Journal of Child and Family Studies, 24*, 3423–3435. https://doi.org/10.1007/s10826-015-0144-4

Osher, D., Cantor, P., Berg, J., Steyer, L., & Rose, T. (2020). Drivers of human development: How relationships and context shape learning and development. *Applied Developmental Science, 24*(1), 6–36.

Padilla-Walker, L. M., Coyne, S. M., Fraser, A. M., Dyer, W. J., & Yorgason, J. B. (2012). Parents and adolescents growing up in the digital age: Latent growth curve analysis of proactive media monitoring. *Journal of Adolescence, 35*, 1153–1165. https://doi.org/10.1016/j.adolescence.2012.03.005

Palladino, V., McNeill, R., Reif, A., & Kittel-Schneider, S. (2019). Genetic risk factors and gene-environment interactions in adult and childhood attention-deficit/hyperactivity disorder. *Psychiatric Genetics, 29*(3).

Parritz, R. H. (1996). A descriptive analysis of toddler coping in challenging circumstances. *Infant Behavior & Development, 19*, 171–180.

Pinto, R., Ashworth, M., & Jones, R. (2008). Schizophrenia in black Caribbeans living in the UK: An exploration of underlying causes of the high incidence rate. *British Journal of General Practice, 58*(551), 429–434.

Plomin, R., DeFries, J. C., Knopik, V. S., & Neiderhiser, J. M. (2016). Top 10 replicated findings from behavioral genetics. *Perspectives on Psychological Science, 11*(1), 3–23.

Polderman, T. J., Posthuma, D., De Sonneville, L. M., Stins, J. F., Verhulst, F. C., & Boomsma, D. I. (2007). Genetic analyses of the stability of executive functioning during childhood. *Biological Psychology, 76*(1), 11–20. https://doi.org/10.1016/j.biopsycho.2007.05.002

Pollak, S., & Wolfe, B. (2020). How developmental neuroscience can help address the problem of child poverty, National Bureau of Economic Research, Working Paper No. 26842.

Posne, M. I., & Rothbart, M. K. (2000). Developing mechanisms of self-regulation. *Development and Psychopathology, 12*, 427–441.

Posner, M. I., & Rothbart, M. K. (2007). Research on attention networks as a model for the integration of psychological science. *Annual Review of Psychology, 58*, 1–23. https://doi.org/10.1146/annurev.psych.58.110405.085516

Rao, N., Richards, B., Sun, J., Weber, A., & Sincovich, A. (2019). Early childhood education and child development in four countries in East Asia and the Pacific. *Early Childhood Research Quarterly, 47*, 169–181.

Reardon, S. F. (2011). The widening academic achievement gap between the rich and the poor: New evidence and possible explanations. In G. J. Duncan & R. J. Murnane (Eds.), *Whither Opportunity*. Russell Sage Foundation.

Richards, B., et al. (2019). A deep learning framework for neuroscience. *Nature Neuroscience, 22*, 1761–1770.

Rudasill, K., Molfese, D., & Molfese, V. (2019). Child sleep and socioeconomic context in the development of cognitive abilities in early childhood. *Child Development, 90*(5), 1718–1737.

Salzwedel, A., Stephens, R., Goldman, B., Lin, W., Gilmore, J., & Gao, W. (2019). Development of amygdala functional connectivity during infancy and its relationship with 4-year behavioural outcomes. *Biological Psychiatry CNNI, 4*(1), 62–71.

Sarason, I. G. (1984). Stress, anxiety, and cognitive interference: Reactions to tests. *Journal of Personality and Social Psychology, 46*, 929–938.

Sari, I. N., & Nugrahani, A. (2022). Level of knowledge, attitude, and behavior of pregnant women in giving stimulation to the fetus. *Open Access Indonesian Journal of Medical Reviews, 2*(3), 234–238. https://doi.org/10.37275/oaijmr.v2i3.192

Schmahmann, J., Guell, X., Stoodley, C., & Halko, M. (2019). The theory and neuroscience of cerebellar cognition. *Annual Review of Neuroscience, 42*.

Schultz, W., Dayan, P., & Montague, P. R. (1997). A neural substrate of production and reward. *Science, 275*, 1593–1599.

Scott, A. B., Reed, R. G., Garcia-Willingham, N. E., Lawrence, K. A., & Segerstrom, S. C. (2019). Lifespan socioeconomic context: Associations with cognitive functioning in later life. *The Journals of Gerontology, Series B: Psychological Sciences and Social Sciences, 74*, 113–125. https://doi.org/10.1093/geronb/gby071

Selita, F., & Kovas, Y. (2019). Genes and Gini: What inequality means for heritability. *Journal of Biosocial Science, 51*, 18–47.

Shah, et al. (2014). Genetic and environmental exposures constrain epigenetic drift over the human life course. *Genome Research, 24*, 1725–1733.

Shin, W., & Li, B. (2017). Parental mediation of children's digital technology use in Singapore. *Journal of Children and Media, 11*, 1–19. https://doi.org/10.1080/17482798.2016.1203807

Stein, J. L., Wiedholz, L. M., Bassett, D. S., Weinberger, D. R., Zink, C. F., Mattay, V. S., et al. (2007). A validated network of effective amygdala connectivity. *NeuroImage, 36*, 736–745.

Stumm, S., Smith-Woolley, E., Ayorech, Z., McMillan, A., Rimfield, K., Dale, P., & Plomin, R. (2019). Predicting educational achievement from genomic measures and socio-economic status. *Development Science*. https://doi.org/10.1111/desc.12925

Surachman, A., Wardecker, B., Chow, S. M., & Almeida, D. (2019). Life course socioeconomic status, daily stressors, and daily well-being: Examining chain of risk models. *The Journals of Gerontology, Series B: Psychological Sciences and Social Sciences, 74*, 126–135. https://doi.org/10.1093/geronb/gby014

Thomas, R. M. (1992). *Comparing Theories of Child Development* (3rd ed.). Wadsworth.

Thomas, M. S. C. (2012). Brain plasticity and education. *British Journal of Educational Psychology—Monograph Series II: Educational Neuroscience, 8*, 142–156.

Thomas, M. S. C., & Johnson, M. H. (2008). New advances in understanding sensitive periods in brain development. *Current Directions in Psychological Science, 17*(1), 1–5.

Toll, S. W., Van der Ven, S. H., Kroesbergen, E. H., & Van Luit, J. E. (2011). Executive functions as predictors of math learning disabilities. *Journal of Learning Disabilities, 44*, 521–532. https://doi.org/10.1177/0022219410387302

Tononi, G., & Cirelli, C. (2014). Sleep and the price of plasticity: From synaptic and cellular homeostasis to memory consolidation and integration. *Neuron, 81*, 12–34. https://doi.org/10.1016/j.neuron.2013.12.025

Ulfig, N., Setzer, M., & Bohl, J. (2003). Ontogeny of the human amygdala. *Annals of the New York Academy of Sciences, 985*, 22–33.

UNESCO (United Nations Educational, Scientific and Cultural Organisation). (2004). *The Plurality of Literacy and Its Implications for Policies and Programmes*. UNESCO Education Sector.

Valkenburg, P. M., Piotrowski, J. T., Hermanns, J., & de Leeuw, R. (2013). Developing and validating the perceived parental media mediation scale: A self-determination perspective. *Human Communication Research, 39*, 445–469. https://doi.org/10.1111/hcre.12010

Van Barell, C., Weiss, A., & Penke, L. (2019). Developing individual differences in primate behaviour: The role of genes, environment and their interplay. *Behavioral Ecology and Sociobiology, 73*, 20.

Van den Bulck, J., Custers, K., & Nelissen, S. (2016). The child-effect in the new media environment: Challenges and opportunities for communication research. *Journal of Children and Media, 10*, 30–38. https://doi.org/10.1080/17482798.2015.1121897

Warren, R. (2003). Parental mediation of preschool children's television viewing. *Journal of Broadcasting & Electronic Media, 47*, 394–417. https://doi.org/10.1207/s15506878jobem4703

Williams, M. M., Kemp, B. R., Ferraro, K. F., & Mustillo, S. A. (2019). Avoiding the major causes of death: Does childhood misfortune reduce the likelihood of being disease free in later life. *The Journals of Gerontology, Series B: Psychological Sciences and Social Sciences, 74*, 170–180. https://doi.org/10.1093/geronb/gby039

Willson, A. E., & Shuey, K. M. (2019). A longitudinal analysis of the intergenerational transmission of health inequality. *The Journals of Gerontology, Series B: Psychological Sciences and Social Sciences, 74*, 181–191. https://doi.org/10.1093/geronb/gby059

World Bank (2017) The World Bank GINI Report. http://data.worldbank.org/indicator/SI.POV.GINI

Wright, J. C., et al. (2001). American children's use of electronic media in 1997: A national survey. Journal of Applied Developmental Psychology, 22, 31–47. https://doi.org/10.1016/S0193-3973(00)00064-2250.

Zelazo, P. D. (2004). The development of conscious control in childhood. *Trends in Cognitive Sciences, 8*(1), 12–17.

Zhang, Y. E., Landback, P., Vibranovski, M. D., & Long, M. (2011). Accelerated recruitment of new brain development genes into the human genome. *PLoS Biology, 9*(10), e1001179. https://doi.org/10.1371/journal.pbio.1001179

CHAPTER 6

Personality Psychology

Introduction

Neoclassical economic theory considers individuals as consumers, with a uniform persona and indistinguishable by personality, categorised as making rational choices based on the availability of perfect information. However, individuals have separate and distinct personalities. For example, in the field of psychology, an individual's personality is associated with a specific set of beliefs which encompasses a thinking processes, values and personality traits. However, in economic theory, while individual preferences persist due to the assumption that individuals make rational choices facilitated by the assumption of perfect knowledge, beliefs arise through the process of equilibrium, through the expression of choice between bundles of different goods. In this case, economists would conclude that an individual's beliefs would have an impact on his/her choices.[1] Moreover, beliefs depend upon ideologies or cognitive frames.[2] To an extent, the latter imposes limitations on the potential data which can be observed and processed.[3] This is because as the environment changes, either by economic crises or by technological change, the beliefs and perceptions of

[1] Hoff, K., and Stiglitz, J. (2010), Equilibrium Fictions: A Cognitive Approach to Societal Rigidity, American Economic Review, Papers and Proceedings, 100, pp. 141–146.

[2] Ibid.

[3] Ibid.

S. Ramesh, *The Political Economy of Human Behaviour and Economic Development*,
https://doi.org/10.1007/978-3-031-12666-6_6

some individuals may change while those of others remain unchanged. The result may be that institutional change in society remains constrained.[4]

Economic theory does not recognise that individuals are different from each other due to differences in personality traits as well as in the formation and organisation of psychological systems such as the brain. The reason for this is to simplify the analysis of the real world, to allow relationships between variables to be mathematically modelled, but with the disadvantage that abstract results are produced. Therefore, for economic analysis to be more realistic, its tools should also encompass the tools of personality psychology, which facilitates an evaluation of how individual differences in traits arise. Traits have a direct impact on how an individual may feel and function. The extent to which an individual will be able to overcome a harsh environment to remain 'feeling good' may impact on an individual's health and contentment. If there is an optimal combination of personality traits which allows individuals to succeed and thrive, leading a contented and healthy life, then it is important to consider how personality traits may form. In this context, scholarly work suggests that the responses of infants are more associated with environmental factors rather than genetic ones. Moreover, the environment in which an infant/child develops is not totally under its control but under that of its primary caregiver. Furthermore, the nature and quality of an infant's/child's relationship with its primary caregiver has a direct impact on the extent of the child's emotional and motivational stability as an adult. The lesson is therefore that the provision of quality childcare is important, and the question arises as to whether the state should have a role and a responsibility for its provision. Economic crises may also impact on the development of personality, with those growing up during tough times being more resilient in adulthood in comparison to those who have had a 'soft' upbringing. From an economics point of view, early intervention to facilitate the development of optimal, balanced personality traits is desired to prevent and reduce the extent of personality and mental disorders in adulthood. Such disorders will have economic impacts such as lower, if any, worker productivity and public spending on the medical care and treatment of those afflicted.

[4] Ibid.

Developmental Perspectives on Personality: From Youth Based to Life Span Models

An individual's personality is best described as resulting from how experiences and behaviour shape internal physiological systems.[5] One of the features of an individual's personality are traits. These may impact on an individual's disposition and determine the level of his/her health and contentment.[6] The development of personality over a lifetime is embedded in attachment theory.[7] This relates to how closely an infant/a child is attached to his/her primary caregiver, securely or insecurely.[8] The degree to which an infant/a child is attached to its primary caregiver will determine the level of his/her motivational and emotional stability in later life, although there may be some volatility during adolescence due to the release of hormones signalling the transition from childhood to adulthood. The nature of an individual's motivational and emotional stability will determine the extent to which they can maintain relations for a period as well as the nature of the relationships.[9] In this case, according to attachment theory, infants/children first begin to become aware of the world and its environment from the behaviour and responses of its primary caregiver to stimuli, especially ones relating to threats and distress.[10] In such scenarios, infants/children would normally seek the protection of their primary caregivers,[11] although the extent of this would depend on the nature of the relationship

[5] Asendorff, J. (2002), Editorial: The Puzzle of Personality Types, European Journal of Personality, Eur. J. Pers, 16.

[6] Costa, P., McCrae, R., and Lockenhoff, C. (2019), Personality Across the Life Span, Annual Review of Psychology, 70, 423–48.

[7] Bowlby, J. (1980), Attachment and loss: Vol. 3. Loss, sadness and depression. Basic Books, New York, NY.

[8] Young, E., Simpson, J., Grishevicius, V., Huelsnitz, C., and Fleck, C, (2019), Childhood Attachment and Adult Personality: A Lifetime Perspective, Self and Identity, Vol.18, No.1, 22–38.

[9] Ibid.

[10] Simpson, J. A., and Rholes., W. S. (2012), Adult attachment orientations, stress, and romantic relationships. In Advances in experimental social psychology, Devine, P., and Plant, A. (Eds.), Vol. 45 (pp. 279–328), Academic Press, Burlington, MA.

[11] Young, E., Simpson, J., Grishevicius, V., Huelsnitz, C., and Fleck, C, (2019), Childhood Attachment and Adult Personality: A Life Time Perspective, Self and Identity, Vol.18, No.1, 22–38.

between the two.[12] A secure understanding relationship between the infant/child and the caregiver will result in him/her seeking the comfort and the security of the caregiver when faced with a threat which may cause distress in order to hold back any negative emotions which may arise.[13] In this case, as a result of positive shared experiences between the caregiver and the infant/child, the latter will learn an identity which is associated with self-worth, while the former is viewed as someone who can maintain that status due their ability to provide support and care.[14] However, if an infant/a child has a negative relationship with a primary caregiver, then this may give rise to feelings of insecurity, in which the caregiver is viewed as someone who is unable to provide love, support and protection, and so the infant/child develops an entirely self-reliant system for protecting itself from situations which may cause harm or distress.[15] Such a self-reliant system will cause a sense of distrust to arise between the infant/child and others as it grows into adulthood and beyond, leading to unstable and short-term relationships with others.[16] However, this is not to say that experiences later in life will not act to change the internal constructs of dealing with stimuli from the external environment in a positive way.[17] Nevertheless, the nature of the attachment patterns experienced by infants and children early in life will have an enduring effect on relationships during adulthood and later in life.[18] However, there is some evidence to suggest that personality traits remain malleable to some extent even in

[12] Bakermans-Kranenburg, M. J., and Van IJzendoorn, M. H. (2016), Attachment, parenting, and genetics. In Handbook of attachment: Theory, research, and clinical applications, Cassidy, J., and Shaver, P. R. (Eds.), Guilford Press, New York, NY.

[13] Ainsworth, M. D. S., Blehar, M. C., Waters, E., and Wall, S. (1978), Patterns of attachment: A psychological study of the strange situation, Lawrence Erlbaum, Hillsdale, NJ.

[14] Bowlby, J. (1973), Attachment and loss: Vol. 2. Separation, Basic Books, New York, NY.

[15] Ainsworth, M. D. S., Blehar, M. C., Waters, E., and Wall, S. (1978), Patterns of attachment: A psychological study of the strange situation, Lawrence Erlbaum, Hillsdale, NJ.

[16] Young, E., Simpson, J., Grishevicius, V., Huelsnitz, C., and Fleck, C, (2019), Childhood Attachment and Adult Personality: A Lifetime Perspective, Self and Identity, Vol.18, No.1, 22–38.

[17] Fraley, R. C., and Brumbaugh, C. C. (2004), A dynamical systems approach to conceptualizing and studying stability and change in attachment security, IN Adult attachment: Theory, research, and clinical implications, Rholes, S.W, and J. A. Simpson, J.A. (Eds.), Guilford Press, New York, NY.

[18] Simpson, J. A., Collins, W. A., Tran, S., and Haydon, K. C. (2007), Attachment and the experience and expression of emotions in romantic relationships: A developmental perspective. Journal of Personality and Social Psychology, 92, 355–367.

adulthood.[19] The way in which early attachment patterns as future indicators of stability have been examined has been by observing the behaviour of infants in the 12- to 18-month age group when left in a room by themselves as well as left with a stranger, with the primary caregiver departing and returning a while later.[20] Those infants with attachment patterns promoting stability tended to calm down much more quickly as a result of being left in unfamiliar surroundings compared to those infants with attachment patterns promoting instability, who took longer to calm down.[21] Studies have shown that the responses of the infants are more associated with environmental factors[22] rather than with genetic factors.[23] The implication is that the environment in which an infant/child grows up and its associated relationship with its primary caregiver has a greater effect on determining the nature of attachment pattern stability than do genetic factors associated with personality.[24] Therefore, the quality of childcare provision during infancy and early childhood is important in determining the level of motivational and emotional stability in adulthood.[25] Moreover, evolutionary models of development also suggest that an infant's exposure to stress early in life will result in lower emotional stability, leading to unstable relationships, fast sexual maturation as well as poor parenting.[26] On the other hand, infants and children exposed to less

[19] Roberts, B., and Mroczek, D. (2008), Personality Trait Change in Adulthood, Current Directions in Psychological Science, Vol.17, No.1.

[20] Ainsworth, M. D. S., Blehar, M. C., Waters, E., and Wall, S. (1978), Patterns of attachment: A psychological study of the strange situation, Lawrence Erlbaum, Hillsdale, NJ.

[21] Young, E., Simpson, J., Grishevicius, V., Huelsnitz, C., and Fleck, C, (2019), Childhood Attachment and Adult Personality: A Lifetime Perspective, Self and Identity, Vol.18, No.1, 22–38.

[22] Bokhorst, C. L., Bakermans-kranenburg, M. J., Fonagy, P., and Schuengel, C. (2003), The importance of shared environments in mother-infant attachment security: A behavioral genetic study. Child Development, 74, 1769–1782.

[23] O'Connor, T. G., and Croft, C. M. (2001), A twin study of attachment in preschool children. Child Development, 72, 1501–1511.

[24] Young, E., Simpson, J., Grishevicius, V., Huelsnitz, C., and Fleck, C, (2019), Childhood Attachment and Adult Personality: A Lifetime Perspective, Self and Identity, Vol.18, No.1, 22–38.

[25] Fearon, P. R., and Belsky, J. (2016), Precursors of attachment security IN Handbook of attachment. Theory, research, and clinical applications, Cassidy, J., and Shaver, P.R. (Eds.), Guilford Press, New York, NY.

[26] Young, E., Simpson, J., Grishevicius, V., Huelsnitz, C., and Fleck, C, (2019), Childhood Attachment and Adult Personality: A Lifetime Perspective, Self and Identity, Vol.18, No.1, 22–38.

stress in early adulthood will find that he/she is able to form stable relationships, mature sexually more slowly as well as become better parents.[27] However, it is now becoming evident that specific infant/childhood environments may actually have an impact on determining motivational and emotional stability in adulthood, as such environments may favour the development of either unstable or stable emotional patterns.[28] The latter is associated with resilience, although this is sometimes viewed as a collective family construct rather than remaining purely individualistic.[29] Those infants/children who have experienced secure attachments early in life may adopt slow-paced, cooperative strategies in adulthood.[30] On the other hand, those infants/children who have experienced less secure attachments may adopt a fast paced, self-reliant, opportunistic strategy in adulthood.[31] Thus, from an evolutionary perspective, the features of an individual's personality may have emerged and developed in response to infant/childhood environments in order to facilitate either a slow- or a fast-paced life strategy depending on the level of emotional/motivational stability he/she developed in response to the nature of the attachment with the primary caregiver.[32] However, historical circumstances such as economic crises may also change the pattern of development of an individual personality and the environmental factors brought about by such crises may actually contribute towards the development of a more robust and stable personality in some circumstances. For example, some children who grew up during the years of the Great Depression of the 1930s prospered as adults.[33] It may also be the case that even if environments are personally selected by individuals, it may not be optimal and some factors

[27] Ibid.

[28] Nettle, D. (2010), Dying young and living fast: Variation in life history across English neighbourhoods. Behavioral Ecology, 21, 387–395.

[29] Hawley, D., and DeHaan, L. (1996), Toward a Definitions of Family Resilience: Integrating Life-Span and Family Perspectives, Fam Proc, 35:283–298.

[30] Nettle, D. (2010), Dying young and living fast: Variation in life history across English neighbourhoods. Behavioral Ecology, 21, 387–395.

[31] Ibid.

[32] Young, E., Simpson, J., Grishevicius, V., Huelsnitz, C., and Fleck, C, (2019), Childhood Attachment and Adult Personality: A Lifetime Perspective, Self and Identity, Vol.18, No.1, 22–38.

[33] Elder, G. (1998), The Life Course as Developmental Theory, Child Development, Vol.69, No.1, pp. 1–12.

within the environment may not be agreeable to the individual, leading to personality changes.[34]

A greater level of stability gained by strong caring relationships with the primary caregiver will lead the infant/child to develop greater powers of cognition, concentration[35] as well as emotional regulation in adulthood.[36] Furthermore, the features of an individual's personality can be characterised by the concepts of plasticity and flexibility.[37] These narrower characteristics will allow for greater association of the development of personality traits with insecure/secure attachments to the primary caregiver during infancy and childhood.[38] Higher levels of stability are associated with more cooperative personality traits, while lower levels of stability are associated with non-cooperative personality traits.[39] Motivational and emotional stability is regulated by the rostral serotonergic system and this has a level of causality, with differences in stability between individuals.[40] Such biological systems may be programmed by early life experiences, leading to the development of varying levels of individual motivational and emotional stability later in life, in adulthood.[41] However, scholarly work has led to the conclusion that the motivational objectives of individuals change across a lifespan, especially in the context of their content and structure.[42] There is also some evidence to support the idea that genetical, social and cultural factors impact on psychological systems through the common pathway of the neural architecture with regard to changes in personality

[34]Caspi, A., and Roberts, B. (2009), Personality Development Across Life Course, Psychological Inquiry, 12, 2, 49–66.

[35]Main, M. (2000), The organized categories of infant, child, and adult attachment: Flexible vs. inflexible attention under attachment-related stress. Journal of the American Psychoanalytic Association, 48, 1055–1096.

[36]Waters, S. F., Virmani, E. A., Thompson, R. A., Meyer, S., Raikes, H. A., and Jochem, R. (2010), Emotion regulation and attachment: Unpacking two constructs and their association. Journal of Psychopathology and Behavioral Assessment, 32, 37–47.

[37]DeYoung, C. G. (2006), Higher-order factors of the big five in a multi-informant sample. Journal of Personality and Social Psychology, 91, 1138–1151.

[38]Young, E., Simpson, J., Grishevicius, V., Huelsnitz, C., and Fleck, C, (2019), Childhood Attachment and Adult Personality: A Lifetime Perspective, Self and Identity, Vol.18, No.1, 22–38.

[39]Ibid.

[40]Meltzer, H. Y. (1990), Role of serotonin in depression, Annals of the New York Academy of Sciences, 600, 486–499.

[41]Ibid.

[42]McAdams, D., and Olson, B. (2010), Personality Development: Continuity and Change over Life Course, Annu. Rev. Psychol, 61, 517–42.

traits.[43] This in turn may be associated with the plasticity of biological systems. But plasticity, on the other hand, encompasses the personality trait associated with an individual's flexibility to his/her external environment. Higher levels of plasticity are associated with an extrovert personality, while lower levels of plasticity are associated with an introvert personality.[44] The level of plasticity is regulated by the dopaminergic system, especially with regard to reductions in the level of inhibitions, which in turn will determine extrovert and introvert personality traits. There is some evidence to support the idea that plasticity and flexibility remain malleable throughout life because emotional regulation patterns may continue to develop into and through adulthood because of learning and experience.[45] However, while some of the latter may be beneficial, some could be detrimental to personality development, leading to the development of personality disorders at any age. As a result, specific therapy and medical assistance may be required throughout life.[46]

The Biology of Personality

In psychology, an individual's personality is represented by specific thinking processes, traits and values which encompass a specific set of beliefs.[47] However, in economic theory, while preferences are individualistic, beliefs are assumed to have formed rationally as a part of equilibrium.[48] Individuals differ based on different aspects of personality, the way in which psychological systems are formed and organised as well as varying behaviour due

[43] Davidson, R. J. (2001), Toward a biology of personality and emotion. Annals of the New York Academy of Science, 935: 191–207.

[44] Gray, J. A., Moran, P. M., Grigoryan, G., Peters, S. L., Young, A. M. J., and Joseph, M. H. (1997), Latent inhibition: The nucleus accumbens connection revisited. Behavioural Brain Research, 88, 27–34.

[45] John, O., and Gross, J. (2004), Healthy and Unhealthy Emotion Regulation: Personality Processes, Individual Differences and Life Span Development, Journal of Personality, 72, 1301–1334. doi: https://doi.org/10.1111/j.1467-6494.2004.00298.x.

[46] Videler, A., Hotsebaut, J., Schulkens, J., Sobczak, S., and Van Alphen, S. (2019), A Life Span Perspective on Borderline Personality Disorder, Current Psychiatry Reports, 21:51.

[47] Dweck, C.S. (2009), Can personality be changed? The role of beliefs in personality and change, Curr. Dir. Psychol. Sci. 17, 391–394.

[48] Engelmann, J., Schmid, B., De Dreu, C., Chumbley, J., and Fehr, E. (2019), On the Psychology and Economics of Antisocial Personality, PNAS, www.pnas.org. doi: https://doi.org/10.1073/pnas.182013316.

to the impact of different experiences.[49] Personality psychology allows for the study of how individual differences in traits arise, and the impact of these trait differences in terms of individual behaviour.[50] However, in their research, personality psychologists have not fully recognised the benefit of applying evolutionary and adaptive techniques as a way of understanding the processes by which trait differences arise between individuals and how they perpetuate and change from one generation to the next.[51] The evolutionary approach to understanding how trait variations arise and persist in a population can be framed in the context of Darwin's Theory of Natural Selection.[52] The latter is dependent on the existence of a population of living organisms which reproduce, individual organisms differ in terms of traits, these traits can be passed from one generation to another, and differences in traits may arise due to reproduction across the population.[53] Mating amongst a diverse population allows for genetic variation, and has an impact on daily family life as well as on the life achievements of individual members of the family.[54] Research suggests that a child will inherit at least 25% of the modified traits of a parent, while another 25% will depend on the interactions of different genes.[55] Traits which persist in the population from one generation to the next at higher levels in comparison to other traits will across time lead to species-wide psychological and biological changes.[56] The entity responsible for natural selection is DNA, which is constructed on the basis of thousands of genes responsible for the production of different types of proteins.[57] DNA sequences act as a programme for the production of RNA, which is converted into polypeptides,

[49] Cloninger, C. (2000), Biology of Personality Dimensions, Current Opinions in Psychiatry, 13, pp. 611–616.

[50] John, O. P., Robins, R. W., and Pervin, L. (2008), Handbook of Personality: Theory and Research, Guilford Press, New York, NY.

[51] Lukaszewski, A.W. (2021), Evolutionary perspectives on the mechanistic underpinnings of personality IN The handbook of personality dynamics and processes, Rauthmann, J. (Ed), Elsevier Press, San Diego, CA.

[52] Ibid.

[53] Ibid.

[54] Buss, D. (1983), Evolutionary Biology and Personality Psychology: Implications of Genetic Variability, Person. Individ. Diff. Vol.4, pp. 51–63.

[55] Cloninger, C.R., Van Eerdewegh, P., Goate, A et al.(1998), Anxiety proneness linked to epistatic loci in genome scan of human personality traits. Am J Med Genetics, 81:313–317.

[56] Ibid.

[57] Penke, L., Jaap, J., Dennissen, A., & Miller, G. F. (2007). The evolutionary genetics of personality. European Journal of Personality, 21, 549–587.

which lead to the assembling of proteins.[58] The gene itself is composed of DNA and may not although control the production of specific proteins but facilitates thought or emotion.[59] As gene expression is entirely dependent on the environment an individual is situated in, so is protein production.[60] However, the expression of specific genes depends not only on the environment but also on genetic factors.

If DNA becomes corrupted during transcription, then mutations will result. Mutations or changes in the original DNA sequence will cause the emergence of new trait/s.[61] A particular trait may become dominant in a population over others if the gene responsible is able to increase the reproductive rate of a generation as well as of subsequent generations.[62] Natural selection will also allow individual species to develop traits which will allow them to adapt to specific habitats or environments.[63] In the context of natural selection, human nature can perhaps be viewed as the biological adaptations and psychological processes which have arisen in order to propagate the reproduction rate of a species at a time when it may have been constrained due to environmental conditions.[64] The biological and psychological adaptations an individual may undergo may be characterised as being either emotions or trait expressions.[65] The former can be triggered due to critical events, while the latter maybe variations in the levels of trait expression due to environmental circumstances. Gene expression and maintenance is entirely dependent on the environment in which the

[58] Roberts, B., and Jackson, J. (2008), Socioeconomic Personality Psychology, Journal of Personality, 76, 6.

[59] Roberts, B., and Jackson, J. (2008), Socioeconomic Personality Psychology, Journal of Personality, 76, 6.

[60] Robinson, G. E. (2004), Beyond nature and nurture. Science, 304, 397–399.

[61] Dawkins, R. (1982), The Extended Phenotype: The Gene as the Unit of Selection, Oxford University Press, Oxford,

UK.

[62] Hamilton, W.D. (1966), The genetical evolution of social behaviour 1, Journal of Theoretical Biology, 7, 1–16.

[63] Marr, D. (1982), Vision: A Computational Investigation into the Human Representation and Processing of Visual Information. New York: Freeman.

[64] Lukaszewski, A.W. (2021), Evolutionary perspectives on the mechanistic underpinnings of personality IN The handbook of personality dynamics and processes, Rauthmann, J. (Ed), Elsevier Press, San Diego, CA.

[65] Tooby, J., and Cosmides, L. (1990), On the universality of human nature and the uniqueness of the individual: the role of genetics and adaptation. Journal of Personality, 58, 17–67.

foetus/child is situated.[66] However, specific behaviours and temperaments such as addiction to alcohol[67] and cigarettes[68] may be affected directly by individual genetic disposition. This may also be true with slimming diseases such as anorexia and bulimia.[69] The genes which may be responsible for individual behaviours and characteristics may interact, leading to the emergence of new behaviours.[70] Therefore, perhaps in analysing personality disorders, we should think of these as arising due to the interaction of different genes rather than due to the sole activity of one gene.[71] However, there is also evidence that adversity encountered during childhood may cause borderline personality disorders (BPD) in adulthood.[72] Borderline personality disorder is often associated with self-harm and mental instability.[73] In addition to genes, differences in cerebral blood flow may also help to explain trait differences between individuals.[74] For example, introversion was observed when blood flowed to the frontal lobes, the left cingulate and the right insula of the brain.[75] However, extroversion was observed when blood flowed to some temporal neocortex and frontal regions of the brain as well as the left amygdala and insula and right-posterior regions of the putamen.[76] Nevertheless, it may be the case that the regions of the brain do not work independently but that

[66] Roberts, B., and Jackson, J. (2008), Socioeconomic Personality Psychology, Journal of Personality, 76, 6.

[67] Thome, J., Weijers, H.G., Wiesbeck, G.A., et al. (1999), Dopamine D3 receptor gene polymorphism and alcohol dependence: relation to personality rating, Psychiatric Genetics, 9:17–21.

[68] Sabol, S.Z., Nelson, M.L., Fisher, C. et al. (1999), A genetic association for cigarette smoking behavior. Health Psychology,18:7–13.

[69] Kaye, W.H., Frank, G.K., and McConaha, C. (1999), Altered dopamine activity after recovery from restricting-type anorexia nervosa. Neuropsychopharmacology, 21:503–506.

[70] Cloninger, C. (2000), Biology of Personality Dimensions, Current Opinions in Psychiatry, 13, pp. 611–616.

[71] Ibid.

[72] Graybar, S.R., Boutilier, L.R. (2002), Nontraumatic pathways to borderline personality disorder. Psychother Theor Res Pract Train, 39:152–162.

[73] Porter, C., Claus-Palmier, J., Branitsky, A., Mansell, W., Warwick, H., and Varese, F. (2020), Childhood adversity and borderline personality disorder: A meta-analysis, Acta Psychiatr Scand, 141, 6–20.

[74] Sugiura M, Kawashima R, Nakagawa M et al. (2000), Correlation between Human Personality and Neural Activity in Cerebral Cortex. NeuroImage 2000; 11:541–546.

[75] Cloninger, C. (2000), Biology of Personality Dimensions, Current Opinions in Psychiatry, 13, pp. 611–616.

[76] Ibid.

regional brain functions overlap in the determination of temperament[77]—although there still remains a causality between specific regional brain activity and the existence of specific temperaments, and personally disorders.[78] For example, small frontal-lobe volumes have been associated with anti-social behaviour.[79] In addition to the differences in the level of blood flow to different brain regions and structures, causing variations and differences in temperament in and between individuals, variations in levels of serotonin transporter activity will also have the same effect.[80] Some research has also determined that the prenatal environment of a foetus may also be important in the development of later traits.[81] For example, maternal depression during the prenatal stage may cause the foetus to lose or not properly develop grey matter in the frontal lobes of the brain, facilitating the development of uncontrolled behaviours later in life.[82]

Trait Theories and the Psychology of Individual Differences

At the early stages of the study of trait theory, it was believed that the best way in which to organise the study of personality was around five basic traits.[83] These traits include cognition, extent of being outgoing, extent of being withdrawn, level of nervousness, affability, and level of diligence and care.[84] The level of openness or being outgoing is seen as a positive effect

[77] Ibid.

[78] Cloninger, C.R., and Svrakic, D.M. (2000), Personality Disorders.IN Comprehensive Textbook of Psychiatry, Sadock, B.J., and Sadock, V.A. (Ed), 7th Edition, Lippincott Williams & Wilkins: Philadelphia; 2000. pp. 1723–1764.

[79] Lyoo, I.K., Han, M.H., and Cho, D.Y. (1998), A brain MRI study in subjects with borderline personality disorder. J Affective Disorders, 50:235–243.

[80] Cloninger, C. (2000), Biology of Personality Dimensions, Current Opinions in Psychiatry, 13, pp. 611–616.

[81] Krzeczkowski, J., and Lieshout, R. (2019), Prenatal Influences on the Development and Stability of Personality, New Ideas in Psychology, 53, 22–31.

[82] Sandman, C. A., Buss, C., Head, K., & Davis, E. P. (2015), Fetal exposure to maternal depressive symptoms is associated with cortical thickness in late childhood, Biological Psychiatry, 77(4), 324–334. https://doi.org/10.1016/j.biopsych.2014.06.025.

[83] Epstein, S. (1994), Trait Theory as Personality Theory: Can a part be as great as the whole? Psychological Inquiry, 5, 2, 120–122.

[84] Young, C. (2010), Personality Neuroscience and the Biology of Traits, Social and Personality Psychology, Compass, 4/12, pp. 1165–1180.

and is often associated with an individual's sensitivity to reward.[85] Moreover, an individual's level of nervousness is seen as a negative effect and is associated with an individual's sensitivity to punishment.[86] On the one hand, one's level of affability indicates the extent to which an individual can sustain hardship rather than exploit others. However, the level of diligence is indicative of an individual's ability to control and regulate one's own behaviour to follow rules. And an individual's level of cognition relates to the extent to which an individual can use information gathered through sensory perception and exploit it for their own advantage. However, it may be possible that differences in dopamine levels, a neuromodulating chemical, may be responsible for differences in both cognitive processes (working memory)[87] and executive control[88] between individuals. There is some evidence to suggest that levels of peripheral dopamine are determined largely by the levels of the enzyme tyrosinase.[89] The categorisation of these five basic traits allows for the possibility of identifying the areas of the brain which would facilitate each trait.[90] Furthermore, it has been claimed that these five traits will lay the foundations for a universal theory of personality which may be able to explain the origins and individual differences in emotions, thoughts as well as motives.[91] This could lead to a better understanding of human behaviour in any context. However, it may be argued that using traits as the foundation for a universal theory is not justifiable and that a distinction needs to be made between 'state' and 'trait'.[92] A trait may be part of one's genetic endowment. However, some may differentiate between trait and behaviour, and suggest that the latter arises from one's environment, and the former may not

[85] Ibid.

[86] Ibid.

[87] Goldman-Rakic, WM. (1995), Cellular basis of working memory, Neuron, 14, 477–485.

[88] Cropley, V. L., Fujita, M., Innis, R. B., and Nathan, P. J, (2006), Molecular imaging of the dopaminergic system and its association with human cognitive function. Biological Psychiatry, 59(10), 898–907.

[89] Eisenhofer, G., Tian, H., Holmes, C., Matsunaga, J., Roffler-Tarlov, S., and Hearing, V.J. (2003), Tyrosinase: a developmentally specific major determinant of peripheral dopamine, FASEB J. 17, 1248–1255.

[90] Ibid.

[91] Epstein, S. (1994), Trait Theory as Personality Theory: Can a part be as great as the whole? Psychological Inquiry, 5, 2, 120–122.

[92] Steyer, R., Schmitt, M., and Eid, M. (1999), Latent State-Trait Theory and Research in Personality and Individual Differences, European Journal of Personality, Eur. J. Pers, 13, pp. 389–408.

be indicative of such outcomes[93]—although early life experiences may determine the development of traits. For example, it is thought that anti-social aggressive behaviours may emerge from the roots of early life experiences.[94] The latter may result in cast-iron cognitive constructs which cannot be changed[95]—although it may be possible to achieve this through a process of self-realisation.

Differences in personality traits between individuals may give rise to genetic variability.[96] Such differences in personality traits between individuals may allow for the genetic retention of adaptive changes to the environment.[97] This itself may lead to the emergence of new species.[98] This could be because adaptive changes in behaviour due to the environment may lead to longer-term genetic change. Scholars of personality trait differences between individuals have always tended to assume that such differences occur due to both genetic and non-genetic factors.[99] For example. Individual social attitudes are likely to be shaped by environmental and cultural factors. However, research evidence suggests that as a child grows, genetic factors are more ascendant in the formation and development of individual traits than are environmental factors. This is especially true after adolescence.[100] Furthermore, theories associated with the development of psychological traits through genetic mechanisms are more robust and useful if they can explain the mechanism(s) which brings about such change.[101] There is some evidence to suggest that biological time-keeping systems are under genetic influences.[102] However, in research

[93] Mischel, W, (1998), Personality and Assessment, Wiley, New York.

[94] Huesmann, L., and Eron, L. (1989), Individual Differences and the Trait of Aggression, European Journal of Personality, Vol.3, 95–106.

[95] Ibid.

[96] Dall, J., Houston, A., and McNamara, J. (2004), The behavioural ecology of personality; consistent individual differences from an adaptive perspective, Ecology Letters, 7, pp. 734–739.

[97] Weislo, W.T. (1989), Behavioral environments and evolutionary change, Ann. Rev. Ecol. Syst., 20, 137–169.

[98] Dall, J., Houston, A., and McNamara, J. (2004), The behavioural ecology of personality; consistent individual differences from an adaptive perspective, Ecology Letters, 7, pp. 734–739.

[99] Bouchard, T. (2004), Genetic Influence on Human Psychological Traits, Current Directions in Psychological Science, Vol.13, No.4.

[100] Ibid.

[101] Ibid.

[102] Hur,Y.M., Bouchard, T.J., Jr., and Lykken, D.T. (1998), Genetic and environmental influence on morningness-eveningness, Personality and Individual Differences, 25, 917–925.

circles, there still seems to be mystery as to why some personality traits are heritable while other personality traits are dependent on the environment for their formation and development.[103] But because both psychological traits and biological traits are dependent on genetic and environmental factors, this may imply that heritability is a biological phenomenon which occurs in all living organisms.[104] Environmental factors cause living organisms to adapt in order to survive, resulting in a pure adaptation to an environmental factor, spillover effects of adaptations and residual effects of adaptations.[105] Indeed, adaptations occur in order to facilitate the survival of a species by sustaining reproduction.[106] These adaptations may be biological, resulting in genetic change over generations, leading to the acquisition of new biological features, for example, walking on two legs. However, some innovative adaptations may result from cognitive processes. For example, the discovery to control and use fire for cooking by *Homo erectus* allowed for the emergence of *Homo sapiens* over hundreds and thousands of years because of genetic change. The use of fire for cooking meat allowed it to be more digestible and over time led to changes in brain capacity and structure, leading to the transition from *Homo erectus* to *Homo sapiens.* This transition signalled an increase in cognitive capacity, which facilitated even greater levels of innovation. Indeed, because of evolution, all humans have the same mechanisms which have allowed them to adapt to environmental circumstances, and it was these mechanisms which allowed for the survival of previous generations.[107] Moreover, it is clear that the adaptations which human psychological functions have undergone during the evolution of the species have been 'designed' by biological processes and represent a response to a specific environmental factor.[108] In addition, the design of specific adaptations to environmental factors may also result in spillover effects which are not directly related to the

[103] Bouchard, T. (2004), Genetic Influence on Human Psychological Traits, Current Directions in Psychological Science, Vol.13, No.4.

[104] Boomsma., D.I., Busjahn., A., and Peltonen., L. (2002), Classical twin studies and beyond. Nature Reviews: Genetics, 3, 872–882.

[105] Buss, D. M., Haselton, M. G., Shackelford, T. K., Bleske, A. L., and Wakefield, J. C. (1998), Adaptations, exaptations, and spandrels, American Psychologist, 53, 533–548.

[106] Buss, D., and Greiling, H. (1999), Adaptive Individual Differences, Journal of Personality, 67, 2.

[107] Ibid.

[108] Tooby, J., and Cosmides, L. (1992), Psychological foundations of culture. IN *The adapted mind,* Barkow, J., Cosmides, L., and Tooby, J. (Eds.), Oxford University Press, New York.

environmental factor. For example, standing on two feet was an adaptation exceedingly early hominin took to be able to see prey and approaching predators while living in geographical regions which had very tall grass. However, walking on two feet also allowed early hominins to walk and run faster, giving them an even greater advantage over predators, helping them to increase their lifespan and thereby increasing the possibilities for reproduction. Adaptations to environmental factors may also result in 'noise' or residual effects.[109] For example, out of a small population, a proportion may be born with leg deformities. It would seem that psychological processes are able to receive inputs from the environment, with the output developing perhaps within a generation or perhaps over a series of generations.[110] While adaptations allow a species to survive its environment and to continue to reproduce, individual trait differences remain due to sources which can be either non-heritable or heritable.[111] The probability of personality traits arising from heritable factors ranges from 30% to 50%.[112] On the other hand, the probability of personality traits arising from environmental factors ranges from 50% to 70%.[113] Adaptations to the environment, rather than heritable factors, may therefore contribute more towards differences in personality traits between individuals—although there may be some interaction between these two sources of differences in personality traits.[114]

[109] Buss, D., and Greiling, H. (1999), Adaptive Individual Differences, Journal of Personality, 67, 2.

[110] Buss, D. M. (1995), Evolutionary psychology: A new paradigm for psychological science, Psychological Inquiry, 6, 1–30.

[111] Buss, D., and Greiling, H. (1999), Adaptive Individual Differences, Journal of Personality, 67, 2.

[112] Bouchard, T. J., and McGue, M. (1990), Genetic and rearing environmental influences on adult personality: An analysis
of adopted twins reared apart. Journal of Personality, 58, 263–292.

[113] Buss, D., and Greiling, H. (1999), Adaptive Individual Differences, Journal of Personality, 67, 2.

[114] Buss, D., and Greiling, H. (1999), Adaptive Individual Differences, Journal of Personality, 67, 2.

The Puzzle of the Self

Self-awareness and self-esteem are distinct and unique features of human behaviour. Self-awareness is the ability to recognise oneself in a mirror.[115] On the other hand, self-esteem is reflective of the level of self-confidence one has in his/her own ability. Self-awareness, the realisation of one's own consciousness, is a behaviour which develops gradually and incrementally over time. [116] The implication is that a growing child may only be able to partially recognise itself in the mirror until it is mature enough to achieve full recognition.[117] Empirical studies have shown that in order to better understand situations which may not be associated with their understanding of reality, toddlers may engage in some form of multidimensional thinking, perhaps drawing on past experiences.[118] This may explain an infant's early behaviour when it is still acquiring knowledge and experiences to fully reflect reality at a time when its brain is developing rapidly. [119] In addition to the distinction between self-awareness and self-esteem, there is also a distinction between happiness and self-esteem.[120] While happiness may be a state of one's mood, the self-esteem may be closely associated with the extent of one's hopes and achievements.[121] It may also reflect feelings about one's own abilities based on peer and parental reaction to one's achievements.

One aspect of human nature is to find ways to make us feel good, in other words, ways to build up self-esteem.[122] Over time, psychologists have tried to establish the link between self-esteem and human development.[123] In order to establish a possible causal relationship between the

[115] Brandl, J. (2018), The Puzzle of Mirror Self-Recognition, Phenom Cogn Sci, 17, pp. 279–304.

[116] Bertenthal, B. I., and Fischer, K. W. (1978), Development of self-recognition in infant. Developmental Psychology, 14, 44–50.

[117] Brandl, J. (2018), The Puzzle of Mirror Self-Recognition, Phenom Cogn Sci, 17, pp. 279–304.

[118] Perner, J. (1991), Understanding the representational mind, The MIT Press, Cambridge.

[119] Bischof-Köhler, D. (2012), Empathy and self-recognition in phylogenetic and ontogenetic perspective, Emotion Review, 4, 40–48.

[120] Lyubomirsky, S., Tkach, C., Dimatteo, M. (2006), What are the Differences Between Happiness and Self-Esteem? Social Indicators Research, 78, pp. 363–404.

[121] Ibid.

[122] James, W. (1890). The principles of psychology (Vol.1), Henry Holt, New York.

[123] Leary, M. (1999), Making Sense of Self-Esteem, Current Directions in Psychological Science, Vol.8, No.1.

two, psychologists have viewed self-esteem as a trait and the differences in this trait between individuals.[124] However, what has become evident is that high levels of self-esteem maybe a way to alleviate the impact of social and psychological problems on individuals.[125] It may simply be the case that high levels of self-esteem translate into positive, tenacious attitudes in difficult times. Without these, individuals may turn to self-destructive behaviours associated with alcoholism, smoking and the consumption of harmful drugs. This in turn could lead to the pathological damage to an individual's internal organs, leading to an early death. Therefore, it can be asserted that low self-esteem is more likely to contribute towards psychological and mental health problems than does positive self-esteem.[126] For example, poor self-esteem may result in deliberate self-harm.[127] Nevertheless, an individual with a positive attitude, facilitated by a high level of self-esteem, may also act as a signal to others that they are independent and able to achieve personal goals and targets.[128] Therefore, it becomes evident that public programmes designed to improve an individual's self-esteem will have not only individual but also societal benefits.[129] This is specifically true in the case of either a child or an adolescent.[130] Moreover, it has also been found that strengthening family bonds can also benefit the enhancement of self-esteem.[131] Furthermore, good parental behaviour in the upbringing of the infant, the child and the adolescent will also have a positive impact on the development of its self-esteem.[132]

Self-esteem may also be regarded as personal feedback in relation to the extent of self-adequacy.[133] The latter can be quantified as to how one

[124] Ibid.

[125] Ibid.

[126] Ibid.

[127] Chapman, A., Gratz, K., and Brown, M. (2006), Solving the puzzle of deliberate self-harm: The experiential avoidance model, Behavior Research and Therapy, 44, pp. 371–394.

[128] Leary, M. (1999), Making Sense of Self-Esteem, Current Directions in Psychological Science, Vol.8, No.1.

[129] Ibid.

[130] Cast, A., and Burke, P. (2002), A Theory of Self-Esteem, Social Forces, 80 (3), pp. 1041–1068.

[131] Verkuyten, M. (2005), The Puzzle of High Self-Esteem Among Ethnic Minorities: Company Explicit and Implicit Self Esteem, Self and Identity, 4, 2, 177–192.

[132] Harter, S. (1999), The construction of the self: A developmental perspective, Guilford, London, UK.

[133] Bednar, R.L., Wells, M.G., and Peterson, S.R. (1989), Self-esteem: Paradoxes and innovations in clinical theory and practice, American Psychological Association, Washington, DC.

currently feels about oneself (dictated by environmental experiences) and how one would like to feel (an ideal state, with positive environmental influences).[134] If an individual is able to achieve the highest possible level of self-esteem, the idealised state, then he/she may be able to dominate in a social setting.[135] In this case, self-esteem may be viewed as an evolutionary mechanism, which at high levels signals dominance to companions and passers-by alike. This will favour natural selection, in the context that dominant individuals are likely to acquire more of the resources, mates, adequate shelter and food. The possession of these factors will facilitate higher levels of probability for reproduction.[136] Self-conscious emotions such as guilt, shame and pride are also important for societal positioning and winning the loyalty of others.[137] Perhaps, self-conscious emotions should be seen as the drivers of self-evaluation in a societal context,[138] allowing for the emergence of self-esteem through the process of human evolution in an environment of danger and scarcity.[139] Individual and group survival in this environment was driven by the strength to empathise with and incentivise group members.[140] Moreover, scholarly work suggests that when an individual has greater control over his/her environment, then he/she is likely to be more motivated.[141]

Another theory on why self-esteem may exist is that it is a necessary buffer between oneself and the anxiety caused by existential threats.[142] An

[134] Leary, M. (1999), Making Sense of Self-Esteem, Current Directions in Psychological Science, Vol.8, No.1.

[135] Barkow, J. (1980). Prestige and self-esteem: A biosocial interpretation IN Dominance relations: An ethological view of human conflict and social interaction, Omark, D.R., Strayer F.F., and Freedman, D.G. (Eds.), Garland STPM Press, New York.

[136] Ibid.

[137] Sznycer, D. (2019), Forms and Functions of the Self-Conscious Emotions, Trends in Cognitive Sciences, Vol.23, No.2.

[138] Ibid.

[139] Burger, O. et al. (2012), Human mortality improvement in evolutionary context, Proc. Natl. Acad. Sci. U. S. A. 109, 18210–18214.

[140] Von Rueden, C. and Jaeggi, A.V. (2016), Men's status and reproductive success in 33 nonindustrial societies: effects of subsistence, marriage system, and reproductive strategy. Proc. Natl. Acad. Sci. U. S. A. 113, 10824–10829.

[141] Zuckerman, M., Porac, J., Lathin, D., Smith, R., and Deci, E. (1978), On the Importance of Self-Determination for Intrinsically Motivated Behaviour, Personality and Social Psychology Bulletin, Vol.4, No.3.

[142] Solomon, S., Greenberg, J., and Pyszczynski, T, (1991), A terror management theory of social behavior: The psychological functions of self-esteem and cultural worldviews, Advances in Experimental Social Psychology, 24, 93–159.

argument also exists which suggests that self-esteem is a characteristic required for successful reproduction. But this may be a flawed argument.[143] It is for this reason that an alternative theory, which to some extent may straddle the previous two theories, emerged. This alternative theory, the sociometer theory, asserts that self-esteem emerged as a gauge with which the self can identify the extent of its relationships with other members of the community.[144] It more likely emerged through evolution to facilitate the survival of an individual, as those belonging more strongly to the community or a group will be more likely to survive and procreate.[145] Intrinsic feelings of the extent of relational quality with others will serve to trigger conscious cognitive processes into taking appropriate action as necessary in order to maintain the optimal balance of relationships and the social acceptance of and with peers so as to optimise survival possibilities.[146] The sociometer has a gauge to personally appraise the extent and nature of one's relationships with others, which can be seen as a pseudo-mental substitute for the trait of self-esteem.[147] Nevertheless, a distinction also needs to be made between trait self-esteem and state self-esteem. The latter relates to the extent of perception by an individual of how others view the extent of a relationship with him/her.[148] On the other hand, trait self-esteem is what an individual believes is the 'norm' about their relationships with others and can be considered to be the equilibrium state of the sociometer in the absence of environmental fluctuations which would enable an individual to reassess their levels of self-esteem.[149] In allowing for a reassessment of the state of an individual's relationship with others in the face of changing environmental conditions, the sociometer theory allows for an individual self-calibration to reduce the probability of

[143] Leary, M.R. (1999). The social and psychological importance of self-esteem, IN The social psychology of emotional and behavioral problems: Interfaces of social and clinical psychology, Kowalski, R.M., and Leary, M.R. (Eds.), American Psychological Association, Washington, DC.

[144] Ibid.

[145] Baumeister, R.F., and Leary, M.R. (1995), The need to belong: Desire for interpersonal attachments as a fundamental human motivation, Psychological Bulletin, 117, 497–529.

[146] Leary, M. (1999), Making Sense of Self-Esteem, Current Directions in Psychological Science, Vol.8, No.1.

[147] Ibid.

[148] Leary, M. (1999), Making Sense of Self-Esteem, Current Directions in Psychological Science, Vol.8, No.1.

[149] Ibid.

rejection by the social group the individual is associated with.[150] The reassessment output of actions required to recalibrate relationships in a more positive manner may involve actions which may not be beneficial to the individual but will contribute in a positive manner to reducing the probability of rejections by peers.[151] In addition to maintaining a positive relationship with one's peers, self-esteem can also be thought of as an identity process by which there can be intrinsic identification of the strengths and weaknesses of an individual within a group, leading to the allocation of specific roles.[152] Public and societal commitments may incentivise individuals to take positive actions by reducing or eliminating negative and harmful behaviour such as alcoholism, and in the process improving their well-being and self-esteem.[153] Self-esteem may also be the result of successful parenting.[154]

Can Personality Change? The Possibilities of Psychotherapeutics

There is increasing consensus amongst scholars that personality disorders may surface in adolescence, although personality remains relatively stable from early childhood.[155] The diagnosis of borderline personality disorders (BPD) in adolescents is considered to be as accurate as is the diagnosis of these types of disorders in adults.[156] BPD is a condition which is characterised as being a condition in which individuals exhibit behavioural dysfunctionality characterised as involving poor relationships with others as well as mental instability. Adolescents with BPD may also be susceptible to self-harm behaviours.[157] Psychotherapy treatment of adolescent BPD sufferers

[150] Ibid.

[151] Ibid.

[152] Cast, A., and Burke, P. (2002), A Theory of Self-Esteem, Social Forces, 80 (3), pp. 1041–1068.

[153] Schilbach, F. (2019), Alcohol and Self Control: A Field Experiment in India, American Economic Review, 109(4), pp. 1290–1322.

[154] Rutherford, M.B. (2011), The Social Value of Self-Esteem, Soc 48, 407. https://doi.org/10.1007/s12115-011-9460-5.

[155] Wong, J., Bahji, A., and Khalid-Khan, S. (2020), Psychotherapies for Adolescents with Sub-Clinical and Borderline personality Disorder: A Systematic Review and Meta-Analysis, The Canadian Journal of Psychiatry, Vol. 65, 1.

[156] Ibid.

[157] Chanen, AM., Kaess, M. (2012), Developmental pathways to borderline personality disorder. Curr Psychiatry Rep. 2012;14(1):45–53.

is less effective than that of adult BPD sufferers. Psychotherapy is a multidisciplinary approach to treating mental and personality disorders by drawing from the tools and theories of the different sciences.[158] Yet initial treatment would suit the individual to prevent income loss and job opportunities not taken up due to the impact of the BPD condition. Moreover, preventing the BPD condition from occurring in either adults or adolescents would also reduce the impact and cost on public health systems.[159] Therefore, it is important to evaluate the efficiency of the various treatments available for BPD in the context of targets and outcomes. In this context, it has been noted that psychodynamic treatments (PDTs) may be an efficient way to treat BPD.[160]

Disorders of the mind pose issues which need to be addressed by public health systems and government policies worldwide.[161] These disorders may lead to significant reductions in worker productivity, increases in public health spending and substantial economic costs.[162] While at an individual level, mental disorders not only cause immense human suffering but also result from genetic transmission from one generation to another.[163] Despite the economic and social costs of the emergence and prevalence of mental disorders on economies and societies, there are no objective tests to determine if someone has a mental disorder, and neither are there any thresholds of behaviour beyond which a mental disorder can be deemed to exist.[164] However, it may be evident from an individual's behaviour that he/she does have a personality or mental disorder, particularly in

[158] Colby, K. (1964), Psychotherapeutic Processes, Annu. Rev. Psychol, 15, pp. 347–370.

[159] Chanen, AM. (2011), Outcomes in women diagnosed with borderline personality disorder in adolescence. J Can Acad Child Adolesc Psychiatry, 20(3):175.

[160] Keefe, J., McCarthy, K., Dinger, V., McMain, S., Zilcha-Mano, S., Sahin, Z., Graham, K., and Barker, J. (2019), A Meta-Analysis of Psychodynamic Treatments for Borderline and Cluster C Personality Disorders, Theory, Research, and Treatment, Personality Disorders, doi: https://doi.org/10.1037/per0000382.

[161] Vigo, D., Thornicroft, G., and Atun, R. (2016), Estimating the true global burden of mental illness, Lancet Psychiatry, 3:171–8.

[162] Bloom, DE., Cafiero, E., Jané-Llopis, E., et al. (2011), The global economic burden of noncommunicable diseases. Geneva: World Economic Forum.

[163] Beardslee, WR., Gladstone, TR., O'Connor, EE. (2011), Transmission and prevention of mood disorders among children of affectively ill parents: a review. J Am Acad Child Adolesc Psychiatry, 50:1098–109.

[164] Cuijpers, P. (2019), Target and Outcomes of psychotherapies for mental disorders: an overview, World Psychiatry, 18, 3.

cases of aggressiveness and self-destructive behaviour. These kinds of behaviours are difficult to treat.[165]

Over time two systems have emerged for the identification of mental disorders. These include the International Classification of Diseases (ICD) and the Diagnostic and Statistical Manual of Mental Disorders (DSM).[166] However, both the ICD and the DSM have been criticised for a few reasons. This is mainly because mental disorders should not be seen as being definitive but varying to various levels among individuals.[167] Moreover, some therapies may be more effective in mediating the effects of some disorders compared to others. For example, in anxiety and mood disorders, pharmacotherapies may be more effective than Cognitive Behavioural Therapy (CBT).[168] The implication is that it may not be possible to identify the nature of mental disorders using either the DSM or the ICD categories of disorders.[169] Due to this, alternative frameworks for identifying the targets and outcomes of interventions are being considered. For example, the National Institute of Mental Health in the United States has developed the Research Domain Criteria (RDoC).[170] The latter associates mental disorders with the primary functions of the brain and associated neural systems rather than with just a description of the features of the disorders.[171] Functions of the brain and associated neural systems can be associated with working memory and fear, for example.[172] With the DSM and ICD categories of disorders, it would be very difficult to determine what the targets and outcomes of a specific treatment should be.[173] In the

[165] Okano, K. (2019), The origin of so-called 'shadowy personalities' in patients with dissociative identity disorder, European Journal of Trauma and Dissociation, 3, 95–102.

[166] Cuijpers, P. (2019), Target and Outcomes of psychotherapies for mental disorders: an overview, World Psychiatry, 18, 3.

[167] Widiger, TA., Samuel, DB.(2005), Diagnostic categories or dimensions? A question for the Diagnostic and Statistical Manual of Mental Disorders – fifth edition. J Abnorm Psychol, 114, 494–504.

[168] Cuthbert, BN., Insel, TR. (2013), Toward the future of psychiatric diagnosis: the seven pillars of RDoC. BMC Med, 11:126.

[169] Cuijpers, P. (2019), Target and Outcomes of psychotherapies for mental disorders: an overview, World Psychiatry, 18, 3.

[170] Insel, T., Cuthbert, B., Garvey, M., et al. (2010), Research Domain Criteria (RDoC): toward a new classification framework for research on mental disorders. Am J Psychiatry, 167:748–51.

[171] Cuthbert, BN., Insel, TR. (2013), Toward the future of psychiatric diagnosis: the seven pillars of RDoC. BMC Med, 11:126.

[172] Ibid.

[173] Ibid.

context of psychotherapy, the outcomes can either be a reduction in the severity of the symptoms or an improvement in the quality of life of the sufferer.[174] However, the findings of empirical studies associated with a reduction in the severity of symptoms have been criticised because of poorly conducted trials[175] as well as researchers' preference towards specific interventions and the theories related to the specific outcomes of interventions.[176] This may be one reason as to why there is no universal agreement regarding whether a reduction in the severity of the symptoms of a disorder as a result of psychotherapy should necessarily be thought of as an outcome.[177] Nevertheless, in the context of the success of the psychotherapeutic treatment, what is important is the nature of the relationship, or a learning process between the patient and the clinician.[178] In fact, successful treatments involves three types of learning.[179] Firstly, there is the learning of the rules of the relationship between the patient and the clinician. Secondly, during the treatment process there is a transference of knowledge between the patient and the clinician. And, lastly, once the patient has been 'cured', the patient learns via interacting with the wider environment.

An alternative to viewing the targets and outcomes of psychotherapies, rather than as a mere reduction in the severity of the symptoms, is from a patient's of view.[180] This approach could be more pertinent because ultimately the objective of the treatment is to help patients overcome their

[174] Ibid.

[175] Cuijpers, P., Karyotaki, E., Reijnders, M., et al. (2019), Was Eysenck right after all? A reassessment of the effects of psychotherapy for adult depression. Epidemiol Psychiatr Sci, 28:21–30.

[176] Leykin, Y., DeRubeis, RJ. (2009), Allegiance in psychotherapy outcome research: separating association from bias. Clin Psychol Sci Pract, 16: 4–65.

[177] Cuijpers, P. (2019), Target and Outcomes of psychotherapies for mental disorders: an overview, World Psychiatry, 18, 3.

[178] Duarte, J., Fischersworring, M., Martinez, C., and Tomicic, A. (2019), 'I couldn't change the past; the answer was not there': A Case Study on the Subjective Construction of Psychotherapeutic Change of a Patient with a Borderline Personality Disorder Diagnosis and her Therapist, Psychotherapy Research, 29:4, pp. 445–462.

[179] Shakow, D. (1962), Discussion of papers relating to definition of variables, IN Strupp, H.H., and Luborsky, L., (Eds), Research in Psychotherapy, II, Am. Psychol. Assoc, Washington, DC.

[180] Cuijpers, P. (2019), Target and Outcomes of psychotherapies for mental disorders: an overview, World Psychiatry, 18, 3.

disorders.[181] The main features of patient-defined outcomes are that the patient stipulates which problems are important, the severity of the symptoms and what treatment improvements can be made.[182] These features would probably differ from one patient to another. This would also hold true of the validity and the reliability of the patient-defined measures.[183] However, the main advantage of patient-defined outcomes of the treatment of mental disorders is that the type of therapy given by practitioners can be personalised.[184] This may allow for the possibility that the treatments will be successful to varying degrees. An alternative to the previously defined outcomes is the quality-of-life–related outcomes. In this case, there is a growing belief amongst scholars and practitioners that the process of the relief of disorders should not be seen in the context of targets and outcomes but in the context of improvements in the quality of life of the patients.[185] In this case, the quality of life may be thought of as being a facet which integrates physical health, mental health and the ability to enjoy the company of others.[186] However, the quality of life of an individual can also be associated with an individual's employability, ability to earn a steady and consistent income, and ability to afford housing.[187] While assistance can be given to those whose mental disorders may affect their employability as well as access to housing.[188] Nevertheless, these kinds of interventions are not associated with psychotherapy.[189] In fact, quality of life is best measured by individual evaluations of physical, mental and social well-being. It is in this way that the changes in the

[181] Wampold, BE. (2015), How important are the common factors in psychotherapy? An update. World Psychiatry, 14:270-7.

[182] Cuijpers, P. (2019), Target and Outcomes of psychotherapies for mental disorders: an overview, World Psychiatry, 18, 3.

[183] Sales, CMD., Alves, PCG. (2016), Patient-centred assessment in psychotherapy: a review of individualized tools. Clin Psychol Sci Pract, 23: 265–83.

[184] McLeod J. (2011), Qualitative research in counselling and psychotherapy, Sage, London.

[185] Timulak, L., McElvaney, R. (2013), Qualitative meta-analysis of insight events in psychotherapy. Couns Psychol Quart, 26:131–50.

[186] WHOQOL group. (1995), The World Health Organization Quality of Life assessment (WHOQOL): position paper from the World Health Organization. Soc Sci Med, 41:1403–9.

[187] Cuijpers, P. (2019), Target and Outcomes of psychotherapies for mental disorders: an overview, World Psychiatry, 18, 3.

[188] Nieuwenhuyse, K., Faber, B., Verbeek, JH. et al. (2014), Interventions to improve return to work in depressed people. Cochrane Database Syst Rev., 12:CD006237.

[189] Cuijpers, P. (2019), Target and Outcomes of psychotherapies for mental disorders: an overview, World Psychiatry, 18, 3.

quality-of-life–related outcomes associated with psychotherapies have been measured. In this context, it has been found that psychotherapy has improved the quality of life of individuals with mental disorders, with an impact on third parties. For example, it has been found that psychotherapy has led to improved parenting and more effective interventions between mother and child.[190]

Different schools of psychotherapy practice have differing beliefs on the outcomes associated with the treatment of mental disorders. Moreover, each type of therapy has its own framework for stipulating the mechanisms which may change the extent of a patient's disorder. However, the form of psychotherapy which is dominant is Cognitive Behavioural Therapy (CBT), simply due the fact that it is the therapy which has been used in several randomised clinical trials.[191] The central premise of CBT is that once the therapy leads to the removal/reduction in the biases to the thinking of a patient with a mental disorder, then the disorder will either show signs of improvement or disappear. In clinical trials associated with CBT to treat patients with depression, it was found that levels of thinking did improve.[192] Nevertheless, the thinking of patients did also improve when they were treated for other disorders with other therapies.[193] It is therefore possible that irrational thinking is a symptom of depression, and as a therapy reduces the levels of depression faced by a patient, thinking at the same time also becomes more and more rational.[194] Therefore, there may be no causality between CBT and improved thinking in patients with specific mental disorders.

Early life experiences and the environments in which a foetus develops and into which an infant is born may be conducive to the development of mental and personality disorders.[195] Early bereavement may cause an infant

[190] Cuijpers, P., Weitz, E., Karyotaki, E. et al. (2014), The effects of psychological treatment of maternal depression on children and parental functioning: a meta-analysis. Eur Child Adolesc Psychiatry, 24:237–45.

[191] Cuijpers, P. (2019), Target and Outcomes of psychotherapies for mental disorders: an overview, World Psychiatry, 18, 3.

[192] Cristea, IA., Huibers, MJ., David, D. et al. (2015), The effects of cognitive behavior therapy for adult depression on dysfunctional thinking: a meta-analysis. Clin Psychol Rev., 42:62–71.

[193] Cuijpers, P. (2019), Target and Outcomes of psychotherapies for mental disorders: an overview, World Psychiatry, 18, 3.

[194] Ibid.

[195] Bowlby, J. (2005), A secure base, Routledge, London.

to develop a self-questioning nature.[196] If untreated, this may lead to a loss of confidence, leading to the infant developing into an adult with mental disorders.[197] Therefore, the symptoms of mental disorders are simply part of wider, deeper psychological problems. Thus, psychotherapeutic treatments should be focused on relieving and remedying these deeper conscious and unconscious conflicts and not relieving the symptoms suffered by the patients. However, to be treated, unconscious and conscious conflicts need to be quantified. With the latter, it should be possible through experimentation and observation. However, with unconscious issues, empirical quantification is debatable, although in some scholarly circles it is thought to be possible.[198]

In addition to reviewing the outcomes of psychotherapy treatments there are other measures besides a reduction in the severity of symptoms and/or an improvement in the quality of life. Specifically, in the context of economic measures, outcomes are quantified through either a Cost-Utility Analysis (CUA) or a Cost-Effectiveness Analysis (CEA).[199] CEA and CUA studies of the outcomes of Internet-based interventions have shown that these are more successful at lowering the cost of treatments than usual CBT techniques.[200]

Conclusion

Human emotions, anger, hate, jealousy, nervousness, fear and happiness are all expressed all of the time in response to the environments we face.[201] Emotions have developed through the evolutionary process in order to facilitate the adaptation and survival of humans in the environments they

[196] Kirwin, K., and Hamrin, V. (2005), Decreasing the Risk of Complicated Bereavement and Future Psychiatric Disorders in Children, Journal of Child and Adolescent Psychiatric Nursing, Vol.18, Issue 2.

[197] Ibid.

[198] Leichsenring, F., Steinert, C., Crits-Christoph, P. (2018), On mechanisms of change in psychodynamic therapy. Z Psychosom Med Psychother, 64:16–22.

[199] Ophuis, RH., Lokkerbol, J., Heemskerk, SC, et al., (2017), Cost-effectiveness of interventions for treating anxiety disorders: a systematic review. J Affect Disord, 210:1–13.

[200] Donker, T., Blankers, M., Hedman, E. et al., (2015), Economic evaluations of Internet interventions for mental health: a systematic review. Psychol Med, 45:3357–76.

[201] Pollock, N., McCabe, G., Southard, A., and Zeigler-Hill, V. (2016), Pathological Personality Traits and Emotion Regulation Difficulties, Personality and Individual Difference, 95, pp. 168–177.

inhabit.[202] This occurs through a sequential mechanism involving the senses, the expression of a subjective feeling (an emotion) and cognitive processes translating the subjective feeling into a related thought, which then triggers a physical response.[203] For example, seeing a wild bear would trigger the emotion of fear for one's safety. This would then be translated by cognitive processing into thoughts relating to an action to take to improve chances of survival. The thought would then trigger the physical response of climbing as far up the nearest tree as possible. However, emotional regulation is important to ensure that one does not either under-react or over-react. In this case, emotional regulation relates to an individual's ability to control an emotional response to an event in the environment which best allows for adaptation and survival.[204] The better the quality of emotional regulation, the better the quality of the relationships an individual has with others, and the better the ability to adapt to changes in environmental conditions.[205] Effective emotional regulation allows individuals to function optimally when there is a change in an environmental condition.[206] Moreover, effective emotional regulation serves as a source of knowledge which will allow an individual to maintain an optimal level of relationship with others.[207] On the other hand, dysfunctional emotional regulation will mean that an individual will not be able to comprehend the implications of emotional states, and this will lead to poor decisions associated with relationships which ultimately do not last.[208] There may also be poor adaptation to the environment, perhaps reducing

[202] Tooby, J., and Cosmides, L. (1990), The past explains the present: Emotional adaptations and the structure of ancestral environments. Ethology and Sociobiology, 11, 375–424.

[203] Ibid.

[204] Gross, J. J., and Thompson, R. A. (2007), Emotion regulation: Conceptual foundations, IN Handbook of emotion regulation, In J. J. Gross (Ed.), Guilford Press, New York, NY.

[205] Gross, J. J., and Muñoz, R. F. (1995), Emotion regulation and mental health. Clinical Psychology: Science and Practice, 2, 151–164.

[206] Pollock, N., McCabe, G., Southard, A., and Zeigler-Hill, V. (2016), Pathological Personality Traits and Emotion Regulation Difficulties, Personality and Individual Difference, 95, pp. 168–177.

[207] Frijda, N. H., and Mesquita, B. (1994), The social roles and functions of emotions. IN Emotion and culture, Markus, H.R., and Kitayama, S. (Eds), American Psychological Association, Washington, DC.

[208] Gratz, K. L., and Roemer, L. (2004), Multidimensional assessment of emotion regulation and dysregulation: Development, factor structure, and initial validation of the difficulties in emotion regulation scale. Journal of Psychopathology and Behavioral Assessment, 26, 41–54.

the chances of survival. The nature and level of an individual's emotional regulation maybe related to the individual's personality.[209] Furthermore, differences in personality traits between individuals may be linked to the personality dimensions associated with the Big Five Model.[210] The five dimensions associated with this model include the ability of an individual to relate to others in society, the level to which an individual is intimidated by the world, the level to which individuals are conscious of their actions promoting efficiency in all the things they do and the level to which an individual is able to cooperate and integrate his/her existence or activities with those of others.[211] Dysfunctional emotional regulation is likely to be highly correlated to the extent to which an individual feels intimidated by the world, whereas an outgoing personality is better associated with an effective and efficient emotional regulation.[212] It has also been noted that the development of dysfunctional emotional regulation during infanthood and childhood may facilitate the development of borderline personality disorders in adolescence.[213] This could predispose individuals to reduced emotional and mental stability during adulthood. This would in turn result in increased economic, social and public costs. This can only be overcome by the state facilitating the development of an environment in which infants and children are able to develop optimal personality traits.

Economic theory asserts that consumers (individuals) make rational choices in an environment characterised by perfect information. Beliefs or perceptions are formed via the process of achieving equilibrium and the expression of choice. However, in asserting that individuals make rational choices, economic theory fails to consider that consumers (individuals) make decisions which are significantly influenced by emotions. Optimal emotional and mental stability occurs only when an individual's personality traits can develop normally without occurrences of either mental or

[209] Pollock, N., McCabe, G., Southard, A., and Zeigler-Hill, V. (2016), Pathological Personality Traits and Emotion Regulation Difficulties, Personality and Individual Difference, 95, pp. 168–177.

[210] Ibid.

[211] McCrae, R. R., and Costa, P. T. (1987), Validation of the five-factor model of personality across instruments and observers. Journal of Personality and Social Psychology, 52, 81–90.

[212] Timmermans, T., Van Mechelen, I., and Nezlek, J. B. (2009), Individual differences in core affect reactivity. Personality and Individual Differences, 47, 510–515.

[213] Rosenthal, M. Z., Gratz, K. L., Kosson, D. S., Cheavens, J. S., Lejuez, C. W., and Lynch, T. R. (2008). Borderline personality disorder and emotional responding: A review of the research literature. Clinical Psychology Review, 28, 75–91.

personality disorders. It has been found that in the development of an individual's personality, the environment in which an infant or a child develops is more important than are genetic factors. More importantly, included within the environment is the nature and extent of the relationship an infant or a child has with its primary caregiver. A positive, calming relationship would favour the optimal development of personality traits, as well as act to reduce the probability of personality and mental disorders developing. Mental and personality disorders are difficult to diagnose but impose substantial economic and public cost on nation states. Therefore, it should be the role of the state to facilitate the provision of an environment which is conducive to the optimal personality trait development of infants and children. This would further facilitate the development of optimal emotional and mental stability, allowing for stable progression into adolescence and adulthood. Optimal emotional and mental stability correlates with higher levels of rationality and better decision making—although this causal relationship is not accounted for by contemporary economic theory.

References

Ainsworth, M. D. S., Blehar, M. C., Waters, E., & Wall, S. (1978). *Patterns of Attachment: A Psychological Study of the Strange Situation*. Lawrence Erlbaum.

Asendorff, J. (2002). Editorial: The puzzle of personality types. *European Journal of Personality, 16*.

Bakermans-Kranenburg, M. J., & Van IJzendoorn, M. H. (2016). Attachment, parenting, and genetics. In J. Cassidy & P. R. Shaver (Eds.), *Handbook of Attachment: Theory, Research, and Clinical Applications*. Guilford Press.

Barkow, J. (1980). Prestige and self-esteem: A biosocial interpretation. In D. R. Omark, F. F. Strayer, & D. G. Freedman (Eds.), *Dominance Relations: An Ethological View of Human Conflict and Social Interaction*. Garland STPM Press.

Baumeister, R. F., & Leary, M. R. (1995). The need to belong: Desire for interpersonal attachments as a fundamental human motivation. *Psychological Bulletin, 117*, 497–529.

Beardslee, W. R., Gladstone, T. R., & O'Connor, EE. (2011). Transmission and prevention of mood disorders among children of affectively ill parents: A review. *Journal of the American Academy of Child and Adolescent Psychiatry, 50*, 1098–1109.

Bednar, R. L., Wells, M. G., & Peterson, S. R. (1989). *Self-Esteem: Paradoxes and Innovations in Clinical Theory and Practice*. American Psychological Association.

Bertenthal, B. I., & Fischer, K. W. (1978). Development of self-recognition in infant. *Developmental Psychology, 14*, 44–50.

Bischof-Köhler, D. (2012). Empathy and self-recognition in phylogenetic and ontogenetic perspective. *Emotion Review, 4*, 40–48.

Bloom, D. E., Cafiero, E., Jané-Llopis, E., et al. (2011). *The Global Economic Burden of Noncommunicable Diseases*. World Economic Forum.

Bokhorst, C. L., Bakermans-kranenburg, M. J., Fonagy, P., & Schuengel, C. (2003). The importance of shared environments in mother-infant attachment security: A behavioral genetic study. *Child Development, 74*, 1769–1782.

Boomsma, D. I., Busjahn, A., & Peltonen, L. (2002). Classical twin studies and beyond. *Nature Reviews: Genetics, 3*, 872–882.

Bouchard, T. (2004). Genetic influence on human psychological traits. *Current Directions in Psychological Science, 13*(4).

Bouchard, T. J., & McGue, M. (1990). Genetic and rearing environmental influences on adult personality: An analysis of adopted twins reared apart. *Journal of Personality, 58*, 263–292.

Bowlby, J. (1973). *Attachment and Loss: Vol. 2. Separation*. Basic Books.

Bowlby, J. (1980). *Attachment and Loss: Vol. 3. Loss, Sadness, and Depression*. Basic Books.

Bowlby, J. (2005). *A Secure Base*. Routledge.

Brandl, J. (2018). The puzzle of Mirror self-recognition. *Phenomenology and the Cognitive Sciences, 17*, 279–304.

Burger, O., et al. (2012). Human mortality improvement in evolutionary context. *Proceedings of the National Academy of Sciences of the United States of America, 109*, 18210–18214.

Buss, D. (1983). Evolutionary biology and personality psychology: Implications of genetic variability. *Personality and Individual Differences, 4*, 51–63.

Buss, D. M. (1995). Evolutionary psychology: A new paradigm for psychological science. *Psychological Inquiry, 6*, 1–30.

Buss, D., & Greiling, H. (1999). Adaptive individual differences. *Journal of Personality, 67*, 2.

Buss, D. M., Haselton, M. G., Shackelford, T. K., Bleske, A. L., & Wakefield, J. C. (1998). Adaptations, exaptations, and spandrels. *American Psychologist, 53*, 533–548.

Caspi, A., & Roberts, B. (2009). Personality development across life course. *Psychological Inquiry, 12*(2), 49–66.

Cast, A., & Burke, P. (2002). A theory of self-esteem. *Social Forces, 80*(3), 1041–1068.

Chanen, A. M. (2011). Outcomes in women diagnosed with borderline personality disorder in adolescence. *Journal of the Canadian Academy of Child and Adolescent Psychiatry, 20*(3), 175.
Chanen, A. M., & Kaess, M. (2012). Developmental pathways to borderline personality disorder. *Current Psychiatry Reports, 14*(1), 45–53.
Chapman, A., Gratz, K., & Brown, M. (2006). Solving the puzzle of deliberate self-harm: The experiential avoidance model. *Behavior Research and Therapy, 44*, 371–394.
Cloninger, C. (2000). Biology of personality dimensions. *Current Opinions in Psychiatry, 13*, 611–616.
Cloninger, C. R., & Svrakic, D. M. (2000). Personality disorders. In B. J. Sadock & V. A. Sadock (Eds.), *Comprehensive Textbook of Psychiatry* (7th ed., pp. 1723–1764). Lippincott Williams & Wilkins.
Cloninger, C. R., Van Eerdewegh, P., Goate, A., et al. (1998). Anxiety proneness linked to epistatic loci in genome scan of human personality traits. *American Journal of Medical Genetics, 81*, 313–317.
Colby, K. (1964). Psychotherapeutic processes. *Annual Review of Psychology, 15*, 347–370.
Costa, P., McCrae, R., & Lockenhoff, C. (2019). Personality across the life span. *Annual Review of Psychology, 70*, 423–448.
Cristea, I. A., Huibers, M. J., David, D., et al. (2015). The effects of cognitive behavior therapy for adult depression on dysfunctional thinking: A meta-analysis. *Clinical Psychology Review, 42*, 62–71.
Cropley, V. L., Fujita, M., Innis, R. B., & Nathan, P. J. (2006). Molecular imaging of the dopaminergic system and its association with human cognitive function. *Biological Psychiatry, 59*(10), 898–907.
Cuijpers, P. (2019). Target and outcomes of psychotherapies for mental disorders: An overview. *World Psychiatry, 18*, 3.
Cuijpers, P., Karyotaki, E., Reijnders, M., et al. (2019). Was Eysenck right after all? A reassessment of the effects of psychotherapy for adult depression. *Epidemiology and Psychiatric Sciences, 28*, 21–30.
Cuijpers, P., Weitz, E., Karyotaki, E., et al. (2014). The effects of psychological treatment of maternal depression on children and parental functioning: A meta-analysis. *European Child & Adolescent Psychiatry, 24*, 237–245.
Cuthbert, B. N., & Insel, T. R. (2013). Toward the future of psychiatric diagnosis: The seven pillars of RDoC. *BMC Medicine, 11*, 126.
Dall, J., Houston, A., & McNamara, J. (2004). The behavioural ecology of personality; consistent individual differences from an adaptive perspective. *Ecology Letters, 7*, 734–739.
Davidson, R. J. (2001). Toward a biology of personality and emotion. *Annals of the New York Academy of Science, 935*, 191–207.

Dawkins, R. (1982). *The Extended Phenotype: The Gene as the Unit of Selection.* Oxford University Press.

DeYoung, C. G. (2006). Higher-order factors of the big five in a multi-informant sample. *Journal of Personality and Social Psychology, 91*, 1138–1151.

Donker, T., Blankers, M., Hedman, E., et al. (2015). Economic evaluations of Internet interventions for mental health: A systematic review. *Psychol Med, 45*, 3357–3376.

Duarte, J., Fischersworring, M., Martinez, C., & Tomicic, A. (2019). 'I couldn't change the past; the answer was not there': A case study on the subjective construction of psychotherapeutic change of a patient with a borderline personality disorder diagnosis and her therapist. *Psychotherapy Research, 29*(4), 445–462.

Dweck, C. S. (2009). Can personality be changed? The role of beliefs in personality and change. *Current Directions in Psychological Science, 17*, 391–394.

Eisenhofer, G., Tian, H., Holmes, C., Matsunaga, J., Roffler-Tarlov, S., & Hearing, V. J. (2003). Tyrosinase: A developmentally specific major determinant of peripheral dopamine. *FASEB J, 17*, 1248–1255.

Elder, G. (1998). The life course as developmental theory. *Child Development, 69*(1), 1–12.

Engelmann, J., Schmid, B., De Dreu, C., Chumbley, J., & Fehr, E. (2019). On the psychology and economics of antisocial personality. *Proceedings of the National Academy of Sciences of the United States of America.* www.pnas.org/cgi/doi/10.1073/pnas.182013316

Epstein, S. (1994). Trait theory as personality theory: Can a part be as great as the whole? *Psychological Inquiry, 5*(2), 120–122.

Fearon, P. R., & Belsky, J. (2016). Precursors of attachment security. In J. Cassidy & P. R. Shaver (Eds.), *Handbook of Attachment. Theory, Research, and Clinical Applications.* Guilford Press.

Fraley, R. C., & Brumbaugh, C. C. (2004). A dynamical systems approach to conceptualizing and studying stability and change in attachment security. In S. W. Rholes & J. A. Simpson (Eds.), *Adult Attachment: Theory, Research, and Clinical Implications.* Guilford Press.

Frijda, N. H., & Mesquita, B. (1994). The social roles and functions of emotions. In H. R. Markus & S. Kitayama (Eds.), *Emotion and Culture.* American Psychological Association.

Goldman-Rakic, W. M. (1995). Cellular basis of working memory. *Neuron, 14*, 477–485.

Gratz, K. L., & Roemer, L. (2004). Multidimensional assessment of emotion regulation and dysregulation: Development, factor structure, and initial validation of the difficulties in emotion regulation scale. *Journal of Psychopathology and Behavioral Assessment, 26*, 41–54.

Gray, J. A., Moran, P. M., Grigoryan, G., Peters, S. L., Young, A. M. J., & Joseph, M. H. (1997). Latent inhibition: The nucleus accumbens connection revisited. *Behavioural Brain Research, 88*, 27–34.
Gross, J. J., & Muñoz, R. F. (1995). Emotion regulation and mental health. *Clinical Psychology: Science and Practice, 2*, 151–164.
Gross, J. J., & Thompson, R. A. (2007). Emotion regulation: Conceptual foundations. In J. J. Gross (Ed.), *Handbook of Emotion Regulation*. Guilford Press.
Hamilton, W. D. (1966). The genetical evolution of social behaviour 1. *Journal of Theoretical Biology, 7*, 1–16.
Harter, S. (1999). *The Construction of the Self: A Developmental Perspective*. Guilford.
Hawley, D., & DeHaan, L. (1996). Toward a definitions of family resilience: Integrating life-span and family perspectives. *Family Process, 35*, 283–298.
Hoff, K., & Stiglitz, J. (2010). Equilibrium fictions: A cognitive approach to societal rigidity. *American Economic Review, Papers and Proceedings, 100*, 141–146.
Huesmann, L., & Eron, L. (1989). Individual differences and the trait of aggression. *European Journal of Personality, 3*, 95–106.
Hur, Y. M., Bouchard, T. J., Jr., & Lykken, D. T. (1998). Genetic and environmental influence on morningness-eveningness. *Personality and Individual Differences, 25*, 917–925.
Insel, T., Cuthbert, B., Garvey, M., et al. (2010). Research domain criteria (RDoC): Toward a new classification framework for research on mental disorders. *American Journal of Psychiatry, 167*, 748–751.
James, W. (1890). *The Principles of Psychology* (Vol. 1). Henry Holt.
John, O., & Gross, J. (2004). Healthy and Unhealthy Emotion Regulation: Personality Processes, Individual Differences and Life Span Development. *Journal of Personality, 72*, 1301–1334. https://doi.org/10.1111/j.1467-6494.2004.00298.x
John, O. P., Robins, R. W., & Pervin, L. (2008). *Handbook of Personality: Theory and Research*. Guilford Press.
Kaye, W. H., Frank, G. K., & McConaha, C. (1999). Altered dopamine activity after recovery from restricting-type anorexia nervosa. *Neuropsychopharmacology, 21*, 503–506.
Keefe, J., McCarthy, K., Dinger, V., McMain, S., Zilcha-Mano, S., Sahin, Z., Graham, K., & Barker, J. (2019). A meta-analysis of psychodynamic treatments for borderline and cluster. *Personality Disorders, Theory, Research, and Treatment, Personality Disorders*. https://doi.org/10.1037/per0000382
Kirwin, K., & Hamrin, V. (2005). Decreasing the risk of complicated bereavement and future psychiatric disorders in children. *Journal of Child and Adolescent Psychiatric Nursing, 18*(2).
Kowalski, R.M., and Leary, M.R. (Eds.), American Psychological Association, .
Krzeczkowski, J., & Lieshout, R. (2019). Prenatal influences on the development and stability of personality. *New Ideas in Psychology, 53*, 22–31.

Leary, M. R. (1999a). The social and psychological importance of self-esteem. *The Social Psychology of Emotional and Behavioral Problems: Interfaces of Social and Clinical Psychology.*

Leary, M. (1999b). Making sense of self-esteem. *Current Directions in Psychological Science, 8*(1).

Leichsenring, F., Steinert, C., & Crits-Christoph, P. (2018). On mechanisms of change in psychodynamic therapy. *Zeitschrift für Psychosomatische Medizin und Psychotherapie, 64*, 16–22.

Leykin, Y., & DeRubeis, R. J. (2009). Allegiance in psychotherapy outcome research: Separating association from bias. *Clinical Psychology: Science and Practice, 16*, 4–65.

Lukaszewski, A. W. (2021). Evolutionary perspectives on the mechanistic underpinnings of personality. In J. Rauthmann (Ed.), *The Handbook of Personality Dynamics and Processes.* Elsevier Press.

Lyoo, I. K., Han, M. H., & Cho, D. Y. (1998). A brain MRI study in subjects with borderline personality disorder. *Journal of Affective Disorders, 50*, 235–243.

Lyubomirsky, S., Tkach, C., & Dimatteo, M. (2006). What are the differences between happiness and self-esteem? *Social Indicators Research, 78*, 363–404.

Main, M. (2000). The organized categories of infant, child, and adult attachment: Flexible vs. inflexible attention under attachment-related stress. *Journal of the American Psychoanalytic Association, 48*, 1055–1096.

Marr, D. (1982). *Vision: A Computational Investigation into the Human Representation and Processing of Visual Information.* Freeman.

McAdams, D., & Olson, B. (2010). Personality development: Continuity and change over life course. *Annual Review of Psychology, 61*, 517–542.

McCrae, R. R., & Costa, P. T. (1987). Validation of the five-factor model of personality across instruments and observers. *Journal of Personality and Social Psychology, 52*, 81–90.

McLeod, J. (2011). *Qualitative Research in Counselling and Psychotherapy.* Sage.

Meltzer, H. Y. (1990). Role of serotonin in depression. *Annals of the New York Academy of Sciences, 600*, 486–499.

Mischel, W. (1998). *Personality and Assessment.* Wiley.

Nettle, D. (2010). Dying young and living fast: Variation in life history across English neighbourhoods. *Behavioral Ecology, 21*, 387–395.

Nieuwenhuyse, K., Faber, B., Verbeek, J. H., et al. (2014). Interventions to improve return to work in depressed people. *Cochrane Database of Systematic Reviews, 12*, CD006237.

O'Connor, T. G., & Croft, C. M. (2001). A twin study of attachment in preschool children. *Child Development, 72*, 1501–1511.

Okano, K. (2019). The origin of so-called 'shadowy personalities' in patients with dissociative identity disorder. *European Journal of Trauma and Dissociation, 3*, 95–102.

Ophuis, R. H., Lokkerbol, J., Heemskerk, S. C., et al. (2017). Cost-effectiveness of interventions for treating anxiety disorders: A systematic review. *Journal of Affective Disorders, 210*, 1–13.
Penke, L., Jaap, J., Dennissen, A., & Miller, G. F. (2007). The evolutionary genetics of personality. *European Journal of Personality, 21*, 549–587.
Perner, J. (1991). *Understanding the Representational Mind*. The MIT Press.
Pollock, N., McCabe, G., Southard, A., & Zeigler-Hill, V. (2016). Pathological personality traits and emotion regulation difficulties. *Personality and Individual Difference, 95*, 168–177.
Porter, C., Claus-Palmier, J., Branitsky, A., Mansell, W., Warwick, H., & Varese, F. (2020). Childhood adversity and borderline personality disorder: A meta-analysis. *Acta Psychiatrica Scandinavica, 141*, 6–20.
Roberts, B., & Jackson, J. (2008). Socioeconomic personality psychology. *Journal of Personality, 76*, 6.
Roberts, B., & Mroczek, D. (2008). Personality trait change in adulthood. *Current Directions in Psychological Science, 17*(1).
Robinson, G. E. (2004). Beyond nature and nurture. *Science, 304*, 397–399.
Rosenthal, M. Z., Gratz, K. L., Kosson, D. S., Cheavens, J. S., Lejuez, C. W., & Lynch, T. R. (2008). Borderline personality disorder and emotional responding: A review of the research literature. *Clinical Psychology Review, 28*, 75–91.
Rutherford, M. B. (2011). The social value of self-esteem. *Society, 48*, 407. https://doi.org/10.1007/s12115-011-9460-5
Sabol, S. Z., Nelson, M. L., Fisher, C., et al. (1999). A genetic association for cigarette smoking behavior. *Health Psychology, 18*, 7–13.
Sales, C. M. D., & Alves, P. C. G. (2016). Patient-centred assessment in psychotherapy: A review of individualized tools. *Clinical Psychology: Science and Practice, 23*, 265–283.
Sandman, C. A., Buss, C., Head, K., & Davis, E. P. (2015). Fetal exposure to maternal depressive symptoms is associated with cortical thickness in late childhood. *Biological Psychiatry, 77*(4), 324–334. https://doi.org/10.1016/j.biopsych.2014.06.025
Schilbach, F. (2019). Alcohol and self control: A field experiment in India. *American Economic Review, 109*(4), 1290–1322.
Shakow, D. (1962). Discussion of papers relating to definition of variables. In H. H. Strupp & L. Luborsky (Eds.), *Research in Psychotherapy, II*. American Psychological Association.
Simpson, J. A., & Rholes., W. S. (2012). Adult attachment orientations, stress, and romantic relationships. In P. Devine & A. Plant (Eds.), *Advances in Experimental Social Psychology* (Vol. 45, pp. 279–328). Academic Press.
Solomon, S., Greenberg, J., & Pyszczynski, T. (1991). A terror management theory of social behavior: The psychological functions of self-esteem and cultural worldviews. *Advances in Experimental Social Psychology, 24*, 93–159.

Steyer, R., Schmitt, M., & Eid, M. (1999). Latent state-trait theory and research in personality and individual differences. *European Journal of Personality, 13*, 389–408.

Sugiura, M., Kawashima, R., Nakagawa, M., et al. (2000). Correlation between human personality and neural activity in cerebral cortex. *NeuroImage, 11*, 541–546.

Sznycer, D. (2019). Forms and functions of the self-conscious emotions. *Trends in Cognitive Sciences, 23*(2).

Thome, J., Weijers, H. G., Wiesbeck, G. A., et al. (1999). Dopamine D3 receptor gene polymorphism and alcohol dependence: Relation to personality rating. *Psychiatric Genetics, 9*, 17–21.

Timmermans, T., Van Mechelen, I., & Nezlek, J. B. (2009). Individual differences in core affect reactivity. *Personality and Individual Differences, 47*, 510–515.

Timulak, L., & McElvaney, R. (2013). Qualitative meta-analysis of insight events in psychotherapy. *Counselling Psychology Quarterly, 26*, 131–150.

Tooby, J., & Cosmides, L. (1990a). The past explains the present: Emotional adaptations and the structure of ancestral environments. *Ethology and Sociobiology, 11*, 375–424.

Tooby, J., & Cosmides, L. (1990b). On the universality of human nature and the uniqueness of the individual: The role of genetics and adaptation. *Journal of Personality, 58*, 17–67.

Tooby, J., & Cosmides, L. (1992). Psychological foundations of culture. In J. Barkow, L. Cosmides, & J. Tooby (Eds.), *The Adapted Mind*. Oxford University Press.

Verkuyten, M. (2005). The puzzle of high self-esteem among ethnic minorities: Company explicit and implicit self esteem. *Self and Identity, 4*(2), 177–192.

Videler, A., Hotsebaut, J., Schulkens, J., Sobczak, S., & Van Alphen, S. (2019). A life span perspective on borderline personality disorder. *Current Psychiatry Reports, 21*, 51.

Vigo, D., Thornicroft, G., & Atun, R. (2016). Estimating the true global burden of mental illness. *Lancet Psychiatry, 3*, 171–178.

Von Rueden, C., & Jaeggi, A. V. (2016). Men's status and reproductive success in 33 nonindustrial societies: Effects of subsistence, marriage system, and reproductive strategy. *Proceedings of the National Academy of Sciences of the United States of America, 113*, 10824–10829.

Wampold, B. E. (2015). How important are the common factors in psychotherapy? An update. *World Psychiatry, 14*, 270–277.

Waters, S. F., Virmani, E. A., Thompson, R. A., Meyer, S., Raikes, H. A., & Jochem, R. (2010). Emotion regulation and attachment: Unpacking two constructs and their association. *Journal of Psychopathology and Behavioral Assessment, 32*, 37–47.

Weislo, W. T. (1989). Behavioral environments and evolutionary change. *Annual Review of Ecology and Systematics, 20*, 137–169.

WHOQOL Group. (1995). The World Health Organization quality of life assessment (WHOQOL): Position paper from the World Health Organization. *Social Science & Medicine, 41*, 1403–1409.

Widiger, T. A., & Samuel, D. B. (2005). Diagnostic categories or dimensions? A question for the diagnostic and statistical manual of mental disorders—fifth edition. *Journal of Abnormal Psychology, 114*, 494–504.

Wong, J., Bahji, A., & Khalid-Khan, S. (2020). Psychotherapies for adolescents with sub-clinical and borderline personality disorder: A systematic review and meta-analysis. *The Canadian Journal of Psychiatry, 65*(1).

Young, C. (2010). Personality neuroscience and the biology of traits. *Social and Personality Psychology Compass, 4*(12), 1165–1180.

Young, E., Simpson, J., Grishevicius, V., Huelsnitz, C., & Fleck, C. (2019). Childhood attachment and adult personality: A lifetime perspective. *Self and Identity, 18*(1), 22–38.

Zuckerman, M., Porac, J., Lathin, D., Smith, R., & Deci, E. (1978). On the importance of self-determination for intrinsically motivated behaviour. *Personality and Social Psychology Bulletin, 4*(3).

CHAPTER 7

Psychology and Youth Development

Introduction

In previous chapters it has been discussed that the pre-natal and post-natal development of the infant as that of the pre-adolescent child is important for what kind of adult eventually emerges into the world. This is especially true in the context of cognitive prowess but also in the context of emotional and mental stability as discussed in the previous chapter. However, it may be possible for corrections to be made to optimise an individual's behaviour as the child transitions into adolescence and youth. There are two frameworks which can be applied to analysing the development of the behaviours of children and adolescents. These frameworks include the Positive Youth Development (PYD) and Resilience Science (RS) frameworks. The PYD framework suggests that individual children and adolescents are both capable and do adapt to their environments. The implication is that adolescent behaviour is flexible, in which case suitable social programmes can be devised which enhance positive behaviours and remove negative behaviours. While the PYD framework asserts the flexibility of adolescent behaviour such that it can be changed for the better, the RS framework suggests that adolescents are resilient in character to overcome any negative aspects of their environment. This resilience may arise in human adolescents because of a psychological mechanism against adversity. If policies which enhance such a mechanism can be devised, then the

S. Ramesh, *The Political Economy of Human Behaviour and Economic Development*,
https://doi.org/10.1007/978-3-031-12666-6_7

implication is that the resilience of adolescents to an adverse environment may be strengthened. Studies have indicated that one such mechanism is access to education. This may allow children to develop advanced cognitive skills which will allow them to reason as to what would be the best action to take in minimising the impact of an adverse environment on their well-being. Moreover, the equal access of education to both males and females will also result in the reduction of gender inequality by giving girls the opportunity to be educated, enter the workforce in a skilled profession and earn an income. This will also help to ensure that women will be able to contribute to the productivity of the economy on an equal par with men. Adolescents may face an adverse environment particularly in the context of having to grow up in a poor socio-economic environment. This may be characterised as families living on low incomes and parents having to work long hours on lower pay. In such a scenario, children may be left to fend for themselves, the nutrition they receive may be sub-optimal and educational opportunities may not be available. Economic crises may also lead to a lower socio-economic condition, which may impact on the development of children as well as of adolescents. This may be because one or both parent lose their jobs, resulting in the other scenarios previously mentioned but also perhaps leading to stress, which may also negatively impact on the family environment. Elevated levels of stress may negatively impact on the nature of the relationship between the child and the caregiver. Studies have found that the predominance of caring relationships within the family, especially between the child and the primary care giver, are important in the shaping of a resilient personality for the child. However, it has also been found that the child also needs to maintain good relationships with not only his/her peers at school but also with his/her teacher to develop a resilient character. The development of the latter is also important in the context of an adolescent being resilient in the face of bullying. The latter may be seen as a behaviour in which a stronger individual intimidates a weaker individual to consciously weaken his/her well-being as well as to deny access to resources. In this case, bullying may be seen as an evolutionary adaptation rather than as a maladaptive behaviour.

Youth Development and Socio-economic Change

The Positive Youth Development (PYD) view of the development of adolescents and children is closely related to the metatheory, a theory about a theory, regarding relational developmental systems.[1] The results of PYD programmes reflect the competencies and characteristics which youths and adolescents should develop in order to become successful in adulthood.[2] Metatheory relates to what concepts should be included in a theory as well as how the framework of the theory should be put together.[3] The metatheory associated with the study of youth and adolescent behaviour is linked to relational development systems (RDS).[4] Under RDS metatheory, the individual is seen as an intricate, conscious creature which is able to adapt to its environment.[5] This implies a flexibility or plasticity of human behaviour, which is the foundation of all PYD-related models.[6] It is important to take advantage of the plasticity of human behaviour during youth and adolescence, in particular, as it is during this stage of human development that there are rapid changes. In doing so, the factors favouring positive development can be enhanced and factors favouring negative development can be denigrated.[7] This can be accomplished by formulating economic and social policies which create opportunities which facilitate the development of the positive aspects of youth development via the individual context relations pathway.[8] The theoretical frameworks of theories

[1] Overton, W. F. (2015), Process and relational developmental systems, In Overton, W., Molenaar, P., and Lerner, R. (Eds.) IN Handbook of Child Psychology and Developmental Science. Vol.1 Theory and Method, 7th edition, Wiley, Hoboken.

[2] Sukarieh, M., and Tannock, S. (2011), The Positivity Imperative: A Critical Look at the 'new' youth development movement, Journal of Youth Studies, Vol.14, No.6, pp. 675–691.

[3] Lerner, R, et al. (2018), The End of the Beginning: Evidence and Absences Studying Positive Youth Development in a Global Context, Adolescent Research Review, 4, 1–14.

[4] Lerner, R. M. (2018), Concepts and Theories of Human Development, 4th Edition, Routledge, New York.

[5] Overton, W. F. (2015), Process and relational developmental systems, In Overton, W., Molenaar, P., and Lerner, R. (Eds.) IN Handbook of Child Psychology and Developmental Science. Vol.1 Theory and Method, 7th edition, Wiley, Hoboken.

[6] Lerner, R. M. (2012), Essay review: Developmental science: Past, present, and future, International Journal of Developmental Science, 6(1–2), 29–36.

[7] Lerner, R. M. (2015), Preface. In Handbook of Child Psychology and Developmental Science, 7th edition, Wiley, Hoboken.

[8] Lerner, R. M., and Overton, W. F. (2008), Exemplifying the integrations of the relational developmental system: Synthesizing theory, research, and application to promote positive development and social justice, Journal of Adolescent Research, 23(3), 245–255.

based on the RDS framework relies upon the relations between the individual and the context. The nature of these relations is both time and culture dependent.[9]

Resilience Science (RS) is another approach to evaluating the development of children and adolescents. Empirical studies had noted that children who had grown up in a bad environment were able to overcome the constraints of such development and go on to lead a successful and healthy life.[10] Resilience in the context of dynamic individual-contextual relations in an ever-changing environment implies the existence of an adversity-withstanding physiological mechanism within humans.[11] The strengthening of such mechanisms would make youth and adolescent resilience stronger, allowing for enhanced positive development during a vital stage in human development. One such mechanism is education, the improvement in access to this would also lead to readdressing gender inequality to opportunity by giving female youths opportunities to positively develop, and this will benefit the economy and society.[12] Resilience at the individual, family and societal levels can be enhanced and developed by social and economic programmes devised by policymakers.[13] Given the lack of resources, community projects to foster and engage youth development should be carefully designed.[14] This would involve firstly to ask the sequentially relevant questions with regard to the project's ultimate outcome. Secondly, suitable and effective administrative structures should be put in place to optimise adult and youth involvement in decision making. Finally,

[9] Elder, G. H. Jr., Shanahan, M. J., and Jennings, J. A. (2015), Human development in time and place IN Handbook of Child Psychology and Developmental Science. Vol. 4 Ecological Settings and Processes in Developmental Systems, Bornstein, M., and Leventhal, T. (Eds), 7th Edition, Wiley, Hoboken.

[10] Masten, A. S. (1999), Resilience Comes of Age: Reflections on the Past and Outlook for the Next Generation of Research IN Resilience and Development: Positive Life Adaptations, Glantz, M., and Johnson, J. (Eds.), Plenum, New York.

[11] Masten, A. S. (2007), Resilience in developing systems: Progress and promise as the fourth wave rises. Development and Psychopathology, 19, 921–930.

[12] Chisholm, L., and Bois-Reymond, M. (1993), Youth Transitions, Gender and Social Change, Sociology, Vol.27, No.2, pp. 259–279.

[13] Southwick, S. M., Bonanno, G. A., Masten, A. S., Panter-Brick, C., and Yehuda, R. (2014), Resilience definitions, theory, and challenges: Interdisciplinary perspectives. European Journal of Psychotraumatology, 5(1), 25338.

[14] Campbell, D., and Erbstein, N. (2012), Engaging Youth in Community Change: Three key Implementation Principles, Community Development, 43:1, pp. 63–79.

those leading the project should have access to many skills and be networked with those of a similar capacity.

The common theme between RS and PYD is that both models focus and emphasise the positive aspects of youth and adolescent development.[15] Moreover, RS is also a strengths-based approach and, like PYD, also has a link to metatheory.[16] PYD developed in the context of the desire of scholars to study and evaluate the positive aspects of the behaviours of developing adolescents.[17] However, such evaluation should be based on the impact on youths of their wider environment, which varies from generation to generation rather than just narrowly focusing on physiological changes which occur due to age.[18] Environmental changes affecting youth development may include demographic changes, structural changes in economies, increased urbanisation as well as advances in technology and the wired economy.[19] It is important to understand that it is a combination and interaction of the personal characteristics of youths and the very facets of their environment which leads to not only successful youth development but also positive externalities impacting on the wider community.[20] Moreover, scholarship seeks to better understand how changes occur in individuals over time and how developmental differences may arise between individuals.[21] The emphasis is on better understanding the positive aspects of the development of adolescents.[22] Knowledge of the factors which enable positive youth development will allow policymakers and practitioners to put in place policies to magnify the presence of these

[15] Lerner, R, et al. (2018), The End of the Beginning: Evidence and Absences Studying Positive Youth Development in a Global Context, Adolescent Research Review, 4, 1–14.

[16] Masten, A. S. (2007), Resilience in developing systems: Progress and promise as the fourth wave rises. Development and Psychopathology, 19, 921–930.

[17] Lerner, R, et al. (2018), The End of the Beginning: Evidence and Absences Studying Positive Youth Development in a Global Context, Adolescent Research Review, 4, 1–14.

[18] Wyn, J., and Woodman, D. (2006), Generation, Youth and Social Change in Australia, Journal of Youth Studies, 9:5, pp. 495–514.

[19] Larson, R., and Wilson, S.(2004), Adolescence Across Place and Time: Globalisation and the Changing Pathways to Adulthood IN 'Handbook of Adolescent Psychology', Lerner, R., and Steinberg, L. 9th ed., John Wiley and Sons INC, Hoboken, New Jersey.

[20] Lerner, R., Bowers, E., Geldhof, G., Gestsdottir, S., and DeSouza, L. (2012), Promoting Positive Youth Development in the Face of Contextual Changes and Challenges: The Roles of Individual Strengths and Ecological Assets, New Directions for Youth Development, No.135.

[21] Lerner, R. M. (2012), Essay review: Developmental science: Past, present, and future, International Journal of Developmental Science, 6(1–2), 29–36.

[22] Lerner, R. M. (2017), Commentary: Studying and testing the positive youth development model: A tale of two approaches. Child Development, 88(4), 1183–1185.

factors, which at the same time reduce the presence of the negative factors associated with youth behaviour.[23] Programmes and policies to promote PYD should include the mentorship of youths and adolescents by suitably experienced and qualified adults as well opportunities for participation in leadership roles within the household and civil society.[24] Role models for youths and adolescents to follow as well as to learn from are also very important.[25] Furthermore, in order for youth participation programmes to positively impact on youths, it is important that the participation is existent in the design and mechanisms and societal structures which affect the lives of youths and adolescents on a daily basis.[26] The common characteristics which emerge from successful PYD include youths being able to perform tasks well, being self-confident and caring about the welfare of others, having a strong moral orientation and being connected with others and with society.[27] The other perspective of PYD is one that reflects the reality that an individual has the potential for change throughout the adolescent period in adapting to his/her environment. An alternative to PYD is the Deficit Model, which views youth development from a negative perspective, viewing positive development as resulting from a reduction in the factors which contribute to negative development.[28] These may in particular arise during times of an economic crisis when youths may suffer the impact of austerity as a result of their parents losing their jobs and/or having to take pay cuts.[29] Despite accumulated scholarly work which suggested that the Deficit Model was not suitable to evaluate behavioural development in adolescents and youths, it continued to be the preferred tool of practitioners well into the last decade of the twentieth century.

[23] Lerner, R, et al. (2018), The End of the Beginning: Evidence and Absences Studying Positive Youth Development in a Global Context, Adolescent Research Review, 4, 1–14.

[24] Lerner, R. M. (2004), Liberty: Thriving and Civic Engagement Among American Youth, Sage, Thousand Oaks, CA.

[25] Assibey-Mensah, G. (1997), Role Models and Youth Development: Evidence and Lessons from the Perceptions of African American Male Youth, The Western Journal of Black Studies, 21:4.

[26] O'Donoghue, J., Kirshner, B., and McLoughlin, M. (2002), Introduction: Moving Youth Participation Forward, New Directions for Youth Development, No. 96.

[27] Lerner, R. M. (2018), Concepts and Theories of Human Development, 4th edition, Routledge, New York.

[28] Freud, A. (1969). Adolescence as a developmental disturbance IN Adolescence, Caplan, G., and Lebovici, S. (Eds.), Basic Books, New York.

[29] Pimlott-Wilson, H., and Hall, S. (2017), Everyday experiences of economic change: repositioning geographies of children, youth and families, Area, 49, 3, pp. 258–265.

However, after this period, PYD began to emerge as a better framework to evaluate youth and adolescent behaviour because of insights gained from youth schemes and research in biology suggesting that an individual's characteristics remained malleable even into adolescence.

Socio-economic Status, Parenting and Youth Development

The impact of the level of socio-economic status (SES) on childhood and adolescent development can be analysed from two perspectives, that of social causation and that of social selection.[30] According to the former, the health and well-being developmental outcomes of children are impacted upon by the social condition associated with the environment of their upbringing.[31] However, according to the social selection perspective, the personality traits and emotional states of the child will have a big impact on not only his/her behavioural development but also the extent of his/her socio-economic environment.[32] The development of adolescents is sub-optimal if they are brought up in a family environment characterised as one being of a lower socio-economic status (SES).[33] A lower SES is often defined as those situated in the lower social classes, characterised by having either no or minimal education and being employed in an unskilled occupation.[34] The result of the occurrence of either one of these factors or both will be a low level of income and a lack of access to the resources a child would need to be given to optimally develop into adolescence and then adulthood. Moreover, the parents may have to work longer hours. This may result in the children being left to care for themselves in the absence of affordable childcare. Childhood and adolescent development may be subsequently denigrated, resulting in poor self-esteem, awkward

[30] Conger, R., Conger, K., and Martin, M. (2010), Socioeconomic Status, Family Processes and Individual Development, Journal of Marriage and Family, 72, pp. 685–704.

[31] Ibid.

[32] McLeod, J. D., and Kaiser, K. (2004), Childhood emotional and behavioral problems and educational attainment. American Sociological Review, 69, 636–658.

[33] Letourneau, N., Duffett-Leger, L., Levac, L., Watson, B., and Young-Morris, C. (2011), Socioeconomic Status and Child Development: A meta-Analysis, Journal of Emotional and Behavioral Disorders, 21(3), pp. 211–224.

[34] Santos, A., Ebrahim, S., and Barros, H. (2008), Gender, socio-economic status and metabolic syndrome in middle aged and old adults, BMC Public Health, 8:62.

social behaviour as well as poor intellectual and linguistic levels.[35] Moreover, childhood development in a low SES level may also result in cumulative mental and physical health issues later in life.[36] However, the measures by which SES can be defined can be broadened to include the marital status of the parents and whether the parents are in receipt of social security transfers from the government.[37] Although a lower SES may negatively impact on the well-being and development of children and adolescents, this is not guaranteed and the eventual outcome would depend on the interaction of a number of variables. Moreover, the low level of SES may have a smaller impact on childhood development than other factors. In this case, it is important to consider the interaction of different kinds of parental behaviours and the nature and type of SES.[38] For example, parents at lower levels of SES may control children more than parents at higher SES levels as well as being more adept at dispatching harsher punishment when the children are naughty.[39] It has been found that poor parenting regardless of the level of SES may have a bigger impact on denigrating childhood and adolescent behaviour.[40] An overtly authoritarian parenting style may lead to children prone to becoming overweight and eventually obese.[41] However, protective parenting is associated with the child developing better health.[42] Nevertheless, living in an extended family

[35] Mendelson, T., Kubzansky, L. D., Datta, G. D., and Buka, S. L. (2008), Relation of female gender and low socioeconomic status to internalizing symptoms among adolescents: A case of double jeopardy? Social Science & Medicine, 66, 1284–1296.

[36] Kroenke, C. (2008), Socioeconomic Status and Health: Youth Development and Neomaterialist and Psychosocial Mechanisms, Social Science and Medicine, 66, pp. 31–42.

[37] Ensminger, M., and Fotherill, K. (2003), A decade of measuring SES: What it tells us and where to go from here, IN Socioeconomic status, parenting, and child development, Bornstein, M., and Bradley, R. (Eds.), Lawrence Erlbaum, Mahwah, NJ.

[38] Hoff, E., Laursen, B., and Tardif, T. (2002), Socioeconomic Status and Parenting IN Handbook of Parenting, Volume 2 Biology and Ecology of Parenting, Bornstein, M. (Ed), Lawrence Erlbaum Associates, Publishers, London.

[39] Ibid.

[40] Berger, L., and Brooks-Gunn, J. (2005), Socioeconomic Status, Parenting Knowledge and Behaviours, and Perceived Maltreatment of Young Low Birth-Weight Children, Social Service Review, 79, pp. 237–67.

[41] Rhee, K., Lumeng, J., Appugliese, D., Kaciroti., and Bradley, R. (2006), Parenting Styles and Overweight Status in First Grade,' Pediatrics, 117, No.6, pp. 2047–2054.

[42] Beach, S., Lei, M., Brody, G., Kim, S., Barton, A., Dogan, M., and Philibert, R. (2016), Parenting, Socioeconomic Status Risk and Later Young Adult Health: Exploration of Opposing Indirect Effects via DNA Methylation, Child Development, Vol.87, No.1, pp. 111–121.

may reduce the impact of low SES on the developmental outcomes of children and adolescents. This may be because in an extended family, aunts, uncles and grandparents may be able to provide support to the parents by looking after the children when they go to work. In this case, the parents may be less stressed and may exhibit good parental behaviours with their children such as patience and providing encouragement to learn and study. In fact, the impact of the level of SES may be mitigated by the child's own personal characteristics as well as the specific characteristics of the family.[43] This may be in contrast to stressed parents, with access to a lower level of social and family support,[44] who may exhibit negative parental behaviours such as beating and shouting at children as well as not providing them with the physical, emotional and intellectual nourishment they may need to develop through childhood and adolescence into healthy adulthood. However, it may be a combination of the parental behaviours resulting from a low level of income as well as the inability of parents to provide the tangible and intangible resources required by children which leads to the sub-optimal development of adolescents.[45] Nevertheless, whether child development suffers because of either parental stress or a lack of access to resources, it is evident that the mental health of parents is affected more if they come from a low SES level compared to a higher one.[46] However, even at a high level of SES it has been found that a child's positive development may be constrained due to emotional deprivation because the parents may not always be available as they are busy making money or enjoying their personal leisure.[47] Moreover, a child growing up in an environment associated with a higher SES level is prone to ill-health

[43] Bradley, R., and Corwyn, R. (2002), Socioeconomic Status and Child Development, Annu. Rev. Psychol, 53:371–99.

[44] Perry, B. (2007), Relational poverty and the impact of trauma on children: A neurodevelopmental view of resilience and vulnerability to adverse childhood experiences. Resistance and Resilience: Helping Children and Youth Survive in the Face of Family Violence. Fredericton, NB, Canada.

[45] McLoyd, V., and Wilson, L. (1990), Maternal behavior, social support, and economic conditions as predictors of distress in children, New Directions for Child Development, 46, 49–69.

[46] Petterson, S., and Albers, A. B. (2001), Effects of poverty and maternal depression and early childhood development. Child Development, 72, 1794–1813.

[47] Luthar, S., ad Latendresse, S. (2005), Comparable 'risks' at the Socioeconomic Status Extremes: Preadolescents Perceptions of Parenting, Development and Psychopathology, 17, pp. 207–230.

in adolescence.[48] This maybe because higher parental and family income levels may lead to greater access to narcotics, tobacco and alcohol—although the opposite may be true of a child brought up in a household which would be characterised in SES standards as being poor.[49]

Government-sponsored developmental programmes to improve childhood development[50] as well as the development of adolescents[51] have been to an extent successful. However, the nature of such developmental programmes may differ between developed and developing countries as well as between countries with income inequality. In countries where income equality is greater, it has been found that government-led programmes to facilitate the cognitive development of children have been successful.[52] This has been particularly true in the case of improved levels of literacy[53] and numeracy.[54] The impact of the level of SES on child and adolescent development is often analysed using the framework associated with the Total Environmental Assessment Model of Early Childhood Development (TEAM-ECD). The latter views the impact of SES on childhood and adolescent development from a number of different angles, ranging from the depth of social contact (individual, community) to the nature and

[48] Beach, S., Lei, M., Brody, G., Kim, S., Barton, A., Dogan, M., and Philibert, R. (2016), Parenting, Socioeconomic Status Risk and Later Young Adult Health: Exploration of Opposing Indirect Effects via DNA Methylation, Child Development, Vol.87, No.1, pp. 111–121.

[49] Ibid.

[50] Olds, D. L., Sadler, L., and Kitzman, H. (2007), Programs for parents of infants and toddlers: Recent evidence from randomized trials. Journal of Child Psychology and Psychiatry, and Allied Disciplines, 48, 355–391.

[51] Dougherty, G. (2007), Ensuring the best start in life: Targeting versus universality in early child development. IRPP Choices, 13(8), 1–52.

[52] Letourneau, N., Duffett-Leger, L., Levac, L., Watson, B., and Young-Morris, C. (2011), Socioeconomic Status and Child Development: A meta-Analysis, Journal of Emotional and Behavioral Disorders, 21(3), pp. 211–224.

[53] Irwin, L. G., Siddiqi, A., and Hertzman, C. (2007). Early child development: A powerful equalizer, World Health Organization's Commission on the Social Determinants of Health, Vancouver, British Columbia, Canada.

[54] Case, R., Griffin, S., and Kelly, W. (1999), Socioeconomic gradients in mathematical ability and their responsiveness to intervention during early childhood, IN Keating, D., & Hertzman, C. (Eds.), Developmental health and the wealth of nations (pp. 125–149). Guilford, New York, NY.

geographical focus of the developmental programmes.[55] Furthermore, the emphasis of analysis of the TEAM-ECD focus is on the development of the child over time.[56] The main facilitators of the development of a child are those which arise from its immediate environment, its family, parents and siblings as well as other close relatives such as aunts and uncles.[57] In this context, it is important to consider family-specific factors such as proneness to domestic violence, alcoholism or health factors which may impact on the development of the child in negative ways.[58] This may particularly be in the case when the health of the primary caregiver to the child is affected. In any case, whatever the family-specific factors affecting child development, the emphasis of the TEAM-ECD framework is to view investments in child development, enabling developmental programmes as an economic strategy based on human capital development.[59] This type of early intervention in human capital will mean that once the child grows up to enter the work force, he/she will be productive and able to contribute to the economy of the country in a positive manner. However, due to a lack of resources, developing countries are both unlikely and unable to put in place developmental programmes which can improve and enhance the social dimensions of the TEAM-ECD framework. Such developmental programmes which support the developmental well-being of children may therefore arise at the instigation of non-governmental bodies.[60]

Impact of Economic Crisis on Youth Development

The proportion of any countries workforce defined as being in their youth is typically within the 15–24 years age group.[61] Economic crises can have a significant negative impact on the ability of individuals to find jobs,

[55] Letourneau, N., Duffett-Leger, L., Levac, L., Watson, B., and Young-Morris, C. (2011), Socioeconomic Status and Child Development: A meta-Analysis, Journal of Emotional and Behavioral Disorders, 21(3), pp. 211–224.

[56] Ibid.

[57] Ibid.

[58] Ibid.

[59] Ibid.

[60] Letourneau, N., Duffett-Leger, L., Levac, L., Watson, B., and Young-Morris, C. (2011), Socioeconomic Status and Child Development: A meta-Analysis, Journal of Emotional and Behavioral Disorders, 21(3), pp. 211–224.

[61] ILO (2010), Global Employment Trends for Youth: Special Issue on the Impact of the Global Economic Crisis on Youth, ILO, Geneva.

especially youths. This has been verified through empirical findings.[62] In general, economic crises will reduce the incomes of households through increasing job losses. As a result of reduced household incomes, households may have to cut down on food expenditures, social outings, as well as potential educational expenditure. This may have a negative impact on the development of infants, children and youths.[63] This may be due to the reduced opportunities for personal development as well as the constraints on psychological and cognitive development, which may result due to malnourishment.[64] These effects would then go towards perpetuating poverty, as children would grow up more disadvantaged than children from wealthier backgrounds. Such children would have weathered the storm of the economic crisis due to the wealth of their parents and family. Youth unemployment may also delay household formation where the youth is able to afford to get married in his/her own household and to start a family.[65] However, while the trajectory from the youth living with parents to his/her own household may be delayed, it has been found that the trajectory tends to remain stable.[66] Furthermore, empirical studies have shown that the youth unemployment rate is negatively impacted for at least 5 years following the onset of a financial and subsequent economic crisis, with the most severe negative impacts occurring in the second and third years.[67] In the case of youths, the added impact would be a reduction in the possibilities to find work. This is because, owing to the economic crisis, it would be particularly difficult for the young and inexperienced to be able to get jobs compared to older adults, who may have not only the skills but also the experience of being able to find work. The situation is made even worse when governments adopt austerity policies which may result in reduced social spending, putting those families living on a

[62] Choudhry, M., Marelli, E., and Signorelli, M. (2010), The Impact of Financial Crises on Youth Employment Rate, No.79, Quaderni Del Dipartimento Di Economia, Finanza E Statistica.

[63] Ortiz, I., and Cummins, M. (2012), When the Global Crisis and Youth Bulge Collide: Double the Jobs Trouble for Youth, Social and Economic Policy Working Paper, Unicef Policy and Practice, Unicef.

[64] Ibid.

[65] Junankar, P. (2014), The Impact of the Global Financial Crisis on Youth Labour Markets, IZA DP No.8400.

[66] Serracant, P. (2015), The Impact of the Economic Crisis on Youth Trajectories: A Case Study from Southern Europe, YOUNG, 23 (1), pp. 39–58.

[67] Choudhry, M., Marelli, E., and Signorelli, M. (2012), Youth Employment Rate and Impact of Financial Crises, International Journal of Manpower, Vol.33, No.1, pp. 76–95.

shoestring budget even worse off. However, countries implementing austerity policies in the backdrop of severe financial and economic crises may face differing responses from their citizens. For example, following the global economic crisis of 2008, both Ireland and Greece had to be bailed out by the International Monetary Fund, the European Central Bank as well as the European Union.[68] In order to receive a financial bailout, the governments of Greece and Ireland were bound to adopt austerity policies which drastically reduced government spending in all sectors of the economy, including social spending. The protests of citizens to the austerity policies were different in these countries.[69] For example, in Greece, youths had always faced elevated levels of unemployment, but in Ireland youths had found it much easier to find work in an economy that had been growing prior to the financial crisis. Moreover, there had been in place greater fiscal equivalents of social protection, while this had not been the case in Greece.[70] And while austerity policies contracted the economies of both countries, it also made job creation much more difficult. As a result, the protests of the citizens of Greece were more vocal than the protests of the citizens of Ireland.[71]

The global financial crisis of 2008 was no exception in impacting negatively on youth employability. Its impact on the latter was significant for years following the crisis. For example, even by 2012, there were still 200 million people looking for work throughout the world and the number of accumulated unemployed had risen by 27 million persons.[72] It would also appear that 40% of the world's labour force is without a job—and into this category would fall many of the world's youth, those in the 15–24 years age group.[73] Furthermore, it is estimated that approximately 120 million workers enter the global labour force annually, 90% of whom are from developing countries.[74] In the 8 years between 2012 and 2020, it is

[68] Papadopoulos, O. (2016), Youth Unemployment Discourses in Greece and Ireland Before and During the Economic Crisis: Moving from Divergence to 'contingent Convergence,' Economic and Industrial Democracy, Vol. 37(3), pp. 493–515.

[69] Ibid.

[70] Ibid.

[71] Ibid.

[72] ILO (2012), Global Employment Trends 2012: Preventing a Deeper Jobs Crisis, ILO, Geneva.

[73] Ortiz, I., and Cummins, M. (2012), When the Global Crisis and Youth Bulge Collide: Double the Jobs Trouble for Youth, Social and Economic Policy Working Paper, Unicef Policy and Practice, Unicef.

[74] Ibid.

expected that the labour force will grow by approximately 1.1 billion workers globally.[75] At the same time as economic crises are reducing job creation, jobs themselves are becoming insecure and more precarious by nature.[76] Moreover, AI and the automation of job roles is also adding further to limiting, restricting and reducing job creation in the traditional industrial sectors of the economies of countries around the world. As a result of the jobs becoming more insecure and precarious, it may be the case that there may be greater negative spillover effects on society, even leading to revolution and social change. During times of crisis, it has been found that youths are likely to express their frustration through social media channels.[77] However, some youths may be able to escape unemployment by, for example, going into higher education to acquire a higher level of skills, which may make them more attractive to hiring employers. But this may put off unemployment for only a brief time, as even upon graduation it may be difficult for educated youths to find jobs. But in developing countries and amongst the not-so-wealthy in developed countries, financial and educational constraints may make it harder for youths to enter higher education. They will be unable to skill themselves and will be unable to earn any income. Therefore, it is imperative that governments, in developing and developed countries, adopt economic policies which have a focus on the creation of jobs, especially in the high technology sectors of the economy. This will also foster economic growth through greater increases in labour productivity—although specific policies may differ between developed and developing economies. For example, in developed countries, the state of the economy may be more amenable to technological development, though this may not be the case in some emerging economies such as Indonesia, for example. In these countries, the emphasis of economic and social policies may be on facilitating the development of agriculture, education and entrepreneurship.[78]

With some countries experiencing an increase in not only the yearly youth population but also the annual youth labour force, it is imperative to have economic and social policies in place which engender job creation

[75] Ibid.

[76] Standing, G. (2011), The Precariat: The New Dangerous Class, Bloomsbury, London.

[77] Iwilade, A. (2013), Crisis as Opportunity: Youth, Social Media and the Renegotiation of Power in Africa, Journal of Youth Studies, 16, 8.

[78] Durotoye, A. (2014), The Crisis of Youth Unemployment in the MINT Countries: Causes, Consequences and Corrections, European Journal of Business and Management, Vol.6, No.24.

to prevent the prevalence of lost generations.[79] In addition to this, living standards would be boosted by increases in economic growth, which would be a spillover effect from economic policies fostering job creation. However, it is also important to consider the quality of the jobs which are being created.[80] For example, rather than creating full-time jobs with the associated full-time benefits, economies may create only short-term jobs, part-time jobs or jobs on zero-hour contracts. Therefore, policy makers should understand the importance of the economy creating quality jobs to foster better social welfare in the context of the nature of the relationship between economic and social policies.[81] For example, while pursuing educational policies to increase productivity and economic growth, education can also facilitate social mobility. However, being educated does not mean that youths will be able to find a job. This will depend on the state of the economy and the relevance of the qualification to the needs of the economy.

There are several policies governments can embrace to facilitate the economy to generate jobs.[82] Firstly, governments could promote industrial policies which facilitate the development and growth of small- and medium-sized enterprises. Secondly, the government could reduce information asymmetry in the labour market by supporting and facilitating the exchange of information between employers and potential employees. This could be achieved through the government-financed job exchanges. Thirdly, government could subsidise the provision of educational programmes, which would allow for unemployed youths and older workers to acquire or retain skills, which would allow them to successfully find jobs with the skills required by the economy. Fourthly, governments could promote entrepreneurial training and educational programmes which facilitate youths to not only develop entrepreneurial skills but also be given the mentorship support and financial resources which would be required to sustain and develop new businesses in the long term.

[79] Ortiz, I., and Cummins, M. (2012), When the Global Crisis and Youth Bulge Collide: Double the Jobs Trouble for Youth, Social and Economic Policy Working Paper, Unicef Policy and Practice, Unicef.

[80] Ortiz, I., and Cummins, M. (2012), When the Global Crisis and Youth Bulge Collide: Double the Jobs Trouble for Youth, Social and Economic Policy Working Paper, Unicef Policy and Practice, Unicef.

[81] Ibid.

[82] Ibid.

Family Connectedness and Well Being of Emerging Adults

Adolescence has often been viewed as the peak of mental and physical fitness in the adult life cycle.[83] However, there has been a shift in thinking regarding how this peak may be harmed from a biological perspective to an environmental one.[84] In order to optimise the development of the child into adolescence and then into adulthood, health and social programmes should be designed to mitigate the poverty and lack of economic opportunities individuals may face in this transition.[85] But in order to design optimal programmes for adolescents, it is necessary to know more about the risk behaviours of adolescents as well as about their health problems. The best way in which this information can be gathered is through population studies.[86] Such studies will also allow for garnering information on the risk behaviours and health problems faced by most adolescents, facilitating the development of programmes which will give relief to the greatest number of adolescents possible. The focus of the health and social programmes should be the development of resilience in pre-adolescent children so that when adolescence is reached, the individual will be better able to cope with any environmental situations which may arise in such a way that the negative impact on mental and physical well-being is avoided. In designing programmes to build the resilience of the individual during infancy and childhood, it is essential to embed the nurturing of caring relationships which are both intra-familial and inter-familial. If this embeddedness can be achieved, then by the time adolescence has been reached, individuals will be resilient to negative factors in their environment.[87] The lack of connectedness between individuals, their families and their peers arises because of the lack of community, engagement and dependence.[88]

[83] Blum, R. (1987), Contemporary threats to adolescent health in the United States. JAMA, 257(24), 3390–5.

[84] Resnick, M., Harris, L., and Blum, R. (1993), The Impact of Caring and Connectedness on Adolescent Health and Well-Being, J. Paediatr. Child Health, 29, Suppl, 1, pp. 53–59.

[85] Dryfoos, J. (1990), Adolescents at Risk: Prevalence and Prevention. Oxford University Press, New York, 1–28.

[86] Resnick, M., Harris, L., and Blum, R. (1993), The Impact of Caring and Connectedness on Adolescent Health and Well-Being, J. Paediatr. Child Health, 29, Suppl, 1, pp. 53–59

[87] Werner, E. and Smith, S. (1982), Vulnerable but Invincible: A Longitudinal Study of Resilient Children and Youth, McGraw-Hill, New York.

[88] Slater, P. (1970), The Pursuit of Loneliness: American Culture at the Breaking Point. Beacon Press, Boston.

Moreover, in Western society, the adolescent is more vulnerable due to the cultural value of individuality, from which may arise loneliness and a lack of engagement with the community.[89] Therefore, a well-developed connectedness programme would allow for the development of resilient personal characteristics, which would result in the development of positive behaviours in the adolescent rather than the harmful negative behaviours associated with delinquency, drug and alcohol dependency and perhaps even crime. However, if positive behaviours have developed, at adolescence, the individual will be able to transition into a stable adulthood. In this context, it has been found that if a child is well connected with its peers at school, with parents and with family members then there is better emotional development and the well-being of the child is greatly improved. In fact, it has been found that the level of family connectedness is central to the positive development of well-being in adolescents.[90] Nevertheless, the degree of this family connectedness need not be widespread. For well-being to be develop in a child to become omnipresent in the adolescent, only one caring and nurturing relationship with an adult would be required.[91] An elevated level of family connectedness would prevent the emergence of adolescent behaviour which is of a disturbed nature. Although to prevent the emergence of delinquency, pregnancy and typical acting-out behaviours during adolescence, well-developed school connectedness was more important than the development of family connectedness. Therefore, education may play a greater role in preventing the emergence of acting-out behaviours.[92] The specific factor associated with education leading to this is not just the child's performance at school but also its attitude to being at school. In circumstances in which the level of family connectedness is low, perhaps due to a stressful environment, a higher level of school connectedness can act as a buffer, mitigating the

[89] Lerner, M. (1992), A platform for the politics of meaning A values-oriented approach to progressive politics, Jikkun, 7(4), 11–23.

[90] Resnick, M., Harris, L., and Blum, R. (1993), The Impact of Caring and Connectedness on Adolescent Health and Well-Being, J. Paediatr. Child Health, 29, Suppl, 1, pp. 53–59.

[91] Rutter, M. (1987), Psychosocial resilience and protective mechanisms. Am. J. Orthopsychfat, 57: 316–31.

[92] Santelli, S., and Beilenson P. (1992), Risk factors for adolescent sexual behavior fertility. and sexually transmitted diseases J School Health 1992, 62(7), 271–279.

impact on the development of the individual's resilience and well-being.[93] But a well-developed family and school connectedness at the same time have been found to be good indicators of how an individual is able to positively perceive his/her future.[94] Moreover, on the whole, it has been found that the control of stress within the family and improvements in the nature of family connectivity are more important for the development of positive behaviours than an improvement in the family's socio-economic status.[95] But this finding may be dependent on the availability of a substantial and accessible social security system. Due to the fact that many countries may not have access to such a system, it would be realistic to assert the importance of reducing and eventually eradicating poverty through the use of suitable economic policies and programmes so that families can prosper and children have access to the resources which will allow them to thrive.[96] Although, for positive behaviours and resilience to develop in children, leading to an optimal positioning for adolescence, a caring and nurturing relationship between child and adult would be required in the longer term, leading to adolescence. But the nature of the extent of connectedness may vary and depend on a range of demographic factors such as race and gender as well as on socio-economic status.[97] Moreover, children who are brought up with parental support, with no coercion but the freedom to express themselves, tend to be well adjusted in adolescence, leading to a stable adulthood.[98] Furthermore, transiting from education into a job also improved the young adults' sense of well-being, while at the same

[93] Wilkinson-Lee, A., Zhang, Q., Nuno, V., and Wilhelm, M. (2011), Adolescent Emotional Distress: The Role of Family Obligations and School Connectedness, J. Youth. Adolescence, 40, pp. 221–230.

[94] Crespo, C., Jose, P., Kielpikowski, N., and Pryor, J. (2013), "On Social Ground": Family and School Connectedness promotes adolescents' future orientation, Journal of Adolescence, 36, pp. 993–1002.

[95] Resnick, M., Harris, L., and Blum, R. (1993), The Impact of Caring and Connectedness on Adolescent Health and Well-Being, J. Paediatr. Child Health, 29, Suppl, 1, pp. 53–59.

[96] National Commission on Children. (1991), Beyond Rhetoric a New American Agenda for Children and families Final Report of the National Commission on Children, US Congress, Washington DC.

[97] Townsend, K., McWhirter, B. (2005), Connectedness: A Review of the Literature with Implications for Counseling, Assessment and Research, Journal of Counseling and Development, Vol.83.

[98] Aquilino, W., and Supple, A. (2001), Long-Term Effects of Parenting Practices During Adolescence on Well-Being Outcomes in Young Adulthood, Journal of Family Issues, Vol.22, No.3, pp. 289–308.

time improving the nature of the relationship between parent and child.[99] It has also been found that family connectedness will be better if parents and children have meals at the same time and place.[100]

There does seem to be a hierarchy in the development of relationships and connectedness.[101] For example, at a primary level, relationship within the family[102] lay the groundwork for relations with peers at the secondary level. The extent of family connectedness acts to instil values in children.[103] These are then transcribed into peer relationships. This in turn leads to laying the foundations for the development of romantic relationships at the tertiary level.[104] The changing nature of relationships can be seen as a hierarchical transition rather than a hierarchical displacement.[105] Moreover, in the transition from child to adolescent to adult, a measure of the development of positive well-being can be ascertained by evaluating how independent the individual has become while at the same time maintaining strong relationships with his/her peers and family.[106]The strength of social connectedness also becomes stronger as people grow older, with the quantity of weaker social relations decreasing.[107] However, in order to maintain

[99] Buhl, H. (2007), Well-Being and the Child-Parent Relationship at the Transition From University to Work Life, Journal of Adolescent Research, Vol.22, No.5, pp. 550–571.

[100] Eisenberg, M., Olson, R., Neumark-Sztainer, D., Story, M., and Bearinger, L. (2004), Correlations Between Family Meals and Psychosocial Well-Being Among Adolescents, Arch Pediatr Adolesc Med, Vol.158.

[101] Guarnieri, S., Smurti, M., and Tani, F. (2015), Attachment Relationships and Life Satisfaction During Emerging Adulthood, Soc. Indic. Res, 121, pp. 833–847.

[102] Aquilino, W. S. (2006). Family relationships and support systems in emerging adulthood IN, Emerging adults in America: Coming of age in the 21st century, Arnett, J.J., and Tanner, J.L (Eds.) American Psychological Association, Washington, DC, pp. 193–217.

[103] Kundu, S., and Adams, G. (2008), Identity Formation, Individuality and Connectedness in East Indian and Non-East Indian Female Canadian Emerging Adults, Identity An International Journals of Theory and Research, 5(3), pp. 247–260.

[104] Allen, L. P., & Land, D. (1999). Attachment in adolescence, IN Handbook of attachment: Theory, research, and clinical applications, Cassidy, J., and Shaver, P.R. (Eds.), Guilford Press, New York.

[105] Furman, W., Simon, V., Shaffer, L., and Bouchey, H. (2002), Adolescents' working models and styles for relationships with parents, friends, and romantic partners. Child Development, 73, 241–255. doi: https://doi.org/10.1111/1467-8624.00403.

[106] Wei, M., Liao, K., Ku, T., and Shaffer, P. (2011), Attachment, self-compassion, empathy, and subjective wellbeing among college students and community adults. Journal of Personality, 79(1), 191–221. doi: https://doi.org/10.1111/j.1467-6494.2010.00677.x.

[107] Chan, M. (2015), Multimodal Connectedness and Quality of Life: Examining the Influences of Technology Adoption and Interpersonal Communication on Well-Being Across the Life Span, Journal of Computer-Mediated Communication, 20, pp. 3–18.

secure romantic relationships, individuals may need to have very good communication and conflict resolution skills. Those individuals who are unable to maintain secure romantic relationships, for example, moving from partner to partner, may be put on counselling and training programmes which develop their communication as well as conflict resolution skills.[108]

Adolescent Development and Bullying

Bullying occurs when one person has greater power over another, causing the weaker individual to be psychologically or mentally harmed through direct and indirect bullying.[109] This kind of behaviour among adolescents is both widespread and of global concern.[110] Bullying can also be seen as a problem associated with maintaining normal, balanced relationships with others.[111] However, the presence of bullying behaviour is not just prominent amongst human adolescents. In this case, such behaviours have also been observed amongst contemporary hunter gatherers[112] as well as our evolutionary cousins, chimpanzees.[113] Contextually, it would therefore seem that bullying behaviour allows the strong to deny the weak access to food, social and mating resources.[114] Thus, bullying behaviours may be an evolved adaptation which allows the strong to survive and pass on their genes through reproduction while the genes of the weak dies out.[115] It has also been observed that adolescent bullies seemed to be much better off

[108] Guarnieri, S., Smurti, M., and Tani, F. (2015), Attachment Relationships and Life Satisfaction During Emerging Adulthood, Soc. Indic. Res, 121, pp. 833–847.

[109] Olweus, D. (1993), Bullying at school: What we know and what we can do, Wiley-Blackwell, New York.

[110] Volk, A., Craig, W., Boyce, W., and King, M. (2006), Adolescent risk correlates of bullying and different types of victimization, International Journal of Adolescent Medicine and Health, 18, 375–386.

[111] Pepler, D., Craig, W., Connolly, J., Yuile, A., McMaster, L., and Jiang, D. (2006), A Developmental Perspective on Bullying, Aggressive Behaviour, Vol.32, Pages 376–384.

[112] Turnbull, C. M. (1972), The mountain people, Touchstone, New York.

[113] Goodall, J. (1986), The chimpanzees of Gombe, Harvard University Press, Cambridge, MA.

[114] Book, A., Volk, A., and Hosker, A. (2012), Adolescent Bullying and Personality: An Adaptive Approach, Personality and Individual Differences, 52, pp. 218–223.

[115] Kolbert, J. B., & Crothers, L. (2003), Bullying and evolutionary psychology: The dominance hierarchy among students and implications for school personnel, Journal of School Violence, 2, 73–91.

than their peers in terms of overall well-being.[116] The implication is in some adolescents, bullying may also be an evolutionary adaptation[117]—rather than just the result of maladaptive behaviour.[118] Furthermore, there is some evidence to suggest that bullying behaviours are genetically transmitted from one generation to another and thus may be part of the composition of an individual's personality.[119] Therefore, in the context of bullying as an evolutionary adaptive behaviour, the link between genes, personality and bullying is important to consider.[120] The main personality characteristics of a bully are represented by a tolerance of violence,[121] neurotic behaviour as well as more sociability.[122] Other studies have revealed that individuals who exhibit bullying behaviour towards others do not show empathy towards others and are also not inclined to show guilt due to their behaviour.[123] The specific characteristics of adolescent bullying are that boys are more likely to bully than girls and that such behaviour reaches its zenith between the ages of 10 and 24.[124] Furthermore, boys and girls tend to engage in bullying behaviour with each other whilst pubertal development is advanced.[125] Girls with attention deficiency syndrome tended to exhibit bullying behaviour more so than those who did not

[116] Caravita, S. C. S., Di Blasio, P., and Salmivalli, C. (2009), Unique and interactive effects of empathy and social status on involvement in bullying, Social Development, 18, 140–163.

[117] Book, A., Volk, A., and Hosker, A. (2012), Adolescent Bullying and Personality: An Adaptive Approach, Personality and Individual Differences, 52, pp. 218–223.

[118] Volk, A., Camilleri, J., Dane, A., and Marini, Z. (2012), Is Adolescent Bullying and Evolutionary Adaptation, Aggressive Behaviour, Vol 38, pp. 222–238.

[119] Ball, H. A., Arsenault, L., Taylor, A., Maughan, B., Caspi, A., and Moffitt, T. E. (2008), Genetic influences on victims, bullies, and bully-victims in childhood. The Journal of Child Psychology and Psychiatry, 49, 104–112.

[120] Book, A., Volk, A., and Hosker, A. (2012), Adolescent Bullying and Personality: An Adaptive Approach, Personality and Individual Differences, 52, pp. 218–223.

[121] Olweus, D. (1993), Bullying at school: What we know and what we can do, Wiley-Blackwell, New York.

[122] Connolly, I., and O'Moore, M. (2003), Personality and family relations of children who bully. Personality and Individual Differences, 35, 559–567.

[123] Barry, C. T., Frick, P. J., DeShazo, T. M., McCoy, M. G., Ellis, M., and Loney, B. R. (2000), The importance of callous-unemotional traits for extending the concept of psychopathy to children, Journal of Abnormal Psychology, 109, 335–340.

[124] Book, A., Volk, A., and Hosker, A. (2012), Adolescent Bullying and Personality: An Adaptive Approach, Personality and Individual Differences, 52, pp. 218–223.

[125] Pepler, D., Craig, W., Connolly, J., Yuile, A., McMaster, L., and Jiang, D. (2006), A Developmental Perspective on Bullying, Aggressive Behaviour, Vol.32, Pages 376–384.

suffer the condition.[126] Moreover, the bullying behaviour of children tended to increase after the age of 10/11 as they shifted from junior school to secondary school.[127] Bullying tendencies were greater when children at school did not relate or associate well with their teachers.[128] However, in older adolescents, there seems to be growing empathy with others and reduced tolerance for aggression from others.[129] But only a few adolescents were likely to intervene when witnessing bullying incidents with those intervening not doing so because they felt the matter had nothing to do with them.[130]

Recent findings suggests that the 10- to 24-year age range may represent the duration of adolescence in human beings.[131] Furthermore, and perhaps more surprisingly, it has been found that bullies have the quality of being agreeable when bullying behaviour is taken into account in empirical analysis.[132] The implication is that a bully can have cordial relationships with peers who he/she may like but more intimidating, harsher and harassing relationships with peers he/she may not like.[133] The deliberate nature of bullying does tend to support the view that it represents an evolutionary adaptive behaviour.[134] However, there may also be cultural

[126] Sciberras, E., Ohan, J., and Anderson, V. (2012), Bullying and Peer Victimisation in Adolescent Girls and Attention Deficit/Hyperactivity Disorder, Child Psychiatry Hum Dev, 43, pp. 254–270.

[127] Pellegrini, AD., and Long, J.D.(2002), A longitudinal study of bullying, dominance, and victimization, during the transition from primary through secondary school. Br. J. Dev. Psychol. 20:259–280.

[128] Nation, M., Vieno, A., Perkins, D., and Santinello, M. (2008), Bullying in School and Adolescent Sense of Empowerment: An Analysis of Relationships with Parents, Friends and Teachers, Journal of Community and Applied Social Psychology, 18, pp. 211–232.

[129] Galambos, N.L., Barker, E.V., Tilton-Weaver, L.C.(2003), Canadian adolescents' implicit theory of immaturity: What does childish mean? IN Exploring Cultural Conceptions of the Transition to Adulthood. New Directions for Child and Adolescent Development, Arnett, J.J., and Galambos, N.L. (Eds), Vol. 100, pp. 77–90.

[130] Cappadocia, M., Pepler, D., Cummings, J., and Craig, W. (2012), Individual Motivations and Characteristics Associated with Bystander Intervention During Bullying Episodes Among Children and Youth, Canadian Journal of School Psychology, 27, 3, pp. 201–216.

[131] Sawyer, S., Azzopardi, P., and Wickremarathne, D. (2018), The Age of Adolescence, Vol.2, Issue 3, pp. 223–228.

[132] Book, A., Volk, A., and Hosker, A. (2012), Adolescent Bullying and Personality: An Adaptive Approach, Personality and Individual Differences, 52, pp. 218–223.

[133] Ibid.

[134] Ibid.

differences with regard to bullying. For example, bullying tends to be more widespread in the United States (US) compared to European countries.[135] In the US, individual freedom and the freedom of expression are valued more highly than in Europe. This may lead to higher levels of bullying and victimisation. Nevertheless, other empirical findings also suggest that bullying tends to be greater in countries with greater income inequality than in countries with lower levels of income inequality.[136] This implies that bullying may result due to deficiencies in the socio-economic conditions, especially low incomes of parents and/or parents having to work longer hours, with children having less access, in which children grow up. However, the presence of social support systems such as the state provision of childcare facilities and transfer papers may mitigate poor socio-economic conditions, which reflects in reduced bullying behaviours in children.[137] This may be because the presence of social support systems allows for children to be better looked after, to have access to better nutrition and to be able to spend more time with their parents. As a result, children may be able to think more positively of themselves and be socially adaptive with reduced or no bullying tendencies as well as being resilient to bullying by others.[138]

The bullying behaviour which emerges during adolescence may develop into a more aggressive behaviour in adulthood and may be exhibited in behaviours such as the beating of partners as well as the beating of children.[139] This may lead to the deterioration in the mental and physical well-being of others, the breakup of families, runaways, deteriorating socio-economic circumstances as well as the perpetuation of such

[135] Hoover, J., Oliver, R., and Hazler, R. (1992), Bullying: Perceptions of Adolescent Victims in the Mid-western USA, School Psychology International, Vol.13, pp. 5–16.

[136] Elgar, F., Craig, W., Boyce, W., Morgan, A., and Vella-Zarb, R. (2009), Income Inequality and School Bullying: Multilevel Study of Adolescents in 37 countries, Journal of Adolescent Health, 45, pp. 351–359.

[137] Barboza, G., Schiamberg, L., Oehmke, J., Korzeniewski, S., Post, L., and Heraux, C. (2009), Individual Characteristics and the Multiple Contexts of Adolescent Bullying: An Ecological Perspective, J. Youth Adolescence, 38, pp. 101–121.

[138] Donnon, T. (2010), Understanding How Resiliency Development Influences Adolescent Bullying and Victimisation, Canadian Journal of School Psychology, 25, 1, pp. 101–113.

[139] Pepler, D., Craig, W., Connolly, J., Yuile, A., McMaster, L., and Jiang, D. (2006), A Developmental Perspective on Bullying, Aggressive Behaviour, Vol.32, Pages 376–384.

behaviours in future generations.[140] Moreover, other negative behaviours may emerge such as alcohol and drug dependency, particularly in the children once they become adults. The economic consequences could also be significant. People may lose their jobs due to their behaviours, there may be an increased dependence on social welfare, lower incomes, rising inequality and decreased productivity in the economy. Therefore, it is important to determine the factors which may give rise to adolescent bullying and devise suitable social programmes to mitigate as well as negate the development of such factors. In this case, the development of adolescent bullying behaviours can be associated with the environment a child develops in, and particularly schools, peers and families.[141] Both bullies and their peers who are bullied show a tendency to be less engaged at school, with less bonding with peers and teaching staff.[142] Furthermore, bullying victims are likely to be less confident of themselves as well as being more introspective and lonely compared to their peers.[143] This type of loneliness is more prevalent during adolescence, leading to greater susceptibility towards becoming the victims of bullies.[144] Moreover, the victims of bullies may become bullies themselves.[145] Therefore, the monitoring of student behaviour by staff and by fellow students, who may be more mature, to prevent bullying is paramount.[146]

[140] Bauer, N.S., Herrenkohl, T.I., Lozano, P., Rivara, F.P., Hill, K.G, and Hawkins, J.D. (2006), Childhood bullying involvement and exposure to intimate partner violence. Pediatrics, 118:E235–42.

[141] Spriggs, A., Iannotti, R., Nansel, T., and Haynie, D. (2007), Adolescent Bullying Involvement and Perceived Family, Peer and School Relations: Commonalities and Differences across Race/Ethnicity, Journal of Adolescent Health, 41, pp. 283–293.

[142] Haynie, D.L., Nansel, T., Eitel, P, et al. (2001), Bullies, victims, and bully/ victims: Distinct groups of at-risk youth. J Early Adolesc 21:29–49.

[143] Unnever, J.D. (2005), Bullies, aggressive victims, and victims: Are they distinct groups? Aggressive Behav, 31:153–71.

[144] Acquah, E., Topalli, P., Wilson, M., Junttila, N., and Niemi, P. (2015), Adolescent Loneliness and Social Anxiety a Predictors of Bullying Victimisation, International Journal of Adolescence and Youth, 21, 3, PP. 320–331.

[145] Barker, E., Arseneault, L., Brendgen, M., Fontaine, N., and Maughan, B. (2008), Joint Development of Bullying and Victimisation in Adolescence: Relations to Delinquency and Self-Harm, J.. Acad. Child. Adolesc, Psychiatry, 47, 9.

[146] Spriggs, A., Iannotti, R., Nansel, T., and Haynie, D. (2007), Adolescent Bullying Involvement and Perceived Family, Peer and School Relations: Commonalities and Differences across Race/Ethnicity, Journal of Adolescent Health, 41, pp. 283–293.

Conclusion

The first few years of a child's life, including the pre-birth stage of development in its mother's womb, may be important for the development of cognitive capacity for the rest of its life; behaviours can be altered even during the adolescent stage of development. This is due to two perspectives. The first, according to the PYD framework, suggests that the character and personality of an adolescent are malleable and remain fluid to change. The second perspective, according to the RS framework, suggests that if a child develops resilience going into adulthood, then this will enable it to navigate a poor environment optimally. The development of resilience is dependent on the presence of psychological mechanisms which will allow the adolescent to overcome adversity in its environment. Therefore, it is evident that if the psychological mechanism which would allow adolescents to overcome adversity could be enhanced, then the adolescent's resilience would become stronger. It has been found that the main mechanism which would allow adolescents to overcome adversity is education. The implication is that giving children access to educational opportunities will help them to develop their cognitive and decision-making skills. This would then allow the adolescent to make the best, optimal decision about what actions should be taken to reduce the impact of a negative environment. The latter may result if a child is brought up in a poor socio-economic environment in which its nutritional, educational and well-being requirements are lacking. Without a resilient character, the child may be negatively impacted, leading to vulnerability into adolescence and into adulthood. The result may be a self-perpetuating cycle of poverty, greater inequality and poor levels of well-being. Resilience is also important in children as well as in adolescents to overcome the negative impact on well-being from bullying by peers. Bully results because the individual is de-connected socially and psychologically from family members, peers as well as teachers. An adolescent may not have strong nurturing relationships with family members who are primary caregivers due to low socio-economic conditions. In such conditions, stress levels within the family may be extremely high. At a policy level, education plays an especially key role in the healthy development of the child as well as the adolescent into adulthood. If educational programmes can be devised such as to support the development of positive behaviours amongst adolescents such as resilience and the maintaining of good relationships within and outside of the family, then the development of the child and the adolescent can be optimised. Moreover, social programmes should also be devised which mitigate the poor socio-economic conditions in which a child or an adolescent may develop. This will further support their positive development into adulthood. At this stage of development, he/she will be able to make a positive contribution to economic activity, leading to a lowering in inequality at a societal level.

References

Acquah, E., Topalli, P., Wilson, M., Junttila, N., & Niemi, P. (2015). Adolescent loneliness and social anxiety a predictors of bullying victimisation. *International Journal of Adolescence and Youth, 21*(3), 320–331.

Allen, L. P., & Land, D. (1999). Attachment in adolescence. In J. Cassidy & P. R. Shaver (Eds.), *Handbook of Attachment: Theory, Research, and Clinical Applications*. Guilford Press.

Aquilino, W. S. (2006). Family relationships and support systems in emerging adulthood. In J. J. Arnett & J. L. Tanner (Eds.), *Emerging Adults in America: Coming of Age in the 21st Century* (pp. 193–217). American Psychological Association.

Aquilino, W., & Supple, A. (2001). Long-term effects of parenting practices during adolescence on well-being outcomes in young adulthood. *Journal of Family Issues, 22*(3), 289–308.

Assibey-Mensah, G. (1997). Role models and youth development: Evidence and lessons from the perceptions of African American male youth. *The Western Journal of Black Studies, 21*, 4.

Ball, H. A., Arsenault, L., Taylor, A., Maughan, B., Caspi, A., & Moffitt, T. E. (2008). Genetic influences on victims, bullies, and bully-victims in childhood. *The Journal of Child Psychology and Psychiatry, 49*, 104–112.

Barboza, G., Schiamberg, L., Oehmke, J., Korzeniewski, S., Post, L., & Heraux, C. (2009). Individual characteristics and the multiple contexts of adolescent bullying: An ecological perspective. *Journal of Youth Adolescence, 38*, 101–121.

Barker, E., Arseneault, L., Brendgen, M., Fontaine, N., & Maughan, B. (2008). Joint development of bullying and victimisation in adolescence: Relations to delinquency and self-harm. *Journal of the American Academy of Child and Adolescent Psychiatry, 47*(9).

Barry, C. T., Frick, P. J., DeShazo, T. M., McCoy, M. G., Ellis, M., & Loney, B. R. (2000). The importance of callous-unemotional traits for extending the concept of psychopathy to children. *Journal of Abnormal Psychology, 109*, 335–340.

Bauer, N. S., Herrenkohl, T. I., Lozano, P., Rivara, F. P., Hill, K. G., & Hawkins, J. D. (2006). Childhood bullying involvement and exposure to intimate partner violence. *Pediatrics, 118*, E235–E242.

Beach, S., Lei, M., Brody, G., Kim, S., Barton, A., Dogan, M., & Philibert, R. (2016). Parenting, socioeconomic status risk and later young adult health: Exploration of opposing indirect effects via DNA methylation. *Child Development, 87*(1), 111–121.

Berger, L., & Brooks-Gunn, J. (2005). Socioeconomic status, parenting knowledge and behaviours, and perceived maltreatment of young low birth-weight children. *Social Service Review, 79*, 237–267.

Blum, R. (1987). Contemporary threats to adolescent health in the United States. *JAMA, 257*(24), 3390–3395.

Book, A., Volk, A., & Hosker, A. (2012). Adolescent bullying and personality: An adaptive approach. *Personality and Individual Differences, 52*, 218–223.

Bradley, R., & Corwyn, R. (2002). Socioeconomic status and child development. *Annual Review of Psychology, 53*, 371–399.

Buhl, H. (2007). Well-being and the child-parent relationship at the transition from university to work life. *Journal of Adolescent Research, 22*(5), 550–571.

Campbell, D., & Erbstein, N. (2012). Engaging youth in community change: Three key implementation principles. *Community Development, 43*(1), 63–79.

Cappadocia, M., Pepler, D., Cummings, J., & Craig, W. (2012). Individual motivations and characteristics associated with bystander intervention during bullying episodes among children and youth. *Canadian Journal of School Psychology, 27*(3), 201–216.

Caravita, S. C. S., Di Blasio, P., & Salmivalli, C. (2009). Unique and interactive effects of empathy and social status on involvement in bullying. *Social Development, 18*, 140–163.

Case, R., Griffin, S., & Kelly, W. (1999). Socioeconomic gradients in mathematical ability and their responsiveness to intervention during early childhood. In D. Keating & C. Hertzman (Eds.), *Developmental Health and the Wealth of Nations* (pp. 125–149).

Chan, M. (2015). Multimodal connectedness and quality of life: Examining the influences of technology adoption and interpersonal communication on well-being across the life span. *Journal of Computer-Mediated Communication, 20*, 3–18.

Chisholm, L., & Bois-Reymond, M. (1993). Youth transitions, gender and social change. *Sociology, 27*(2), 259–279.

Choudhry, M., Marelli, E., & Signorelli, M. (2010). The impact of financial crises on youth employment rate. *Quaderni Del Dipartimento Di Economia, Finanza E Statistica, 79*.

Choudhry, M., Marelli, E., & Signorelli, M. (2012). Youth employment rate and impact of financial crises. *International Journal of Manpower, 33*(1), 76–95.

Conger, R., Conger, K., & Martin, M. (2010). Socioeconomic status, family processes and individual development. *Journal of Marriage and Family, 72*, 685–704.
Connolly, I., & O'Moore, M. (2003). Personality and family relations of children who bully. *Personality and Individual Differences, 35*, 559–567.
Crespo, C., Jose, P., Kielpikowski, N., & Pryor, J. (2013). "On Social Ground": Family and school connectedness promotes adolescents' future orientation. *Journal of Adolescence, 36*, 993–1002.
Donnon, T. (2010). Understanding how resiliency development influences adolescent bullying and victimisation. *Canadian Journal of School Psychology, 25*(1), 101–113.
Dougherty, G. (2007). Ensuring the best start in life: Targeting versus universality in early child development. *IRPP Choices, 13*(8), 1–52.
Dryfoos, J. (1990). *Adolescents at Risk: Prevalence and Prevention* (pp. 1–28). Oxford University Press.
Durotoye, A. (2014). The crisis of youth unemployment in the MINT countries: Causes, consequences and corrections, European. *Journal of Business and Management, 6*, No.24.
Eisenberg, M., Olson, R., Neumark-Sztainer, D., Story, M., & Bearinger, L. (2004). Correlations between family meals and psychosocial well-being among adolescents. *Archives of Pediatrics & Adolescent Medicine, 158.*
Elder, G. H., Jr., Shanahan, M. J., & Jennings, J. A. (2015). Human development in time and place. In M. Bornstein & T. Leventhal (Eds.), *Handbook of Child Psychology and Developmental Science. Vol. 4, Ecological Settings and Processes in Developmental Systems* (7th ed.). Wiley.
Elgar, F., Craig, W., Boyce, W., Morgan, A., & Vella-Zarb, R. (2009). Income inequality and school bullying: Multilevel study of adolescents in 37 countries. *Journal of Adolescent Health, 45*, 351–359.
Ensminger, M., & Fotherill, K. (2003). A decade of measuring SES: What it tells us and where to go from here. In M. Bornstein & R. Bradley (Eds.), *Socioeconomic Status, Parenting, and Child Development.* Lawrence Erlbaum. Socioeconomic and experiential influences on the ...
Freud, A. (1969). Adolescence as a developmental disturbance. In G. Caplan & S. Lebovici (Eds.), *Adolescence.* Basic Books.
Furman, W., Simon, V., Shaffer, L., & Bouchey, H. (2002). Adolescents' working models and styles for relationships with parents, friends, and romantic partners. ("(PDF) Furman Simon Shaffer Bouchey2002 - academia.edu"). *Child Development, 73*, 241–255. https://doi.org/10.1111/1467-8624.00403
Galambos, N. L., Barker, E. V., & Tilton-Weaver, L. C. (2003). Canadian adolescents' implicit theory of immaturity: What does childish mean? In J. J. Arnett & N. L. Galambos (Eds.), *Exploring Cultural Conceptions of the Transition to*

Adulthood. New Directions for Child and Adolescent Development (Vol. 100, pp. 77–90).

Goodall, J. (1986). *The Chimpanzees of Gombe*. Harvard University Press.

Guarnieri, S., Smurti, M., & Tani, F. (2015). Attachment relationships and life satisfaction during emerging adulthood. *Social Indicators Research, 121*, 833–847.

Haynie, D. L., Nansel, T., Eitel, P., et al. (2001). Bullies, victims, and bully/ victims: Distinct groups of at-risk youth. *Journal of Early Adolescence, 21*, 29–49.

Hoff, E., Laursen, B., & Tardif, T. (2002). Socioeconomic status and parenting. In M. Bornstein (Ed.), *Handbook of Parenting, Volume 2 Biology and Ecology of Parenting*. Lawrence Erlbaum Associates.

Hoover, J., Oliver, R., & Hazler, R. (1992). Bullying: Perceptions of adolescent victims in the mid-western USA. *School Psychology International, 13*, 5–16.

ILO. (2010). *Global Employment Trends for Youth: Special Issue on the Impact of the Global Economic Crisis on Youth*. ILO.

ILO. (2012). *Global Employment Trends 2012: Preventing a Deeper Jobs Crisis*. ILO.

Irwin, L. G., Siddiqi, A., & Hertzman, C. (2007). *Early Child Development: A Powerful Equalizer*. World Health Organization's Commission on the Social Determinants of Health.

Iwilade, A. (2013). Crisis as opportunity: Youth, social media and the renegotiation of power in Africa. *Journal of Youth Studies, 16*, 8.

Junankar, P. (2014). The impact of the global financial crisis on youth labour markets, IZA DP No. 8400.

Kolbert, J. B., & Crothers, L. (2003). Bullying and evolutionary psychology: The dominance hierarchy among students and implications for school personnel. *Journal of School Violence, 2*, 73–91.

Kroenke, C. (2008). Socioeconomic status and health: Youth development and neo materialist and psychosocial mechanisms. *Social Science and Medicine, 66*, 31–42.

Kundu, S., & Adams, G. (2008). Identity formation, individuality and connectedness in East Indian and Non-East Indian female Canadian emerging adults, identity. *An International Journals of Theory and Research, 5*(3), 247–260.

Larson, R., & Wilson, S. (2004). Adolescence across place and time: Globalisation and the changing pathways to adulthood. In R. Lerner & L. Steinberg (Eds.), *Handbook of Adolescent Psychology* (9th ed.). Wiley.

Lerner, M. (1992). A platform for the politics of meaning A values-oriented approach to progressive politics. *Jikkun, 7*(4), 11–23.

Lerner, R. M. (2004). *Liberty: Thriving and Civic Engagement Among American Youth*. Sage.

Lerner, R. M. (2012). Essay review: Developmental science: Past, present, and future. *International Journal of Developmental Science, 6*(1–2), 29–36.

Lerner, R. M. (2015). Preface. In *Handbook of Child Psychology and Developmental Science*, (7th ed.). Wiley.
Lerner, R. M. (2017). Commentary: Studying and testing the positive youth development model: A tale of two approaches. *Child Development, 88*(4), 1183–1185.
Lerner, R. M. (2018). *Concepts and Theories of Human Development* (4th ed.). Routledge.
Lerner, R., Bowers, E., Geldhof, G., Gestsdottir, S., & DeSouza, L. (2012). Promoting positive youth development in the face of contextual changes and challenges: The roles of individual strengths and ecological assets. *New Directions for Youth Development, 135.*
Lerner, R. M., & Overton, W. F. (2008). Exemplifying the integrations of the relational developmental system: Synthesizing theory, research, and application to promote positive development and social justice. *Journal of Adolescent Research, 23*(3), 245–255.
Lerner, R., et al. (2018). The end of the beginning: Evidence and absences studying positive youth development in a global context. *Adolescent Research Review, 4*, 1–14.
Letourneau, N., Duffett-Leger, L., Levac, L., Watson, B., & Young-Morris, C. (2011). Socioeconomic status and child development: A meta-analysis. *Journal of Emotional and Behavioral Disorders, 21*(3), 211–224.
Luthar, S., & ad Latendresse, S. (2005). Comparable 'risks' at the socioeconomic status extremes: Preadolescents perceptions of parenting. *Development and Psychopathology, 17*, 207–230.
Masten, A. S. (1999). Resilience comes of age: Reflections on the past and outlook for the next generation of research. In M. Glantz & J. Johnson (Eds.), *Resilience and Development: Positive Life Adaptations.* Plenum.
Masten, A. S. (2007). Resilience in developing systems: Progress and promise as the fourth wave rises. *Development and Psychopathology, 19*, 921–930.
McLeod, J. D., & Kaiser, K. (2004). Childhood emotional and behavioral problems and educational attainment. *American Sociological Review, 69*, 636–658.
McLoyd, V., & Wilson, L. (1990). Maternal behavior, social support, and economic conditions as predictors of distress in children. *New Directions for Child Development, 46*, 49–69.
McMahon, R. J., & Peters, R. D. (Eds.). (2002). *The Effects of Parental Dysfunction on Children.* Kluwer Academic/Plenum.
Mendelson, T., Kubzansky, L. D., Datta, G. D., & Buka, S. L. (2008). Relation of female gender and low socioeconomic status to internalizing symptoms among adolescents: A case of double jeopardy? *Social Science & Medicine, 66*, 1284–1296.
Nation, M., Vieno, A., Perkins, D., & Santinello, M. (2008). Bullying in school and adolescent sense of empowerment: An analysis of relationships with parents, friends and teachers. *Journal of Community and Applied Social Psychology, 18*, 211–232.

National Commission on Children. (1991). *Beyond Rhetoric a New American Agenda for Children and Families Final Report of the National Commission on Children*. US Congress.

O'Donoghue, J., Kirshner, B., & McLoughlin, M. (2002). Introduction: Moving youth participation forward. *New Directions for Youth Development, 96*.

Olds, D. L., Sadler, L., & Kitzman, H. (2007). Programs for parents of infants and toddlers: Recent evidence from randomized trials. *Journal of Child Psychology and Psychiatry, and Allied Disciplines, 48*, 355–391.

Olweus, D. (1993). *Bullying at School: What We Know and What We Can Do*. Wiley-Blackwell.

Ortiz, I., & Cummins, M. (2012). *When the Global Crisis and Youth Bulge Collide: Double the Jobs Trouble for Youth, Social and Economic Policy Working Paper*. Unicef Policy and Practice, Unicef.

Overton, W. F. (2015). Process and relational developmental systems. In W. Overton, P. Molenaar, & R. Lerner (Eds.), *Handbook of Child Psychology and Developmental Science. Vol. 1 Theory and Method* (7th ed.). Wiley.

Papadopoulos, O. (2016). Youth unemployment discourses in Greece and Ireland before and during the economic crisis: Moving from divergence to 'contingent Convergence'. *Economic and Industrial Democracy, 37*(3), 493–515.

Pellegrini, A. D., & Long, J. D. (2002). A longitudinal study of bullying, dominance, and victimization, during the transition from primary through secondary school. *British Journal of Developmental Psychology, 20*, 259–280.

Pepler, D., Craig, W., Connolly, J., Yuile, A., McMaster, L., & Jiang, D. (2006). A developmental perspective on bullying. *Aggressive Behaviour, 32*, 376–384.

Perry, B. (2007). Relational poverty and the impact of trauma on children: A neurodevelopmental view of resilience and vulnerability to adverse childhood experiences. Resistance and Resilience: Helping Children and Youth Survive in the Face of Family Violence. Fredericton, NB, Canada.

Petterson, S., & Albers, A. B. (2001). Effects of poverty and maternal depression and early childhood development. *Child Development, 72*, 1794–1813.

Pimlott-Wilson, H., & Hall, S. (2017). Everyday experiences of economic change: Repositioning geographies of children, youth and families. *Area, 49*(3), 258–265.

Resnick, M., Harris, L., & Blum, R. (1993). The impact of caring and connectedness on adolescent health and well-being. *Journal of Paediatrics and Child Health, 29*(Suppl 1), 53–59.

Rhee, K., Lumeng, J., Appugliese, D., & Kaciroti., and Bradley, R. (2006). Parenting styles and overweight status in first grade. *Pediatrics, 117*(6), 2047–2054.

Rutter, M. (1987). Psychosocial resilience and protective mechanisms. *American Journal of Orthopsychiatry, 57*, 316–331.

Santelli, S., & Beilenson, P. (1992). Risk factors for adolescent sexual behavior fertility and sexually transmitted diseases. *Journal of School Health, 62*(7), 271–279.

Santos, A., Ebrahim, S., & Barros, H. (2008). Gender, socio-economic status and metabolic syndrome in middle aged and old adults. *BMC Public Health, 8*, 62.
Sawyer, S., Azzopardi, P., & Wickremarathne, D. (2018). *The Age of Adolescence, 2*(3), 223–228.
Sciberras, E., Ohan, J., & Anderson, V. (2012). Bullying and peer victimisation in adolescent girls and attention deficit/hyperactivity disorder. *Child Psychiatry & Human Development, 43*, 254–270.
Serracant, P. (2015). The impact of the economic crisis on youth trajectories: A case study from Southern Europe. *Young, 23*(1), 39–58.
Slater, P. (1970). *The Pursuit of Loneliness: American Culture at the Breaking Point*. Beacon Press.
Southwick, S. M., Bonanno, G. A., Masten, A. S., Panter-Brick, C., & Yehuda, R. (2014). Resilience definitions, theory, and challenges: Interdisciplinary perspectives. *European Journal of Psychotraumatology, 5*(1), 25338.
Spriggs, A., Iannotti, R., Nansel, T., & Haynie, D. (2007). Adolescent bullying involvement and perceived family, peer and school relations: Commonalities and differences across race/ethnicity. *Journal of Adolescent Health, 41*, 283–293.
Standing, G. (2011). *The Precariat: The New Dangerous Class*. Bloomsbury.
Sukarieh, M., & Tannock, S. (2011). The positivity imperative: A critical look at the 'new' youth development movement. *Journal of Youth Studies, 14*(6), 675–691.
Townsend, K., & McWhirter, B. (2005). Connectedness: A review of the literature with implications for counseling, assessment and research. *Journal of Counseling and Development, 83*.
Turnbull, C. M. (1972). *The Mountain People*. Touchstone.
Unnever, J. D. (2005). Bullies, aggressive victims, and victims: Are they distinct groups? *Aggressive Behavior, 31*, 153–171.
Volk, A., Camilleri, J., Dane, A., & Marini, Z. (2012). Is adolescent bullying and evolutionary adaptation. *Aggressive Behaviour, 38*, 222–238.
Volk, A., Craig, W., Boyce, W., & King, M. (2006). Adolescent risk correlates of bullying and different types of victimization. *International Journal of Adolescent Medicine and Health, 18*, 375–386.
Wei, M., Liao, K., Ku, T., & Shaffer, P. (2011). Attachment, self-compassion, empathy, and subjective wellbeing among college students and community adults. *Journal of Personality, 79*(1), 191–221. https://doi.org/10.1111/j.1467-6494.2010.00677.x
Werner, E., & Smith, S. (1982). *Vulnerable But Invincible: A Longitudinal Study of Resilient Children and Youth*. McGraw-Hill.
Wilkinson-Lee, A., Zhang, Q., Nuno, V., & Wilhelm, M. (2011). Adolescent emotional distress: The role of family obligations and school connectedness. *Journal of Youth and Adolescence, 40*, 221–230.
Wyn, J., & Woodman, D. (2006). Generation, youth and social change in Australia. *Journal of Youth Studies, 9*(5), 495–514.

CHAPTER 8

Conclusion

The aim of this volume is to evaluate whether differences in upbringing represent a source of persistent inequality in society. The objective of this volume is to determine how the social and economic policies of governments should be focused to eradicate the emergence of such inequalities at source. If a government's social and economic policies are not so attuned and correlated with the realities and needs of human development, then the implication would be that there will be increases in inequality because of economic growth. Therefore, changing the emphasis of government policy from facilitating economic growth to promoting improvements in the quality of life and well-being may not have much effect if the causes of inequality are due to differences in upbringing. This will give rise to differences in the trajectory of human development—With children nurtured in a caring and loving environment with access to educational and other resources faring better later in life in contrast to those children who are destitute of love and resources. The former will develop to be more resilient into adolescence and then into adulthood while the latter will not. It may be this category of children who develop mental and emotional stability issues later in life as a result of converging with an adverse environment.

Contemporary economic thought, theory and practice try to analyse, evaluate and better understand the causes as well as the consequences of rising inequality amongst the population of a country despite rapidly

S. Ramesh, *The Political Economy of Human Behaviour and Economic Development*,
https://doi.org/10.1007/978-3-031-12666-6_8

rising economic growth. The result of this is that prosperity and wealth fall into the hands of the few while the many remain poor, struggling to make ends meet as well as the needs of day-to-day existence. However, a little recognised feature of human behaviour is that some are able to overcome the chains of poverty, whether in developing countries or in developed countries, to do well and prosper in life—while most succumb to inequality, which then shifts from one generation to the next in a cyclical self-sustaining manner. The question arises as to how some can overcome inequality while others succumb to it. Moreover, it also has to be recognised that in the context of economic systems, the capitalistic economy does allow for more opportunity while the command/planned economy does not. However, it is interesting to note that after the collapse of command economies, people from these countries migrated to developed Western countries to seize the opportunities of the capitalistic system. The implication is that the elements of human behaviour required to rise above inequality despite living in a country lacking in the equality of opportunities emerge regardless of the nature of the economic system into which people are born. The question is how it does this happen?

After the end of World War II in 1945, a consensus had arisen amongst economists and policymakers that the policy objective of maximising GDP would lead to an improvement in human welfare through rising incomes. Although prosperity would be in the hands of the few initially, it would diffuse or trickle down to the rest of society in any particular country. However, the increase in globalisation in the last four decades has seen income becoming even more concentrated in the hands of the few, while the many remain poor or experience a stagnation of income, both within countries and between countries. This may be either because there is a lack of opportunity for individuals to progress and climb the ladders of prosperity or due to a lack of capability amongst individuals themselves. The growing disparities in income and the increasing inequality both in developing countries and in developed countries have led to a shift in the thinking of economists, policymakers and practitioners as to whether the maximisation of economic growth is the best way to deliver economic prosperity and opportunities for all the citizens of a country. This one-dimensional approach to economic development seemed to be a necessary but not a sufficient condition to ensure that there would be improvements not only in the well-being but also in the development of opportunities for all the citizens of a country. The shift in thinking led to the embracement of human well-being and its enhancement as the ultimate objective of economic and social policy, which would require a multidimensional strategy. This is because the dimensions of human development and well-being include longevity, literacy, enforceable human rights, freedom of thought as well as the ability to respect oneself in a tolerant socio-economic environment. The focus of the shift to the human development multidimensional approach reached a zenith in 1990. At this time, there was a shift in thinking regarding the purpose of economic activity and whether this should just emphasise the capitalist ideology of making money and profits. Undeniably human existence requires much more than either a free market economy or the opportunities to make money. Some might say that capitalism is an economic ideology with no soul, but some religions are seen as a way of life. The emphasis of capitalism is on economic growth, a measure of the level of economic activity, in the context of increases in productivity. Economic activity is only a secondary requirement to human existence, whilst spirituality and its enhancement and development is paramount. This is clearly evident in the way the caste system is divided, with those being responsible for the spiritual and learning needs of society at the top (Brahmins—priests and teachers), who are then followed by those required to maintain power and security of the state (Kshatriyas—warriors and rulers). The Kshatriyas are then followed by those required for economic activity, the Vaishyas (farmers, traders and merchants). The Vaishyas are then followed by the Shudras (labourers), who are in turn followed by the Dalits (outcastes—street sweepers, latrine cleaners), who occupy the lower rungs of the Hindu caste system. On the other hand, in the context of capitalism, the division of labour is solely associated with production, increases in productivity and economic growth. In this case, it is evident that capitalism takes a very short-term view of human existence which only relates to making money, while Hinduism prepares an individual through earthly existence for the life beyond. Thus, it is evident that the role of economic activity in capitalism and in Hinduism has different purposes and outcomes. Capitalism represents the means of existence, whereas Hinduism relates to a way of life which is supported by a means of existence.

The multidimensional approach to economic development should focus on the use of policies to maximise economic growth and GDP as well as policies to enhance and improve the factors associated with human well-being and development. In other words, human behaviour should be better aligned with economic activity such that economic development is facilitated, enhanced and sustained. Nevertheless, empirical studies evaluating the relationship between economic growth and human development have produced mixed results. For example, in Nigeria, it has been found that there is a one-way causation from economic growth to economic development. This may be because economic growth will create jobs, which in turn will increase household incomes, leading to an improvement in the well-being of people in the household. If parents are able to gain employment, the higher household income may benefit children in the household, who may gain access to better educational opportunities as well as better nutrition. However, access to these opportunities may not benefit the child if the relationship with the primary caregiver is not good and/or if the primary caregiver is unable to facilitate the cognitive and non-cognitive development of the child. Moreover, the primary caregiver may use the income from newly created jobs for their own benefit rather than that of the children in the household. Nevertheless, in some countries, increased public spending on female health and education tended to strengthen the link between economic growth and human development. This is because if females are given access to health and educational opportunities, infants may be born healthier and may benefit from the better decision making of their mothers during their infant, childhood and adolescent development. Therefore, it is evident that the way in which economic growth impacts on human development is dependent on the amount of public funds spent by the government as well as what the money is spent on. For example, in Latin America it was found that public spending on health promoted economic growth through income generation. The implication is that, with better healthcare, workers would less likely be absent from work. The result would be that healthy workers would be able to take any job and as a result generate income. However, in African countries it was found that the levels of human capital stock were more important to economic growth than government spending on health and education. This may be due to the fact that in Africa infrastructure is not widespread and does not play a significant role in income generation, whereas human capital stock has a more significant impact on income generation. On the other hand, in eastern European countries, it was found that early public intervention with a focus on human development not only facilitated economic growth but also sustained it. This early public intervention, in providing early years schooling, may be the post-communist legacy of many, if not all, eastern European countries. An access to education would mean that children would be able to acquire skills and knowledge from a very early age to further the cause of human development. Moreover, access to educational opportunities from a very early age may mean that children develop the characteristic of resilience which will enable them to optimally navigate life's difficulties during adolescence and beyond into adulthood. Nevertheless, in Saudi Arabia, at least in the short term, there is a negative relationship between economic growth and financial inclusion. This may be because financial inclusion is leaning towards private sector firms rather than individuals in the short run. If financial inclusion is limited to individuals, then consumption expenditure will be constrained, leading to lower levels of economic growth—although economic growth and financial inclusion do have a causal relationship over the long term. This may be because in the long run more individuals gain access to financial products such as bank and savings account. Finally, the nature and extent of political processes in a country as well as the nature and role of global institutions may dictate the rate at which human welfare and development progresses, if at all. Political processes as well as the work of global institutions shape the nature of economic activity, which may affect human behaviour in different ways. Economic activity may take place either in a free market economy, a mixed-market economy (a mixture of government intervention and free market forces) or a command economy. The free market economy is one in which there is little, if any, government intervention in the economy (the US economy before the 1930s), while the command economy is one in which there is total government control of the economy, including the fixing of prices and determining of what goods should be produced in the economy. The extent of individuality also varies from one type of economic system to another. In a free market economy, the level of individuality is much great than that in a command economy. But in both systems, some children may enjoy better nurturing and a better environment to grow up in compared to other children. So, children may have the potential for optimal development in terms of emotional stability and cognitive and non-cognitive skills, whether they were born in a country with a command economy, a free market economy or a mixed-market economy. Evidence supporting the hypothesis that optimal human development is possible in command economies is represented by the numbers of people who have grown up in such systems but, when allowed, have migrated to more developed countries, where there is better infrastructure, institutions and greater opportunities for personal and professional development. But the extent of the opportunities available to individuals are dependent upon the nature of the economic system. The mechanism for optimal human development may not be the result of an inherited genetic profile an individual is born with, but its interaction with the individual's socio-economic environment, culture and relationships. The implication is that human behaviour, economic activity and economic development need to be evaluated and studied using an integrated approach encompassing the fields of biology, neuroscience, psychology and the social sciences. The implication of this integrated approach into analysing childhood and human development is that genes are 'followers' and are triggered into action only by environmental stimuli, which may differ from one person to another. This, in the context of childhood upbringing, has not been integrated into any human development policy framework sufficiently enough to have an impact on society in the context that the roots of inequality in life arise from differences in childhood upbringing. A childhood upbringing which nurtures the qualities of resilience and adaptability in individuals may lead to a reduction in inequality later in life. The development of cognitive skills is important for the development of resilience. Therefore, such socio-economic policies should be developed, designed and implemented that create an environment in which opportunities are available to activate an individual's cognitive capabilities. Economic activity should be focused on improving human well-being (by improving and toning resilience) as well as the development and enhancement of cognitive capacity. It is here that there can be found the link between economic development and human behaviour.

The sources of inequality in adulthood may lie in the poor development of the cognitive and the non-cognitive in the early years of a child's life due to the lack of effective development of its brain. This may be because of a number of factors. For example, an individual may be born with poor-quality inherited genes or have to grow up in a poor socio-economic environment due to limited parental income. Children growing up in such an environment may have constrained access to education, poor nutrition and limited opportunities for social engagement with their peers. In this case, it therefore becomes critical to better understand brain development in the early years of a child's life. Such knowledge will allow governments to devise policies which allow for the optimal development of a child's cognitive and non-cognitive abilities. Furthermore, the link between motor development and cognitive development has been noted as far back as the 1950s. Motor development may also facilitate the acquisition and the use of language by a child because such development may also lead to changes in the brain. The development of both language and motor systems undergoes inter-related development because the same resources associated with cortical processing are shared. The development of language processing skills in an infant as well as in a child is based on an integrated functional system which encompasses motor development. The latter may represent crude forms of linguistic development in the infant before speech emerges, in which the infant will use hand signals or facial expressions to engage with its carers. It is therefore evident that it is the area of the brain associated with motor development which is also associated with the processing of language tasks. Moreover, as a child develops the ability to use language, its self-awareness will also develop as well as an awareness of others. In theoretical terms, this is regarded as a development of the Theory of Mind. Thus, in the development of early years education policies, governments should consider the relationship between motor development in infants and the development of cognitive abilities later in life.

Critical to the development of a child's brain are the genes it inherits from its parents. In this case, genes play a key role in the body's production of specific proteins. Genes which produce brain-specific proteins are therefore critical to the development of the cerebral cortex. The structure and function of the cerebral cortex support human cognitive functions. There are four main aspects of cognitive ability which all interact in the development of general cognitive ability. These aspects of cognitive ability include the speed which can be associated with the processing of information, the capacity of memory as well as the verbal and spatial ability. On the other hand, the non-cognitive intelligence of a child encompasses a wide range of skills and behaviours which interplay with its cognitive abilities in order to facilitate its academic performance. The features of non-cognitive intelligence include the individual's character traits, the level of self-belief as well as the motivation to achieve. It is the non-cognitive contribution of motivation and focus on achievement which allows them to succeed in their cognitive endeavours as measured by academic performance. Furthermore, some non-cognitive skills such as tenacity and the ability to self-control one's emotions may be entirely dependent on personality traits. However, these traits may not be malleable like other traits—although the brain is most malleable at younger ages, during which the environment faced by a child is quite different from the world faced by an adult brain. Nevertheless, observational evidence supports the claim that the brain remains malleable to change even later on in life. For example, patients recovering from brain injuries may need to relearn not only their language skills but also their ability to walk. The implication is that through mentorship and guidance, behaviours can also be altered even during the adolescent stage of development. This can be seen from two perspectives. The first, according to the PYD framework, suggests that the character and personality of an adolescent are malleable and remain fluid to change. The second perspective, according to the RS framework, suggests that if a child develops resilience as she/he transitions into adulthood then this will enable an ability to optimally navigate through a non-conducive environment.

In the case of a young child however, a socio-economic environment which degrades the development of a child's non-cognitive skills may constrain the development of a child's cognitive ability. Furthermore, a child's short-term memory may be strained and limited when the child is using its cognitive capacity to deal with stress and emotions caused by environmental factors. In the transition from childhood to adult, the human brain becomes less and less malleable as it develops. Therefore, it is not difficult to see why poverty in childhood may have lifelong impacts. Empirical research suggests that the conditions of poverty under which a child grows up will lead to not only low levels of educational attainment but also behavioural and mental health problems later in life. Moreover, a poor environmental upbringing may also lead to poor control of emotions, leading to stress and a negative impact on cognition. The stress-induced epigenetic mechanisms may cause the body to produce proteins which will enhance gene expressions of negative personality traits. Moreover, the lack of a stressful childhood will lead to the optimal development of the amygdala. This is necessary for the development of normal behaviour and the mental well-being of the child. The latter is due to the fact that the development of the amygdala is associated with the emergence and development of self-emotional regulation mechanisms of the child. Furthermore, investment in childhood programmes to foster mindfulness may allow a child to become better at emotional self-regulation by allowing itself to separate self from circumstance. This will allow the child to enhance its own academic achievement as well as future skill formation.

It has been previously stated that critical to the development of a child's brain is the nature of the genes it inherits from its parents. However, more directly associated with a child's inherited genes is a better-educated mother. The latter would be able to select the best male from a pool of potential suitors. Furthermore, a better education leads to better decisions. The extent and nature of school resources also impact on the development of a child's cognitive and non-cognitive skills. Empirical research suggests that small class sizes helps to develop a child's non-cognitive skills. Moreover, some teachers are better than others at facilitating the development of a child's cognitive skills—although other teachers may be better at developing a child's non-cognitive skills.

Traditional economic theory reduces the human contribution to economic activity with regard to the identification of the role of labour and rationality. This has been accomplished in two specific ways. Firstly, the construction of specific criteria centred on the behaviour of indifference curves allows for a preference ordering. This allows for the theoretical formalisation of self-interest. Secondly, preference orderings are constructed on the basis of observed choices. On the other hand, the newly emerging field of neuroeconomics takes a different approach based on the empirical findings of neuroscience. The aim is to better understand the actions of an economic agent based on human motivation. In this case, neuroscience seeks to amend existing economic theory by using research findings on the development of the human brain and emotions to construct models of human behaviour which are more realistic. However, an analytical framework which allows decision making to be conceptualised is the Somatic Marker Hypothesis (SMH). The SMH framework recognises that reasoning as a decision-making process is reliant upon several layers of neural operations which are dependent on non-cognitive factors (emotions, attention) as well as cognitive factors (processing of stored information). SMH represents a suitable framework for integrating the findings of neuroscience and neuroeconomics, allowing for a consistent way in which human motivation and behaviour can be analysed and explained. Principally, it must be recognised that human behaviour and reasoning are dependent on bio-regulatory processes, which are themselves based on physical structures such as the brain which make up human physiology. The bio-regulatory processes are themselves based on primary emotions associated with survival, for example, fear and secondary emotions. The latter are more complex and associated with planning and reasoning, and include emotions such as sympathy and jealousy. Primary emotions are experienced when the hypothalamus, the basal forebrain and the brain stem are triggered in consecutive order. Once this has happened, secondary emotions are experienced when the ventromedial prefrontal cortex of the brain is activated. Human emotions, whether primary or secondary, are exhibited due to the specific environments faced by individuals. Emotions have developed through the evolutionary process in order to facilitate the adaptation and survival of humans in their specific habitats. This occurs through a sequential mechanism which involves the senses and the expression of a subjective feeling such as an emotion, with cognitive processes translating this subjective feeling into a related thought. This in turn will trigger a physical response. For example, seeing a lion in a forest results in fear, which may cause an individual to either climb a tree, run or seek safety in some other way. However, emotional regulation is also important to ensure that an individual does not either under-react or over-react with regard to a given situation. Emotional regulation is effective when its subconscious use allows an individual to behave optimally in response to a specific environmental factor or change. Furthermore, effective emotional regulation will allow an individual to maintain optimal relationships with others. However, emotional regulation which is dysfunctional will mean that an individual will not be able to understand the consequences of a specific course of action taken in response to a given emotional state. In such a scenario, relationships will be unstable and not long-lasting. Dysfunctional emotional regulation is most likely to occur when an individual is introverted and likely to be easily intimidated—although an outgoing personality may likely be more emotionally stable with better emotional regulation as he/she is less likely to be intimidated by the world. Optimal emotional and mental stability only occurs when an individual's personality traits can develop normally without the occurrence of either mental or personality disorders. There should be a role for the state to facilitate the provision of an environment which is conducive to the optimal personality trait development in infants as well as in children. Economic theory ignores the role of emotions in decision making because of its assertion that consumers make rational choices in an environment in which a condition of perfect information is assumed.

The first few years of a child's life are the ones in which there is significant development of the brain, the nervous system as well as motor development. This is specifically in the context of not only the addition of new neural connections but also the strengthening of existing ones. Mental stimulation is particularly important during the infant stage of a child's development, as it is during this period that there is the most significant development of the brain. This will lead to a corresponding increase in cognitive ability due to the exponential growth of synaptic connections. Furthermore, it has been found through neuroimaging techniques that movement (motor activity) and the completion of tasks which require thinking processes serve to simultaneously activate two regions of the brain—the dorsolateral prefrontal cortex as well as the neo-cerebellum. Moreover, the simultaneous motor activity and the completion of tasks requiring thinking and the stimulation of brain areas is not a coincidence. Theories associated with the development of cognition rely upon this causality. For example, Piaget's theory of cognitive development is dependent upon the causality between simultaneous thinking and physical movement and the actuation of areas of the brain. Thus, it is evident that Piaget's theory promotes the idea that as incremental psychological changes occur in the brain, leading to a change in its overall structure, cognitive processes also develop as a result. In contrast to Piaget's theory of cognitive development, which emphasises modular changes in the psychological cognitive system, Vygotsky places greater emphasis on the development of the entire psychological system. In this case, according to Vygotsky, the development of one component in the psychological system changes the functionality of the entire system. For example, the development of memory may change the way in which the brain functions because it will be able to 'store' more information. It may be the case that with more information, the functioning of the brain can lead to better decisions being taken by an individual. This may be because more experiences could be stored as memories, and decisions and actions taken on the basis of these based on expected best outcomes. In contrast to either the Piaget or the Vygotsky perspective, according to the Kohlberg perspective the structure of thought is more important than is content awareness (psychological system changes) for the development of moral reasoning. Therefore, according to Kohlberg, the cognitive processes which lead to content awareness (psychological system changes) are more important than the automatic recognition of content awareness (psychological system changes) with regard to the development of moral reasoning. In other words, according to Kohlberg, the development of moral understanding and reasoning leads to cognitive development due to psychological system changes. In this case, it may be important for early school learning programmes to be designed and delivered in such a way that they allow for the infant/child to develop moral understanding and reasoning skills. As a result of acquiring these skills, psychological system changes will occur which will facilitate cognitive development.

Poverty and inequality are inextricably linked. This may be because poverty gives rise to poor nutrition, a lack of educational opportunities and stressed parents. As a result of these factors, an infant may not be able to develop his/her cognitive ability as the full functionality of the brain will not be optimised. Therefore, integral to any educational development programme for infants and children implemented by governments, there should also be complementary policies and programmes associated with enhancing and facilitating the infant/child's nutritional and primary care-giver needs. In this case, the availability and uptake of educational opportunities will facilitate the development of a child's cognitive ability as the neuronal connections in the brain are rewired as learning takes place and new skills and experiences are acquired. The lack of educational opportunities is more likely to be widespread in developing countries. Moreover, this lack of educational opportunities will be compounded by poor infrastructure as well as a lack of access to resources due to low levels of parental incomes. Furthermore, in such cases the relationship between the parents and the infant/child may not develop as well as they should because the parents may need to work longer hours. This situation is made worse when other family members, such as grandparents, uncles and aunts, are not around to help with the upbringing of the child.

Women may in particular be denied the right to an education even to achieve basic levels of literacy. The productive non-integration of women into the economy will lead to a loss of productive capacity and will act as a contributor to a reduction in economic growth. Moreover, when a mother is uneducated she may not always be able to make decisions which lead to the optimal development of an infant/child. In this case, the mother's life choices for her children may simply be irrational as these will simply arise from emotions. Furthermore, an uneducated mother is likely to have only a low level of skills. The implication is that she may only be able to undertake menial low-paying jobs, which may require a lot of effort and time. As a result, she may be away from the infant/child for a long period of time during the day and be tired when she gets home. In this case, the environment and circumstances may not be optimal for the development of a good and stable relationship between the primary care-giver, the mother, and the infant/child. This role will be of primary importance in circumstances in which the male, the traditional breadwinner, in many cultures and societies is either physically incapacitated or addicted to the consumption of alcohol. In such cases, the mother will be responsible not only for looking after the children and providing for their needs but also for the care of the father. However, in the case of addiction to alcohol, the father may actually leave the family home or die relatively young. The father may also be addicted to gambling, in which case the circumstances of low-income families may be particularly dire.

Racial discrimination in a country may also lead to harmful impacts on the development of the infant/child. This is because it may grow up to believe that it is inferior to others because of the way it has been treated during its upbringing. The lifetime impact may be that the child develops into adulthood with a lack of confidence and neurotic behaviour. A racial divide and discriminatory politics may also harm the long-term economic growth and economic development of a country. In some countries, Malaysia, Sri Lanka and India, for example, politicians from the majority population may play the racial card in elections to win power. This has led to the current demise of Sri Lanka, where politicians have played the racial card, to separate Tamils from Sinhalese, in order to win power. Playing the racial card would have meant using hired thugs to ferment racial tensions, leading to riots and other acts of violence against the minority population. Furthermore, in the current situation in Sri Lanka, the corrupt practices of the Rajapaksa family have led to the economic meltdown of the Sri Lankan economy. As of 20 May 2022, Sri Lanka has only £40 million in its foreign exchange reserves and is unable to pay for the imports of food, fuel and medicines (Ashworth, 2022). The racial divide in countries such India and in particular countries such as Malaysia and Sri Lanka has hindered economic development by contributing to an inefficient allocation of human capital and a brain drain due to outward migration to more developed countries. This loss of human capital will further contribute to the damage to the economy through a lack of economic growth and economic development. Lower levels of GDP per capital will also constrain positive childhood development. Therefore, educational policy by itself will not be enough to ensure that infants are given the best opportunities, environment and circumstances to develop cognitively and non-cognitively through childhood, adolescence and adulthood. In this case, government should create an environment which promotes a secular society in which individuals respect each other as human beings under the rule of law. This would be an additional requirement in association with complementary policies associated with nutrition, gender equality and primary caregiver development and assistance. Nevertheless, at a policy level, education plays an especially key role in the healthy development of the child as well as the adolescent into adulthood. If educational programmes can be devised such as to support the development of positive behaviours amongst adolescents such as resilience and the maintaining of good relationships within and outside of the family, then the development of the child and the adolescent can be optimised. Furthermore, social programmes should be devised which mitigate the poor socio-economic conditions in which a child or an adolescent may develop. This will further support their positive development into adulthood. Governments should also follow policies such as investment in infrastructure and the facilitation of entrepreneurship in order to create an economic environment in which opportunities will be created for employment creation and innovation. As a result, human behaviour and economic activity will facilitate economic growth and economic development.

Reference

Ashworth, J. (2022). Voices: Sri-Lanka's President Rajapaksa makes Boris Johnson Look like a paragon of virtue, The Independent, Voices: Sri Lanka's President Rajapaksa makes Boris Johnson look like a paragon of virtue (msn.com).

Index[1]

[1] Note: Page numbers followed by 'n' refer to notes.

S. Ramesh, *The Political Economy of Human Behaviour and Economic Development*,
https://doi.org/10.1007/978-3-031-12666-6

T

U

The manufacturer's authorised representative in the EU is Springer
Nature Customer Service Centre GmbH, Europaplatz 3, 69115 Heidelberg,
Germany. If you have any concerns regarding our products, please
contact ProductSafety@springernature.com

Printed and bound by CPI Group (UK) Ltd, Croydon, CR0 4YY
30/09/2026
02225490-0010